THE
HONESTY
OF THE
PSALMS

SIMPLE REFLECTIONS, THOUGHTS, AND CHALLENGES
ON THESE TIMELESS THOUGHTS FROM CHILDREN OF GOD

THE
HONESTY
OF THE
PSALMS

WRESTLING WITH
THE **WORD OF GOD**
IN A **BROKEN WORLD**

Kelly Vander Woude

credo
house publishers

Published in the United States by Credo House Publishers,
a division of Credo Communications LLC, Grand Rapids, Michigan
credohousepublishers.com

ISBN: 978-1-62586-180-1

Cover and interior design by Frank Gutbrod
Editing by Donna Huisjen

Printed in the United States of America

First Edition

WHAT THIS IS

I've found over the years that every one of us struggles in our relationship with God. Some of those struggles are small, and some of them can be epic battles that would make for a great movie. Some of those struggles are still going on to this day. I've also come to realize that many of us not only need to hear that but also need to hear that it's okay. That our relationship with God is going to have highs and lows but that we should never feel as though, if we're not frolicking in fields of lilies toward candy cane plains with butterflies flapping their wings all around us, there's something wrong with us. Or, even worse, . . . that we're "bad" followers of Christ. The truth is that following God can be messy. Not because God drags us into messy situations but because we find that our messy selves follow us into whatever situation we're in. The truth for me is that it feels as though half the time I don't even know what I'm doing. So, how in the world am I to know what God wants of me? There are times when I'm angry with God and can find bitterness creeping into my heart because he seems to be ignoring my plea. I long to be held by him but just "know" that won't happen unless I die or he comes again—whichever happens first.

Yes, our relationship with God has its highs and lows, but for some reason we've morphed into a Christian culture that feels as though our space with God needs to be refurbished so that it's always cheery and on good terms with God and everyone else. But whose life and relationships really are that way? Mine aren't, and I certainly have never met anyone else who can say theirs is. And so, what do we do? Are we to live a false life and exist in a false narrative with God (which wouldn't work because he knows us better than we know ourselves)? Do we tell people to just "pray about it," assuring them that "it will all work out" (praying is great—but those kinds of clichés have never been helpful to me)? Or can we actually wrestle with a holy God and not walk away with the limp of all limps (think Jacob in Genesis 32:22–32)? My take on this: let's be real and authentic. I affirm that we *can* legitimately wrestle with God, all the while knowing this in no way makes us a horrible, subpar, or "bad" Christian. If we affirm that God knows us already, then why hide? And if we affirm that God is big and wise enough to handle sin and death and resurrection—then I'm sure he can shoulder the burden of my wrestling with him (Job reminds us of that). I say let's enter into the truths expressed by the psalmists and work to understand their wrestling with God.

The psalms are a roadmap to an authentic relationship with God. Through the experiences of others, we are invited to share an insider's glimpse into their sorrow, joy, fear, anger, and a whole host of other emotions. When we read and engage with the psalms, our eyes become open not only to the psalmists' plight but to the constancy of our God. Through the psalms we are given the freedom and encouragement to allow the space in which we're currently residing—whatever that may look like— to be lifted up to God above, who hears us, knows us, and has already answered our deepest pleas and needs through the death and resurrection of his Son, Jesus Christ, and the indwelling of the Holy Spirit within each of our hearts.

It was for this reason that I began writing these reflections. What started as a simple blog on the psalms years ago for the youth and leaders of the MIDWEST B.A.S.I.C. Bible Camp in Iowa has developed into something much bigger. My prayer for you is that—wherever you may find yourself in life, you will carve out time each day to spend with the God who loves you and has given his life as a ransom for you. That no matter where today (or any other today) may find you, you will make sure to spend time alone in his company. What you'll find in the following pages is this:

1. An encouragement to read each of the 150 psalms.
2. A bit of history, context, and meaning of the psalm (if the information is available).
3. Words and reflections that stood out for me (my own wrestlings and wonderings).
4. Three questions for each psalm that encourage *you* to dig a little deeper into the text and listen for its voice in your life.

Parenthetically, I've chosen with respect to Psalm 119 to spend multiple days plumbing its depths, one day for each of its 22 eight-verse sections, all dealing in one way or another with the topic of God's Law. Sound repetitive? You'll actually be amazed by the rich connections between the Old Testament Law and the New Testament Jesus.

I pray that this book will remind you of the freedom you have to be in an authentic relationship with God and that my own reflections and challenges will help you navigate these treasures and give breath and breadth to your own dialogue with God. Worship journal, anyone?

I pray that this book may remind you that, no matter the space in which you find yourself, God loves you more than you will ever know—so much that he offered the life of his own sinless Son, Jesus Christ, in sacrifice for yours.

I pray that, as you walk this journey with me, the Holy Spirit will continue to open up your heart to his life-giving Word—a Word reminding us daily, with every stroke of the pen, that these writers thrust us forward into God's limitless love and the hope he offers.

Finally, I pray that you will be reminded that nothing can remove from you the love of God and the hand he has placed on your life. You cannot undo the cross, you cannot undo Christ's justification, and you cannot undo God's love. So, no matter the wrestling or the limp, no matter the scrapes or the bruises, no matter the words uttered in the throes of anger or angst—remember that God can handle it . . . and that he will not think any less of you, his child!

Thank you for taking this journey with me through the book of Psalms. My prayer is that this book will offer you an opportunity to wrestle with God through engagement with my simple words and reflections.

A PSALM OF
WELL-DRINKING

L et's start at the beginning and read together Psalm 1!

What's interesting about this psalm is that it is very general in its purpose. In its simplicity it becomes the basis for understanding what all the other psalms are going to declare: God is good, . . . and all other things outside him are bad. Life with God is good, life without God . . . yeah, good luck with that! What God asks of his children and how they are to treat others and live life vs. what society says. So, which do you chose?

We live in a world that is trying to gain control of your thoughts, your mind, your actions, your decisions—and, ultimately, your heart. A world that is wanting you to live and drink from it rather than living and drinking from the goodness of God. And I absolutely love this image of a tree and how the person who walks in the light of God is like that tree, planted next to streams of water. So, what does that mean? The image is beautiful and cool, but it has to speak to us, mean something to us, find a peace within us; ultimately, it must take root in our hearts (pun intended).

A tree that is healthy not only drinks from its healthy source, but as soon as that water becomes tainted it is no longer a healthy tree. No longer is refreshing, cool, clean water being pulled into its roots. Now, because the water is infected, the tree, too, is infected. All the pathogens, chemicals, and nasty runoff from the fields that made their way into the water are now circulating throughout the life of the tree. What's really cool is that, when you cut down a tree and look at its rings, you can see these things. You can see the stamp of the years that were lean and dry. You can see when the tree started getting diseased and infected. Why? Because the water, the life-giving source of the tree, means something.

The psalmist refers in verse 4 not to the good but to the tainted tree—a reference to ourselves, each one of us—because we have become just that. We are influenced and misguided each and every day. Even when we see the healthy water, the good things, we for whatever reason still are drawn to that which hurts us. Pornography, sex, violence, hatred, self-interest, and a myriad of other evils could be talked about forever! But I also think that so often what starts off as clean quickly becomes polluted. It's the brokenness that we've come to know and experience. And so, the tree and water become a beautiful metaphor for you and me (trees) and holy and good water (God and his Word) vs. you and me (trees) and stink-u-bus water (sin, destruction, everything outside the goodness of God).

So, here's the truth: one cannot drink from the Word of God, from the Spirit of God, and also drink from things outside him. Nor can we get healthy and be strong and true while still ingesting the poisons that are around us. Just as a doctor would not give you medicine *along with* the poison that brought you in to see them in the first place, we must drink solely from God and him alone and stay away from harmful things.

So, how? How does one move from the nasty water to the good water? Well, first off, the psalmist declares that we must simply be in the Word of God. We must read the Scripture, chew on it, and see its truth and relevance in our lives. But we must also carry it with us and let it circulate throughout our bodies. We cannot just read our Bibles and then say, "Whew! I'm done now!" Just as we don't just take a sip of water when we're parched, we don't just take a one-time sip of the Bible. We drink it in. Because just as water strengthens, cleanses, nourishes, and gives us what we need—so too does God's Word.

Because you and I, believers of God's good Word, know that the drinking doesn't stop there. The truth is that our sins and decisions in life seem to push us further and further from the water. Somehow these trees (you and I) have grown legs and walked away from our source of goodness. The truth is, though, that God has picked up his stream and run it right through our trunks. By way of Christ, God gave us exactly what we need: refreshing, life-giving, soul-restoring, eternal water.

THREE QUESTIONS FOR YOU TO CHEW ON:

1. Which source do you tend to drink from? Why?
2. How is your time alone with God and his Word? Is it important enough for you?
3. What are some things you can do to drink more of God and less of this world?

A KINGDOM BATTLE
PSALM

Begin your reading today with Psalm 2.

Psalm 2 is a really difficult application text for our day because it's not a lament or confessional psalm but a "coronation psalm" that was used for kings back in the day. It's an exhortation (an urging by someone) on how a king should act—especially in light of the covenant given by God (the claim that he alone is in charge).

We must remember that the Davidic Covenant stated that God promised David through Nathan the prophet (2 Samuel 7; 1 Chronicles 17:11–14; 2 Chronicles 6:16) that the Messiah (Jesus Christ) would come from his lineage and from his tribe, Judah, and that not only would this King endure forever, but his kingdom would as well. So, when we read this psalm, we not only understand the issues of the day but also look forward to what was to come, via the Messiah, in the future.

So, what does that mean for us? We must always first understand what is happening in the text so that we can understand what it means for us today. Whereas Psalm 1 deals with light and darkness between *people*, Psalm 2 looks at it via contrasting two kingdoms: the kings and kingdoms of darkness (and of this world) vs. the King and his kingdom of light.

Unless we're going to talk about you, or me, becoming a "ruler" in this world, we really need to read this as God's asking of us (as he does of David) to make a decision as to which kingdom we are going to live and work and serve in. That which calls us away from God or that which calls us to him? That which "plots evil" and serves itself and our own needs, or that which works toward reconciliation, love, and grace and puts others first?

I'm going to assume that most of you have had it ingrained in you that there are things of this world and things above it. Attitudes, actions, and desires that this world seeks and acts upon that reflect living a life for "me," and then things *outside* this world that speak of attitudes, actions, and desires that look toward heaven and reflect living a life for others. This may seem repetitive, but it is so for a reason. The Messiah of which this text speaks came for this very reason. Jesus Christ came to restore and redeem a world that had collapsed in on itself instead of blossoming outwardly and opening up unto others (I picture a rose; when it is closed up it does not do anything but fill its own need, but when it blossoms it produces beauty, food, and color into the world that are hard to match).

I want to close with us looking at something truly honest. This psalm ends with the proclamation, the call, to take "refuge in him." To fight against the kingdom of this world that you battle against day in and day out . . . and rest in God. Fall into him; allow your shoulders to slough off their burden and relax. Allow his shelter to give you peace. I picture one of those great Midwest Iowa storms when the rain comes pounding down and it's so heavy and thick and fast that the earth doesn't even have time to drink it up before it starts to flood. Can you imagine having no way of finding shelter from this kind of storm? Can you imagine having to stand underneath a tree or overpass simply to find refuge from the onslaught of rain? That's what we have in this text, but it's not a storm from which we seek refuge— it's a world and society that say we have to be prettier, skinnier, taller, more athletic, more focused on self, and more willing to step on all those who may try to stop us from reaching the top, . . . because the "top" is the only place to be. Christ tells us not only that with him this isn't so but the very opposite, that we are to serve the Lord, whose value system is opposite that. We serve a Lord who healed the sick, gave his life for the lowly, and put all of them above himself.

THREE QUESTIONS FOR YOU TO CHEW ON:

1. What in this psalm speaks to you? To what are you drawn? Why?

2. How can we live in this world and yet still be in that world to which God calls us?

3. If we firmly believe that the kingdom of God is now (which we do), what are some tangible things *we* can do to help live this out in a world that is pushing against it and us?

A PSALM OF
FLEETING PETITION

Please turn with me to Psalm 3.

David's son Absalom is vying for the crown, which means that he's looking to get rid of the current king—his father. So, David is on the run, fleeing from his enemies, fleeing from his courts, fleeing from his son, fleeing from his home. And while on the run he calls out to God for help. On the run, when people say that God will abandon him and not answer his prayers for deliverance, he calls out to God because he knows God. He has a relationship with him.

So, what does this all mean? It means that there is only one place where we can find comfort and strength. There is only one person who does not seek to remove you by force from where you are. There is only one person who truly comes to you in your time of need, and it's not your best friend or sibling—it is God. Don't get me wrong, Mom and Dad and family and friends will be there for you and will have your back, but they cannot truly give you refuge. They cannot give you the peace that lasts.

What I find truly interesting (and encouraging) is that in this fleeing of David from his son and his son's army, in his time of ultimate need, in his worries about what will happen, and most likely in his anger over what is taking place, he doesn't seek out God's wrath, nor does God bring it. David doesn't ask God to go out and avenge him. He seeks God to protect him, to give him strength to hold fast without fear; he asks for deliverance (removal from this moment). Yes, David asks God to "strike all my enemies," but this is a defensive move—not an offensive one. Maybe it's because David is running from family, and we know that David loves his son tremendously and doesn't want him hurt. Maybe David understands that *this type* of petition is not one God will act upon. Or maybe he simply understands that, regardless of where he is or who is after him, the Lord will continue to sustain him and give him what he needs.

I like that word *sustain*. It's a verb that means to strengthen or support physically and/or mentally. We can be sustained by food or nutrients; we can be sustained by the prayers and petitions of people; and we use this verb to express that something "worked," that it gave us what we needed for the duration of a trying time.

For David, being "sustained" by God included protection ("shield around me" in v. 3), God's voice answering him at all times (v. 4), God waking him in the morning (ordaining the days of his life), and God giving him the protection and comfort he needed to actually lie down at night (one must be "at peace" in order to fall asleep). A synonym for *sustain* is "support." God supports his people by giving them what they need when they need it—which is daily.

I love how this psalm ends: "From the LORD comes deliverance. May your blessing be on your people." This moves from David and his needs to God's people and *their* needs. I would argue that the text isn't actually about David at all—it's about God and what he does for his people. His flock. His children. David understood that his position was over God's people and that it was God who had put him there for a specific reason (and God who would remove him if he so desired)—it wasn't, ultimately, about David at all. David had made it about himself numerous times, but after each sinful incident he had been corrected and reminded of God's charge to him to lead God's people—to serve them and him—never himself.

That is ultimately where we, too, must go. David used his final few words of this psalm not to continue to plead his own need or even affirm his own faith; he used the last bit of ink in his pen and the last space on his parchment to ask God to simply bless God's people. To sustain them in all they need. Again, it's a movement from the individual to the corporate.

I think David's on to something . . .

THREE QUESTIONS FOR YOU TO CHEW ON:

1. What in this psalm speaks to you? To what point(s) are you drawn? Why?
2. Have you ever asked God to help others when you yourself were the one in need?
3. Why is it so difficult for us to put others before ourselves?

A PSALM OF
CHAOS AND FOCUS

Begin today's reading with Psalm 4.

When I was learning to ride a motorcycle, the instructors told us that when we rode, we were to *look at* where we were wanting to go. The reasoning behind this is that our body will naturally follow in the direction our head and gaze are focused. I am unsure why this happens, but for some reason it makes sense to me. This analogy works for the rest of life as well. When we focus our attention on something that happens in life, all other things get wrapped up and tag along as well. When my high school girlfriend broke up with me and I became angry and sad, everything else in my life became affected as well. How I treated others, how I responded to others—all of this was affected by that one storm. I see it when my kids have had a rough day at school. Their emotions take over and then spill over to all other relationships and activities for that day. The rest of the night is simply harder on us all because they are consumed by something else. I still do this when I've had a rough day at work.

For some reason, when we find ourselves in the storms of life and gaze into the angry and dangerous elements, we are drawn in and consumed. It's like the red, evil eye of Sauron in *The Lord of the Rings*. Its gaze is strong and powerful and simply sucks us in! We can't see anything else or do anything else . . . it simply takes us over. David, in our psalm, is in the midst of that storm. There is a crisis at hand, yet even while David is seeking relief from his distress, he is able to turn away from the opposition at hand and focus his gaze Godward.

David writes that *because* he has a relationship with God, he knows that God hears and will answer his prayers and have mercy on him. *Because*

God is in his life, the light of his face will shine upon him again (a great relief when you are in the midst of darkness), his heart will fill with joy, he will find peace and be able to rest—and, ultimately, he will dwell in safety. God will not forsake him or abandon him.

I think this is something we all know, but something that is hard to remember when we have been sucked in and are being consumed by a life event that is painful. The death of a loved one can bring anger—especially when it's unexpected. The divorce of parents or a rift in a marital relationship can bring anger and questions. If God is in full control, why would he allow this? Why would he even bring two together if they are simply going to be ripped apart later on? So many storms in life try to fracture our faith, and when we fear getting sucked into the storm and focus on it, we begin to steer our ship *into* that storm instead of steering for safety. Instead of looking for God and his promises, our heads get turned, . . . then our bodies follow suit, . . . and then our thoughts, emotions, and the rest of us. Pretty soon, we feel ourselves to be swallowed up. While I think David recognized this (it's not said, but it's implied), he also recognized that the same kind of "following" that our body does when our heads and gazes are turned toward the storm happens when we gaze upon God and seek *his* shelter, *his* safety, *his* comfort.

The storms are still going to happen. Death and destruction will threaten us all in many ways, . . . but darkness cannot cast out darkness—only light can. In the middle of a lighted room you will not find a speck of darkness creeping in and slowly taking over. Instead, it is light that shatters any darkness and begins taking over. We must always focus on the light.

In the midst of the pain and chaos that can surround us, we must focus on him. Always focus on God, and he will always bring you safely home.

THREE QUESTIONS FOR YOU TO CHEW ON:

1. What in this psalm speaks to you? At what point does the psalmist hit home? Why?
2. Have you ever been fully consumed by a storm of life that then spilled over into other areas of your life?
3. What are some ways/things by which we can refocus our attention when that "eye of Sauron" is drawing us in?

A PSALM OF TWO PATHS

Open your Bible with me to Psalm 5 and take a moment to read it.

I don't know about you, but I am not very good at listening to people moan, whine, and complain. I just don't want to hear it. I am a "do something about it" type of person. You have a problem . . . then respond! Take some action. *Do something about it.* That's easier said than done sometimes—and we know that. What do you do when you've taken action and the results have not changed? What do you do when circumstances are simply outside your control? What do you do when you've banged your head against the wall in frustration because things simply are not changing? You go to God in prayer. Not only do you go to God in prayer, but you ask him to lead and take over. Not only do you ask God to lead, but you ask him to lead *you* in what steps *he* would have you take. It's the "Make your steps my steps, Lord" type of request.

I remember having a coworker years ago (when I was outside of ministry) with whom I simply did not get along; it seemed as though every interaction we had with each other made my feelings toward her become more negative. With every conversation, every email, I just felt anger brewing. She simply was not a nice person, and it seemed as though she was consistently trying to get people to "bite" and respond in a negative way that she could use against them. I remember finally taking the bait and responding to something she had done by doing exactly what it was I so despised *about* her. Instead of taking the right path of response, as I had for so long, I took the incorrect one. It did not turn out well.

In the midst of all the chaos that is happening around them, all the lies being told, the arrogance being poured out, . . . in the midst of all of this the psalmist responds by asking God to lead them. He knows that God will deal with things the way God will deal with them, but he is neither God nor able to do what he does. So, he cries out for help and asks for one thing: to be led in righteousness. Set the right path before him, he prays, so he can walk it and not fall trap to the destructive, wicked ways of those who surround him. Yes, he asks for protection and refuge within God's arms—but that can happen only when one walks that right path and falls in line with living a godly life.

I find it interesting that this request to have the Lord set the path "straight" (v. 8) had nothing to do with its being an easy or a flat path—it was simply straight, . . . which means that it could also have been really, really difficult. I knew the straight and right path before responding to my coworker; I had been walking along it for quite some time, but it was getting hard, so I took an easier path and then learned that the easy path wasn't the right path. Ultimately, I found out that getting *back* on that right path (the way of righteousness) was much harder. The apologies, the conversations, the humility—none of that was easy.

We all, throughout life, will interact with many different people, and oftentimes our gut response won't be the right one. Yet we will make that gut response and regret it later on more than once. Still, we believe in a God of love, grace, and forgiveness. We believe in a God who allows us to wander off that path in order that we may learn his ways and know what the right path was and is and why it's better. Making mistakes may be hard, but it's through that process that we learn. And, ultimately, we must declare that a God who actually *gives us the right path* is One who is not only deeply in love with us and wants us to make the right decisions but also is intimately involved with our everyday affairs and watching out for us.

THREE QUESTIONS FOR YOU TO CHEW ON:

1. What in this psalm speaks to you? To what verse(s) are you drawn? Why?
2. How do *you* respond when you don't know what to do? What is your go-to action?
3. When was the last time your path was "straight" and yet not easy? What did you learn from that experience?

A PSALM OF
PAINFUL WAITING

Open your Bible with me and read Psalm 6.

Context. Well, our Bibles tell us it's David, and, clearly, he has been in some pain, as he speaks of being faint and needing healing because his bones are in agony. Is he sick? Is he on the run? Is he in hiding? Is he in the middle of war? David cries out to God to "hold up" before acting on his discipline. Why? Because he is repentant of his sins. Psalm 6 is part of a list of psalms that are considered "the Penitential Psalms" in that the writers are repenting and seeking forgiveness. So deep is their sorrow that they feel faint, their bones are in agony, their soul is in anguish, and they spend the nights groaning and weeping—so much so that, should they continue to lie in bed crying, the volume of tears would probably create a river and float them away!

What's interesting is that all this pain and suffering is *on them*. God isn't forcing them to flood the earth with their own tears. God isn't hurting their bones or making their souls anguish. It's all the psalmist. Bringing the psalm into the context of the reader praying with the psalmist, she is the one in her own pain and sorrow. I think she is expecting God to immediately respond, in anger, and punish her for her sins; it's almost as though she is waiting for it. As though this wrath of heaven will come down as a bolt of lightning and strike her dead at any moment!

Have you ever felt that way? Have you ever felt as though you were waiting for God's righteous anger to come crashing down and smite you off the face of the earth? Or maybe it's not God you can relate to. Maybe you came from an abusive home, where the threat of your mom or dad coming home to "deal" with you was made. Maybe the threat hasn't been made, but you've been there enough times to know that once _____ gets home you will be severely punished.

The psalmist, as he writes—as he laments, as he cries out for forgiveness from God, as he goes through his own struggles over what he has done and begins living out the punishment that *he himself* has not only brought on but handed down to himself—knows that God is listening and will hear and respond. He knows that the Lord accepts his apology—his prayer for deliverance from his woes (v. 9).

This is the grace we find in this psalm. We do not believe in a God who doesn't listen, doesn't help, doesn't extend love/grace/mercy, and doesn't respond. And nowhere in Scripture would we find the support of a nonexistent, never-present, aloof God. From Genesis through Revelation we see this complete, beautiful story of God's work amongst his people. And in that story, as well, we see God's wayward children constantly breaking his laws. And through that story we see God consistently responding to them—not with anger but with love. But that's only the tip of the story. The complete story is about God's *complete* love of his children, a love that is seen, experienced, shown, felt, observed, and given in our Lord and Savior Jesus Christ.

Which leads me to verse 5, where the psalmist asks, "Among the dead no one proclaims your name. Who praises you from the grave?" Well, in short: we do. The grave is where we were, and yet through Christ we are no longer. So, we praise him. Yes, the psalmist is asking this rhetorical question, as the grave is where he sees himself going—but while that may *seem* like our destination, we praise God that it is not. Can you see how all of this points to Christ?

- *No* grave because of Christ
- Cry for mercy: Yes—enter Christ
- God accepting our prayers: Yes—Christ is our ultimate prayer need.
- Overwhelming enemies? Yes—because of Christ

So yes, I absolutely get that David is in this painful waiting period as he waits for the work of God to come to fruition in his life. And I definitely have been in that place/space—but what exactly are we waiting for? Not only has God already responded (by way of Jesus), but God's grace and mercy have been poured out upon us—not his wrath and destruction (thank you, Jesus, for that too).

THREE QUESTIONS FOR YOU TO CHEW ON:

1. What in this psalm speaks to you? At what point are you drawn in? Why?
2. Why does it seem that even though we declare God's goodness we are still waiting for possible wrath from him? Where does this belief come from?
3. I love the image of "unfailing love" in verse 4. But is "unfailing" an accurate adjective? God simply *is* love. It doesn't "fail" or "succeed"—it simply *is*. Is there a better way to understand God's love?

A PSALM OF
REAPING AND SOWING

Consider with me the words of Psalm 7.

Holy Cow, this is intense! Someone is needing some deliverance—*now!* Someone is being pursued—about to be torn apart like a lion with its prey—and is there no one to rescue him? If you've ever watched a nature show and seen how lions hunt and then eat said prey, you can sense the intensity here! We get a feeling of the chaotic frenzy that is surrounding the writer.

We've all been "wronged" before, but have you ever been accused of something you didn't do? Or maybe rumors were spread that you *did* do something when in fact you were innocent. Was someone trying to ruin your reputation or name? For whatever reason, people seem to feel the need to hurt others and bring them down because their own reputations are being threatened. It's a kind of power struggle. From petty squabbles that get out of hand to simple misunderstandings. It's not only your word against mine—but it's either you or me, and I'm going to do everything in my power to bring you down before you get to me!

David is on the run for his life. He is seeking refuge from the lion that hunts him and wants to take him down. Scratch that. He's on the run from a lion (we assume Saul) that wants to rip him to shreds and utterly destroy all that he has and is. That wants him to cease to exist. And what's really interesting is that, while David is running for his life, he asks God not only to rescue him but to actually allow this devouring to happen, should God find fault or evil within him. If he has brought this on by something he has done, then he asks God to allow the lion to catch him and feast on him: "Let him trample my life to the ground and make me sleep in the dust" (v. 5).

Let's be honest here: none of us are innocent in life. All of us, David included, have blood on our hands. Maybe David didn't deserve having Saul come after him, you probably didn't deserve the rumors spread or the hatred thrown at you, I never deserved some of the things that happened to me, . . . but I did deserve others that I *was* punished for. Not only that, but we deserved much worse for things that were never caught or seen.

The fact of the matter is that David fully knows he is not innocent of sin. Yet, there is a difference between that and what he is seeing here: *intention* to sin and hurt. David uses the term of someone being "pregnant with evil" (v. 14). And Jesus says in Matthew 26:52 that "those who draw the sword will die by the sword." Essentially, someone who conceives trouble will have that same evil fall back upon them. Evil produces evil. Paul writes in his letter to the Galatians (Galatians 6:7) that you "reap what you sow," which is pretty much the same thing Jesus says but broader in sense and inclusion. What I find fascinating here is the idea that the person who so passionately sought out David could have used that passion and intensity for good. What if those who worked so hard to spread lies about you would use their effort instead to spread *love* and kindness about you and others? What if we didn't desire to "conceive" evil but instead desired to conceive and produce love? Would this not have that same and, yet opposite, effect that both Jesus and Paul speak of? Reaping love and sowing love should produce love in others and myself—right? Yes, it does (read vv. 8–9 of Galatians 6 for exactly what Paul writes).

So, what does this mean for us? I think there are a few takeaways:

- Remember that you are not as innocent as you think. This doesn't mean you deserve whatever hard thing is happening to you right now, but neither does it mean that you are as good as you think you are (hard pill to swallow).
- Do not pay back sin with sin, hatred with hatred, and anger with anger.
- Reap and sow love. It *will* be difficult—nearly impossible, but it can be done.

THREE QUESTIONS FOR YOU TO CHEW ON:

1. What in this psalm speaks to you? To what are you drawn? Why?
2. How can you, wherever you are, "conceive and produce" love?
3. In verse 8 the psalmist asks to be "vindicated . . . according to my righteousness." How does that even happen? Are any of us truly "righteous"? Do we even have the right to ask this?

A PSALM OF "YOU WANT ME TO DO WHAT?"

Begin today's reading with Psalm 8.

For me, it is really hard not to see contrasting images in this text. From the grandiose to the tiny—and even in the smallest there is still this majestic massiveness. The moon and the stars are huge and vastly complex, and yet there is a simplicity, I suppose, in comparison to us humans. In fact, we have been crowned with glory and honor—we have been made rulers over the works of God's hands. Here is God, the majestic Creator of all things, who has intimately used his fingers to place stars and planets in the sky and then created all these immense galaxies that we are only beginning to discover and understand, . . . and those same fingers formed you and me! Not only that, but he has asked us, the "crown" of his creation, *to rule over* that which he has created! That is amazingly beautiful and yet frightfully scary in terms of our accountability!

I suddenly feel as though the weight of said planets is upon my shoulders! Why, God? Why have you asked us (or in this case *me*) to take on such a task! Actually, you didn't ask—you simply enabled and entrusted us to do so! I concur with David here when I shout out (as it is in the rhetorical question in v. 4): *Why?* (In case David wasn't asking why and was simply amazed, I will ask *for* him: Why!?)

We are unsure where David was in his life at this point or what was going on when he penned this psalm—but I cannot help but picture him writing this as he reflects on his youth and all that he has done. I see the shy boy who was a shepherd of sheep. A young man full of compassion and dedication to the Lord, a young man who was a protector and defender at heart! A young man who eventually would run to the front lines of the battle between the Philistines and the Israelites and decide to take on the Philistine giant Goliath, whom nobody else could beat (read 1 Samuel 17 for that story)! A young man who would eventually become king. I wonder whether at any point in David's life he ever wondered why God had in mind all that was going to happen through him. Why God would use him for such a task. Who picks a shepherd of sheep to lead a nation of people?

So, I ask again—Why, God? The reason is simple—it's because God cares and loves us. And even more so because God knows us. He created us!

I frequently am amazed at all that God is and does, and yet he still asks me to take part in his plan. I am utterly flabbergasted that the Maker of heaven and earth *entrusts* me with the care of his people. Who am I that you are mindful of me, God? I have a hard enough time taking care of *myself*, and you ask me to take care of others? To watch over them, lead them, guide them, encourage them, teach them, share with them, and love them? If God had called me on my phone to tell me this, I'm pretty sure I'd have hung up, thinking it was a prank call or he had simply dialed the wrong number!

But that's just it, isn't it? God absolutely knows what he is doing and has invited us into the care of his world. God has intimate knowledge of you and me and has blessed us with gifts and attributes that are to be used to care for his kingdom, his people, his animals, his world. Everything and anything in it. If you are in it, if you are in this world, . . . then you are a steward of it.

I don't think this psalm was meant to overwhelm; instead, it invites us to marvel at God's immensity and yet his intimacy with us. If you're anything like me, this becomes compounded when we remember that this same majestic, vastly powerful God entered into our lives later on through that line of David and came to earth as a human—with the sole purpose of dying for you and me. I don't think anything more intimate could ever be done.

For me this begs the question: God has entrusted you with gifts. How are you using them in his kingdom and for his purposes?

THREE QUESTIONS FOR YOU TO CHEW ON:

1. What in this psalm speaks to you? Where does it draw you in? Why?
2. Do you ever find yourself asking, "Why me, God?" Why do you think God chooses us for certain tasks and not for others?
3. How are you being a steward of this world?

A PSALM OF "REFUGENESS"

B egin today's reading with Psalm 9.

First off, this is most definitely a psalm of praise and thanksgiving. But it's very specific in its praise and thanksgiving in that the psalmist is praising God for his *vindication*. For his being proven "right" in the sight of those who oppress the palmist, those who desire to harm him, those who desire to ruin him. He has not only been proven innocent—to vindicate also means to set free from. So, all those words, all that harm that the enemy has wanted to place upon him, God does something about. But when? When does vindication happen?

As we read through this psalm, we begin to see that part of this vindication is in God's "refugeness" (that's not a word, but it works in my head). Numerous times in this psalm we see this image of what it looks like to have God as our refuge. God, as he is enthroned on high, acts as a refuge by rebuking and destroying enemies (vv. 3–5), is a "refuge for the oppressed" (v. 7), is a "stronghold" (v. 9), and lifts us from the gates of death (v. 13). Not only that, but there is "salvation" in him (v. 14). All of these images speak of God's "refugeness." God, in his majesty, in his holiness, is our safety and security—our stronghold and fortress in *all* times. He is our place to flee for protection, as well as security.

But let's be clear here: whatever vindication we think we need, we really do not deserve. This is the whole point of the gospel, is it not? This is our whole understanding of grace, is it not? You, me, your parents, your neighbors, your brother and sister (you probably already knew that one)— are not "innocent" by any definition of the word—and this is understood in the last two verses of our psalm when the psalmist speaks of "mortals."

While he definitely cries out for God to not let his foes triumph, this must be widened with the understanding that God must not let *any mortal* triumph. Again, we must be clear here: allowing mortals to triumph and not be judged by God would be detrimental to the human race (this is where we come to understand that none of us are innocent). You and I, we are vindictive, spiteful, and harmful people, not only to ourselves but to each other, and left to our own devices we would consistently harm each other, overtake each other, uproot each other, ensnare each other, . . . and eventually perish, either at the hands of each other or of ourselves (which is what the psalmist is asking God to rescue him from).

But God is our fortress—is he not? God is our refuge—is he not? He doesn't let our foot slip (Psalm 121:3), nor will he allow you to stumble (John 11:9). He hears the cries of the afflicted, the oppressed, the hurting, and he responds by securely wrapping us up and being our refuge.

The psalmist closes by asking God to judge the nations—and by the grace of God, he has. It is *because* of how we harm others and neglect those for whom we are to care that we have been found guilty and sentenced to death. But it is at the same time *because* of who God is (the One and only judge) that in our guilt God has stepped in and taken our sentence of death *upon himself*. Why? Because he is our fortress and stronghold. It is in him, and him alone, that we find refuge. He does not forget the needy and the afflicted—and he will not let them perish.

Psalm 9 is a psalm that reminds us to simply give thanks to God for what he has done—from the little to the large things, and then all that space in between. But I think this psalm needs to stand as a reminder for us that throughout life we will have challenges. That even a life fully given to the divine doesn't mean we won't still need refuge. The biggest mistake we can make as Christians is to think that life is going to be one grandiose, happy day for us, frolicking in lush fields filled with fluttering butterflies and bluebirds chirping on our shoulders. Life is rough; some of this we bring upon ourselves, and some of it is brought upon us by others. But we give glory to God, our Fortress, in whom we find rest. Both now and for eternity.

THREE QUESTIONS FOR YOU TO CHEW ON:

1. What in this psalm speaks to you? Where are you drawn? Why?
2. We read (vv. 7–10) that God reigns forever and rules the world in righteousness—and yet it seems plain that this is *not* our reality. It's the hope and knowledge we have as we declare that his righteousness will reign over all else, and yet the current corruption, anger, and hate that are in this world don't seem to match up with those verses. Or do they?
3. Someone hurting may read verse 12 and feel that God *does* ignore their cries. What might be your response to people with such feelings?

A PSALM OF WAITING FOR GOD'S RESPONSE

Begin by opening your Bible and reading Psalm 10.

When "bad" people are being bad, the last thing we want is for them to appear to be thriving in their badness. So, why is it that oftentimes bad people have their ways "prosper," while the "good" people do not? Why is it that, despite their lies and threats and vulgarity, they seem to have the Midas Touch?

Great question—but, unfortunately, we don't get an answer in this text.

What's even more painful than that question is that the psalmist paints the picture that this wicked person, the one he is crying out to God to do something about, is *blatantly* doing evil in the eyes of God. Such people know who God is, and they scoff at him. They "revile the LORD" (v. 3), making "no room for God" (v. 4). Such a person rejects God's laws (v. 5) and laughs at even the notion that God would look down and see what he is doing and care (v. 11).

I remember watching the movie *The Ghost and the Darkness* (1996) and learning about these "man-eating lions of Tsavo" that not only terrorized a camp of railroad workers back in 1898 but killed and *consumed* at least 35 people for nine months! Two lions—that knew of the harm that could come upon them by humans—waited near the village, crept in at night, caught the helpless victims, and dragged them off and ate them. This is what I picture in this text—and I'm not sure which disturbs me more, this scoffing at God by this horrible person or the fact that he is waiting in secret for victims and then catching the helpless and dragging them off and crushing them under his strength!

Regardless of our feeling with regard to the evil person, I find a few truth nuggets that we need to see here.

First off, kudos to the psalmist for seeing this horrid person and what he was doing to the poor and helpless and then responding! The psalmist is pleading with God to rise up and defend him, help him to never be a victim again! Also, he declares not only the closeness of God to his children, not only the anger that comes upon God when the poor are oppressed and victimized, but also how he absolutely cannot stand for it and *must* act!

But wait—we see in verse 1 that the psalmist is pleading with God to not "hide" himself in times of trouble. So, how is this working? How is God working when it looks as though that is actually the problem—that God is *not* working?

We must remember that simply because we observe something to be happening or not happening with God doesn't mean that's actually true. Simply because it *appears* as though the wicked triumph over all the weak does not mean that they actually do or ultimately will. Simply because evil and greed and horrid schemes seem to increase in number and the rich are getting richer does *not* mean that the work of God has ceased to be. God is not indifferent to the troubles and plights of his people—we, in fact, proclaim otherwise, as did, and does, the psalmist.

So, how is it that God is not "hiding"? That is the ultimate question here. When evil sets out to invade the hearts of people, when they begin to become greedy, wicked, and lawless, . . . where is God? Why is he not responding in the way we would wish? In a way that we could see?

That is where I question my own motives on what God should do. Should he smite them? Should he rein down lightning and strike them where they stand, right there with eyes wide—frozen and blank—blinking a couple of times and then disintegrating to ash upon the earth (as in the cartoons)? Should God send plagues or floods or other forms of his Old Testament work? What about having the wicked become poor and desolate or any other type of payback for what they have done?

That's precisely the point at which I'm stuck . . . and struck . . . and convicted. *My* desire would actually be for "eye-for-an-eye" retribution—but how would that be any better? Is that not the same vile evil that the psalmist is wanting God to do something about? Dealing with sin and evil is what God is really good at—not me. Me dealing with sin simply involves *more* sin.

Does this mean, however, that we are to do nothing? Not at all! As Eugene Peterson says, when we come to God it puts us "in attentiveness to human needs, developing a compassionate response to every kind of distress.[1] "We need a heart for the oppressed and the victimized—but our hearts need to speak *for* them and *to* them, as well as *against* the oppressors. Our energy needs to be poured out *to* the hurting and not the hateful evil person—knowing that God, in his time, is at work. That's where I am taken with this psalm.

THREE QUESTIONS FOR YOU TO CHEW ON:

1. What in this psalm speaks to you? To what are you drawn? Why?
2. Does God call us to sit and cry out for him to act—or to do something ourselves—or both? Why and how?
3. What are some ways in which God calls *you* to help the oppressed? Do you have any fears about what God has placed on your heart for his people?

---

1   Peterson, Eugene H., *Praying with the Psalms: A Year of Daily Prayers and Reflections on the Words of David* (New York: HarperOne, 1979).

A PSALM FOR THOSE
WAITING

Open your Bible with me and read Psalm 11.

The opening sentence sets the stage for the rest of this short psalm: "In the LORD I take refuge." Game. Set. Match . . . I win.

Have you ever had a conversation with yourself? A few years ago, I was asked to climb Long's Peak in Colorado with a buddy. A few hours into the hike it began to be painfully evident that I was not cut out for this. Every step felt horrible in my legs, back, butt, . . . everything! Every step I took brought me closer to wanting to quit, even though it also brought me closer to the top. I constantly was telling myself, *"Just go 10 more feet . . . 10 more feet . . . ,"* but then I was also telling myself, *"There's no shame in quitting. All you have to do is tell them you're done and you can go home! It's that easy . . ."*

This is what I picture is happening in this text, an inner-monologue argument:

Voice 1: Hey, look at all those archers, all those wicked men who are attacking us. They look strong. They look well defended, . . . and look! They don't even come out to face us—they hide in the shadows to attack!

Voice 2: Yeah—I see it. They do look strong and fierce. Oh, man, . . . this isn't good.

V1 (Voice 1): We should run. Flee. Head to the mountains for safety! We can be protected there. This is something tangible *we* can do. They will slaughter us if we don't!

V2 (Voice 2): Are you kidding? The mountains can't protect us—only God can. He knows my heart, he knows my thoughts and desires—he knows me better than I know myself (Romans 8:27–37). He is righteous and just. He watches over and examines all people—me included!

V1: Listen, I'm telling you: it's okay to do this—God will understand. Plus, what is God going to do here, honestly? You call yourself "righteous," but what can *you* do? What can the righteous person do? You're scared—it's fine. Let's flee this place! *That* is something *you* can do!

(LONG PAUSE)

V2: No . . . the Lord will protect us however he deems fit. Only God will be my shelter, my refuge, my safety. Those archers haven't shot yet . . . I will hold true to God, and in him I'll find comfort.

What's difficult about many of the psalms is that we have no context, no backstory to tell us what exactly is happening and why—all we can really do is speculate. But what we *do* know is that there is a temptation here—a strong temptation.

In truth, we don't know whether this was an actual battle or something else. It could have been simply David or someone else faced with a scenario in which evil people were trying to bring him down. Think of a group of people spreading rumors and lies about someone, and he feels tempted either to join in to save himself or to fire back, and so he's talking to himself. We simply do not know the context, but temptation is temptation—and temptation, in its simplest form, is doing something "unwise," which clearly means that "temptation" is not good.

Temptation, in its Christian understanding, is being pulled in or having a desire to do something that is not good for us, that will harm us *even if* it brings pleasure now. Temptation is a choice that stands before us, asking us to either choose God and his ways or to be unwise and take that path which is *against* God and his desires for us. Temptation is not truth. Temptation is not factual. Temptation is a hidden lie behind the promise of immediate pleasure. Temptation is tricky, nasty, and brutal . . . and can cause more harm than anything else.

What makes this difficult is that we desire immediate outcomes and responses. We are fed by immediate gratification—but oftentimes God does not work that way; too often we want God working in our time and not his. We want refuge now instead of when God chooses to bring it. We want our enemies to be smited (smoted, smotten, smitten . . . you get what I'm saying), to be "dealt with" now instead of later. We are like children in this sense. As Jim Gaffigan says, children simply *hear* the words "ice cream" and want it now. "And make it chocolate!"

But the fact is, if we are wise, if we affirm who God is and that he sits enthroned in his holy temple and observes all things and is in control of all things, and that it is wise to listen to him instead of to temptation—then we must also affirm that it is wise to allow God, in his own time, to do what he will do. What is great is that we see this relationship with the psalmist and the Lord and know that he too wrestled with what it means to be in a relationship with God. The psalmist, too, struggled with temptation. He, too, wanted an immediate response—even if that initial impulse was fleeting.

This psalm reminds us of who we are and what it looks like to trust in the Lord. It reminds us to trust him, . . . and a massive part of that trusting may even mean waiting.

THREE QUESTIONS FOR YOU TO CHEW ON:

1. What in this psalm speaks to you? To what are you drawn? Why?
2. Do you struggle with temptation? If so—how do you overcome it? What steps do you put in place to avoid succumbing to temptation's voice?
3. Verse 5 states that God "hates with a passion." How does the claim that God "hates" sound? As though God is doing something outside his character?

A PSALM FOR HOLY WORDS

Next in line comes Psalm 12.

Every year we go to the polls—sometimes twice a year. And every four years we hit those polls trying to find out who our next president of the United States will be. We'll have taken in all that was given to us via TV and radio commercials, mail flyers, email, Spam, news reports, mass-produced phone call recordings, internet sites, and even television debates. Somewhere, in all that was said by the candidates, is, presumably, the truth. The problem is that it's deep in there. One must wade through dirt and grime to find, see, and hear what a given candidate really believes. The problems are that "no one is faithful anymore," . . . "everyone lies to their neighbor," . . . "everyone flatters each other with their lips," . . . and "every person harbors deception in their hearts."

Both candidates do this, . . . and I do, too.

We tell people lies, we tell them what they want to hear or whatever is needed so that we can save face or get a leg up on the competition. The corporate world so often preys on the weak, then oppresses them because, . . . well . . . they're weak, and why not!? The problem is obvious: this goes against everything we believe in terms of how we are to treat each other. The problem is that so many people simply do not care.

The psalmist finds this abhorrent. How could people be this way? How could people treat others in this manner? Taking this into today's context, I picture her walking down the street and seeing all the suffering people. Behind them stand the swindlers and the people who have hurt them. I see the man telling a bald-faced lie to his neighbor about something he did to him, or maybe a hurtful word he spoke to someone else about him. I picture people spreading rumors, while others say whatever seems expedient to someone in front of them—all while their heart slowly turns to stone with hatred.

Who cares about the man and woman suffering in pain, being taken by swindlers? There are plenty of people who have lots and give lots—they'll be taken care of, right? Who cares if the neighbor stole something or hurt the person next door—it's not as though they have to be friends! Plus, the neighbor can easily replace what was taken or work to dispel the rumor! Actually, who cares about rumors or telling lies? All of those issues can be fixed. Plus, it's only words! Right?

I remember Thumper, from *Bambi*, saying, "If you can't say nuth'n nice, don't say nuth'n at all." And while that's true, the problem is that *not* saying anything can also be bad. And saying something nice when you don't mean it or believe it is bad as well. The problem with all of this is that no matter what our words, they are so often used to hurt and break others down. Our lips flap, our tongue gets going, and everyone needs to watch out because it's me against the world!

The problem is that our words need to speak truth. Our words need to speak for our heart, and too often they don't. But this psalm isn't a lesson in who we *ought* to be; it's a reminder of who God is!

God's words are right and true and flawless. God's words are like "purified silver and gold." God's Word is spoken and done. He doesn't go back on his word, nor does he contradict what he has already said. While we use words to get what we want, God uses words to help those in need. We lie, cheat, and steal with our words. God speaks truth, loves, and gives by his.

The human race has become vile and corrupt, but God says that he will fix it. He says that he will redeem us (Isaiah 43:1; 47:4; Luke 1:68; Romans 3:23–24; Colossians 1:13–14) and restore us once again. Restoring us from sin; restoring us from, and to, each other; restoring us from, and to, ourselves.

This psalm not only becomes a reminder of those around us but should remind us of ourselves and the destruction we, too, can cause when we put "me" before "you." This psalm serves as a prayer, a petition, and a call to action, a reminder that God has placed us here on his earth, in his kingdom, to *be* his heart and hands and feet, as well as his lips. So may his words freely come from our lips. And may our lips clearly speak from our heart, which beats for him.

THREE QUESTIONS FOR YOU TO CHEW ON:

1. What in this psalm speaks to you? What draws you in? Why?
2. Are there any situations when a lie is okay?
3. Were there any times in your life when God spoke the truth to you even though it was hard for you to swallow?

A PSALM FOR THE WRESTLING MIND

G et started today by reading Psalm 13.

When I read this psalm, I personally am drawn to the opening two verses. This feeling of pain and sorrow and confusion, . . . of longing for the Lord to answer, respond, . . . *do something!* And because the psalmist is waiting without a response, the worst thing happens: his mind begins to wander and go to assumptions. He begins wrestling with his own thoughts, his imagination, his speculations. And we have all seen enough police dramas and lawyer TV shows to know that speculations don't hold water.

When we are hurting and in pain, the last thing we need is to allow our minds to do what they do best—think. Thinking is good—it helps us each and every day—but our thinking can also get us into a lot of trouble. Not physical trouble, but emotional trouble. Wrestling with our emotions and our thoughts at the same time can lead to stress, anger, feelings of hopelessness, and a feeling of being ignored and even forgotten.

David feels forgotten. In the midst of an enemy that surrounds him, he feels distressed and cast aside. He seeks answers from God. He wants him to respond and bring down his foe so that the enemy does not "rejoice over him" any longer. Many of the psalms convey this feeling of being forgotten or rejected. Even though the words shared by the psalmist are rhetorical in nature, the feeling still stands. There are times when we simply feel abandoned. There are times when we feel far away from God. There are many times when we feel the pressing need for a response.

After this crying out from the psalmist, he proceeds to acknowledge that, even while he doesn't know why God doesn't answer, . . . even though he *feels* the way he does, he *trusts* in the unfailing love of God (v. 5). His *heart rejoices* in his salvation. He will *sing* the Lord's praise, for God has been good to him (v. 6).

We who are believers know that this speaks of Christ. That, while God has never whispered in our ears that we are going to be in this place of pain for another two weeks, thirteen hours, and forty-five minutes (give or take a few seconds), instead God's unfailing love sent his Son, Jesus Christ, to earth to *be* our salvation (Romans 5:11; Colossians 1:20). God's answer to our plight, to our destruction of ourselves, to the pain and suffering that had come upon us (by our own hands—which is a whole other discussion altogether), was to save us. No longer is God's face "hidden." No longer must we speculate as to why God does not answer—he did. He has. He still does.

What's tough is that still today we struggle with our own thoughts. We want answers to the abandonment we feel, the pain we are enduring—and oftentimes our minds bring us to a place we know in our hearts isn't reality. We know that the Holy Spirit draws near to those who are brokenhearted and in pain, and yet our minds wrestle, questioning whether this is true. The psalmist even declares this in Psalm 34:18, so we know that he knew it, felt it, was aware of it—and yet he still wrestled. Our minds, when left to their own devices, go down toward the deep end. Assumptions can hurt us. Wrestling with our own thoughts can damage us.

What if God *did* tell us and consistently repeats, "*You will be in this trouble or state of feeling abandoned for the next week and a half*"? Would that make it any easier? Maybe. Would that change the outcome? *Not at all.* Our time in this state of feeling is the same whether God tells us the outcome or not. The knowledge actually doesn't change anything. It may make us feel better knowing "Okay, just three more days, . . ." but it really doesn't change anything. The length of the term was always going to be a set time. What this is really about is *trust*.

Do we really trust God more if we know the duration of our suffering? Maybe—maybe not. I know that I need to be better at trusting God in the unknown. My trust is really good with the known—it's that opposite trusting action that I need to be better at. I'm not saying God allows these things to happen so that I will trust better—and that's not what the psalmist is proclaiming, either. This psalm is about trusting in God's unfailing love— even when we don't know what is happening. Trusting with our hearts, even when our minds try to speak otherwise.

THREE QUESTIONS FOR YOU TO CHEW ON:

1. What in this psalm speaks to you? At what point are you drawn in? Why?
2. Is it hard for you to trust God? Why or why not?
3. Many people are uncomfortable with demands placed upon God (as in v. 3). Are we permitted to make a demand of God? *Is* it even a demand?

A PSALM OF
FOOLISH WAYS

Pick up your Bible and read Psalm 14.

As with all things, when we read Scripture we must try to take in all that is being said (and usually there is a lot). Drawing in context, not allowing feelings to get in the way of the intentionality of the text, and so forth. Really, it's a matter of simply allowing the text to speak and teach us something—or remind us of something. To reveal not only truth but fact. And ultimately, to declare who God is, and what he not only *has* done but *is* doing in response to what we *have* done and *continuously* do.

What's hard for me is that when I read texts like Psalm 14, I am automatically struck by their hard-hitting opening declaration: in this case that the fool says "'There is no God.' They are corrupt, their deeds are vile; there is no one who does good." Wait a minute—the psalmist intimates that only a fool says there is no God. His words are focused on the fool, but then he takes one big swing at *all* people and says not only that there is "no one who does good" (the end of v. 1) but that "all have turned away, all have become corrupt" (v. 3), going on to restate that "there is no one who does good, not even one."

Hold up here! I may not be the "best" Christian out there, but I don't consider myself a fool when it comes to knowing God. I have *never* said "There is no God," and I pray that those words never run across my lips! I have never uttered the words "I do not believe in you any longer, God!" Nor have I ever done anything remotely close to that kind of blasphemy. So, what's the deal, Psalmister?

I think we need to understand that it's not about what we verbalize—it's about what our heart speaks (as noted at the beginning of this text).

And honestly, our hearts don't fully speak of our love of God. Not always. Our hearts don't always beat in tune and step with his. The psalmist is right when he says, "The fool says in their heart, 'There is no God.'"

Do any of us seek God (v. 2)? Honestly seek and search and live lives in response to him?

Our lips may not say it, but our hearts reveal it: we are all under sin—and the world *is* guilty before God.

We, you and I, are the fools. There's no way around it. In Hebrew the word translated "fool" is pronounced *na-bal*, and it can have a wide range of meanings: godless, futile, worthless, good-for-nothing, miser, fool, unbeliever—the list is somewhat long. It's hard for us to throw all of those together because we look at that list and see something different in each word—and never would we actually admit that *we* were, or are, one of those nabal-ers. But this is the reality we live in. And, in a way, the first half of this psalm is laid out that way. We are all these fools. God does look down and sees that *all of humanity* fails to understand. *All* of humanity has turned away and become corrupt. Even the good we try to do is tainted with ego, dirt, loathing, hatred, anger, indifference, and many other things.

And that is the problem.

We have become so corrupt within that oftentimes we don't want to see what we do and what we are capable of. Sin and self-love are so deeply entrenched in us that they hit us at the core; they have affected our heart. Paul says in Romans 3:11 that nobody understands, . . . because there is no one who seeks God. But this, ultimately, isn't about *us* seeking God—it's about God's response to our failure to seek him. God's response to our failure to love and live lives with hearts that beat as his. So, yes, God looks down, . . . and sees all this corruption and hatred and disgust and contempt, . . . but he doesn't just sit there. He doesn't ask us to stand up and come *up* to him—for he knows we cannot. Instead, he comes to us (this is Christ's birth).

This, as verse 7 reminds us, is the salvation that comes out of Zion—and not only for Israel but for the world. The Lord doesn't simply come and restore his people, the people of Israel, but he expands the understanding and restores all people who perceive the state of their heart, understand that in Christ that heart can be better, . . . and turn to him. But it's not *their* turning that actually happens—it's God turning their hearts to him. It's God "healing" us with his love so we can thus *give and be* his love to others.

Evildoers never do learn, because learning, turning away from harming others, is something we see and experience only in God, the source of all good (Matthew 19:17; Mark 10:18). But thanks be to God that, even in the midst of our own hearts having a hard time learning, God has given us his

Spirit of truth, his Spirit of peace, of reconciliation, of love to act upon our hearts and to lead them into being good stewards of each other, lovers of God Almighty and each other, . . . people who view others as above ourselves (Psalm 143:10).

THREE QUESTIONS FOR YOU TO CHEW ON:

1. What in this psalm speaks to you? What draws you in? Why?
2. Why do we often choose to ignore our personal sins?
3. If God looks down upon all humanity and doesn't find a single person who does good, then why does he stick with us? Why doesn't he just wash his hands of us?

A PSALM OF
NEEDING MORE

Begin this reading with Psalm 15.

Psalm 15 is an interesting one. It starts off with a question, a rather simple one: "Who can dwell where you dwell?" Who can live where you live? Who can be in your presence day and night? And, while this may seem like a simple question, those who know God know that the answer is not easy. Well, it is, . . . but it isn't. The answer is easily answered: nobody. None of us can. And the reason is simple: look through verses 2–5a, and if you can answer "Yes, that is me," then you're in (or is it out?)!

But here's the thing: you can't just answer "yes" to any one of them—you must affirm and do them all. And not just once or periodically, but always. Forever.

Speaking truth from the heart—that's easy, right? And we are good at honoring those who fear the Lord. I never lend money and expect *any* interest, nor have I ever taken a bribe. So, I'm good there! And, I suspect, if you're anything like me, maintaining your word, an oath, even when it hurts, is maybe like 80/20, . . . and then we have the rest.

Blameless? Nope.

Do what is righteous? Most of the time?

No slander on the tongue? Oh boy, is it getting hot in here? . . . I'm feeling a little uncomfortable . . .

Doesn't wrong their neighbor? I haven't today—does that count? Probably not.

So, great—this is a psalm that reminds us of who God is . . . and that we have no ability to dwell in his presence, . . . nor are we able to approach him. We must remember that the understanding of the Israelites was that

God was set apart from them and that, when he came into their presence, he rested upon the temple and the sanctuary. Specifically—in Jerusalem. That was where God was. And even to this day we must remember that *in a way* that still holds true. God cannot be around sin. Perfect holiness can be surrounded only by perfect holiness (outside of Jesus and the Holy Spirit—but that's a different conversation).

The question pondered by David is a spiritual one: Who can visit you, God, where you live? Who can be a guest in your house? Who can come to your table and simply hang out with you? Who is holy enough, good enough, right enough? No one. Not one. Not even David.

I've always thought highly of my desire to be kind and considerate of people, regardless of who they are or aren't. I can remember clearly as a kid (sixth grade, to be exact) playing football with a bunch of my friends, and there was one kid who was playing with us (I'll call him Scott). Anyway, Scott had some mental limitations, and I clearly remember him being so emotionally charged and angry that he kind of lost it. All my friends circled around him and started making fun of him—which, of course, made it worse for Scott. So, I broke up the group, calmed Scott down, and got him away. I share this with you not to pat myself on the back or to toot my own horn but for you, and me, to understand that this isn't enough. Actually . . . this is to be expected. We *should* do this. Every day to every single person we meet.

And here's the thing: even this isn't enough. Because while I am not breaking any other commandments at this time or any other issues on the list here from David, . . . I know that I will. Either earlier in the day I did, or later on I will.

There is no way around it—we should not and *cannot* approach God's sanctuary. We cannot dwell with him or come near him or even be a guest of his. We are incapable. But the beauty of all of this is that when we understand that, we understand the impact of Christ so much better.

Christ came to *us* so that we could come to *him* (John 3:17). Christ came to earth so that he could cleanse us from our sins, so that we could be united with him and God the Father and the Holy Spirit when our time on this earth is up. Everything Christ did was so that we, and this world (God's kingdom), would be restored to what they once were. To a place where people would be blameless and righteous, where people would speak truth with a reverent tongue. Where nobody would despise or hurt others. Plainly put, God worked everything out to make it so that we could be with him in his presence. Through Christ, who allowed that to happen when he died for our sins, and through the Holy Spirit, who fills us up *to speak and to act* in love, since we are incapable in our own power of doing so.

Until then, we must understand that this is where we *will be*—we ain't there yet. And since we ain't there yet, we got some love'n to do here until then. So, walk blamelessly, as best you can. Love all people as much as you can, regardless of class, creed, color, or belief. Because she who does these things will not be shaken.

THREE QUESTIONS FOR YOU TO CHEW ON:

1. What in this psalm speaks to you? Where are you drawn in? Why?
2. With social media these days, it seems as though we feed off those "good" stories, and, inevitably, there is a remark by someone that we need to see more of this. Why do we act so positively to these acts of goodness and kindness? Why don't we just expect people to be kind and not make such a big deal of it?
3. How are you "walking blameless" each and every day? What actions are you taking to love, serve, and be kind to people?

A PSALM OF
"ALL OR NOTHING"

Pick up your Bible and read Psalm 16.

Can you be "safe" hiding behind a rock, all while leaving a part of you exposed—even just a little part showing?

We're unclear exactly what is happening in Psalm 16, but verse 1 is the summary of the whole 11 verses. David seeks refuge in God. David declares that it is only in Yahweh that safety is not only granted but carried out. While most of this psalm speaks of that safety, we do read a few verses of what David sees happening around him.

There are those who are running around looking for safety in other gods, . . . but they only suffer. They go around making sacrifices and doing more and more, and yet nothing but hurt and sorrow come upon them. David is so convinced of the scope and magnitude of this harm that he won't even utter the names of other gods. It's such a toxic scene and such a septic thing to be a part of that even the names of these gods will never come across his lips. It's not that he doesn't want to chance it—it's just that he knows that he simply cannot.

This makes me wonder: How *bad* could something as simple as speaking be? I mean, we talk about how people have "sold themselves to the devil"—but is simply uttering a name as drastic as David makes it seem?

David, as well as the rest of the faithful Israelites, knew and understood that their loyalty either was or wasn't to God. They had a long history of bringing false gods into their homes. In fact, *our* whole history as a people goes back to this consistent acquiring of more and more "house" gods and other little gods that we've picked up as we've migrated through life—hoping one or two of them will do this or that for us. This is actually what made Yahweh so distinct from all the other gods. God was setting the Israelites apart to be *his* people, and he *their* God. Nothing else. Nothing more. We must understand that for a faithful follower of Yahweh there was no swaying back and forth. We see this again in the New Testament. In John's revelation (Revelation 3:15–16) we actually get God's words, saying that we must either be *for* him ("hot") or against him ("cold")—"hot" meaning that you are all in and God is happy and all is good, and "cold" meaning that you aren't for him at all—but at least that gives God something to work into. But this middle ground, neither hot nor cold? Yeah—not good.

And today is no different. You are either for God or against him. You are either a follower of Jesus Christ or you are not. And honestly, I think that's part of the problem we have today. We are losing our commitment to God in many ways. We want to accept only *this* and not *that* when it comes to Scripture. We want to speak of God's loving grace and forgiveness, and yet we don't want to hold to his commandment to love others above ourselves (Philippians 2:3). We know what God desires of us to do and be and know so that we can come to him seeking restoration and forgiveness, but then we begin to live lives that are opposite what Scripture says—doing things against God, all the while knowing and declaring that we can simply come to God later on and ask for forgiveness in prayer.

It doesn't work that way. In a sense it does—God grants his forgiveness—but we are called to be more than that. Live better than that. To be "alive in Christ" (Ephesians 2) means that what we *were* is no more—because what we *are* is something new, good, beautiful, and complete. We are to count ourselves "dead to sin but alive to God in Christ Jesus" (Romans 6:11). And to be truly alive in Christ means that we have to truly *be for* Christ.

Trusting God means that you simply trust him. You obey him. You seek him and nothing else. This is the first and greatest commandment. And it's something we all struggle with each and every day. We worry, we get anxious, we try to do things our own way. We know what we *should* do, and yet we do something completely different. All of these things do nothing but harm us. All of these things tell God, and others, that we "trust" God . . . but not fully. And in the end, all of these things begin to harm us and chip away at our faith. Faith isn't faith only when it's easy and convenient.

Paul writes in Colossians 3:17 that all we do, whether in word or in deed, we are to do in the name of our Lord Jesus Christ. Which means that all our eggs need to be in the same basket—the one marked "faith in God."

Always. Every time. If you think about it, how can God keep you safe if you don't actually allow him to be your refuge? If you don't allow him to protect and lead and guide you in all circumstances?

Don't leave part of yourself exposed behind the Rock of Salvation. It's all in, or nothing.

THREE QUESTIONS FOR YOU TO CHEW ON:

1. What in this psalm speaks to you? To which verses are you drawn? Why?
2. It seems as though, if we're truly honest with ourselves, everything we do is against God to begin with. So how does this even work?
3. David states in verse 8 that with God on his side he will never be shaken. Do you agree? Is David saying that we'll never go through hardships that test our faith? That we will never wonder, "Where are you, God?"

A PSALM FOR A
HOPEFUL TOMORROW

B egin this reflection by reading Psalm 17.

Psalm 17 is, in a lot of ways, very similar to Psalm 16. In both psalms the writer feels the pressure of enemies, their anger, and their hatred, and seeks out God's hand to deliver and protect. But what's different about Psalm 17 is that, where Psalm 16 speaks of all of this *beginning* to happen—Psalm 17 is a cry out, as this enemy has surrounded him and is closing in. It's the difference between seeing your enemy in the distance . . . and feeling their hot breath all around you.

The big difference I see and feel between Psalms 16 and 17? Whereas in Psalm 16 the author is looking around and seeing his foes coming in—in Psalm 17 I get this image that he has fallen to his knees and is praying to God for his deliverance. And what's really interesting is that the vast majority of these 15 verses (1–12) are about what is immediately happening. The plea to God to listen, the request to examine his heart and who he is, his call for God to see all the evil that surrounds him and to protect him from his enemies. It's all about *now*. All about things that he sees happening, and thus he comes to God in the present, seeking a response in the present. However, in verses 13–15 the prayer petitioner switches to the future. He asks God to "rise up and confront that which they see before them." The need is for God to save him from what *will* come . . . tomorrow . . . from his foes.

Verse 15 expresses this calming additional "known" that when he wakes in the morning he will see God.

Theologians are a little unclear as to what verse 15 exactly alludes to. Is this an allusion to Moses, who saw something *like God* (without seeing him face-to-face) at the burning bush—where he came into God's presence and still walked away alive? Is he thinking that he will die during the night and thus anticipating that he will wake in his spiritual body to see the face of the Lord? Or is it simply the feeling that *because* he is not like the sinful people who surround and close in on him he is more *like God*—"righteous," as God is righteous?

While we may disagree on exactly what verse 15 means, theologians all agree on what it declares: the presence of God is good. And not only "good"—it is great. And not only "great"—it is safe. And not only "safe"— it is peace. And not only "peace"—it is what we declare, as the psalmist does; it is where our future is placed.

We read in Revelation 2:3–5 that our future is with God. A future in which we will not only be in a place where there is no more night, no more pain and suffering—but we will see the face of God, and his name will be upon us.

None of us are promised tomorrow. None of us are even promised today or the next minute. You may not make it through this day or this night or even the next hour, but if you believe and declare and call upon the Almighty King of kings and Lord of lords—then your future is in his presence. Not only his "presence" in the sense that you feel him (as we do today with the Holy Spirit), but God will be before you and next to you. You will have an opportunity to walk and talk with him in the cool of the day.

Followers of Jesus Christ know that we are not guaranteed today— that it could all easily be taken away or lost or simply forgotten. This is a struggle that even Christians have—we know that our future is held firmly by the One who has given us that future: Jesus Christ. And that even if we die today, we will fully live tomorrow.

THREE QUESTIONS FOR YOU TO CHEW ON:

1. What in this psalm speaks to you? To what are you drawn? Why?
2. How does our hope for tomorrow help us through our fears of today?
3. Reading verses 10–14, there is something that stands out, at least for me, about God and his use of his "sword." Is he slaying someone? Is he harming his enemies? Is God shedding any blood? Have you ever asked God to save you—but to do so without harming your enemies?

A PSALM OF
SINGING UNTO THE LORD

egin your reading today with Psalm 18.

Psalm 18 may seem long—may seem "wordy"—but wouldn't you, too, be wordy and wanting to sing a nonstop song unto the Lord if you had been saved from your enemies? Would you not sing a song of joy after being delivered from death? I think I would!

In order to begin to grasp this song of joy, one needs to go back into history to read what was going on between David and Saul, . . . to see and hear why the Lord God would split apart the heavens and move the earth in order to fight for David.

A *very* brief history: before David there was Saul, the son of Kish from the tribe of Benjamin (one of the original tribes of Israel). Saul was king before David became king. In the books of 1 and 2 Samuel we can read about the rise of Saul into the throne, but God eventually rejects Saul as king, and Samuel tells Saul that God will anoint a *new* king—David, the son of Jesse, from the tribe of Judah. David will replace Saul as king . . . and Saul does not like this. Thus begins the battle between the two—well, more from Saul's side than David's, as David has multiple opportunities to kill Saul but never does (he never fully understands why Saul hates him so much), even though Saul continuously tries to kill David. We read in 1 and 2 Samuel of the conflicts between the two, the fierce battles, the hiding, and eventually Saul dies. And then in 2 Samuel 22 we read nearly this *same* song of praise that we have here in Psalm 18. David's enemies have been delivered to him, and Saul is no more. So, David sings a song of joy (even though he mourns the death of Saul).

Why is this important for us to understand? Because it is through this line of David that we get Christ. Because, just as David saw God as his "rock and deliverer," his "fortress" and "shield," so too may we. Just as David saw his enemies as "cords of death" that entangled him and overwhelmed him, so too there are cords of death that entangle us and try to bring us down. Sin interweaves its nasty web of cords all around us each and every day. Lust, greed, lying, hatred, anger—those all weave a nasty web around us, constantly trying to coil around us and bring us death and destruction.

But, just as in David's song, God responded and did something about it.

Think about it: When in our past (as read in the Bible) did the earth quake, with the foundations of the mountain shaking? When did all of these "tremble" (check out Matthew 27:45–53)?

What about God parting the heavens and coming down to us? We see something similar in the birth of Jesus.

When did God reach down and rescue from their foes those who would die without his intervention? When Christ came and overcame sin and death (1 Corinthians 15:55–57).

When did God turn darkness into light? When Jesus came. We read in John 1:1–5 that Christ *is* the light and that darkness cannot overcome him.

David's song wasn't sung about Christ, but it was a song about the love and desire of God to step in and save his people. While this song in Psalm 18 is not specific to us as it was to him, it still is *our* song! Yes, David's song is very specific to him and what he saw and how he felt—but David sings of how God saved him from death and destruction and that none of this would or could have happened if it weren't specifically for God's hand delivering and redeeming him.

This psalm invites us to sit in David's sandals and listen to his heart sing about what God has done . . . and then ultimately invites the reader/listener to sing *their own* song about God's redeeming love and grace!

So, let me ask: What is your song? What song would *you* sing unto your King, your Lord and Savior, your Redeemer and Sanctifier who split the heavens for you, who crossed oceans and valleys for you, who overcame sin and death for you, who died upon the cross for you? We know all the names and work of Christ—it's just a matter of seeing *where* those have been in your life.

The music is here; the lyrics are here as well. It's just a matter of adding your own words of gratitude and proclamation . . .

THREE QUESTIONS FOR YOU TO CHEW ON:

1. What in this psalm speaks to you? At what point are you drawn in? Why?
2. There are a lot of beautiful images we get of God from the psalmist (v. 2). Using your context and vocabulary, what images would you add to this list?
3. Along similar lines, verses 8–15 give us images of God's coming down to save (clouds, cherubim, the "wings of the wind," etc.). How do you envision God's commanding of the universe as he heads down to save his people? Me? I like to picture God with a lasso around a cloud or maybe even surfing a lightning bolt.

A PSALM OF
THE REVEALINGS OF GOD

Read with me Psalm 19.

Who is the Lord, and what do we know about him? That's really what this psalm comes down to—well, that and your response to that knowledge! And it's not really a question that the psalmist is asking you and me; instead, he is simply proclaiming. And he is doing so from a large to small perspective (grandiose to tiny).

The psalmist begins this song by observing that the heavens declare the glory of God, the skies proclaim the work of his hands—and they do so each and every day. While they may not physically speak about God, the way the clouds move, the way the sun sets and rises, the way everything in nature is so perfect in what it does . . . all of these things, and so much more, declare the splendor and glory of God.

But the psalmist doesn't end with the things seen above—he moves on to the other things we are given by God that are perfect and good, primary among them his Word. From what is seen and observed to what is felt and held in and refreshing to the soul (v. 7)—all of it is from God. All of them are meant to instruct and share and work together to his glory. That's what his Law does and his Word is—food that nourishes and refreshes the soul. Through nature (called "natural revelation") and through Scriptures and the Law (also called "special revelation"), we are given glimpses of who God is and what he does and has done for us.

What's really tough about this psalm, to me, is that it invites us to rethink what we need and desire from God. I'm not talking about food on the table or shelter over our heads—or even my wife and kids. While I am grateful and feel so blessed that God has allowed me to love them and watch over them for the time he has given them to me, this isn't really about those *things* (or people), nor are they necessities in life. What I'm talking about is our constant need to "see" God and "hear" from him.

I can remember a few times as a kid having a sleepover with a buddy and just talking about how great it would be to talk with God. To ask him questions, to hear his voice—to ask him why he had made this or that (like mosquitos—I understand they are food for animals, but they are a pain to me!). This psalm challenges us to really *look*—because all we *need* from God is actually given unto us and right before us.

Look up to the heavens and see the splendor of God's hands and mouth as he spoke and things were created (Genesis 1:1–2). God spoke and made and parted the waters and created land—everything with his voice. Isaiah writes (40:12–31) that it was God who measured the waters and weighed the mountains and the hills so that they would be balanced just right. They weren't sporadically placed—they were put in place with thought, love, and knowledge.

But that's just what we can see—those are things we are supposed to observe to be reminded of God's love and passion and glory. Things that our *eyes* and *heads* need. But then he went above and beyond, and he created what our *hearts* need: his Word.

David writes that the "law is perfect, refreshing the soul" (v. 7). The commands of the Lord are "radiant" and "trustworthy, . . . and not only that, but they are more precious than gold or silver or money or credit and sweeter than honey—and chocolate! Simply put: the Word of God is everything we will ever need and much, much more.

Everything God has given to us (his special revelation) and everything he has given to us to observe (his natural revelation) is about showing us who he is and what he has done and giving us what we need each and every day. In a world where we want to see more and feel more and know more, the psalmist encourages us—reminds us—that all we need has already been given.

You want to *feel* God? Go stand outside on a cool morning, just as the sun rises. The warmth of the rays and the radiance of the sun remind us that God created this day unlike any other. And that this day will bring new and beautiful opportunities for you to feel God's love and share it as well. Or take a walk in the woods and see the beauty and splendor of the trees and bushes and animals—how everything works perfectly together and, when left to its own, balances itself and holds itself perfectly.

You want to *hear* from God? Read your Bible, be in prayer, talk to a trusted friend. All those (and so many more) are ways in which God speaks to us. God uses friends to help guide us in our anxious and confused states. God uses prayer to communicate with us and soothe our souls (James 1:5), and he uses his Word to open up and reveal his heart, his will, and his passionate love and grace (over 3800 times we encounter "God said..." type of moments in Scripture). All of this, as you and I both know, culminates today with God revealing himself through his Son (Hebrews 1:1–2), who died upon the cross for our sins and now through his Spirit reconciles, sanctifies, and comforts us each and every day (Romans 8:18–30).

In a world that wants to *see* more and *feel* more from God, maybe it's time we simply open our eyes just a little bit wider—drawing in what stands before us.

THREE QUESTIONS FOR YOU TO CHEW ON:

1. What in this psalm speaks to you? To what are you drawn? Why?
2. Do you ever stare up at the night sky, or lie down in the grass during the day and stare up at the sky, and see not only the beauty of God's creation but the fact that what you see declares God's glory? How do the stars and clouds declare God's glory or the work of his hands?
3. Verse 13 asks that God keep the psalmist from "willful sins." What are those? How are those different form *un*willful sins?

A PSALM OF PRAYER AT THE CROSS

To begin today's reading, turn to Psalm 20.

Our psalm for today is an interesting one—verses 7 through 9 definitely have this "war" flavor—and rightly so. The author speaks of how some people trust in chariots and some in horses, whereas, really, trust should be placed only in God. And those who *do* trust in horses and chariots? They will fall, because horses and chariots fall themselves—but God does not. One should never place her trust in anything *but* God.

But what's really interesting is that everything leading up to verse 7 has a "Gethsemane" feel to it, which is probably why Christians throughout the ages have seen this psalm as a prayer at the cross.

Verse 1: Christ is in distress and is in prayer to God before being arrested (Luke 22:39–46).

Verse 2: Obviously needing help, Christ, in his prayer, asks for it—and not only for himself but for those who put him there and the thief next to him.

Verse 3: Christ's death *is* the ultimate sacrifice and offering offered up to God, as it becomes available to all those who believe (Romans 3:23–26).

Verse 5: Christ becomes victorious as he takes on sin and death and overcomes it—not only for himself but for you and me as well (1 Corinthians 15:55–57).

Verse 6: The whole point of Christ coming to earth was to save. The whole point of Christ leaving his throne on high was to save. To me, this is the essence of the story, not only of Christ but of the Bible. It is God's story of saving not only his children but this world and restoring it—and doing so by answering the daily prayers of stress and chaos that are lifted up to him.

What I find really fascinating and challenging and beautiful is that multiple Gospel authors give this picture of the cross and the prayer lifted up in that time and in the sight of those who were there, and not only in the sight of those who were there but to those of us who, two thousand years later, can *put* ourselves there. During Lent and Good Friday, we are drawn to the scene at the cross, and our prayer intertwines with Christ's prayer. Understanding fully in our time what Christ was doing way back then, our prayer would have been to add our voice to his so that his prayer would be heard. We would have prayed that his voice be heard (vv. 1, 4), that he be protected and defended (v. 1), that he be strengthened to make it through and endure what he was doing for us (v. 2), that God would see and remember the work and devotion of his Son (v. 3), and that all of this—what was meant to happen—be fulfilled and come to fruition (v. 4).

I declare each and every one of those things, but so often when I see someone in need or hurting or suffering, I want, I feel that I *need*, to do something. I need to act. I need to *react*. I like to think that, if I had been there, I would have pushed those soldiers aside and climbed up that rugged cross and ripped those nails out! I would have fought tooth-and-nail for my Savior. I would have been just like Peter and drawn my sword in the garden and cut off more than an ear of a soldier! (John 18:10).

But then again, part of me feels as though I would have sat back and watched. I'd like to think that would have been because I knew what Christ was doing and that it had to be done, but I think there's some selfishness on my part, along with an instinct to protect *myself* first. But this isn't a psalm about my failures or what I would or wouldn't have done; this is a psalm about God hearing a plea for help and working out salvation *through* those prayers.

David and his people knew that their safety came because they knew that God listened to his children and saved them if that was his will, so they prayed for God's will to be done. To save the anointed one, David. To save those who put their trust in him and not themselves or chariots or horses or anything else. But you and I know that salvation truly comes through Christ and his work upon the cross.

What's really interesting is that, in view of that cross, in that horrible, bloody, and painful scene, we don't pray for God to "take it all away" but for God to fulfill and complete his work. Have you thought about that before? I know I haven't. My focus so often is to stop the pain, end the hurt, send down a balm to be placed upon my own or others' sores; while I fully know that Christ *is* the One who ends all pain and all hurt and *is* the balm of Gilead, I have never tried to put myself *at* the scene. I have never thought of giving thanks *in that moment* for what Christ was about to do. That seems odd and strange and wrong. But without his sacrifice, there would be no future for us. Without the cross, there is no redemption. Without the pain, there is no joy. Without Christ there is no future.

In the end, I'm reminded that this is a psalm of prayer and petition, but also a declaration. I'm reminded that our crying out to him with our requests and thanksgivings is heard, is responded to, and is ultimately the reason for Christ and his suffering and death.

THREE QUESTIONS FOR YOU TO CHEW ON:

1. What in this psalm speaks most vividly to you? At what point are you drawn in? Why?
2. As this psalm is very reminiscent of Good Friday, how do we take verse 5 and its encouragement to "shout for joy" over Christ's victory? As he was dying, as he was still working toward the victory over sin and death, how could we have shouted for joy?
3. Put yourself at the cross—What do you see? How do you feel? What happens to our feelings when we don't already know that victory will come three days later?

A PSALM OF
EXUBERANT PRAISE

Before considering this devotion, read Psalm 21.

Wow. Psalm 21—read simply on its own—seems off to me. Off because it *sounds* egotistical. It sounds "self-loving." It sounds like everything opposite what I was ever raised to be and/or have tried to teach my kids. King David has been given the "desires of his heart" (v. 2). He's been welcomed with "rich blessings" and a "crown of pure gold" (v. 3). All his enemies have been taken out, and blessings upon blessings have been granted. He has received "eternal blessings" (v. 6) *and* great "glory" (v. 5). While those are right and true and good, it almost sounds as though the king is gloating—almost bragging because of this.

So, what's up with that?

In order to understand what is happening here, we actually have to go back and reread the previous psalm (Psalm 20). These are "partner" psalms, and thus we need to reread the corresponding psalm to understand what is happening. When we do that we can then, hopefully, *not* think that the king is egotistical. So, do me a favor and read Psalm 20. I'll wait.

If you recall from Psalm 20, David and his people are praying for safety as the king is about to go into battle. In Psalm 20 the king and his people are standing before the Lord and waiting to go to battle, but before they *throw down*, they *lift up* their prayers to God. They get it that they aren't going to put their trust in people or manmade things or even animals, for it is God and God alone in whom we are to place our trust. So, it's a psalm that is a prayer request.

If there were a psalm between 20 and 21, it would be a psalm about the battle itself, because Psalm 21 finds us post battle. The war has been won. The battles have been fought, and David stands victorious, with his foes being either sent to the hills, overrun, or destroyed. So, Psalm 21 is a psalm of victory. That's what we get at the beginning and the end of this psalm—cries of rejoicing because of the strength of the Lord, because of the victories he gives.

But I'm still a little disturbed about the gloating going on. Maybe "disturbed" isn't the right word—then again, maybe it is. Part of me, again, is annoyed with the way David reacts. Again, this is not the way I was raised. But then again, times were, and are, different. I'm not going to battle for my kingdom and my life. I'm not fighting people who want me dead or who want to take the crown from my head. I'm not fighting people who are anti-Yahweh. When my parents schooled me on proper responses to winning, it was all in regard to the soccer field, basketball court, tennis court, football field, and baseball diamond. This is the same thing I teach my own kids. Mine, and ours, were about competition; this, however, was about life and death.

With that said, I simply can't put my own feelings into this text. None of us ever should. The Bible isn't a collection of stories on how "*I* would react," nor is it filled with stories and accounts of how I would do things differently. We have to allow Scripture to stand and say what it does—and *be* what it is. We must remember that the Bible is about God and what he is doing, even while others do not respond appropriately. The Bible is about God and *his* redeeming of his people, his creation, and his world through his Son, Jesus Christ, who did this via leaving his throne on high and taking the form of a human—Jesus Christ of Nazareth.

With that said, we also must remember that when Christ came into this world he did so via the lineage of David (David is attributed as the author of this psalm). As Matthew 1:1–17 tells us, there were 14 generations in all from Abraham to David and then 28 generations from David to Christ. Yes! David was the great-great-great (add a bunch more "greats" here . . .) grandfather of Jesus Christ.

So, what does this have to do with anything? Well, David must succeed, his lineage must go on because that line runs smack-dab into Jesus Christ. God *must* deliver David from his foes, for this is the lineage he has chosen to lead to Christ. It's the lineage that leads to the birth, to the cross; it's the lineage that brings salvation.

The more I think about it, the more I realize that it is not my place to say that David's response is inappropriate or over the top. I'm pretty sure I'd be overjoyed if I had been delivered from death and given life, too.

Oh, wait! We have . . .

THREE QUESTIONS FOR YOU TO CHEW ON:

1. What in this psalm speaks to you? To what are you drawn? Why?
2. Put yourself in this psalm and replace all the references to David with yourself—doing so in light of Christ's victory. How does this psalm *now* feel?
3. David asked for life and length of days, as well as victories over his enemy. What would *you* ask of God in response to God's victory in your life?

A PSALMFUL DECLARATION OF HOPE

Let's begin by reading Psalm 22.

This psalm is one of the more popular out there; the reason is not only that we typically think of it as a Lenten/Good Friday text, not only that there are at least eight different Scriptures that quote it, but I suspect that many of us have felt "forsaken" at one time or another. As with any relationship, we've had our ups and our downs with God, and just as with David here, our downs can be pretty low. Feelings of God being far away, or that we have been forsaken, or that God simply is not answering our pleas and cries—those are only the tips of the iceberg of emotions that have befallen almost all of us at some point in our lives.

When we look at this text, there is a beautiful weaving of emotions. Verses 1 and 2 are full of anguish, and then verses 3 through 5 are hopeful. Verses 6 through 8 have David ripping into himself, 9 and 10 declare "good" feeling, but then 11 through 18 channel back to fear. I see a wave of emotions, a rollercoaster of emotional life, all twizzled together.

I see me . . . and you . . . and our life and prayers with God.

I came across an author who said that he can easily imagine a 21st-century psychologist reading this psalm for the first time and calling it "the bipolar psalm" because of all the mood swings—it's almost as though there were two different people sounding off! Well, guess what? There are. Not in the sense that there isn't really just one voice and person—but this bipolar emotional rollercoaster we weave is the type of relationship we have with God. And it's not his fault—it's 100% ours.

We're the ones who choose sin over goodness. We're the ones who dig the hole so deep it appears that we cannot see God from the pit of it. We're the ones who wait so long to come to God seeking his help. We're the ones who want help in a specific way—so much so that when God *is* helping us, we fail to see it or simply do not *want* to see it. It's like looking to the right for God to come and save us, when he's already clearly helping us but we're refusing to look to the left.

But I'm rambling—this psalm isn't about our inability to see God; this is a psalm about God's response. I think we've taken Psalm 22 to the destination we know best (the cross), and we fail to see what else happens in this psalm. Almost as if we read the first verse and then simply stop. I know I'm guilty. Those first nine words speak of anguish and death and a feeling of abandonment, and I immediately think of Christ's crying out upon the cross (Matthew 27:46; Mark 15:34), but we cannot stop at the first verse and feel as though we understand and know what is happening. If we did, we'd fail to see that verses 19 through 31 feel different. David steps away from the rollercoaster of lament and praise and simply moves to praise and adoration. What's interesting is that there are some who feel that this psalm is actually two separate psalms based on this transition, but I would argue against that. What we get in verse 19 and beyond is a peace amongst the storms of life. An understanding and declaration that, regardless of what is happening, God is in control. It's as though David is in the dark with a flickering flashlight, but then, all of a sudden, a blaze of light comes through . . . and stays on. No more swaying, no more rollercoaster of waves—only hope.

To me, psalm 22 is a psalm of hope and grace. Hope and grace, as seen and experienced throughout life. It's the realization that at your lowest low God is your high. And at your highest high God still is high. That, when you're in the tank and see no way out, God is the hand that reaches down to rescue you. But Psalm 22 is also a reminder that what Christ did upon the cross was so that my lows will not stay low—they eventually will be lifted. *I* will be lifted. Through his willing sacrifice of his life, the grip of death has been released from my throat.

But here's the thing: David is onto something here. David, in his crying out, makes this declaration: that he will praise God. Not only to himself, but in the "assemblies," he will praise him (v. 22). *That* is our challenge.

We know what God has done; we easily declare it to our friends and neighbors and even in church—but how about at school? How about at work? Verse 27 says, "All the ends of the earth will remember and turn to the LORD, and all the families of the nations will bow down before him." I very easily sit here and tell you that when Christ comes again, people will bow before him (Romans 14:11). That's an easy one, and it puts everything on God. The problem with looking only at Paul's text in Romans 14:11 is that Christ clearly tells us that *we* have work to do. *We* must tell the ends of the earth about God and his work. *We* must allow the earth to "feast and worship" in this truth (v. 29). In short, *we* have some God-sharing disciple making to do! (Matthew 28:16–20). But I want to remind us that *in* that discipleship making we must be honest about that relationship. We cannot deceive people into thinking that life with God is easy and that all burdens and troubles will be cast away (if it were only that easy!).

Just as Psalm 22 shows us what life looks like in an honest way—so, too, our words must be truthful as we share our hope. For hope is realized only when we recognize that we constantly need it—and have been given it.

THREE QUESTIONS FOR YOU TO CHEW ON:

1. What in this psalm speaks to you? Where are you drawn? Why?
2. Why is it that our emotions run all over the place in our relationship with God? We know who he is, the promises he gives (and keeps), and yet, while God is consistent in his relationship with us, we are not consistent with him? Why, when we know it's not true—why do we still feel forsaken?
3. Our psalmist speaks of fulfilling his vows before others. What does that look like for you in your context?

A PSALM OF PEACE

To begin, please read Psalm 23.

Is there any more timeless psalm out there than this one? This psalm is quoted at funerals, in times of trouble, and as praise when people come *through* trouble! This is just a really, really good psalm of peace and hope!

For the psalmist, there is an understanding that God is in control and is looking out for him—and that is all we need to know. And because of this feeling, because of the words he uses, this hopeful, peaceful psalm begins to show just how much trust David has in God.

Not once does the psalmist ask God to explain why the valley is so dark and why he is being led there. Two of my favorite books in all of Scripture are Lamentations and Job—both are heart-wrenching and at times almost demanding in tone, but here, in this text, the psalmist is simply at ease, knowing that God does all these things and is in full control. Not only is God in control, but he is present and walking alongside, leading, guiding, watching over. And *that* is more than enough to know.

It's the *presence* of God that brings peace. Not answers. Not reasons. Not knowing the future—simply God's presence.

How many of us can fully be at ease with something like that? I think we can say we can—and say so rather easily, . . . but how about putting it into practice? Because for all that we read, we must understand that the writer wasn't writing these words because he *intended* to do this trusting; he penned the words because he'd *been there*. The waters had *not* been calm, the pastures were *not* green and lush, . . . and yet he still fully trusted.

That's life. Right? Hard times abound. Marriages split. Bills can pile up, mortgages can go into foreclosure, jobs are lost, family members get really sick and even die. Friendships are broken up—and so much more. It literally can feel as though we're in this valley of death.

But what really makes this text hard? There is no explanation. For a society that thrives on explanation and has a felt need for things to be explained, it ain't happen'n here, and that's really hard for me personally. I like explanations. I like to know why and when. But Psalm 23 isn't gonna give it to me—and I think that's the point.

Hope and peace must be understood, even when there is no explanation. Trust is called trust for a reason. Trusting the Good Shepherd—and being comforted by the fact that he *is* the Good Shepherd. And that's what this psalm brings to us. That even when we cannot see or know or understand where we are at or why things are happening, our knowing that the Shepherd is near and that he is good brings us to peace and calmness—and ultimately, rest.

I love this last line: "and I will dwell in the house of the LORD forever." And I will *dwell*—I will live, I will rest, I will be ever-present—in the house of the Lord, in his presence, in his place, at his table, *forever* . . . for the rest of my days and *then* some. God's presence—his love—will go everywhere. The blessings of God will remain no matter what happens. No matter what trials and tribulations come.

No matter what the circumstances, this amazing Shepherd will protect me, and I will be in *his* presence forever. This is the comfort the psalmist has while in the midst of the valley and while lying in green pastures, . . . and it's the exact same comfort we are given today. God doesn't abandon us when times are tough, nor does he take us to green pastures simply to let us feed and then watch him walk away. The life of a shepherd is one of sacrifice, commitment, love, and dedication. It's a life you live while giving up all other things. Your thoughts, emotions, actions, and inactions are all focused on that which you shepherd—and having the Lord as our Shepherd means that there isn't anything he wouldn't do or hasn't done for us. There is nothing he wouldn't take on to make sure we are given what we need.

One of the reasons this psalm is so special is that everything we know about the Lord is wrapped up in it. Commitment, love, sacrifice, comfort, . . . all of his attributes and all of these realities find fulfillment in understanding Christ and what he has done. John 10:10 states that Jesus Christ came so that "we may have life, and have it abundantly." Abundant life—not death, not starvation, not constant fear and trembling—but life!

Psalm 23 hopefully reminds you of all that the Lord has done for you.

THREE QUESTIONS FOR YOU TO CHEW ON:

1. What in this psalm speaks to you? To what images are you drawn? Why?
2. Our society/culture has a definition of what abundant life looks like, but how does that match up with "abundant life in Christ"?
3. Calling/seeing God as the Good Shepherd was an analogy that made sense back then—but what about today? Does it fit with our understandings? Is there a better analogy for our times?

A GLORIOUS SONG-PSALM

Begin by reading Psalm 24.

When I first read this text, I cannot help but get hung up on the first two verses, which deal with creation. The author, David (it's assumed by most people that it was David who penned this), makes a statement at the beginning that should be carried throughout the rest of the text. God is the Creator of the world and all that is in it—as well as all who are in it. And since God is the Creator, the earth is his, and everything that is within the earth is as well. This seems like pretty basic 101 stuff, but again, if we proclaim that creation is the Lord's, then everything else we say and do must be said and done with that same caveat.

If it truly is the Lord's, there are ramifications; it goes without saying that it *really is his*. You want to see God and ascend the mountain? Then you must declare it is his and play by his rules. You want to stand before God? Then you must understand that wherever God is *is holy*. Thus, only holy, clean people with pure hearts who do not trust in idols or swear by false gods—only *they* can stand before God in his holy place. These are God's rules, and we must obey them.

The most common belief out there is that this psalm was penned by David while the ark was being brought back from the house of Obed-Edom to the tabernacle that David had prepared for the Lord on Mount Zion (2 Samuel 6:12). It's that David wrote this psalm in a call and response format, either between different choirs or soloists and the people who were there—with each group "answering" the other. Picture a soloist singing verses 1 and 2, then a different soloist singing verse 3, with then a choir responding in full voice on verse 4. Or maybe there was a soloist leading the group as they were entering the city, and as they passed through the gates and down through the shops and homes they would sing back and forth in preparation for coming near the temple of the Lord.

But if you are anything like me, this song also reminds you of how far we've really come and all that God has done. While I fully declare this psalm to be right and good and true, I'm instantly reminded that the only ones who could ascend the mountain, the only ones who had "clean hands" and a "pure heart," were those priests who not only received the sacrifices of the people but then offered them up to God on their behalf. Through the sacrifice of animals and the shedding of their blood, hands were made clean. Hearts were made pure. Thoughts were wiped clean of anything and everything that wasn't directly focused upon God. So, this "song" they sang was a preparatory song, an anticipatory song, a song of joy and hope—but also, in a way, a call out to the priests to prepare themselves to go in front of God on behalf of the people.

Praise God that times have changed. While God still is the God of creation, the One who created the heavens and the seas and the earth and all within (Genesis 1), the One who still requires us to play by *his* rules—while God still is the same God who required animal sacrifices to pay for human sins so that the people could draw near to him and be in his presence, thus being forgiven for their sins (Leviticus 4:35; 5:10) and being given "clean hands and pure hearts"—what God ultimately has done, in his grace and mercy and forgiveness, is send his One and only Son, Jesus Christ, to *become* the *final* lamb who died for the sins of the world (John 1:29).

What's really beautiful is that Psalm 24 now becomes not a song of hopeful anticipation that the priests would atone for the sins of the people on their behalf, but this song now becomes a declaration that it was Jesus Christ who did this for his people. And where the priests had to do this every day, day in and day out for the people (since humans can never *not* sin)—Jesus Christ paid the price one single time. It took only one death, his own, to complete the atonement (payment for the penalty of sins) for your and my sin.

Psalm 24 is a declaration of hope and praise in just how marvelous this King of glory is. It's a song I love to sing—knowing that this King of glory *descended* that mountain and came to us. It is *that* King of glory who washed me clean and is daily, by His Spirit, giving me a pure and clean heart.

There are many wonders and beauties that we will live into and explore when we finally come into his presence once-and-for-all when Christ comes again. And I know that no matter what I do in heaven, no matter where I go—this surely is a song I will be singing—and hopefully, a song I can sing responsively and joyfully with many people for eternity to come.

Who is this King of glory? The Lord Almighty, Jesus Christ—he is the King of glory.

THREE QUESTIONS FOR YOU TO CHEW ON:

1. What in this psalm speaks most directly to you? At what point are you drawn in? Why?

2. "God is the Creator" can be a hard statement for nonbelievers to swallow. In a broken world, how does the truth that God is the Creator and that all is his bring you peace and comfort?

3. Even with Christ ascending the mountain for us and giving us the clean hands we need—that still doesn't give us an excuse not to live our lives as he has called. So how are you living a life with clean hands?

A MEDITATIONAL PSALM
OF UNDERSTANDING

L et's begin today by reading Psalm 25.

I frequently find myself coming to the conclusion that I just don't get it. I fully proclaim that God's ways are not my ways (Isaiah 55:8) and that there is *no way* that I can fully understand why God does what he does, but what I am finding is that I am having a harder and harder time fully comprehending, and even defining, some simple terms that pertain to who he is and what he does.

If I say that God is full of grace (John 1:16), which I do, this comes with some limitations for me in that the grace I try to bestow is fractured and incomplete. That's because I am limited by sin, not only in terms of what I can comprehend, but my feelings get all messed up inside there, too.

If I say that God is fully forgiving and that he holds no records of wrongs (an attribute Paul tells the church to have in 1 Corinthians 13:4–8), then why do I struggle with guilt? Why does forgiveness look so complicated and messy for me?

Psalm 25 is a meditation that tries to work through understanding who God is, as well as who we are. It's a meditation that reflects on who we are as understood by who God is. It's a revelation that can fully take place only when one comes to the understanding of who they are, what they have done, who God is, and what he has done, as well. What's really cool (and we lose this in our English translations) is that the psalmist works through this meditation through what is called an acrostic format—meaning that each new verse begins with the next letter in the alphabet (Hebrew, not English).

Why is this cool and important? Because it speaks of a "complete," comprehensive unit.

We have a saying that when we cover our bases completely, or that when something is completely known, it is done from "A to Z." Meaning that there is nothing left out—all is there. This confession, this meditational writing, is simply saying, "I am setting it all out there, playing all my cards, leaving it all on the table: you are God, I am not. You are whole, I am incomplete. You are holy, I am sinfully fractured. You forgive and have forgiven, and yet I do not forgive and should not be forgiven. But in your mercy—here are my errors—remember who you've made me to be and are making me to become, . . . and remember *that* instead of my past."

Meditation has always been hard for me—and it's not because I cannot do it; it's simply that I cannot do it (that makes sense in my head). I have a difficult time sitting still, a difficult time staying focused. I almost need to be doing something else in order to focus on something (that makes sense in my head as well). But what is more of a struggle for me is that I know I should; I know that with practice things get easier, though that is a difficult pill for me to swallow. Bottom line: I don't do it . . .

We all need to learn from the psalmist here. He understands who he is. More importantly, he understands who God is and his need for him— that realization can come only through prayer, reading, and some form of meditation or reflection. I say this because if we don't *think* about who God is and what he has done—don't just "think" but *think*—then how are we to fully grasp the situation we are in and the work God has done? The cross means nothing to us if we don't actually look upon it and see the large, heavy wooden beams; the jagged nails; the thick, coarse rope, the blood-soaked holes in the wood, the quickly scrawled words, "Jesus of Nazareth King of the Jews" above it—words scratched out in truth but also with ridicule (John 19:19).

The psalmist understands that the humble need to be led by God—for without God's guidance there is no understanding of what is right (v. 9). And not only that, but he is declaring in that same voice that God's right way is the only way; *the* right way is *his* way. It's what Paul declares in Romans 7:7, that if it weren't for the Law, the Word of God about how to act and interact and show love and goodness to others and him—if it weren't for *that* Word (Law), then Paul wouldn't even have known he was in sin. How could Paul have known that he was wrong and that God was right had he not meditated and worked through it?

Meditation and reflection aren't supposed to be difficult or complex. In truth, we do this all the time. When we pray—when we take a walk and simply listen and hear, when we look outside and see the snow gently fall, or the pouring rain pound the earth or the lightning light up the night sky—we are engaging in forms of meditation and reflection that allow us to see, hear, feel, and listen to God, to sense who he is and what he is doing.

We proclaim that all areas of our lives are to be given to God and that there is no space in this world over which he doesn't claim: "mine" (a reference to Abraham Kuyper's famous quote; see Psalm 24:1; Acts 1:24; Colossians 1:17). I think it's time for me to start working through that, meditationally, as I already proclaim it verbally.

With meditation and reflection, I may not be able to fully comprehend these differences in terms, but in my struggle with those words comes the assurance and peace I seek.

THREE QUESTIONS FOR YOU TO CHEW ON:

1. What is there in this psalm that particularly speaks to you? Where are you drawn? Why?
2. Verse 11 seems, well, odd—doesn't it? Why would God do something good for the "sake of" *his* name? Isn't it about us (the answer is "no" there—just say'n)?
3. Jesus, and his work, is all over the place in this text! As you read it, how many requests of the psalmist do you see that are answered in Jesus?

A PSALMFUL PLEA FOR VINDICATION

Open your Bible today and read through Psalm 26.

Wow—I'm stuck by that first half verse. Vindicate me—*vindicate me*? Really? But as I stare at those two words, I'm not sure exactly what it is I'm stuck on. Do I have the gall to demand that God vindicate me? Do I feel I'm *worthy of* being vindicated? Have I led a blameless life? Have I trusted in the Lord without wavering? Do I really want to be tested and examined in my heart and my mind?

Our understanding of "vindicate" means to be cleared of suspicion. We often see this when someone was convicted of a crime they never committed and years later are vindicated as new evidence comes out and the sentence was overturned. They've been cleared of any wrongdoing, but in Hebrew this word has its roots in "judgment." So, really, shouldn't we be reading this as "Judge me, O Lord"? That makes sense as the rest of the psalm has David giving *up* his defense.

Against evil
- Verse 3b: I walk continually in your truth and not lies.
- Verse 4: I do not sit with deceitful people or consort with hypocrites.
- Verse 5: I abhor (hate) groups of evildoers and will not associate with them.
- Verse 11: I lead a blameless life.

For goodness
- Verse 6: I come to your altar clean and cleansed.
- Verse 7: I proclaim your name aloud and praise you—sharing this with others.
- Verse 8: I love your temple, your dwelling, and look fondly to it.

Does David really think he is perfect? Does David really think he is blameless, walking continuously in God's truth and never straying to the left or to the right? He may not sit or consort with hypocrites, but I'm pretty sure making that statement means that he is, in fact, a hypocrite. Right? His life definitely isn't blameless—is it?

What about adulterously looking at (and coveting) a naked Bathsheba? (2 Samuel 11:2)

What about committing adultery? (2 Samuel 11:4)

What about the fact that, since he was the king and she was not, one can easily make the case that this was, in fact, rape? (2 Samuel 11:4–5)

What about the planned death of Uriah the Hittite (husband of Bathsheba)? (2 Samuel 11:14–15)

What about the fact that David's own son Amnon raped his sister Tamar—and beyond being "furious" David didn't do anything about it? (2 Samuel 13:20–22)

The fact of the matter is that for every "good" thing we see from David, for every "good" deed he professes, for everything he *thinks* he does that is good and righteous, there are just as many "bad" things in his life. But are we to look critically at what David has done? Is that the point of this psalm? To pile up all his sins on one side of the scale and then pile up all his good deeds on the other and make sure that his good deeds are so overriding and heavy that the whole thing topples down? No. We must remember in Scripture that we have to understand the voice being spoken (in this case David's) and the greater work being done (always *by* God).

One author (H. D. M. Spence) writes that the understanding for David was different from ours in that Old Testament believers simply didn't understand, as we do today, what it means to have human imperfection. In a way there was an understanding of sin, but unless it was a blatant sin that got called out and was seen as such—it simply was never understood in that way. So, David sees deceitful men and women, hypocrites running around, wicked people joining together, and he looks in the mirror and says, *That's not me, so I must be 'good'—and not even just good but blameless.*

But what is really interesting about this psalm is that, while David proclaims this "goodness," and seeks God to judge him for the good he feels he has done, he also asks that God have mercy on him (vv. 9–11). Why? I think it's because, no matter what faults God does find—and he knows God will—he still asks that God look past them.

This text encourages us to reflect upon the fact that, even though David isn't as "good" as he thinks he is, he still seeks out goodness. He sees those who ignore the truth, who are deceitful, who are hypocrites, who are evil and wicked (those who do not go by what God desires), and he wants nothing to do with them or their ways. Instead, he grounds himself in truth, righteousness, and mercy—all of which come to us and stand before us *from* God. It's the ways of the world vs. the ways of God.

In this psalm we see a man who simply wants to do, and be, in the right, and he knows that right is found only in God. As Christians we proclaim that we can do no good without God's guiding hand, without the Holy Spirit working the good in us. Does this mean that we are perfect, since we are believers? Nope. Does it mean that we are at least "somewhat perfect"— maybe a smidge or a skosh? Not at all. What it does mean is that the Spirit is daily sanctifying us and making us closer and closer into his image—*into* that perfection.

Judgment for our sins will take place—and the truth is that we've all been found guilty of untold sins against ourselves; each other; and more importantly, God. But through Christ we have been redeemed of our sins (Titus 2:14) and made blameless (Ephesians 1:4), . . . even if that "blameless" status won't come to fruition until we stand before him. And there's nothing scary about that.

THREE QUESTIONS FOR YOU TO CHEW ON:

1. What in this psalm speaks to you? Where are you drawn? Why?
2. It sounds as though David abhors all things, and people, that do not act in accordance with (or acknowledgment) of God. So how is one to witness to nonbelievers if they don't "sit" with them, *see* them, and do life with them? Is David declaring that he avoids all nonbelievers like the plague? Is that how *we* should act and live?
3. Verse 12 is really interesting, as David declares that "he stands on level ground." What does that mean, and why is that important? Is the "level ground" the Word of God? Is it the way he lives and the life he leads? Maybe both? How hard is it to stand, and stay balanced, on uneven and rocky ground—especially when the wind blows? Any implication there for our faith and life journeys?

A PSALM THAT FIGHTS
FEAR WITH TRUTH

Open your Bible and read with me Psalm 27.

As I read this psalm, I cannot help but sense fear. So many times, within the psalms, we get a picture of what the whole psalm is about simply by the first couple of lines, and in this text we are told that darkness and death are fearful; weakness in one's life based on oppression and harm from others: fearful. But how can one have fear when there is the Lord? How can one have fear from darkness when, in fact, it is the Lord who brings light? How can one fear death when salvation comes from the Lord?

What's really interesting is that when we look at this psalm, we see this proclamation of the ability to be strong in the midst of what *could* be fearful *because* the Lord is who he is (v. 1), but then in verse 7 we seem to have a shift in mood. No longer does the psalmist sound confident. No longer does he sound strong—he now sounds scared. Dare I say it: fear*ful*.

There is a really interesting dynamic with fear. To some, *facing* fear is strengthening and confidence-building. Fear brings out something they have never known they have. To many, however, fear is debilitating and crippling.

So, what do you do when you're struck with fear and your knees have buckled? What do you do when you appear strong and courageous, but then the reality of the situation smacks you upside the head, and the next thing you know you're curled up in a ball and rocking yourself in the corner (yes—I've been there)? You trust. You trust God for who he is, what he's said, and what you know to be true.

The psalmist knew that there was life beyond his current situation. He knew that he could "dwell in the house of the LORD all the days of" his life (v. 4). He knew that he would gaze upon the beauty of the Lord and find him in his temple (v. 5). That is—he could come to God and be in his presence—and that he ultimately would be given shelter.

What's really difficult is that in the midst of fear, hope can seem far off. In the midst of darkness light can seem as though it takes forever to appear. When fear strikes, when darkness sets in, it seems nearly impossible to focus on anything *but* that which is directly before us: fear, abandonment, darkness, chaos, pain, and suffering for many.

To the psalmist, coming to this "point" of *seeing* the light was a matter of proclaiming what he knew to be true, over and over . . . and over again. Yes, there is this moment in the text when fear appears to creep in, but fear doesn't have the last say—his confidence in God does (v. 13). His strength and knowledge of God pull him back from the fear that was beginning to creep in. The psalmist borders on falling into despair, were it not for his faith.

Faith is an interesting thing. Faith is easily obtained when things are good and continue to be good. Faith is great when you see it blossom because things are going right, but faith can feel as though it cowers when things are tough. Faith can feel as though it becomes fleeting when times are dark and lonely. Faith can, well, feel as though it leaves us. But the thing is, that's not faith. Faith doesn't work that way.

There are some who feel that it is in those moments of fear that faith is actually being tested, but I'm not sure I agree with this. To me it feels as though my faith is never tested; I am simply *reminded of* my faith when I need to be reminded of it most. Because loneliness, fear, and doubt are so strong and work off what we can see, feel, and hear, we easily succumb to them and allow them to take over. But the smallest amount of faith can shatter the deepest of fears. Because where fear holds to nothing and grasps at everything, faith anchors itself in one thing: truth.

I don't know. Maybe I need to work a little harder on where I fall in line with "faith testing" in the midst of fear. But one thing I do know for sure, when times *were* dark and lonely for me, I sure was thankful that the truth of God was anchored deep within. Because *that* became the only true thing I knew: God and his love and the truth of the Word that gives it to me.

I frequently, during these times, just needed someone to talk to. Sometimes just having someone to talk to and hear you and pray for and with you can help push the darkness away and remind us of the light and truth of Jesus Christ. Too many people have lost their lives due to depression and feeling the darkness take over. Every battle is different and unique—but no battle is to be fought alone.

I have some information down below to help any who are interested. Again—we all need someone to talk to, listen to, and lean *into*. So, use them—your pastor, youth pastor, parent, friend, therapist—anyone.

Some Scripture to help:

- Philippians 4:8
- Deuteronomy 31:8
- Psalm 23
- Romans 8:38–39

A phone number of people who are there to listen and help: 800-278-8255 (National Suicide Prevention Lifeline)

THREE QUESTIONS FOR YOU TO CHEW ON:

1. What is it in this psalm that speaks to you? What draws you in? Why?
2. The psalmist has one request in verse 4. What is it? What about you? If you could have one request of God, right now, what would it be?
3. The last verse encourages us to "wait for the Lord" and to be "strong in heart." How does waiting" work for you, because I'll have to admit that it doesn't for me (I'm *very* impatient—just ask my wife or parents). What does waiting do for us? Why is it good?

A PSALM TO
FIGHT HYPOCRISY

Turn in your Bible to Psalm 28 and read it.

Our psalm today is one that is typically seen as a "partner" with Psalm 26. Where Psalm 26 is a proclamation of the differences between those who declare and live by the Lord and those who do not, Psalm 28 finds the writer either in the midst of danger or being surrounded by evildoers.

This psalm is not like many others in which we have a historical context to pull from, or even an understanding of worship (some liturgical use), but this psalm is simple in its desire: may my heart and my mouth proclaim the same message: *your* truth.

And, for how short this psalm is, *that* focus in verse 3 is the heart of the problem: Lord, . . . do not surround me, or lump me in, or find me in the midst of or even in the party of . . . hypocrites.

But what's really interesting here is that, where we see a plea for this not to happen, there is also a request for judgment in relation to those issues. We may not flat out read "Judge me, Lord, and find my heart and my actions clean," but what we *do* see here is the psalmist crying out to God for help—which essentially is asking *to be* judged. To be judged and found to *not* be wicked or have malice in his heart.

This is really where I am struck. How many of us have spoken out of the "side of our mouth"? How many of us have talked badly about one person, only to say something different to the person's face? How many of us have appeared two-faced in such situations? How many times do we find ourselves going along with others in our actions, even though our hearts speak of something different? I think we need to acknowledge both situations that we so easily can find ourselves in, because oftentimes our hearts and our mouths don't line up. To me this is one of the biggest issues facing Christians. Our words, our actions, and our heart simply are not lining up with each other.

A hypocrite is not only a liar, but also a pretender, a deceiver, a phony, a fraud, a sham, and a fake—and none of these have any place with God. They have no place with God not only because none of these are attributes or actions *of* God but also because *we* are called to be ambassadors of Christ (2 Corinthians 5:20), to be prophetic in our work—speaking out for those who have no voice, lifting up those who have not the strength to lift themselves, healing the sick, praying for our enemies and friends, giving love when hate is thrust upon us. We are to be Christ in all situations to all people—but we cannot do that if we are hypocritical in this world. Too many times I have heard from my non-Christian friends that followers of Jesus really aren't *following* Jesus. Mahatma Gandhi said it best: "I like your Christ, I do not like your Christians. Your Christians are so unlike your Christ."

That should sting. And if it stings, . . . then you know it's true. If it stings—then you probably also find yourself, as I do, in that area of being hypocritical. It's not that I mean to, but I do. And we know that those actions simply serve ourselves (Romans 16:18)—not God or the other person.

I had a conversation with someone recently in which they said there seems to be a disconnect between their own heart and head. Their heart is screaming of what God desires of them, what Christ calls them to do and be, . . . and yet their head is battling that truth. I think we can all find ourselves in that paradoxical conundrum.

So, what do you do? I think we need to take a clue from our psalm reading. In verse 2 we have the psalmist crying out for mercy, for forgiveness, for God's wrath to relent and not find them at fault, as they know they deserve. He closes out that verse by lifting his hands toward God's Most Holy Place. This is important—because the holy place was a place of goodness, forgiveness, healing, and strength. And then, to top it all off, the psalmist uses the last three verses to simply speak the truth of who God is. So, it's a cry for God's judgment, for God to see who they are, to have mercy, to cleanse and heal, and to guide them (as a shepherd does).

Not only is God our strength and shield (v. 7), not only is God our joy and fortress of salvation (v. 8), not only is he our shepherd forever (v. 9), but he is love, grace, mercy, and compassion. And so, even while we declare those truths (just a few of the truths of who God is), we also must acknowledge that *we* are to be those truths too. Those are truths and character traits, that

God instilled inside us. Those are truths the Holy Spirit breathes into us each and every day. Those are truths we are filled up with, encouraged to use, and strengthened to give and live out in our actions with each other and with him.

That is God's truth; that is also our truth. Understanding those realities and living them out are going to be the only way to stop the hypocrisy, as well as the disconnect many observe between Christ and those who claim to follow his example.

THREE QUESTIONS FOR YOU TO CHEW ON:

1. What in this psalm speaks to you? Where are you drawn? Why?
2. In verse 1 the psalmist asks God to not be silent or turn a deaf ear to him. Why would a believer ask that? Do we believe God does, would, or ever has responded, or "failed" to respond, in this way? Where is this question/request coming from?
3. Is it wrong that the psalmist is asking for repayment toward evildoers? Should those kinds of words ever come across our lips? Or can we just chalk this up to our being sinners and the assumption that such sin is going to happen?

A PSALM FOR
STANDING IN AWE

Begin your reading today with Psalm 29.

We lived in Iowa for a number of years, and it wasn't until we lived there that we came to truly see the beauty of lightning and thunderstorms. Whereas back in Washington the thunder would crack and there might be one whip of lightning (maybe a few), out there in the Midwest you fully understand, see, hear, and feel the bolts of lightning and sheets of rain. Lightning that not only lights up the whole sky but comes as a wave of numerous bursts. And the power. Wow! The house-shaking power is unexplainable. You almost feel it shake inside you. It's phenomenal.

David may or may not be experiencing such a deluge (I'm not sure about the types of storms they experience in Israel), but he is experiencing the power and might of the God who controls all things, weather included. And, as David stands and watches this thunderstorm roll in, he is lost in its beauty, power, and strength. Not the strength of the lightning but the strength of God, who controls it. And he is so moved by it that he calls upon the angels to praise God (as well as all those people who might have been with him). Maybe he's even scared by this magnificent storm.

I think this is something we all do quite often. We watch as a lightning storm cuts across our town. We see the power of the waves crashing against the rocks. We see how the rain can erode the land and how the wind can strip away even rock. All these things are part of what we call the "natural" world. Things that happen that are outside of our control—but not God's.

Back in Psalm 19 we learned that the God of the universe, the God of the expanse, the God of all things that are great and beyond us, is also the

God of the Word. It's an understanding that the all-powerful God of these great and magnificent, *large* things is also the God of the small things. The God who seems to be beyond me is also the God who draws near me.

Think about *that* for a second. The God who created the heavens and the earth (Genesis 2:2) is also the God who created you (Genesis 1:27. The majestic God of all things, the One who cares for the mightiest of things, cares even more deeply for you! The God who created the mountains is also the God who planted the tiniest of hairs on my bald head. The God who created the different galaxies (and at this point we don't know how many there are) is the same God who created the quark and even smaller things yet to be discovered. No wonder David found himself praising God as he saw the storm rolling in! No wonder, we can surmise, he tried to calm any people who were around him who may have been terrified by what they saw, felt, and heard. No wonder he called upon even the angels to give glory to God!

This makes sense because when you understand fully who God is, what he is capable of doing, what he *does* do and *what he has done for you*, then your natural response is going to be one of worship and praise to God.

The God of the universe is the God who entered into humanity, as a babe, to save it from sin and itself. The God who speaks with a voice that shatters trees and shakes deserts and causes oxen and lambs to leap, who is enthroned on high and is King forever, is the very same King who left his throne next to the Father and humiliated himself, temporarily setting aside his power and majesty, who humbled himself so that *we* could be restored. What king sacrifices himself for his people? Only one: God.

I am utterly at a loss for words. David found words to call out praise for the work of God, and I, too, think about that work and come away unable to speak. Honestly, I don't even know what else to type at this moment, because no words can express my gratitude and humility for who he is and what he *could* have done . . . but *chooses* to do instead.

And maybe that's where we need to be at. Awe-struck by his power. Grateful for his might. Humbled by his desire to do something about his sin-ravaged people. A God so powerful, so above all things, still desires you and me. Still desires to give us an everlasting peace (v. 11).

Maybe next time I see one of these beautifully intense lightning storms, I'll take an example from David and call out how majestic God is, how strong he is, and how blessed I am that he calls me his own and has blessed his people with eternal peace.

THREE QUESTIONS FOR YOU TO CHEW ON:

1. What in this psalm speaks to you? To what are you drawn? Why?
2. When my kids were younger and the storms rolled in, my wife and I frequently found it difficult to calm them; in contrast, the people in God's temple praised him during the same kind of time (v. 9) during which we were in fear and child-calming mode. How would you encourage someone who was fearful to see the beauty, power, and strength of God during times of great thunder, lightning, and fear?
3. It's interesting how the psalmist speaks of all these powerful things that God does, and yet ends the psalm with a last word of peace. How do the power and strength of God give peace?

A PSALM FOR AUTHENTIC PRAISE

Begin your reading with Psalm 30.

Like so many psalms before it (and after it), Psalm 30 is simply a psalm of praise—and we see that as this exaltation is not only at the beginning and the end but also in the middle of the psalm and everywhere else. Under the title, "Psalm 30," you will also read that this psalm is a song for the "dedication of the temple." Which means that it would have been sung, and even led, *at* the temple, with possibly thousands and thousands of people. If not more.

Imagine that for a second. David has gathered before the temple thousands upon thousands of worshipers, musicians and everyone else, and he leads them in this song and proclamation of how good God is and how they should all praise and worship him. But then, with everyone listening to him, waiting on what he will say next, he is led to confession. *In front of everyone!*

- David did something (we aren't sure what) that angered God. (v. 5)
- David felt "secure," and probably got a little arrogant and did something sinful—and God "hid his face" in response. (vv. 6–7)
- David did something that possibly should have caused God to wipe him off the face of the earth, sending him to the pits of hell. (v. 8)

I stand in front of a congregation week in and week out, sharing with them the love of God, as given to us and seen throughout Scripture. I speak of what it looks like to repent and turn to God, to be filled by the Holy Spirit when we allow him to use us for his purposes; many times, as we work through texts, I do this by giving examples from my own past and struggles. But even for me, there are some things I cannot imagine sharing—and there are some things I've shared that required me to muster up more courage than I could ever have thought possible. But why? Why would I hide my sins from others? If God knows them, . . . if I do them knowing God knows them and sees them, . . . and if they are sins I committed, why is it that embarrassment so easily leads me to silence?

Here is David—standing before the people of God—expecting them to respond to all the goodness and grace and love he pours out. David is leading them *in* that praise, . . . and he does so by sharing with them some of that which has hindered his relationship with his Maker. David fully understands not only who God is (we see that in the text) but that in order for people to be helped in *their* worship, he is required to be authentic with them.

What's really fascinating to me is that we know this. If you have spent any time with *anyone ever*, then you know that the best and most authentic relationships come when people let down their guards and show who they are. This is really hard for me. Not only as the type of person I am, but because of the area of ministry I am in. Some people like it when a pastor shares personal information—others do not. It's the nature of the beast. But I think we can learn something here. In this call to praise David knows who he is surrounded with, but it doesn't matter. He doesn't care because it's not about them. Yes, he's trying to bring all those around him to worship God and do so because the Lord has turned "wailing into dancing," not only for him but for others—but it's not about them. It's about God. It's about *his* relationship with God and whether he can help others in their walk, in their faith, by sharing and living it out in his. Then that's what he'll do. We even get a glimpse of this when David returns with the Ark of the Lord (2 Samuel 6); as this massive procession is entering the city, he is dancing and leaping with every ounce of might he can muster. Saul's daughter (David's wife) comes out and is simply appalled by what she has seen him do—for this is *not* what a king does! And David's response? "I will celebrate before the LORD. I will become even more undignified than this" (2 Samuel 6:21–22).

We are communal people—we simply are. When God created Adam, he saw that he was "good," but he knew that Adam could be *better*. So, he made Eve. We were created *for* relationships. Authentic relationships. I would add authentic *godly* relationships. With God and us . . . with God and each other. And those can only happen when we allow people to *be* people. When we allow them to sing when they need to sing, confess when they need to confess, dance when they need to dance, and cry when they need to cry. I guess that what I'm saying is that I like what David does. I like how he is authentic in his worship. That he is leading by example. And if it helps others—if his sins help others see their sins and acknowledge before God their relationship, then so be it.

I think that, ultimately, we become better people and have healthier relationships with each other *and* God when we stop trying to hide things. My relationship with God can be messy, . . . and I'm pretty sure yours can be, too—so let's agree to share in the messiness of faith together.

THREE QUESTIONS FOR YOU TO CHEW ON:

1. What in this psalm speaks to you? Where do you find yourself drawn in? Why?
2. Oftentimes we find that we want others to share their "messiness" with us, but we struggle to share ours with them. Why is this so? How can we overcome this?
3. How can Psalm 30 be hopeful/helpful for someone who is still enmeshed in their sins of the past? Can we use this psalm in our current darkness, even though David writes as someone who is now on the *other* side of darkness?

A PSALM OF HOPING
IN THE LORD

Begin today by reading Psalm 31.

All the psalms are special, and we can learn something from each of them. It strikes me as I read this psalm that there is a lot of similarity in terms of feelings here to many of the other psalms we have considered. Once again, the author (David) is in distress, scared, and lost, . . . and yet he fully trusts the Lord, seeks him for restoration, cries out that God is good, and seeks him for his shelter. But what I am really being struck by is that David is experiencing all this fear and loneliness—paranoia, it would almost seem—*and he's the king.* David has all the money he could ever need, more friends than he could ever ask for, more servants than he could ever require, more homes than needed, more space than necessary—there literally is nothing in this time that he couldn't get if he wanted it—and yet, here he sits.

I'm not sure why—but I picture David sitting in a dunk tank full of fear, anxiety, and paranoia. Which reminds me that even a king can feel scared, lonely, depressed, and anxious. Even someone whom we would place on the highest of pedestals, someone who has everything anyone could ever want or need in life, can feel as though they are in the loneliest of places.

David's life has been one of ups and down. Persecuted by Saul, on the run from his son Absalom, waging wars, and fighting battles—so much of what we see in Scripture has David on these highs and lows of life. It had to be rough being the king! It had to be rough having someone consistently trying to kill you. It had to be rough watching family members turn against you. So much of what we see in life and say to each other (whether warranted or not) is that the higher up in status you are the easier life must get. Money, fame, fortune—all of these "things" must make living in the world easier, . . . or so we tell ourselves.

The fact of the matter is that simply because you have more stuff doesn't negate the reality that life can be a struggle. The fact of the matter is that money doesn't solve problems and that having more friends doesn't necessarily mean that you won't feel lonely. All the stuff in the world still is only stuff—and people are still people. We may *think* that having more means fewer problems and issues—but strip people away from what they "have," and in the end we're all the same. Stand me next to Bill Gates, and strip us down to our undies (sorry I put that picture in your head), and you'll find that we aren't any different. We may look different, but we consist of the same material. Society may *say* we're different, but are we? I say no.

Psalm 31 is laid out in chunks (sections) as David is traversing a wave of emotions that go from being scared and seeking the refuge of God (vv. 1–8) to a petition for God to rescue him from all that he has done and all that he sees happening around him (vv. 9–18) and then to triumphant praise that he gives to God and encourages others to do as well (vv. 19–24). I think this is why the psalms are so encouraging and used daily by millions and millions of people. David is simply just like you and me, and we see that. And since he is just like you and me, there are some things we can learn from this text.

- In David's stress over what was happening, even though he was scared and possibly even paranoid, everything still came down to trusting God. (positive thing)
- David knew that God intimately saw in and through him (vv. 6–8) and that because of this God kept him safe. (positive thing)
- When we are in the deepest of depths, ravaged by guilt and anguish—we tend to pile on feelings on top of feelings. Our friends may or may not run from us, they may or may not talk about us, but we can very easily convince ourselves that they do. (negative thing)

Psalm 31 reminds us that we all struggle in life and that life isn't always happy and pleasant—and it doesn't always end pleasantly, either. Life is rough, . . . and it is rough for all people at some point or another. And in a psalm like this—where darkness creeps in, when all your friends seem to be against you, when your enemies are your neighbors and hateful, lying words swirl around you like a tornado of harmful tongues—there is always one thing that remains. There will always be one constant throughout life's ups and downs: God and his faithful love.

It's in that faithful love of God that we know that, even if David were sitting in that dunk tank, even when we are in the deepest of pits and our emotions are in the darkest of places, our cries out to God still find their target. Because they don't have to travel far when the One you cry out to is already with you, observing what you see, feeling what you feel, and holding you tightly through it all.

Be strong and take heart, all you who hope in the Lord!

THREE QUESTIONS FOR YOU TO CHEW ON:

1. What in this psalm speaks to you? To what are you drawn? Why?
2. David remained fairly positive (as much as one could be) while in the midst of all that was going on. How do you remain positive, and focused on God, when your life seems to be in a downward spiral?
3. How do you work through your emotions when it *feels* as though you are far off from God? As though your prayers, petitions, and requests have to travel a long distance (even though we know they do not)?

A PSALM BLESSING
THE FORGIVEN

egin your reading with Psalm 32.

What does it mean to be blessed? Initially, to me, that is an easy answer. I feel blessed because I have a roof over my head, a job that pays the bills and puts food on the table, a family whom I love tremendously and who loves me, my health, and a church and community that I love to serve with and alongside. I truly feel blessed in that sense. The problem is, that's *not* what David is talking about. To David, being "blessed" is seen and experienced only through forgiveness.

We're not *too* sure of where David is coming from here—i.e., which sin is he speaking of—but most feel that it's safe to say he's reflecting on the sins of adultery and murder, as seen in 2 Samuel 11 with regard to Bathsheba and her husband. Regardless of whether this is where we find David—the fact remains that his sin was so heavy it was as though he simply could not function. He couldn't get up and walk around, had no energy to be or do anything—he had relegated himself to simply sitting. There was just no living in this space. And maybe that's where we need to see David in this psalm. David is reflecting back on that moment *before* Nathan came to him and called him out for his sins. So, while he's moved to rejoicing for the forgiveness of God, he's remembering *back* to the feelings between the sinful act and the confession, recalling the emotions and the fact that, *in this* space, there was no quality of life.

Have you ever done that before? Taken a step back and thought about how you were feeling *after* you had sinned and yet *before* confession and repentance took place? I can't say that I have. I cannot count how many times I have sinned—I definitely recall the "doozy" ones—but more often than not after confession I've wanted *nothing* to do with reflecting on why I did what I did or how I felt afterward. It's just not something I want to feel. Now, I've made *tons* of mistakes in my life—and some of those would also be chalked up as sins—and I've learned lessons because of them (just as David did here). But what would it look like for me to take an internal temperature or feeling gauge of those moments? It makes perfect sense *to* do it—right? I mean, all sins are committed for the same reason: they make *me* feel _____. It's about the *feeling*. Right? The more we chew on it, the more we can all acknowledge that we've been in that moment before confession and after sin—right? *Especially* as we're "dwelling" on how to approach the person we sinned against and ask their forgiveness. There is *nothing* fun about those moments!

David has felt the chastening of God, but he has felt the weight of sin upon himself as well. Not liking either of these experiences, and believing in a God who forgives, he comes to the understanding that this feeling is *not* where he is supposed to dwell. And let's be honest, it's probably not where we'd like to be, either. It is here that we find the two states of feelings of this psalm. While one is depressed and heavy, the other is full of rejoicing and praise.

Why?

I think that, on the one hand, we all understand that it is not enjoyable being in a place of knowing we need to seek forgiveness and then actually doing it. Dwelling upon the sins is really crushing to our heart, mind, and soul. And if you've ever sinned and tried to sweep it under the rug without addressing it and seeking forgiveness, then you know as well how that feels. It simply is not good, it's not healthy, and it's not right. David experienced a release of pressure and weight when he confessed—when he brought the sin out into the open and sought forgiveness, and that's the place this psalm encourages us to come to.

I think we need to remember what forgiveness really is. We seek forgiveness when we've realized the harm we've caused and the damage we've done, not only to the person we've harmed, and not only to God, but to ourselves as well. And so, forgiveness becomes the neutralizer in our lives. Think of forgiveness as the extinguisher of the flames of sin and destruction we cause each and every day. We were not created to be bringers of sin and chaos; we were created with quite the opposite desire on God's part. To be loving, peaceful, grace-filled bringers of God's love. But when we do the opposite of that, when we hurt and harm, we cause destruction—and the only way to right the wrong is to seek forgiveness. To have the flames of sin extinguished.

Again—we are *not* to be either in the ash heap because of our sins or still in the fire. God's desire for us is to simply be in beauty and life, not destruction and death.

I want to come back to verses 1 and 2, because those are the key points. We need to understand that in life there are really only two understandings and ways to live by: God's way and the way that is *not* God's. You are either blessed and being blessed because you are walking in the ways of God, or you are not. You are either heavily burdened because of your sins and have not sought forgiveness, or you are free from sin and guilt because you've sought forgiveness from God.

David's recollection of the pain of being pulled between the two places is written here because he's being open about his personal struggles. He writes to encourage you and me to acknowledge our sins and place them at the throne of God—not only because we're supposed to, not only because forgiveness comes only when we seek it from him, not only because God is the only one who *can* fully forgive, but because on top of all those things that place of blessing is where we want to be and live into.

God has given us life through forgiveness. God has given us blessings through reconciliation. God has given us both of those through his Son and Holy Spirit. Psalm 32 simply is the reminder that it is offered to those who seek it.

THREE QUESTIONS FOR YOU TO CHEW ON:

1. What in this psalm speaks to you? Where are you drawn? Why?
2. I asked it above, and I'll ask it here: Do you ever go back and reflect on your feelings *after* the sin and yet before the repentance? Can we even do that?
3. Verse 7 states that God is the psalmist's hiding place—and yet when we sin, our hiding is usually *from* God and not *in* him. How does our working through our sins change when God becomes our hiding place instead of the One to hide from?

A PSALM OF THANKS

Open your Bible with me and read Psalm 33.

"Sing joyfully to the LORD, you righteous; it is fitting for the upright to praise him. Praise the LORD . . . Sing to him a new song." These are the words that begin our psalm—and words that we frequently find throughout the psalms; these are words that struck me this morning as I was reflecting upon them.

If you recall, the psalms were written not only by believers of God, but they were written with the understanding that those who read them are believers as well. So, when you and I read them, we might do well to think of them as a gateway into a life so long ago—and yet a challenge to your life today.

So, let me ask you: Have you, today, sung joyfully to the Lord? The author is claiming that you who are "righteous"—you who walk with the Lord, you who sing of his praises—that *you* and *I* are to sing joyfully. Right now. So, *have* you? He's given us tons of examples of *his* praise (the word of the Lord is right and true, v. 4; he loves justice and righteousness and justice, v. 5; earth is full of his *unfailing* love, v. 5; and then simply a call to look at his creation and the work he has done!).

Again, . . . I ask you: Have you joyfully sung to the Lord?

I woke up this morning with a new week ahead of me. One during which I'm scheduled to have meetings with people who are in despair due to the death of a loved one, a meeting with someone who has some limits to their body and mind, a meeting with people who sacrifice their lives daily for others, meetings with people in ministry, and meetings with other pastors. I have kids who have soccer practices and swim practices and music lessons. I am still reflecting upon the previous week, when I performed a funeral, and I have one coming up this week, too. My week so often is full of "stuff" that I wonder, Where is *my* time?

Terrorism is still happening all over the place; there is death here within the US; people are going hungry and are without shelter, without love, without hope. So many tragic things outside my influence and things that are within my reach as well . . .

So many things to worry about, . . . and yet, we're called to praise God? To sing joyfully to him? To *thank* him for the things he does? How can that be, when there is so much pain going on? When there are so many big catastrophes taking place?

I think we can easily get overwhelmed by the *big* things in life and fail to see the little things. Like the fact that I have an opportunity to be and do all these things with people in the congregation I serve and the community I live in. Like the fact that my kids have opportunities to engage in activities and figure out who they are and who God is making them to be, and the fact that I get to support them in that journey as well. Yes, I still worry about what is happening around the world, but I praise God for the simple fact that, as God looks down and sees all humanity, the Lord will deliver us from death (vv. 13, 18, 19).

There are so many things that we can praise God about on this day, and for me it's all those little things that we can see and feel that add up to become something bigger than the big things that drag us down. It's really easy to be so consumed by the big things that we fail to see the little things, and yet those little things are what will sustain us when the big things in life try to take over.

I had a talk this morning with a sister in Christ whom I value, and she mentioned that she thanks God for the trees and the grass. She'll simply stop and thank God for those, or for a bird. It's the little things that can bring us hope. It's the little reminders of who God is that help us each and every day.

So, what are you singing joyfully about on this day? That God raised you up for one more day? That your loved one who suddenly passed away knew the Lord and knew that their hope was in him and that he took the sting of death and destruction way? That you have a roof over your head, or one more breath in your lungs? One more opportunity to tell all the people you know that they are special, mean something to you, and that you love them?

This text is a psalm of encouragement for us to see who we are and respond appropriately for all that God has done, continues to do, and will do. It's a psalm that requires us to look past our consistent focus on things around us and firmly place our trust in him and thank him for the simple fact that he is who he is and does what he does.

THREE QUESTIONS FOR YOU TO CHEW ON:

1. What is it in this psalm speaks to you? To what are you drawn in? Why?
2. I love the challenge of verse 3, when the psalmist is encouraging people to "play skillfully" for the Lord. *Is* that important? Why?
3. The final verses speak of hope and waiting—which are things we carry with us throughout our whole lives. What are you waiting and hoping for in God today?

A PSALM FOR
A LONG LIFE LIVED

To begin today's reading, consider with me the words of Psalm 34. If your Bible is like mine, you'll see some text just below the title "Psalm 34" that reads something to the effect of "Psalm of David. When he pretended to be insane before Abimelek, who drove him away, and he left." What in the world? David pretended to be insane? It's funny how we can miss some things. First Samuel 21:11–14 recounts the story of David fleeing into the hands of the enemy, . . . and then feigning madness.

But is this a story advocating pretend madness? A suggestion that we, when in trouble, simply need to pretend to be insane and we'll be let go? That, when in trouble, we can simply pretend and God will deliver? Not at all. The words of Psalm 34 find their mark in verses 11–14. The invitation to "Come, my children, listen to me" show us that this is a psalm of life's teachings. The words contained in these 22 verses are words of life. Words of salvation. Words that remind us that throughout life we are to trust, see, and remember that it is the Lord who saves. It is the Lord who delivers. It is the Lord who rescues.

I googled "how to live a long life" (funny how a search engine name is now an actual word and term), and I got 87,500,000 results! You'd think that, with that many hits and instructions, we *could all* live a long life. Some of the results even come with pictures! We should exercise, be proactive with health problems, avoid high risk behavior, avoid toxic substances (not sure whether that's drugs or anything else in life that the FDA says is bad for me), avoid drinking to excess, quit smoking, and avoid street drugs (and no—the pictures didn't help).

Science says that I can live to be like the oldest person ever (Jeanne Clement), who lived to be 122—in fact, she smoked until she was 117! So, toss out what those "7 Habits of Healthy People" and just hope you have good genes! We're learning that the average life span *is* increasing, but in order to get to 122+ we'll have to have "super genes" and somehow modify our body chemistry. The problem? While science and medicine *can* help us and prolong our life, is that really "living"? Is there necessarily happiness there? Is there joy? All those "healthy lifestyle" people may be right in that those suggestions *should* be part of my daily life, but will doing these things guarantee me a long life? Ultimately, . . . what *is* a long life? My grandmother is in her nineties, and according to her words she's been here too long. I have a friend who's in his early fifties, and from his perspective he has already lived a good, "long" life.

David isn't giving us instructions on how to exist longer on this earth; his words, instead, are on how to *live* longer. Not by numbers, but by joy and hope. Abundant living comes to us when we are given life in God. For David, living came when he "sought the LORD, and he answered" his cry, delivering him from all his fears. His "face," beaming with the radiance of God, was delivered from its troubles, rescued from the pit of hopelessness (vv. 4–7). Living is knowing that you are cared for and loved, watched over and rescued. Living is knowing that when you are in need, the Lord rescues. Living is feeling and observing and breathing into the goodness of God. To live is to be kept from evil and turned toward the face of goodness. Living is seeking and finding peace.

The reason David seeks to instruct children, the reason we also instruct children, is that we want them to know what is right and true—because we've experienced pain and heartache and know that there is no "living" in that emotion, in that place, in that fear. Living a long life is relative. I get that. But I think we need to understand that it's not the quantity of days but their *quality* that we've been given.

With that said—here is something good and true and a rule to live by that will not necessarily grant you a long life but will help you truly live each and every day: "Give thanks always and for everything to God the Father in the name of our Lord Jesus Christ" (Ephesians 5:20).

THREE QUESTIONS FOR YOU TO CHEW ON:

1. What in this psalm speaks particularly to you? At what point are you drawn in? Why?
2. What, to you, constitutes a long life? Is it things you've done, accomplished, and experienced, or is it about a number?
3. I'm struck by verses 2 and 3, where David encourages the afflicted to hear his words and rejoice with him in God. Does God only hear the afflicted, or is David stating something else—like that the afflicted *know* they are afflicted and thus turn to God (while those in denial of sin do not turn to God)?

A PRAYING PSALM FOR PERSECUTORS

Begin today's reading with Psalm 35.

This psalm is broken up into three sections or parts (vv. 1–10, 11–18, 19–28), with each part moving further along in terms of the context of the lament—the backstory of the request for God to deliver the author from such hate. The reason for the request? The hatred simply is not justified. The words and actions of those surrounding the author are without cause (in this case, we believe it is Saul who persecutes him; see 1 Samuel 24).

If you take a minute to read the 1 Samuel 24 text (which I hope you do), you'll notice that Saul experiences a "coming to Jesus moment" (Okay, he obviously doesn't come to Jesus, but you get my point) toward the end. He realizes the goodness that David has sought on his behalf—that more than once he was within David's grasp, and David *could* have killed him but didn't. And this fits exactly with our psalm reading today, where David proclaims (beginning at v. 11) that, while he consistently prays for his persecutors, they simply never relent in their persecution of him. His goodness, time and time again, is being repaid with evil. When they were sick, he openly grieved for them and fasted in the hope of God's healing them (v. 13). Why? Why, with all this goodness that God's servant sought and lived out for other people—why was none of that being returned to him? Why was goodness not being reciprocated?

That's a hard question to answer—though I think many of us find ourselves asking it. Why is it that there are people who simply dislike us? That no matter how hard we try, or how good we are to them, they simply cannot find it in their hearts to be kind in return? Why does it seem as though, when they are sick and I pray for healing for them, it is in their healing that they are reinvigorated to attack me more? As though their healing brought them a second wind in their horribleness!?

One answer: I don't know.

Another answer: Some people are simply that way.

A more complete answer: I don't know; some people are simply that way—and, regardless, . . . we still seek goodness *for* them.

I don't know which is more painful. That some people are genuinely harmful to us, or that deep down inside I know that no matter what *they* do to me, I can control *myself* and what I am called to do and be: a seeker of peace. That means peace between us but even more so it is a reference to people who find peace with God.

Everything we do is supposed to be for God and others. We are called to sow seeds regardless of where they may land (Matthew 13), and as we see and read and know, we are also called to pray for our enemies. Christ says that we have been told that we are to love our neighbors and hate our enemies, but we're actually called to love our enemies *and* pray for them (Matthew 5:43–48). And that is the context in which we need to see this lament of a psalm. Yes, while David is under Saul's persecution and laments over what is happening *to himself*, his lament is not so deep that he doesn't seek restoration for the one who wants to kill him.

We do see that David isn't happy with what is happening to him and that it doesn't make a lick of sense to him. And yes, he wants God to make the enemies' paths dark and slippery, "with the angel of the Lord pursuing them" (v. 6). Yes, he cries out for God to "not be silent" (v. 22), but in that lament, in that crying out of one's despair, there is an understanding that God is doing more than only things *for you*. His grace goes where it goes. His word lands where it lands and upon those upon whom it does. That's a hard, and yet important, truth to swallow.

I think there are a few things we need to remember and a few lessons we can take away. We need to remember that there are bad people in this world. But simply because someone is bad doesn't mean they aren't a child of God. And because they are a child of God, we must consistently recognize that they will receive his blessings as he sees fit. *And because they are a child of God*, we must pray for them. That's one takeaway. Another one? We do not repay evil with evil (1 Peter 3:9) because it is not darkness that drives out darkness—only love can do that.

Even when it pains us, . . . we pray for others. Even when it hurts us and feels as though it goes against every fiber within us, it simply doesn't matter. What matters is that *our adversaries* deserve saving just as much as we do. And simply because we are trying to be godly people now doesn't mean that those who torment us will not become godly people later on.

So, until that day comes, we shall pray.

THREE QUESTIONS FOR YOU TO CHEW ON:

1. What in this psalm speaks to you? To what are you drawn? Why?
2. Why is it so stinking hard to pray for someone who is so harmful and hateful toward us? How do you move past your negative feelings about someone and into a hopeful prayer for them?
3. How do you forgive someone you feel is "unforgiveable"?

A PSALM FOR
THE GOD-MINDED

B egin today's reading with Psalm 36.

I'm struck by verses 2 through 4. They stand out not only because they are so drastically different from the other nine verses, but, whereas six of them speak to who God is (vv. 5– 10), verses 2–4 speak of how good people think *they* are. And the psalmist doesn't pull any punches here. He simply responds to what he sees, hears, and knows. The wicked people:

- Flatter themselves
- Don't see their own sin and faults
- Spew out all kinds of vitriol from their mouths
- Plot and accept evil, even when they lie down.

In case you've noticed in those three verses, it's all about the individual. These people are stuck on themselves, love themselves, find no fault within, spew hate and evil, and want nothing to do with wise decisions or good deeds; again, even while they are at rest, they continue to drum up plans of evil and harm. These people are the epitome of what it means to be mean. The world revolves around them, and they, themselves, are their best friend.

How lonely must this be? I ask because everything about those verses screams of having nobody. Nobody to show love to or from whom to receive it. Nobody to enjoy any moments of life with. Nobody to simply trust because the person who is like this is not only always scheming and planning, but since all they do is spew hatred and think harm, not only does nobody want to be around them, but they themselves don't trust anyone. What's even sadder is that I can name a few people who fit into this category. And while I've previously been angry with them for the things they do, I am now beyond that and simply sad for them. It pains me to know there is that much anger, hatred, and poison in someone's life.

Two things I want to point out here quickly. First off—this psalm is considered an "oracle": a message given prophetically to someone. So, we can see this psalm as a message from God on an evil way of living (in this case, it's the "unbeliever," as opposed to the believer, who acknowledges love, righteousness, justice, and peace).

Second, simply because this is an oracle doesn't mean that we simply blow it off as a prophetic word. I say this because I think that:

- We possibly all know someone who does these types of things
- We've all personally done some of the things we read about in verses 2–4 (and yes, I'm included in that).

Don't we all at some point (even sometimes currently) think more highly of ourselves than we ought? Flattering ourselves so that we feel better? Have we not all lied and said harmful, wicked things, purposefully deceiving others, even when we know the right thing we should be doing? Haven't we all lain in bed and thought about how we were going to pay someone back or plotted a "plan B," should _____ happen? Yeah—that's called plotting evil and committing ourselves to a sinful course. Shoot, . . . I've been there, too.

While David is praying to the Lord to be held securely against people like this who plot against him, and while you and I should pray that, too—we also must live into verses 5–11, lest we fall *back* into verses 2–4. When we're in those times of verses 2–4, we must cling to verses 5–11 to help us get out of the funk. Here's what I mean: one simply cannot dwell in God's love and righteousness when one seeks evil and hatred and self-love. One simply cannot understand how priceless God's unfailing love is when it's not of interest to you, when you are, instead, filled with your *own* love for *you*. And here's the biggest thing: you simply don't want to dwell in the house of the Lord and drink in his river of delights (v. 8) when all you want to do is live for yourself.

Everything we are to do in life is in response to what God has done. Understanding yourself and your sin and evil desires, yourself and your actions and inactions toward others—everything you do: it's all in response to God's love. Because God loves, because of everything Christ has done, God has done, and the Spirit continues to do, . . . simply respond with *love*.

As I have stated, as I continue to preach from the pulpit week in and week out, our response is always to *be love*. Not love for me but a love of others. Love of God. As God sacrificed for others, we sacrifice for others, too. As God shows mercy upon us—we show mercy on others. Paul writes in Romans 12:9, "Let love be genuine. Abhor what is evil; hold fast to what is good." In other words, seek life and living in God and not in yourself. Love him, obey him, follow him, and do unto others as not only he has done for *them* but as he has done for you.

So, here is our challenge:

- Lift up others and encourage them with love and kindness.
- Understand your own limitations and sins and seek restoration and help from God.
- Speak love and truth with an abundant amount of grace.
- If something is wise and right, *do it.*
- While lying in bed, be in prayer about all you have done and where God wants you to share his grace and love the next day—*and do it.*

Be God-minded today, tomorrow, and in all situations in response to people. I'm pretty sure that if we all did that, . . . we could start a revolution.

THREE QUESTIONS FOR YOU TO CHEW ON:

1. What is there in this psalm that speaks to you? Where are you drawn? Why?
2. How can we be "God-minded"? What does that even mean?
3. Why is it important to see yourself in others? How does doing that break down walls and unite, as opposed to putting up walls and dividing?

A PSALM OF
PRESENT VS. FUTURE

Today's psalm is Psalm 37.

Our psalm today is a continuation in thought from Psalm 36, as they both speak about those who seek God and those who do not. And a constant theme throughout both of these psalms is that of the difference between the wicked and the righteous.

Fifteen different times we see the adjective "wicked" coming up here. And *wicked* strikes me, because I don't think we use that word very often. In fact, unless I'm referring to a "wicked witch" or we're speaking of *The Wizard of Oz* or someone dressing up for Halloween as a witch, . . . I simply never use that word! But a wicked person, by definition, is someone who *knows* they are doing wrong, knows they are guilty, and chooses to go on anyway. It's all about knowing your evil actions and desiring to do them anyway.

Let's hold that thought for a second, this decision to do things. We'll come back to it shortly.

This psalm pushes us to simply trust in God (v. 3). To be among those who know that God is faithful and that he watches over those who put their trust in him. Who wait for the Lord and keep his way (v. 34), who try to walk by being upright and blameless (v. 37), and who simply do not worry about the *perceived* prosperity of those who are wicked.

There are a lot of things we worry about in life, . . . and "fairness" is definitely one of them. At the beginning of our text today, David says not to "fret" about these things. Three different times (vv. 1, 7, and 8) we are told not to be angry, not to be enraged or burn with fire against the wicked—because God is at work. God doesn't simply allow those things to happen. What we need to remember is that these perceived achievements of the wicked (all those status symbols we would consider evidence of prosperity), are issues we worry about *now*—and that the wicked are concerned about them now as well. But while God *is* concerned about the now, this text reminds us that it is the future that really is at stake.

But what really strikes me about our text is this word *fret*.

To "fret" simply means to worry, . . . but it's actually more than that—it's more complicated than worry because it takes the worry of your mind and adds physicality to it. Fretting is a full-bodied experience. But something we need to understand is that we're actually losing something in the Hebrew-to-English translation of this word. The meaning of the Hebrew word is actually "hot with anger"; it speaks of "kindled rage." Think of it as a coal burning inside you until it becomes so painful that the only way to snuff it out is by the water of *envy* (that word should make us all shudder). Fretting, to me, seems to be a combination of worry, envy, and actual anger.

Let's now come back to "wicked" and bring it all together, because I think *choice* is a tether between the two.

Just as a "wicked person" knowingly *chooses* to do wicked things, do we not also choose to allow envy to creep in? Isn't getting angry a choice? Isn't worrying a choice we make? Obviously, there are some drastic differences between being wicked and fretting, but both come down to choice. Come down to decisions. Come down to actions. And something else to consider: How easy is it to go from fretting to sinning?

It's all about trust. And trust is hard to come by when you perceive inequalities. Trust is hard to have when you see a blatantly horrible person "succeeding" in life. Trusting and having patience in God are extremely difficult when we fully understand that our desires are not necessarily his; our "plans" are not his plans, nor does God work things in *our* time or way. And yet, we're still called to trust him through all of this. But what does the psalmist say about our trust when we're angry with God for not acting in a way we want or for allowing something to happen that goes against every ounce of what we believe? What does it say about our trust when we become envious of someone else? I'm saying this to myself as much as to you: *we need to stop worrying and holding on to things of the present and instead hold (and live into) the things to come and the promises we've been given.* Dwell *in* the future and not *on* the present.

David writes to remind those reading this psalm that, as children of God, we must think and hold to our future and not our present. We must dwell and drink into the blessings of eternity with God, where prosperity and wealth mean absolutely nothing. For we go to a place where money has no value; goods and commodities are free; and all people are loved, cared for, and considered equal. Where love and goodness flow like a stream; joy and happiness are like a spring that never ends; and there is no death, crying, or despair.

We can get hung up on the evil and wickedness of people, but this does no good, for their destination is fully as known to God as ours is. And, really—worrying, fretting, getting envious or angry over what is going on in other people's lives does you no good, . . . because it's their life, not yours.

Ultimately, we need come back to verse 8 of our text, which should also answer the question I asked earlier: "Refrain from anger and turn from wrath; do not fret—it leads only to evil."

THREE QUESTIONS FOR YOU TO CHEW ON:

1. What in this psalm speaks to you? At what point are you drawn in? Why?
2. What are some things you can do to avoid focusing on the "now" of life and live into the hope of what is promised to come?
3. How does our anger over not getting what we want from God work against our trusting him and his ways?

A PSALM FOR FINDING
REST IN FORGIVENESS

Begin today's reading with Psalm 38.

One of the internet sensations has to do with animal shaming. The owner comes home and sees that their beloved family member (a dog or a cat—usually a dog) has utterly destroyed the home. The couch is ripped up, pillows have had their innards pulled out, the walls have been chewed on and scratched up, shoes have been destroyed, and it looks as though a tornado has dropped down inside the house; destroyed all it could; and then, just as quickly as it had arrived—poof, . . . it disappears. Then the shame comes. The dog simply looks guilty. She knows what she has done. He knows he will be caught. Even in those instances when there are multiple dogs in the home, the guilty party looks ever so guilty, and the other dogs appears to want nothing to do with them—they have distanced themselves from the guilty home-wrecker of a friend they once had.

David is ever so guilty for his sins, and his friends, his companions, those he is normally with are avoiding him (v. 11). It's so bad for David that in verses 13 and 14 he feels as though he cannot speak or hear. He's simply at a loss. He's in *grief*—which is a powerful word and emotion, especially when you grieve for the pain and sin *you* have caused.

We don't know what sins David has committed, but what we do know is that his pain is real, his anguish is deep, and his grief is all-consuming (as it usually is). What could someone do that would cause God to be angry (v. 1)? What could we ever do to make ourselves feel as though God would shoot arrows at us or to cause God's hand to come down heavily upon us (v. 2)? What could we ever do to cause guilt so strong (v. 4), wounds so deep and infected (v. 5), back so sore from bowing in guilt (v. 6), and a heart so full of anguish that even the "light" of our eyes has flickered out (v. 10)? Again, we simply don't know in this instance, but I would ask whether it matters. Do specifics help us? Nope.

I think we can all relate to the feelings David has. We know what it's like to do something so bad that we feel there is no hope for us. We've been in that place where guilt, shame, grief, and agony are ever present. Maybe you betrayed a friend. Maybe you did something to save your own skin at the expense of a coworker. Maybe you lied, stole, or even turned your back on God. Again, the specifics don't matter here, because we've all felt the sting of guilt realized as grief.

The worst part? It seems as though the deeper we sink into our guilt, the more pain we feel. The deeper the pit, the darker the anguish. Our grief over our sin could even lead to our feeling far from God. As if our guilt has created this massive chasm that not even God could cross. Scratch that. My shame is so bad *because* of what I've done that God simply doesn't seem to even *want* to cross over to me. Instead, he shoots arrows at me—and his shot is true. His anger appears so strong that his hand just weighs me down. His disappointment is so strong that it rings in my head to the point that I cannot hear or speak.

Again, I ask: Does it matter that we don't know where the psalmist's pain is coming from? I would argue no, because the psalm isn't about the sins committed. The psalm is about the *understanding* of the pain caused and the *guilt* felt; even more so, this psalm is a reflection of the forgiveness that comes. Did you catch that? It's not about the guilt or shame—it's about the forgiveness!

David knew he had sinned and caused God pain, and that pained *him*. We need to allow David to feel what he's feeling because that guilt and shame speak not only of his actions but also of how deeply he loves God. Grief and personal torment fall upon us only when we truly love the one we've hurt and feel remorse for what we've done. Caring about what we have done is actually a sign of caring for the one we've hurt. And there is an acknowledgment that *must* take place when we've hurt God. We have to come to him, we have to acknowledge our sins, we have to name what we've done because it is only in that space, it is only in that understanding, that we can truly begin to heal. *Forgiveness can happen only when we seek forgiveness.* Restoration can take place only when we face the music. And this is what David eventually does. After twenty verses of pain and anguish, he closes this psalm with two verses (21–22) that ask for forgiveness: "Do not forsake me," . . . "do not be far from me," . . . "come quickly and help me," . . . "O Lord my Savior."

That last declaration is everything to us. "Savior" means someone who saves—right? Saves us from our guilt; saves us from our fear of abandonment from God; saves us from *ourselves*; saves us from our anguish; and most importantly, saves us from that heavy hand or those piercing arrows. Did you catch Jesus there at the end? The psalmist declares God their Savior, . . . and what does God do? He saves, by way of Jesus.

It's interesting that our Savior is also the One we fear we've hurt the most (and in most cases, if not all, we *have*). And that's simply how God works. For all the pain we cause him, he wants no pain to be inflicted on us. Christ takes all that we suffer, all the anguish we place upon ourselves, all the guilt we harbor and live into, all the grief we swim in because of the harm we've done; and Christ says, "Give me all of that . . . and I will give you rest" (Matthew 11:28).

I think guilt and shame over what we have done can be a good thing—but only if we allow them to help us learn from our past mistakes. But never should we dwell in the past or in the present guilt. We are to find rest in forgiveness. And, ultimately, we need to recognize that God *is* our Savior—which we see in full fruition with Jesus Christ.

THREE QUESTIONS FOR YOU TO CHEW ON:

1. What in this psalm speaks to you? Where are you drawn? Why?
2. We read that every sin is a sin against God—even the ones toward other people. How is that so?
3. Is there any sin we can commit that would keep us from God's saving?

A PSALM OF
HOPE AMID DESPAIR

O pen your Bible with me to Psalm 39, and take the time to read it. The feeling of this psalm is that David is now at ease from wicked people who were around him. However, simply because they are gone doesn't mean he isn't in pain—for the belief is that he is now trying to recover from whatever afflictions have befallen him. And it is in this recovery (or hope *for* recovery) that he fully understands how brief our time on this earth is. It is in this time that David begins to wonder why we do what we do. We go back and forth, acquiring more and more (or at least trying to), but in the end where will it go? We certainly cannot take it with us—so, why do we even bother?

It's in these moments of clarity (frequently as we struggle with illness) that we begin to reflect. It's in these moments of finding truth in life that all other things are put in their true place. Money doesn't matter in the end. Our lives *are not* as long as we think they are—and we don't even know how much time we have. We can "heap up wealth" (v. 6), but when we die, we cannot take it with us. And I've seen more families ruined over someone's Last Will and Testament than I'd like to count.

Things of this world bring out the worst in us. Funny, and ironic how that works—that this world is full of things that are not wholesome and good and good *for* us, . . . and yet . . . *and yet* while we know this—we still seek them. This is why many people feel that the psalmist, while in this state of despair over worldly and other than worldly living, is more or less pulling a Job. Maybe he's reflecting on Job's life and his words in Job 7, or maybe he gets what Job has been saying this whole time, that life is hard, and asking, "When, God, will you take me home so I can leave this pain and suffering?" (*brief pause*) "But until then, . . . please bring me peace in my pain and suffering."

It is really hard to go through pain and grief and suffering when it seems as though there will be no end. The days can seem darker, the pain deeper—and that's only for what we're going through per se. Then we tack on the guilt we can swim in, too. All of this consumes us. All of this pushes even the sanest person to reflect not only on the *meaning* of life but *their own* life and choices as well.

It's interesting how perspective works. I read an article from a gentleman who didn't truly understand his relationship with God until his own mortality was put in jeopardy. It took battling leukemia for him to understand what Christ means when he says we are to offer up our lives in service to him—and that in our relinquishing our lives we actually *gain* life (Matthew 10:5–42). David is having this same moment of perspective. Those things we acquire; those friends we consistently want to impress; that job for which we sacrifice blood, sweat, and tears simply so we can take a paycheck home? They mean nothing. For "each man's life is but a breath" (v. 5).

David also recognizes that he needs to swallow his own pill. Back in Psalm 37 David spoke wise words to others, telling them that they needed to trust in the Lord. To wait, . . . to wait patiently for what the Lord has been doing and is about to do. And yet here we find David in that same moment, needing to swallow that pill he offered to others. Again, that's really hard to take when our pain consumes even the acquisitions we've come to love to know so much.

What I appreciate about this psalm is that, while David prays for God to bring him healing and an end to his suffering, he fully understands that God understands his lament and frustration and invites it upon his own shoulders. So, this psalm becomes an invitation for all of us to offer up to God our frustrations in where we are, what we are experiencing, our opinion of his evidently ignoring our cries—and even our thinking that he *brings* the pain *to* us (that's a whole other discussion!). But it's also a reminder that this space isn't where we are to be—and that God doesn't work that way. His love and grace are not such that he just sits back and says, "Yeah, . . . she can handle this. I'm just gonna throw this at her now too."

David writes his psalms to those of us who firmly believe that when we leave this sinful earth our souls will join with the many souls who have gone before us, and we will be in bliss with Christ—awaiting his final coming to earth, when he will restore *this* earth to the garden it once was. Ushering in eternity in the new heaven and new earth. David writes to those of us who believe this, hope for this, cling to this with every fiber of our being, and yet still struggle with the worldly things of today.

Psalm 39 is a beautiful song, often used at funerals, which speaks of struggle, pain, and hope. And in a world that is full of struggles and pain, hope is exactly what we need. We are eternally grateful that God not only hears our prayers, not only listens to our cries for help, not only is attuned to our weeping, but has done something about it.

THREE QUESTIONS FOR YOU TO CHEW ON:

1. What is there in this psalm that speaks to you? Where are you drawn in? Why?
2. When you are in despair, where do you see God's hand of hope? How does God help you when so often we do *not* hear his voice or see his hand?
3. Why does it seem that it is in the darkest of places that we find, and understand, our relationship with God (like the example given above about the man who was diagnosed with leukemia)?

A PSALM OF
CRY AND RESPONSE

Open the psalms with me and read Psalm 40.

As I read this text, I'm profoundly struck by the opening three verses. We read that David is in some slimy pit, covered in mud and mire. I instantly think of the quicksand scene from *The Princess Bride*—or, better yet (since that was sand), something more like that scene from *Blazing Saddles*. But, unlike the men in *Blazing Saddles* (or even Princess Buttercup and Westley). David waited patiently. Or did he? We also read that he waited patiently for the Lord and that the Lord turned to him and heard his cry (v. 1) So, is he patiently waiting, or is he crying out to the Lord? Well, in verse 9–17 (over half the psalm), David goes back to crying out to the Lord, for he is in utter despair. So, what's going on here? We have what seems to be a psalm of thanksgiving at the beginning (vv. 1–8), and then this crying out for help with the rest of the 17 verses? What's the deal here?

Many people feel that this psalm is a "Christmas" psalm—a birth of Christ psalm—and that makes sense. Hebrews 10:5–10 reflects back to verses 6–8, as Christ utters those same words that David speaks in our psalm. God truly *did not* desire the Old Testament sacrifices and offerings but established them anyway (full, sinless following and living were what God required, and the offerings became a way to appease for sins). Ultimately, Christ *did* come to accomplish only one thing: the will of God. To fulfill the law and write it upon our heart.

If you remember way back to my introduction, the psalms are divided up into five different "books" (or sections). We are nearing the end of the first book (Psalm 41 is the last), and so something that is starting to show up is an understanding of our depravity; pain; suffering; lament; and, ultimately, our need for redemption. These first 41 chapters work the reader through all the different emotions of life, as well as God's great and loving response to our needs. That's why they are joyful and hopeful—even while painful and penned in the midst of despair.

David is experiencing pain and a need of being saved, as death is surrounding him. And so, he cries out to the Lord to save him; because he knows the Lord ultimately will, he waits patiently for that saving. For David, it isn't a disconnect to have cries going to the Lord while also waiting patiently for him to respond. Can you see the connection to Christ? If not—I invite you to look some more.

- Where is your trust? David states that it shouldn't be in others but in the Lord (v. 4). Whom do we trust—humans or God? Hopefully it's God, for our ultimate trust can only be in his work, love, and sacrifice (aka: Jesus Christ).
- What does the Lord have planned for us (v. 5)? Goodness, grace, mercy, love, forgiveness, redemption, hope, joy, . . . and so much more. And how do we get those? Christ.
- We talked about verses 6–8 already, so see above for that one.
- What is it that we, as Christians, are called to do? Proclaim righteousness (v. 9)? Speak of God's faithfulness, as well as his salvation, and share his love and truth beyond the walls we worship in (v. 10)? Yeah—all of those! Matthew 28:18–20 states that we are to go out and *speak* of all those things! Share the love of Christ, his salvation, and bring hope to those who have no hope and know of no such love!

Those are things we know that God does and tells us to *be* to others and *do* for others. But David then goes into his own need. Just as David understands all this hope and joy as known only in the Lord, that doesn't mean our own hard trials cease to exist. One of the joys of the Lord is knowing that, while he asks us to do all these things on his behalf, he doesn't neglect the needs of his children.

We believe in a God who wants us not only to share of his love but to experience it, too. And this is where I fall deeper in love with David. In verse 12 David comes back to the pain he started with. We read, "For troubles without number surround me; my sins have overtaken me, and I cannot see. They are more than the hairs on my head, and my heart fails within me." Again, we don't know what sin or trouble David was in, but whatever it is, whatever sin he had committed, he has committed it again, and again, and again. David is no better than me . . . or you (I think this is why I love the story of David, Bathsheba, and Uriah the Hittite in 2 Samuel 11:1–5; 12:1–15 so much. Not that I love what he did (these sins are horrible), nor that I have done what he has done, but David is a man of brokenness—and *that* I can relate to).

This psalm reminds us that Christ came for all of us Davids (would Davida be the female version? Probably not). Christ came for the broken, the lost, the sin-repeaters, and the scared. God heard our cry once we left that garden, and he placed our feet firmly upon the Rock—our Lord and Savior Jesus Christ. What is truly beautiful (and, admittedly, scary) is that Christ uses those same people to share not only why all of us broken sinners need him but why *you* need him, too.

David closes this psalm not only with the understanding of who he himself is but by proclaiming the joy he has found in the knowledge that God thinks of him. And not only thinks, but extends his help and deliverance from on high.

You, . . . me, . . . David, . . . we are not deserving. And yet daily I find myself in complete thankfulness for God's grace.

THREE QUESTIONS FOR YOU TO CHEW ON:

1. What in this psalm speaks to you? At what point are you drawn in? Why?
2. Have you ever thought about how God thinks of you? What good things do you think God would say about you (nothing negative— only positive)?
3. How can we wait patiently for God when we are in a dark place of despair and grief?

A PSALMFUL REMINDER OF THE LOVE CAMP

Begin today's reading with Psalm 41.

Here we are. We've made it to the 41st psalm—the last in the group that are dedicated to, and reflective of, the pain and suffering that endure and the ultimate need for a savior and redeemer. Forty-one chapters that speak of what we go through (by our own hands or at the hands of others) and how God is working to bring healing to and through it.

Our psalm today, Psalm 41, is reflective of Psalm 38 in that David is meditating on his own illness or sin and the isolation it brings. But it's not only Psalm 38 that focuses on this theme; so do Psalms 39 and 40. With that being said, a pretty strong case can be made that all four of these psalms speak of the same incident—very likely of the time when David's son Absalom was advancing against him. It is only now, in hindsight, that David finds rest from his attacker.

But what's really interesting is that this isn't a psalm *for* the weak; it is more a psalm for those who *help* the weak. For those who have regard for the weak. For those who love, serve, pray for, sustain, feed, clothe, love (did I say love?) the weak. It's almost as though David is recalling all those who have helped *him* in his time of need. But what's interesting is that this feeling pertains only to the first three verses, because in verse 4 David switches and looks at the other side of those he's been in contact with. At his enemies and those who have abandoned him in his true time of need.

There are two kinds of people in this world—those who love and those who do not. I wish it were more complicated than that, but, unfortunately, I do not see it that way (and I would argue that God doesn't see it any other way, either). And, unfortunately, each interaction we have with people puts

114

us in one camp or the other. We see that in verse 9, where David reflects on someone whom he had always thought was in the love camp (camp A). Someone he ate with, shared food and laughter and joy with—someone to whom he opened up his home. That person is no longer in the love camp, for when David was in need it was abandonment that was offered and given. And not only that, but this individual turned his back against him. That friend didn't act in love. That friend was no longer in camp A but was now in camp B.

What's interesting is that David has been in both of these camps himself! He most *definitely* knows what it's like to *disregard* the weak and prey on them (*ahem*, . . . need we mention Uriah the Hittite or his wife, Bathsheba?). But David also knows what it's like to disregard the fact that one is his enemy and instead to spare him from death (as he did Saul more than once, not to mention Absalom, his own son). Instead of killing Saul, David opens up his house to his disabled grandson and not only provides for him for the rest of his life but feeds him, clothes him, and gives him all he will ever need and much, much more (look into the story of David and Mephibosheth in 2 Samuel 9). Still, David isn't perfect in his ability to show love to others, and that also means he's not perfect in showing his love to God.

But this isn't a story about David or even those who have loved him or abandoned him—or have done a little of both (which would include you and me). This *should* be a reminder to you and me that we are called to simply love. It's a reminder that if we find ourselves in camp B, then we need to love and love and love . . . and love some more so that we become *known* for love and not for anger, hate, or abandonment (which we are *really* good at).

Again—this isn't a story about where we find ourselves in relation to each other; it's about where we find ourselves in relation to God and his grace. This psalm is a psalm of God's sustaining love, mercy, healing, restoration, redemption, and *more* love. And the reason I can say that is not only that David ends the psalm with God's love and grace but that, as David reflects on all the types of people he's been in contact with, as David stews in the love and anger he has received, as David remembers that he even was abandoned by someone who was probably as close as a brother or sister to him, it's only natural that he *also* look at his relationship with God. When we do that, we quickly realize that God doesn't jump from camp to camp, depending on how he feels. God delivers us in times of trouble—and he delivers you to goodness, peace, rest, and hope. Always. God is constant and consistent in his response to all things.

I think we all know this, and while I fully proclaim that this is *not*, at least directly or primarily, about you or me, I am drawn to verse 2 because this *is* a psalm about you. No, wait! It can't be a psalm about you, . . . because it's a psalm about me.

Look at verse 2—Who are blessed? Who are preserved? In whom does God find favor and take joy and delight? Those who have regard for the weak (v. 1). This is a proclamation of God's goodness—but it's also a battle cry for love, service, compassion, and grace *for others*. This is about remaining in camp A, away from camp B. Ultimately, since we *must* take this back to God—is this not all about what Christ has done for you and me—even when *we* have shifted every day from one side to the other, becoming "serial" campers? Yeah. Thought so.

Don't be the friend who abandons. Don't find yourself running away from an opportunity to serve. Don't cower upon hearing evidence of pain. Be the comfort your neighbor needs. Be the voice for the one who has lost it. Be the crutch for those who need support. Love the unloved. Serve those on whom society turns its back (and there are a lot of them). Take in the refugee, clothe the naked, and feed the hungry. "For when you did this to the least of these brothers and sisters of mine, you did it for me" (Matthew 25:40).

THREE QUESTIONS FOR YOU TO CHEW ON:

1. What in this psalm speaks to you? To what are you drawn? Why?
2. Have you ever been betrayed by someone whom you thought was on your side? Have *you* ever betrayed someone? How do you move past that? How do you forgive someone who was so close to you and yet harmed you so intentionally?
3. What does it mean to have regard for the weak? Is it just that we *think* of them, or does it entail something more?

A PSALM FOR UNDERSTANDING YOUR NEED

Begin your reading with Psalm 42.

We have transitioned into Book 2 of the book of Psalms. Whereas the first 41 chapters focused on the relationship and need for a redeemer and really use a Genesis-type lens, so Book 2 (Psalms 42–72) now brings us to an Exodus-type focus, becoming more group focused than individual. What we'll find are psalms that were meant to be used and sung at the tabernacle and later the temple. Songs that focus on God's rescue of his people.

When the Israelites left Egypt and began their journey as God's chosen people—they did so in the desert. For forty years they wandered (in their minds and vision they also wandered, but with God they never did). Forty years of understanding who they were and who God was and not only why they needed him but why they needed him and *only him*. This all makes sense when we read the opening verse (which has become one of the more popular verses out there): "As the deer pants for streams of water, so my soul pants for you, my God."

There are two different focuses coming into this psalm that are extremely important (something that it took the Israelites forty years to understand). *We*, you and I, have needs. Be it water, be it food, be it clothing and shelter—every single one of us has need. The problem we have, however, is that those needs are all temporary. Food lasts us only a little while before we'll need more. Clothing eventually wears out, or we eat too much and need more of the fabric; shelter eventually needs to be replaced; and water is the most important need of all—but even that can go only so far because our bodies use and need continual replenishment.

The image we get in verse 1 is of a deer that is panting for water. Not stale water, not stagnate water, but *streams* of water. Moving water, healthy water, fresh water. So why would deer pant for water? Because they have a thirst that needs to be quenched. Because they are parched and experience dry mouths. Because they are in the desert and in danger of dying of thirst (the word *pant* is associated with a state of exhaustion). The only thing that will keep the deer alive is water. The only thing that keeps us alive while in the desert—the wilderness—is water. Or is it?

The water image takes us right into verse 2, where the psalmist declares that, just as the deer does all this for water, so too does the believer's soul thirst for the only thing that can quench it—and that's God. This takes us to the second need we have—God.

The psalmist knew and understood that the constant we really need in life is God; he fully understood that the only provider of all our needs, including that life-giving refreshment, is God. So, God is technically both the need and the answer for all that is good and necessary in life.

What is it we *truly* need in life? God—and only him.

- How do you go from dying to living? God. (v. 2)
- How do we move from pain and sorrow to joy and happiness? God. (v. 3)
- Where does protection come from? God. (v. 4)
- Where is hope? God. (v. 5)
- Where is pure good and perfect love? With and from God. (v. 8)

It took the Israelites forty years to learn that everything they needed was given by God. It took them forty years to understand that all requests should be placed *in* and *before* God. And why? Because when *we* try to do things, or when we try to put our hope in other things, we fail. We Christians see, declare, and proclaim that all good things come from God, as given to us by the love and work of the Son upon the cross and as continuously poured out into us by the Holy Spirit. So, what does all this mean?

We, perhaps especially in the United States, like to fill our lives with things we think we need (as did the Israelites—funny how things don't change). When we don't have new clothes or shoes and we see that others have those things, we take out credit to buy them or somehow find the cash to make sure those new kicks make it to our feet. We convince ourselves that we *need* them. New gadgets, new technology, new toys—all these things that we convince ourselves make our lives easier (trust me, I've used all the excuses in the world for them, too). But honestly—what *do* you need in life? It's not shoes, it's not tablets, it's not an Xbox or cars or anything else—*except for* Jesus. He is our living water (John 7:37). And *his* water is never used up or depleted; those who drink of it will never thirst again (John 4:14).

It took the Israelites forty years to learn this lesson, and that seems like a long time, but take it from someone who is now in their mid-forties—I still haven't fully learned it. Let me rephrase that. I *have* learned it, but it's the practicing it each and every day that seems to be the struggle.

THREE QUESTIONS FOR YOU TO CHEW ON:

1. What in this psalm speaks to you? To what point are you drawn? Why?
2. In what area do you see the biggest struggle in your generation between need and want? Why do you think that is?
3. During the season of Lent people give up conveniences and other things they enjoy, as the desire is to refocus on God and his giving of what we truly need. It's a way of reorienting our priorities. What would it look like for you to give up something you depend on for a week? Maybe a month. Could you? Would you?

YOUR CALL WAS HEARD

L et's begin today by reading Psalm 43.

As often with me when I read Scripture, there is a line or two that jumps out and grabs my focus—and in this case I'm drawn to verse 3: "Send me your light and your faithful care, let them lead me; let them bring me to your holy mountain, to the place where you dwell."

The image I get is of someone lost. Someone so deeply into going the wrong direction that their only hope is a sign from God—a light that illuminates the path home and brings comfort to their panicked soul. What compounds the sense of anxiety in this psalm is that not only is there this image of being utterly lost and panicked, but when we add verse 2, we get this feeling that the psalmist is at the same time surrounded by enemies. So now he is not only lost but has rounded a corner he had thought would lead him home and instead walked directly into the wrong crowd. Surrounded, outnumbered, panicked—what would you do? The only thing you *can* do: cry out to God.

I've never been lost to the point of panic, but I know what I would do if a loved one ever found themselves in that position. Anything and everything. I wouldn't sleep till I found them, and the only food I'd eat would have to be portable, so I could continue to search, and energizing, giving me the energy to keep on searching. I would send up beacons, hire flight crews to canvas an area. I would put up flyers, knock on doors, cry out to God, and never stop praying. No mountain would be too steep for me to search and no valley too low. They say that we've explored only five percent of the world's oceans. I would search the deepest depths of the ocean simply to find you and bring you home. And I would pray. Continuously.

I know that this psalm is not written from the perspective of the seeker but of the lost. But I cannot relate to David and his feeling of being lost and scared and needing hope to light the path home. But you know what? That's okay, because understanding what I would do for those I love begins to help me understand what God has done for his children who were lost—what God has done for *me*, whether or not I acknowledged it at the time or can now recall my dilemma.

The whole story of Scripture is about God and his unfailing love and desire to *be* with his kids. As we read Scripture, we're invited to see that *we* are those lost children and that God, throughout time, has sent out flares and beacons in response to our S.O.S. signals. Prophets after prophets have come to help us find our way home. David asks for God's light to lead him. Yeah, . . . I don't think we can count how many times God has done that. And then, finally, the largest search party, and most successful *ever*, came in the person of Jesus Christ. Imagine yourself in the middle of the woods, surrounded by massively heavy trees and rocks and cliffs, when all the sudden a path appears out of nowhere. And not only a path—but you can actually see home from where you stand—as though space had folded itself in half, and your home has suddenly been moved close to you. By Christ's coming to earth, by Christ's dying on the cross, and by the Holy Spirit's empowering strength and love poured into our lives, we are given light and faithful care. We are led and brought home to our joy and delight: God. What did God do to bring you and me home? He sent his One and only Son, Jesus Christ, to find us. It was a mission that would lead to his death, but it was a mission he gladly took on. It cost him his life—but it gave you yours.

I may have never *felt* lost, . . . but I sure was lost. We all were, and many of us still are today—but that doesn't stop God. That doesn't stop the work of the Holy Spirit, who gently but mightily calls us out of the lostness and into his state of "foundness."

THREE QUESTIONS FOR YOU TO CHEW ON:

1. What in this psalm speaks to you? Where are you drawn in? Why?
2. Why is the story of our being lost and then found so important to Christians?
3. How do we know that we'll never be lost again? Are there words of Scripture that affirm that God won't need to go on yet another rescue mission on our behalf?

A PSALM OF
FEELING ABANDONED

L et's begin today's reading with Psalm 44.

Perspective is an interesting thing. And it's interesting because it always comes *after* the fact. You jump to harsh conclusions and react in a certain way, but it's only later when you see the situation from a different perspective and gain new insight. Maybe you see how silly you were in your reaction or how you've gained new understanding from someone else's point of view. But does that work when you're dealing with God? It should.

Job eventually gains perspective at the end of his book when the Lord speaks (Job 38–42), but it comes only after he keeps pushing God for an answer regarding his current state. What I find healthy and good about the book of Job is that so many of the questions Job asks are questions I, too, want to ask of God. But, ultimately, just as Job finds truth and peace in who God is and what he is doing that is beyond Job's ability to comprehend, I too am reminded that I am not insignificant, even though there are so many things I cannot fathom—and that I am okay with not knowing the whole of what God is doing.

The psalmist is taking a page out of Job. He is declaring how good God is and how he simply trusts in him alone and nothing else (vv. 6–8), but despite all of that God, from his perspective, has evidently rejected him. God has, in his mind, given him over to be "devoured" like a sheep (v. 11), has allowed him to be scorned and taunted by the people and nations around him. The psalmist is so confident in his faithfulness to God that he sees himself as almost perfect in his worship of him. He doesn't stray to the left or right, hasn't forgotten God's name (v. 20), and has strictly adhered to his covenant (v. 17). So, what's the deal, God? Why are you doing this to him? Ultimately, the end of the psalm verbalizes the question he (and we) are struggling with: "Why, God, have you abandoned us?"

Here's how that feels:

- Me: (praying) "God—I really need you right now."
- God: "Hello! Thank you for calling! I'm away from my phone right now, but leave me a message and I'll get back to you as soon as I can. And remember, . . . wait for the beep!"
- BEEEEEP

Do we really think or believe that it works this way?

Ultimately for me, this isn't the right question—nor is it a fair one. Has God ever abandoned his people? Has God ever forgotten who they are? We see numerous examples of the Israelites *thinking* they were abandoned— but simply because God doesn't answer or save them when they want him to doesn't mean he's off running errands and can't (or, worse, doesn't want to) be with them right then.

We believe in a God who is omnipotent, omnipresence, and omniscient. Who is everywhere, knows everything, and is above all things. There is no end or beginning to his name or his power or knowledge. And so, how could God not *be* somewhere, or how could he "forget" something if we just proclaimed those eternal attributes? To say that he has "forgotten" or is busy is to say that he *cannot do* something or that he changes his mind about wanting to. So, the real question is *Why?* Why would God allow his psalmist to "live in disgrace" (v. 15) and be "plundered" by his neighbors (v. 10)?

We need, for one thing, to understand that this was in Old Testament times. The Israelites were surrounded by hostile nations. And just as they regularly attacked others, they too were subject to being attacked. It is in the midst of this chaos that they remember what God had done in the past (protecting, carrying them through, providing for their ancestors), and they begin to lament and cry out for *that* kind of work again now.

I think this is a really good theological discussion that one should have—but this isn't the time or space for it here. It does, however, bring up a really good question: Why? If I am in prayer with God daily, if I give thanks to him consistently, if I worship him and him alone, *why* is it that things happen that seem outside his goodness? Why do I lose my job? Why does my mortgage fall through? Why are all these health issues happening to me and my family? Why are my parents getting divorced? Why did my cousin, who was so young, have to die?

Can you relate?

The fact is that bad things happen. And many things happen that we wish did not. Simply because we are "good Christians" doesn't mean we are thereby protected from all of life's blows. And if you're anything like me, even the smallest hurdle is sometimes hard to see beyond. We see a challenge before us, and we lament and struggle and sometimes even succumb to the pain and agony. We fail. Even when just over that hill could have been rest and peace—we don't see it because all we see is that which stands before it: the hill that is blocking our vision of it. I'm reminded of Dori in *Finding Nemo*; even when in the worst situations, she tells herself to "just keep swimming, . . . just keep swimming . . ." I think we need to be Dori at times.

Paul writes in Romans 8:31–39 that we are more than battle-hardened fighters. We are more than people who fight day in and day out. We are conquerors. Because Christ died for our sins and justified us by his blood, we have already been given what is beyond what we can see. Because Christ loved and died for us, there is nothing that can separate us from his presence and the ultimate glory that awaits us.

The psalmist reminds us that even the most ardent and faithful believer can struggle when things seem dark—but let us *never* forget who God is and what he has done. Let us never be so bold as to shout aloud that God has forgotten or abandoned us. And let us *always* remember that Christ paid the ultimate price for us. And not only that, but remember Pentecost! Remember the presence of God, through his Holy Spirit, coming *to* us and dwelling *in* us.

How can we be abandoned or forgotten when the Spirit is living in us? How can we be forgotten or abandoned when God did everything, even dying, to pull us back in? Yeah—I need to remember that. Always.

THREE QUESTIONS FOR YOU TO CHEW ON:

1. What in this psalm particularly speaks to you? What draws you in? Why?
2. How do you "just keep swimming" when you're exhausted, spent, and feel as though you cannot go on?
3. What are some things we can do to remind ourselves that God is still here, even when we feel so far away from him?

A WEDDING-SONG PSALM

Open your Bible and read with me the words of Psalm 45.

Our psalm today is one that seems out of place—even though it is not. Where many of the psalms speak of joys and needs, our psalm today is one that simply speaks of praise. But it's not praise in light of David's delivery from his enemies but a simple praise for who God is and what he has done.

The image we get is of the kind of praise that would be initiated by a joyful, royal wedding. The king is now married, and a young man stands before the king and his queen to sing their praises. He sings a song of joy and encouragement and hope about the king in verses 1–9 but then transitions to a focus on the queen in verses 10–17.

Now, this may seem odd and even out of place from our viewpoint, but if you put yourself in the sandals of the writer (or the singer), you get the sense that he is in a state of absolute delight, not only about his king but about the fact that he has taken a bride. Roger Ellsworth writes that he is "bubbling" with joy.

As we work through the opening half of this psalm, we start to read about all the things the singer found delightful and important in his king. He is excellent (v. 2); the words he speaks are full of grace, and he has been blessed by God (v. 2); he is equipped to defend and attack with his sword and is clothed in majesty and splendor (v. 3); he rides in truth, humility, and righteousness, and all he does (his work) is good (v. 4); all the nations bow before him (v. 5); and his throne will never end (v. 6). This king is honest and truthful, and because of this God has placed him above all other things. Not only that, but of all the things this king could have—and of all the women who might have been available to him—he desired *this* royal bride, the one who sits beside him (v. 9).

And the bride? What about her? The place in which she dwells is glorious (v. 13), and she has been given everything she could ever want or need by her groom (v. 14); yet the writer has a challenge for her—which is interesting. He tells her to focus on the king, and only him. Not to look to others who may come to her for favor, who may try to please her; not to take her eyes off the king. For these others *will* come (v. 12). And, finally— she is not to hold to the place she came from but to focus on where she is going, on the one she is with now (v. 10).

Again, this may seem weird to us, but it makes absolute sense in at least two ways:

- Context. The king and his stability, compassion, and strength on the throne was everything to the Israelites. And having him take a bride brought long-term strength and stability to the house, too. When we remember this, and put ourselves in the place of the writer/singer, we get it.
- From a Christian standpoint. This should make absolute sense when we remember that the king is none other than the King of kings: Jesus Christ (Hebrews 1:8; Revelation 19:7–8), and the Bride is his Church.

When we come to this psalm with joy and delight (as does the author who has penned this song and has been invited to sing for the king and his bride), I begin to wonder what words I would have written. In what do I find joy and delight in Christ? What words of praise from my mouth would be meaningful, honest, hopeful, and true? Would I launch myself into an aria of strength, power, and might, never forgetting his love, compassion, and grace?

And what about his bride? The Church? Do I sing a song, as the psalmist has, that challenges, encourages, and reminds the Bride of where she has been, where her focus should be, and the hope for her to come? How she could be swayed by others and yet must stay true to Christ, true to his Word and true to all he speaks of? Just as Christ would frequently speak to his disciples, in the presence of other followers and onlookers, encouraging words of service and revelation, so I know that the psalmist is singing this song in front of a massive crowd of people who are listening and wondering what he will say. What words would *I* choose to sing of my King and to encourage his Bride *while* others are listening? What words would I choose that would help others come to know my King and his Bride?

To be honest, as I think about this, I am getting goose bumps. Just the prospect of singing a solo to Christ makes me nervous. Would I articulate the right thing? Would I say enough? *Could* I say too much? How *long* would I sing? Would there be an appropriate length? Scientists have found that the top one hundred songs move along for an average of 180 seconds before "bloat" starts to set in (their beginning to seem repetitive and tiresome). Would two minutes be long enough? Or would I offer something comparable to the longest song ever recorded as having been written—which is a sixty-nine minute song containing over five-hundred verses?

In honesty, neither of those seems right. I *should* be able to sing a song *less* than two minutes in length because I can easily sum up the splendor of my King in a few short words, and yet sixty-nine minutes doesn't seem long enough in that my whole *life* must be one extended song of joy and hope and splendor about my King that I share with others.

In the end I'm not sure where I should end the song, so I guess I'll simply keep singing. Because, let's be honest: he never ceases to amaze me with things about which I simply want to continue singing his praises.

THREE QUESTIONS FOR YOU TO CHEW ON:

1. What is it in this psalm that touches you? To what are you drawn? Why?
2. The psalms are supposed to be about God, so why do you think this psalm is even here?
3. Put yourself in the shoes of the psalmist. What words would you offer the King, and what words would you sing to his bride (the Church)?

A PSALM FOR PEACE

Begin your reading today with Psalm 46.

Maybe I'm being a little morbid—but I've thought about things that *could* happen that would make my world collapse. When I was a kid, it was me not being around my parents. And not only not being around them but their actually being fully removed from my life. I couldn't imagine not having my protectors, my providers, my love and support physically around me, doing all those things I needed them to do and be. And it wasn't only that I needed them for those things—it was that they were my everything. I even remember quite vividly those half dozen or so months when I was in the seventh grade when my dad was deployed and away from us. Even *half* my support system being gone led to some really tearful nights. And I think about my life today, with regard to my wife, my kids, my friends, my church, my family—those fears are still prevalent.

We don't know much about what the psalmist is experiencing, except for the fact that all the things that represent chaos and destruction in his life are present in the current situation. Waters roaring and foaming (v. 3); mountains quaking and surging (again, v. 3); nations and kingdoms attacking, defending, and falling (v. 6)—all of these things represent terrific strife, chaos, pain, suffering, sadness, and worry.

And to the people of Israel, all these things represented issues that were beyond them—not to mention massive in scope and intimidating. If you are anything like me, when you think of these things you, too, feel somewhat intimidated and insignificant. Mountains are massive obstacles. When they tremble, fear and chaos ensue—the same with waters that roar and foam. I've been whitewater rafting enough times to know the destructive power those waters wield. And nations and kingdoms? To the Israelite life was about war, death, and battles—consistently. Again, I've seen enough on the news and internet to see all the pain, death, suffering, and destruction that are still going on.

So, what does one do? When your world is turned upside down, when circumstances are beyond your control, where do you turn? God. There can be, and should be, nothing else in this world that brings us peace, comfort, and solace other than God himself. His presence, as well as his promises.

I get it. My hope and trust as a kid were in those who were tangible and daily in my life: my parents. As an adult I grew in my faith, grew in my understanding, and grew in my walk. I slowly began to understand that my comfort was never truly in people—it was in God, who surrounded me with his presence and love via those people. I don't mean to say or come across as though I am saying that those things aren't deeply important to me—but I've learned that the only stable constant in life is God. Not others or things. And, when all else fades away—and it will— God still remains.

Everything that we have, the only thing that we cling to in times of worry must be God. Who he is and what he is doing. And in the end, as we grow in our faith and our walk, we begin to understand that our hope is in *his* security and in his promises.

And that's exactly what we have here: God's promises = Comfort/Peace.

And what we need to always remember is that the promises God gave to Israel, the comfort that Israel had in who God was and that he held to his covenantal promise to them, is still available to us today. The psalmist was brought to peace because of the Lord and his promise to never abandon his people (Deuteronomy 31:6), . . . and he never did. He consistently brought them to peace and security. Yes, we can find countless texts in which it *seemed* as though God was not protecting them—but in all those instances it was the *people* who walked away from God. And so, while they may have *felt* abandoned, God was in fact always there. Waiting for them to truly seek his hand of comfort—and when they did, he was there. Even in his silence he was still present. Ever watching, ever waiting.

This is a comfort and peace we have today, as fulfilled in Jesus Christ and the Holy Spirit. Christ descended to this world so that we could be in final peace and comfort with him *instead* of doomed to the death and destruction toward which we were heading. Christ's death pulled us in and reminds us that, even when we try to walk away, or run away, or focus on things other than him, he will never let us out of his grip. And then God said he would give us his Spirit to continue to bring peace and comfort into our chaotic lives (John 14:16–21). Filling us with his presence in the storms, as well as in the peace in our lives.

The question I find myself asking, the question I want *you* to think about—is this: When your life does seem to be in a downward spiral, how is your fear stilled? When those mountains in your life crumble, when a sudden squall sets in, when the rivers slosh and foam and toss you about, where is your peace?

Answer: "Be still, and know that I am God" (v. 10).

THREE QUESTIONS FOR YOU TO CHEW ON:

1. What in this psalm speaks to you? At what point are you drawn in? Why?
2. What, in life, do you fear? Why do you fear it? What is there about it that speaks more strongly than your comfort in God?
3. This psalm, ultimately, speaks of the fear of death. Why do we fear death, when all of our hope is in what comes next?

A PSALM OF
THANKSGIVING FOR
DELIVERANCE

Before launching into today's reflection, take the time to read Psalm 47. Our psalm today is what is called an "enthronement" psalm. A psalm that speaks simply of God's throne over all things. Seen and unseen. Said and unsaid. Living and nonliving. This psalm reminds us that there is not an inch, not a space, not a place, and nothing else that exists that is not governed, ordained, created, and ruled by him.

I love the image of the promises of a future that are given to us in Revelation 7:9–14. Reflecting on the fact that John sees what he calls the "multitude"—a group too vast and wide to count or see, all engaged in the worship of God—is simply beautiful. And that this great number of people represents every tribe, tongue, and nation, past and present? Glorious.

The people of Israel were constantly at war with those around them. Time and time again they were taken over by the Babylonians; the Philistines; and countless other tribes, nations, and people. And, from their side, the people of Israel, under the guidance and protection of God, did the same to their neighbors. That's how things worked. And so, when we read this psalm, we *must* understand context. We *must* see that, to the people of Israel, *they alone* were the children of God, for it was with Abraham that God had made his covenant (Genesis 17). That time after time God delivered his covenantal people (Israel) out of the hands of those who would try to wipe them out, or defame God and work to destroy his name. And through it all, even though Israel herself frequently did those exact same things, the fact remained: God continued to be the Lord of all creation.

As stated earlier, we are in a grouping of psalms (Psalms 42–72) that reflect the exodus—God's removing his covenantal people *out* of Egypt and *into* the promised land. A time when God would protect them from their enemies, provide all necessary needs for them to live each and every day (food, clothing, shelter, water, . . .). These psalms also show us a "worship" aspect of the relationship with God, a prayer of thanks and worship for his deliverance. Psalm 47 is a psalm of thankfulness for deliverance.

So, that begs the question: What, today, are *you* thankful for in terms of *your* deliverance? Christ redeemed you, he called you by name, he knows every ounce of you (inside and out), and he paid for *you* with the price of his blood. Have you lived into that today? Have you experienced truly what that means? I'd hate to think of what *could* have been for my own life . . .

So, what *are you* thankful for? I know that there is much evil I have never experienced—much trauma that I have never felt—but that doesn't mean those kinds of trials don't exist or aren't along the journey and path I'm on. But I know that, in it all and through it all, God is the One who reigns over all things, both seen and unseen. And that regardless of what I experience now, regardless of what still is coming down the road, my only comfort is that my Lord and Savior is over it all and through it all.

There is no journey, no path, no place that I can go where God isn't already reigning.

THREE QUESTIONS FOR YOU TO CHEW ON:

1. What in this psalm speaks especially to you? To what aspects are you drawn? Why?
2. When you think of what deliverance means, and what you've been given, what in particular are you thankful for?
3. If the New Earth will be filled with people from every tribe, tongue, and nation—that also, at least for me, means that we'll have an abundance of cultural opportunities at our fingertips. My being a "foodie" thus means that I can try so much amazing food and cook with ingredients I have never before encountered! What are you looking forward to in the New Creation?

A PSALM THAT
BOASTS IN GOD

Begin by reading Psalm 48.

Our psalm today is a reflection and praise on the city of Jerusalem. A praise on the magnitude and beauty of the city that was the epicenter for the Jewish people. But it's more than that because Jerusalem was *more* than a city—it was believed to be the very place where Abraham prepared to sacrifice his son Isaac (Genesis 22) and the place where the holy of holies was. Jerusalem was sacred, holy, and seen as the very apple of God's eye. To the Hebrews, it was the center of the world. It's where God dwelled; it's what God considered sacred and the very place he gave to his promised children and their descendants. In essence, outside of God himself, Jerusalem equaled *everything*.

As we read Psalm 48, we need to understand a few things about history. To the Hebrews during this time the city was not only Zion—the place for God and his people—but it was their protection; their stronghold; their past, present, and future. It was a city that was more glorious and important than anything else in their lives or religious system. So, to honor God and show his might and strength (and to intimidate all the surrounding people and nations), they built walls, towers, a temple—anything and everything that reflected not only the magnitude of the living God but anything and everything that would tell her neighbors "Don't mess with Jerusalem!" So, it made perfect sense to have a psalm that sings of the grandeur of such a place. It made sense to have a reflective psalm (which we aren't sure who penned) that sings of the walls; the terror the very mention of this city could produce; and the fact that it was the only living God, Yahweh, who stood and made the city secure forever (v. 8). *That* is the point at which I'm struck—and stuck. Boasting—it's just not part of me.

One of the many lessons I was taught by my parents and learned in other ways over time is that one shouldn't boast. One shouldn't be brash or arrogant in life. Nobody likes the person who is cocky. It's almost as though they are begging to be brought low. Begging to be knocked off their pedestal! And, oh, have the people of Jerusalem been brought low—time and time again. Numerous times the people have been seized, captured, driven off, and nearly wiped out.

So, why are they so brazen here? Why does the psalmist give the impression that they are walking along and almost egging on all other people and nations to "just try" to attack her? Try to bring her down! "Give us your best shot, Babylon! All you kings, join your forces—bring the best of your best. Advance together; you will flee in fear once again!" (vv. 4–5). I'm not sure. But what I do know is that when the people of Jerusalem were faithful to God, nothing could destroy the city. When the people were faithful to God, nothing could bring them, or their beloved city, to her knees. When the people of God worship God and him alone, there is nothing, in life or in death, that can bring fear. That almost begs the question for me: Do I boast about God and his love, protection, and safety? *Should* I?

Times have changed, so that no boasting about the security of the city needs to happen. We affirm that Christ has become the living temple, the holy of holies—and that it is in him that we put our security. So, maybe we should boast in Christ. Paul says we shouldn't. This was the problem with the church in Corinth (1 Corinthians 1:29), but he also says that if we *do* boast—we are to boast in the Lord (1:31). But we must understand that there is a difference between boasting in the Lord and boasting in oneself. The people of Jerusalem boasted in the Lord, whereas the people of Corinth boasted in themselves. So, let me ask again: *Should* we boast in Christ?

Well—I'd say yes and no. But let me ask about *how* and *why* you boast. Do you boast to puff yourself up or to egg people on? Then no. Do you boast to challenge or make yourself seem, and appear, better than others? Then no. Boasting in Christ means understanding that it is he and he alone who fills our every need. Through Christ God tore down walls, citadels, towers, and everything else that makes us feel secure. Boasting in Christ, especially from a Greek understanding of the word, simply means to rejoice and find glory. Those are the things that the Hebrews were doing—those are the things that we do, too—just manifested in our time in Christ and not the city of God.

So, boast away—as long as your "boasting" is rejoicing. Boast away—as long as your boasting is of God's glory and grace. To *him* be honor and glory and praise. We boast in *his* work and love, . . . not in ourselves, who are the recipients of that love and grace.

THREE QUESTIONS FOR YOU TO CHEW ON:

1. What in this psalm stands out for you? Where are you drawn? Why?
2. "Boasting" often feels as though we're trying to make ourselves appear better than others. Should we do that? Isn't that very tendency responsible for so much of the pain nonbelievers receive from believers?
3. Instead of boasting, what other actions can we take to *share* what God has done, and does, for his people?

A PSALM TO
BE MESSENGERS OF HOPE

egin your devotional reading today with Psalm 49.

It only takes engaging with different people to fully realize the extent of death. Death doesn't play by societal rules. It doesn't matter who you are, where you come from, how much money you make, or how kind or mean you are, nor does it matter your ethnicity or cultural background. Death simply doesn't care. If you are alive now—death will hit you.

Picture our psalmist walking down the street, observing people to his left, right, and all around. He sees the rich walking down the street with their gold and jewels dangling and clanging loudly against each other as they walk. A veritable tambourine of jewelry. People walking with their heads held high, as they are proud of all they have accomplished. And as they walk down the streets, low and humiliated are the people who have no jewelry, the ones who have no soft, bright, and beautifully crafted clothes: the "low" people. The psalmist sees both groups (v. 2).

And as the psalmist continues to walk, he sees all those whom society considers either wise or foolish. One group is foolishly living lives of haste and waste. Not really understanding what they have or where they are going or even what they need—they waste and throw away what they have— maybe even going about making mistake after mistake. This, in contrast to the other group the psalmist sees: the wise. They are sages, thinkers, and philosophers. They sit and reflect on words, actions, people, and things considered "high above" all others (v. 10). The psalmist sees both groups.

And it is in this moment that the psalmist is convicted. I picture him quickly looking around and finding a wooden crate. Something that will allow him to stand up above others so that both the tall and the short can see him. Maybe he searches around and quickly creates a makeshift cone—something he can use to amplify his voice. He needs to be seen. He needs to be heard. This message is so devastatingly important that no matter the person, the place, or the status, . . . all must hear what needs to be said. There is a truth that must be shouted: anything and everything . . . *will not last* (v. 12).

That's a message we all must hear.

We may count our money and possessions (v. 12), we may trust in what we can and cannot do (v. 13), we may look to the rich and be envious (v. 16), we may count ourselves blessed by what we have and what we know (v. 18), but in the end, when we die, we die. We cannot take what we have with us (v. 17), nor can we do anything about it. Death . . . is death. And death hits us all.

And why is the psalmist so convicted? He has realized this "wisdom" for himself and simply cannot continue to see people and society going down this path of forsakenness. He can't continue to see people seeking and trusting in themselves and things of this world, when, in the end, these things simply don't matter.

I remember seeing a bumper sticker years ago that said, "He who dies with the most toys . . . still dies." And that's the truth. But what we need to see here is that the psalmist is trying to give wisdom to others. He isn't trying to be a downer—he simply wants people to put trust in the true source of hope. Verse 15 tells us that "God will redeem me from the realm of the dead." God will not leave the psalmist in decay but will raise him up—and take him to himself.

This is a reality that all of us have faced and will face time and time again. That everything we, as a society and culture, deem as important simply is not. We are a worldly society that appraises nearly everything based on status, and yet time and time again we see that status means nothing in the end. This begs the question: What *does* matter? If we are called to not gain status, or wealth, or worldly things, . . . what *should* we do?

First off, the psalmist simply wants us to *turn* to God—the only One who *does* endure. To put our trust in God (v. 15) and nothing and no one else.

Second: love. Love as though there is no tomorrow. Love as if there are no barriers (FYI: there *are* no barriers in true, authentic love—like God's love). Love like God. Love in action, love in time. Love exactly how *you* are loved by God.

That's it! Those two things: put your *hope in God* and simply *love.* Sounds easy, right? *It is!* However, we make it difficult in the way we've sought worldly things and worldly actions. But it's really not that hard.

Oh, . . . and here's one more thing: *share your hope!* Take a cue from the psalmist and speak of true hope, true love, and true grace. Let people know that God has *not* left them in the realm of the dead, that Jesus Christ overcame sin and death and redeems those who call upon his name. Give them hope and clarity, for things of this world will simply drag us down. Take a soapbox and a megaphone. Grab some posters and flyers. Plaster Facebook and Twitter with "hope" messages of God and his grace.

Do something. Be the messenger of God's grace that we all were created to be.

THREE QUESTIONS FOR YOU TO CHEW ON:

1. What is there in this psalm that speaks to you? To what are you drawn? Why?
2. Within today's culture, and your current reality, what's the most effective way to share God's love?
3. People respond to authentic love. Why is that? What is there about love that elicits a response? Or is it simply the fact that there is a lack of love in so many places, and so to finally *see* love changes people?

A PSALM OF INSTRUCTION

Open the book of Psalms and read with me Psalm 50.

Our psalm today is a "didactic" psalm—a "teaching" psalm, and it's attributed to Asaph (he was a musician). The goal of this didactic psalm is to teach or instruct all those listening. As we read through Psalm 50, we can see three different movements: introduction, instruction/charge to the righteous followers, and instruction/charge to the wicked. And all of this is framed around *who* God is.

As I read this psalm, I can't help but be drawn to the third of the three sets of instructions. I know who God is (vv. 16), and I fully understand that God doesn't *need* our sacrifices and our gifts to him. Really, all of our life is about fulfilling our vows, not only to him but to each other (vv. 7–15), but it's that third instruction (vv. 16–23) by which I'm struck.

We can see in verse 16 that the wicked are reciting the laws of the Lord and speaking of the covenant he has made, and yet they obviously are wicked because they are giving lip-service to God and to their brothers and sisters. They see bad things happening, and they join in. They speak lies and evil, they speak harshly against others and their actions, and yet they still profess God and his love. So, why does God even care?

God is concerned with those who speak of his name but do so wrongly, because being in a relationship with him means living out that relationship in all aspects of life. If we are called to be his hands and feet, then we simply must *be* his hands and feet. We must love those he loves and serve those he serves. God gives us very specific commands on how we are to act and be (see the Ten Commandments from Exodus 20), on how we should love and serve him, as well as others—and *not* doing those simply is breaking those commandments. But we also must realize that, not only does God care about *how* we are functioning as his hands and feet; God does not want us to know and believe what he demands of us and then simply refuse to do it. God does not want people who give only lip service.

Active worship of God requires actively following his commands. Nodding and speaking the words to people that God is love requires us to *be*, to embody, that love in all situations. We can't say that God is _____ but that *that characteristic or essence* is him and we don't have to abide by it, . . . cuz, well, we're not him. We are called to emulate him in all we say and do. Which means we can't choose who we want to love and who we do not. It simply doesn't work that way.

What about how we speak to people, the words we use to build up or break down? What about our giving and withholding of finances to people in need? What about how we *think* of people and the conclusions we draw about them? All those things (and so much more) speak to the importance of life—for they all manifest the value of life.

I don't want to sit here and say that all those who *don't* speak of those things are wicked, but we need to understand, we need instruction and reminders from each other that God calls his children to be active worshipers—and, really, we should be challenged by Asaph's words in verses 16–21. We know that God speaks of love, but are we practicing it? Really living it out?

This instruction from Asaph is here because we all need reminders and instructions. Paul reminds us in Romans (1:32, as well as 2:21–22) that what we teach and say must not only be words for others—but words for *us* as well. We must be obedient in words, heart, and actions. Hypocrisy has no place in the kingdom of God.

So, what does this mean? To me, this means that we must join forces with Asaph. That we must listen in on the words we ourselves speak when we speak of God—that we must truly take them to heart. That we must fully understand the words we use and why we use them—but it's not as though we may stop there. Our actions back up our words, and we live into the commands and grace of God each and every day. But we also must do what Asaph is doing here for us: agreeing with his challenge to those who do *not* live godly lives, we, too, are to speak into each other's lives and remind each other just want it means to follow God (to be my "brother's keeper").

THREE QUESTIONS FOR YOU TO CHEW ON:

1. What in this psalm speaks to you? To what are you drawn? Why?
2. Are there commands of God that you find you tend to follow more strongly or easily than others? Why is that?
3. What are some things we can do to daily follow the will of God and his commands for his children? What are some ways to better walk in his path and live, and love, as Jesus lived and loved?

A PSALM OF
SIN AND FORGIVENESS

Take a few moments to read Psalm 51.

Our psalm today reflects an emotional plea from someone who gets it. Someone who knows what life is all about. An emotional crying out from a man who is reflecting on a recent past that has been full of deceit; lies; adultery; and, eventually, murder (you can read the whole sordid story in 2 Samuel 11). A man after *our* own heart, someone we can all relate to—whether we want to or not. Because, truthfully—we all deceive, we all lie, we all commit adultery with our hearts and our eyes. We murder with our thoughts and feelings. You, me, none of us are any better than this sinful man, King David.

Psalm 51 is a prayer for cleansing and a realization that true cleansing happens only when we have been forgiven. When we have allowed God in, allowed our sins to be exposed, truly repented for them, and asked God to intervene—to take over. It is the laying down of our sins that are weighing heavily on us, that which burdens us, and asking God to remove the weight from our chest. Sins and heaviness hit us from every angle—every day—every hour. It's not just a "I have done something bad and I must now repent"; it's a daily repetition. A daily repentance. Because we might as well have a sign on us that says, "Sins Live Here—But Are Not Welcomed. Forgiveness in Progress."

Psalms are written in reflection of something real—something personal—but something honest as well. And they are intentionally ahistorical. That is, they are applicable both at the time written and today—eternally relevant. While we read about David's thoughts, we are encouraged to reflect upon our own thoughts with regard to the sinful actions we, too, commit. But what's encouraging is that in this moment of reflection we do not dwell on the negative, because we are *also* reminded that we are delivered from those pits. *That* is what this psalm is about—and this is what our lives are about. Let me explain.

Everything we do is riddled with sin. It's who we are. It's in our nature. Now, that is not an excuse and should never be used as a crutch, either. This doesn't mean that we are to go out and sin freely. What it does mean is that our festering stink-u-bus of sin must be understood, realized, acknowledged, and addressed, because ultimately all sins are a direct attack against God—And David realizes it.

In verse 4 he says, "Against you, you only, have I sinned and done what is evil in your sight."

Even in David's case, where the sin included adultery and murder, David realizes that all sins are against God. Because the true nature of a sin is an offence against the beauty and perfection of God—against his majesty. This is what David is lamenting! Ahhhh—but it is also what he is thankful for! Because God is able to do something about it.

When we neglect our families or friends or neighbors, or anyone else, we are breaking the commands of God. When we act on our own impulses, as David did, we are going against God because he deserves to be the focus of our emotions, our thoughts—and he requires us to be holy—to be "set apart." We are here to love, to serve, to take care of each other, but this is at the same time an accountability we cannot completely follow through on. Because my own personal desires and thoughts always get in the way. And it isn't until we realize that we are in this predicament that we then can realize that we need Christ. We need a Savior to save us from ourselves and to save us from God's judgment.

As Paul says in Galatians 5:17, "The desires of the flesh are against the Spirit, and the desires of the Spirit are against the flesh, for these are opposed to each other, to keep you from doing the things you want to do." This is why we have this lament—why David pours out his heart on this rollercoaster of emotions. Psalm 51 is a teeter-totter, where we have the extreme sins that David committed juxtaposed against the extreme love and pardon he receives from God. It's an emotional plea that is bordering between this low of reflection and this high of knowing that God can, and will, do something about it. David sees his humanness— his mortality—and everything that makes him a sinner—but he also sees everything that is our Father. His love. His forgiving nature. His demands, and yet God's own personal sacrifice he made for David—as well as for you and me.

I like how we read about needing to be "washed thoroughly" and "cleansed." When we wash things, we don't do so halfway. It's not a wash only on one side, or a willingness to leave a stain here, a speck of dirt there. It's a complete washing. When we take a shower, we don't wash only a leg—we clean our bodies thoroughly. That's what David is asking for. And this is what David realizes God can do and knows he does do for us. He completely washes us anew. God completely forgives. Completely takes away that which makes us dirty (1 Corinthians 6:11).

I want you to see something else here, too. David uses this verb phrase "have mercy" in verse 1 because *this is a prayer to God*. A prayer for God to act in accordance with who he is—according to his character, his nature.

But David realizes that he does not deserve any forgiveness. That his sins are his own—that he cannot blame anyone else. We do not deserve God's forgiveness—but it comes because of God's grace. A grace given to us by the love of the Father, the action of the Son, and the continuous work of the Spirit. Thanks be to God!

THREE QUESTIONS FOR YOU TO CHEW ON:

1. What in this psalm speaks to you? Where are you drawn in? Why?
2. Can you define grace? What does grace look like?
3. David's plea for God to "have mercy" is also a declaration of the depths of the sin he has committed, not to mention the depths of God's grace. What *should* be the price of sin? Why does God not give that to us—and why did Christ take it all upon himself?

A PSALM OF ANGER

Begin today by reading Psalm 52.

My first thoughts and impressions on this psalm are that David is really bitter and angry. While you read this psalm, you get this impression of someone who is harboring immense hatred and disgust toward someone. But then we come to know the backstory, and it begins to make sense.

We read in 1 Samuel 21–22 that Doeg the Edomite was a man who, unlike David, was *not* after the heart of God. Doeg was Saul's chief shepherd and someone who, by all accounts, appears to have been bent on harm, pain, and murder—and toward taking pleasure in inflicting this harm (as seen by all the boasting he does). When we read 1 Samuel 21, we see that David has taken off to Nob to visit Ahimelek, the priest, and it is while there that he comes across Doeg. Doeg in turn goes to Saul and notifies him of David's whereabouts—which eventually leads to the death and destruction of many people. So, say what you will about the tone of bitterness and anger in this text, but let's not forget that Doeg would eventually massacre numerous priests and others who helped David when he came to Ahimelek. This psalm is a response from a passionate someone who is angry with a man who is full of hate and murder—who not only kills priests but also other men, women, children, infants, and even cattle.

David's opening question gets right to the point—it's actually not a real, serious question at all but a rhetorical one. A rhetorical question that is asked in disgust. Doeg was boasting of his murderous work. And while that is bad enough, we need to remember that this man worked for Saul— ostensibly a man of God! A man who "plots destruction" and practices evil—loving it more than good—is *not* a good person—not someone whose heart beats in sync with God's. The gist of David's assessment:

You call yourself a mighty hero? You . . . who practice deceit and destruction—whose words cut like a razor!? You who love evil, lies, harm, and inflicting pain on others!? A hero, you love yourself! You boast in *you*. Your so-called strength came by your own thoughts and building yourself up and came at the cost of others!

God requires men and women who work for goodness. Men and women who practice love and sacrifice—who think of others—who forgive. People who seek *his* heart and nobody else's. People who do not lie—and do not take joy in causing pain to others. David's words hit the mark here: *No* man can do these things and be this way and get away with it (and I would add that no *woman* can, either). God *will* deal with such a person.

While David is spot on in his calling out of Doeg and showing him that evil will not win—I wonder what David's intentions were here. Did he write this to simply vent? Did he pen words to ease his troubled mind? Maybe David writes because he realizes that, while it was Doeg who did the harm, none of the deaths of women, children, and animals would have happened had David not gone to Ahimelek. We don't know what David was wanting to do here by penning these words, but it's obvious that, not only was his heart broken by what had transpired, but his anger was fueled as well.

Someone after the heart of Satan, the father of lies, is impossible to deal with. When you boast in yourself, when you take joy in the harm of others, there is nothing you or I can do about the outcome—and that itself causes me some grief. I like to think that there isn't a soul out there to whom love cannot break through. I cling to the hope and knowledge that, since every person was created by God and in his image, there is some part of them that is still available to be reasoned with, to give hope to, to find love in. Even the terrorist who is planning to bomb and kill innocent people, even those who take credit for mass suicide bombs—I cling to the hope that not all is lost with them.

Maybe that's a stretch for you—maybe that was a stretch for David, too. I don't know. What I do know is that in this psalm David has some pretty honest moments, as well as harsh words. I'm reminded, as I read verses 5–6, that we should not pass judgment or tell people what God will do to them. That's not our job—even when we want to.

David is spot-on on his reflection of what God *does* require and what *does* happen to those who work and scheme and seek the father of lies, . . . but the judgment for that type of living is not up to you and me. We need to allow David to feel what he's feeling here (that's what an honest relationship with God must look like), but we also need to be aware and understand that we need to allow these words to be words—words that were spoken to God.

David's words, while honest and true, are harsh and angry; ultimately, those kinds of feelings need to be placed upon God. Not directed *at* God— but given to him. That's really what a relationship with our Father looks like. In our anger, he listens. In our hatred, he listens. It is much better to release those honest emotions to him than to let those words and feelings loose upon one another.

THREE QUESTIONS FOR YOU TO CHEW ON:

1. What in this psalm particularly speaks to you? Where are you drawn in? Why?
2. What do you think David's intentions were here with this psalm?
3. Have you ever had something negative happen that caused you, in retrospect, to wonder whether it would still have happened had you done something differently? Is this healthy? Is it right for us to go through these "what ifs" of life?

A PSALM OF UNCOMFORTABLENESS

Start your reading today with Psalm 53.

"There is no one who does good." Ouch, David! Way to start off the psalm—that's such a downer!

Not much is really known about this psalm, and why David essentially copies his already released proclamation on "nobody is good" from Psalm 14 nobody really knows. If you're anything like me, when you read this psalm you probably feel yourself smacked upside the head and slightly depressed. Let's look at all the less than positive things David has to say:

- Nobody does good. (v. 1)
- Nobody understands. (v. 2)
- Nobody seeks God. (v. 2)
- Everyone has turned away from God. (v. 3)
- All men (and women) are corrupt. (v. 3)
- Nobody does good. (Yeah, . . . we already got that, David, from v. 1—but thanks for telling us again here in v. 3.)
- Evildoers never learn—which is you and me and all other people. (v. 4)
- We drum up dread. (v. 5)

So much—un-joy! What this all means is that the entire human race, all of humanity since the fall, is corrupt, hateful, and evil. There are no ifs, ands, or buts here. It's almost as though David is being given an opportunity to see humanity through God's eyes. To look upon the people of earth and see just how vile and self-loving we are. And, obviously, this is something David recognizes in himself as well.

That's a really interesting place to look. It's this intro-, outer-spection" (you're right, that's not a word) that tethers you to every other person on God's green earth, . . . and when you think about it, that kind of stings. You see the person who lies, and no longer can you see someone who is vastly different from yourself. You see the person who battles addiction (whether it be to drugs, sexuality, or anything else), and no longer can you place them opposite you. Or think of the worst person you've ever seen or met. The bottom line: *you are no different*. The sins *they* commit make them no worse than you. The sins *you* commit make you no better than them. Now, let that sink in for a second! Yeah. You either are ready to argue against me and make a case for *your* "goodness" and "righteousness"—or you are shifting in your seat because you understand the full magnitude and reality of sin.

Every action that goes against God's will and desire for us declares to those around us that "there is no God." Why and how? Because you are seeking your own will, your own love, your own desires and placing them above God. If this weren't so, then we wouldn't have texts like Genesis 6:5; 8:21; Isaiah 53:6; and John 3:3–5.

Nobody does good. We do things that are *partly* good. There are things we do that hold out a hope of goodness—but we are so riddled with sin and corruption that so much of what we do that is less than good, or less than well motivated, overshadows and taints even the best of intentions and actions (Romans 3:23). *Everyone* has turned away from God. On our own, we cannot seek God. But because of the Holy Spirit, we are able to seek and turn to him (Romans 3:12).

For some reason you and I have amnesia and never seem to learn from our mistakes, our sins, our corrupt hearts, and our desires to keep doing what *we* want. The reason? We are full of sin. David sees it, God sees it, and we need to recognize it as well. But as David is looking down (just as God has looked down), he sees a glimpse of the glory to come: the restoration of God's people.

For all the uncomfortable vibes Psalms 53 and 14 give us, we must hold to the hope that is declared and given. That even though we stink in our attempts to be godly men and women, our sins will not have the final say. That even though sin has tainted every area of our lives, God redeems and gives salvation, thus restoring his people (1 Corinthians 1:30). He does so not because we're good enough and deserving of it but simply because he loves.

The beauty I find in his psalm is that it puts me in my place. I think the worst thing we can do is try to rank people and sins. The worst thing we can do is put ourselves or others in some type of an order in terms of sinfulness—or try to convince ourselves that we're good enough for God's love and grace. It doesn't work that way. What this psalm also does for me is give me space to reflect on Judas and what he did to Christ. His betrayal, for many, is unforgiveable and even "un-graceable" (not a word, . . . but, once again, you get it). But where I consistently find myself, when it comes to Judas and his actions, is that I am overcome with grief, pain, anger, . . . compassion, and hope. If the God of love, grace, and mercy can find it in his heart to look past my sins—then why not Judas's?

THREE QUESTIONS FOR YOU TO CHEW ON:

1. What in this psalm speaks to you? What draws you in or hits home? Why?
2. Why do you think we tend to rank sins?
3. What about Judas? Was his sin unforgiveable? If it hadn't been Judas who did the betraying, would/could it have been someone else? Would the cross have happened without Judas?

A PSALMFUL JOURNEY OF PRAISE

I stink at this journey. Okay, sorry—I'm getting ahead of myself. Do me a favor and please read Psalm 54.

We read in 1 Samuel 23:14–26 that David, in fear for his life, is hiding from Saul and his army, who are trying to kill him. Not only that, but with him in this place he is hiding are men who will turn out to be traitors. David has lost the favor of King Saul because Saul knows that he will be overthrown as king, that God intends for David to take the throne from him (we see this even from Jonathan, David's son, as he makes a covenant with David to watch and protect him *because* he knows his friend will be king). So, what does the king do when he sees his kingdom pulled from under him? He goes after the threat himself.

The battle between Saul and David is played out for quite some time. More than once David has an opportunity to kill Saul and end this cat-and-mouse hunt, but David never does. He loves Saul and understands that God's favor was with him and that it was God who anointed him king of Israel—even if God's favor has left him now.

Psalm 54 is a very short prayer of David that speaks of an immediate need (vv. 1–3), a proclamation of God's help and strength (vv. 4–5), and a promise of deliverance and the joy that will be experienced and proclaimed when God does deliver (vv. 6–7). It's very simple in its layout and is meant to get right to the point. David is so confident that God will keep him alive and protect him that he promises to praise God with a freewill offering once this is all done.

I really appreciate how short this psalm is because, to me, the pointedness matches the feeling I personally would have if I were hiding amongst those who were seeking my head. I would be on my toes, quick with words and actions, and with all my movements being concise and to the point. And, obviously, through it all I would be praying to God for his protection and guidance, while at the same time confidently proclaiming the joy I'd know when all was said and done. To me, this psalm matches the thought-process David *could* have been in.

David knows that God is watching over him and that God's faithfulness will never be broken. God has promised David that he will be anointed King (1 Samuel 16); obviously, if Saul is still king, then David's time has not yet come, . . . but it will. David knows that he has done nothing wrong, and so his request for vindication (to have his name cleared and any blame or suspicion removed) is justified. It is here that David knows that God protects and has a plan for him—and that *nothing* will thwart any plan of God.

I think it's often difficult for us to relate to biblical people in instances like this. If you are anything like me, you have never heard a clear-cut call or word from God that leads you down a certain path, affirms the direction God is taking you, or speaks clearly to what you are needed and required to do. And so, it can be difficult to relate to David, who clearly has been told "This is who you will become," and "I will make a covenant with you" (2 Samuel 7). I've said this numerous times throughout these psalm reflections: *how much easier life would be if God would simply tell me his plan for me!* However, the fact that we may have never *heard* the voice of God speak directly to us doesn't mean he does or doesn't do so, nor does it mean that God doesn't have a plan for us or that he won't protect us.

I think we often mistake the lack of clear direction from God as a lack of love or even a lack of input from him, but that isn't the case. I've tried to stick to 700–900 words for each of these psalm reflections, and I could easily fill up that space with promises, affirmations, desires, hopes, and guidance that Scripture gives us. Words that build us up and are to lead us each and every day. Words that the Holy Spirit affirms are what we need each and every day. These words are clear and give us direction. You and I are the ones who muddy them up and fail to listen intently. So, what's the problem (beyond my bad listening skills)?

The problem is that I am wanting *more*. The problem, if I'm truly honest with myself, is that for all the trust I proclaim to have, I'm really not all that trusting. And, honestly, I don't know why, because time and time again God's Word has been true, on target, and exactly what I needed right when I needed it. So, really, I have no excuse.

Maybe that's exactly what we need to see here: no matter what the situation we find ourselves in (like David here, when these men betrayed him to Saul), we seek, through prayer and guidance, God's protection but also an affirmation that when it's all said and done we will praise him and give thanks for what he is doing. Maybe I need to stop worrying about what or where and be comfortable in the knowledge (which I do have) that *regardless* of what happens I will praise God yet again and give thanks for his love, protection, grace, and work in my life.

This is still a journey for me—even as a pastor. And it's a long journey in which I am continuously learning. So, God, be patient with me! (yes, that is part of my prayer).

THREE QUESTIONS FOR YOU TO CHEW ON:

1. What in this psalm speaks to you? Where do you find yourself drawn in? Why?
2. Do David's words ring true in your life? Do you find it easy to praise God even when you are scared and wondering about tomorrow's unknowns?
3. Why is worrying so powerful—even when we know it gets us nowhere?

A PSALM OF BETRAYAL

Open your Bible and read with me Psalm 55.

Think about that one person in your life who knows you. I mean *really* knows you. They know the most intimate details of who you are. What you love, what you hate, what pushes your buttons, and what makes you cry. If you were sick, they would run to the store and know exactly what your favorite food is that, though it would probably not cure you, would sure make you feel better. But even more than this, you've entrusted them with the most intimate of information that you've otherwise always held close to your heart. You're wary about trusting just anyone with this information, but they know it all. Now picture them betraying that sensitive, shared information. This is where David finds himself.

For David, sharing any information like this would have been treacherous for so many reasons. You are the king, and you already have people who want you dead—your own family is betraying you, and now this, too? An ally, a friend, a companion wants the same? Someone you've most likely had at your house for pot roast, some cheesy mac, and probably ice cream and cookies? Your closest friend, who knows your story, knows your past, your hopes and dreams, . . . knows where you sleep—maybe even has a key to your home. Who knows your routines and every intimate detail about you!

This issue has simply broken David. He cannot fathom that someone would do this. My translation says that David is "distraught," and while I think this is accurate, the Hebrew translation also uses "restless" in a wandering aimlessly kind of way. I picture David as so beside himself that he's in a daze. Not sure what to do, not sure where to go, . . . so he simply prays.

We care about what people say about us—for those who may disagree with me, . . . well, I think you're in the minority. But what about when it's someone close? Someone who is more than an acquaintance but is in truth a friend and companion? When it's someone I care about, then their words mean more—and thus their betrayal runs deep. And, honestly, it's not the words they said but the betrayal made. Again, for David it runs much deeper and means much more, because for him it's life and death. For you and me the betrayal is probably limited to words, and thus the effects are going to be minimal. Maybe some whispers from others, maybe some disgrace and embarrassment, . . . but we won't die from it. I'm not saying it doesn't sting and hurt—just that it's not potentially lethal. David, on the other hand, is ready to run away into the desert, hide in the mountains, flee from any and all people, and just be with his protector: God. And so, this psalm becomes an all-out prayer of utter grief and despair. The first part is broken up into sorrow, fear, distress, and pain (v. 1–8); part two comes from the pits of anger, which I know we all can relate to (vv. 9–15, 20–21); and, finally, the psalm ends in the hope and peace of God (vv. 16–19, 22–23).

Betrayal is a really tough thing to work through because not just anyone can betray you—only someone who is close, with whom you have an intimate relationship, can hurt you in that way. And what's tough, too, is that Scripture doesn't include a whole truckload of information on betrayal; it states merely that it *will* happen and that we *must* forgive when it does (forgiveness is a major theme throughout Scripture).

But, honestly, David isn't saying any forgiving words here—so why should I? Again, when we read the psalms, we must remember that these are authentic words and feelings from someone already in a relationship with God; we need to take their words and feelings at face value. This doesn't mean we have to emulate them—but it does mean that we can relate to them because their feelings are universal (they speak to all and in all times).

I take all these feelings of betrayal and say, "Yeah, I would feel that way too." I may not have felt it before, but I can relate to the fears and anger. I, too, would want God to take that person out and deal with this situation in the way only God can. I would want them to feel what I feel and experience the betrayal and hurt they have caused, too. And, ultimately, my place of comfort would be knowing that God will not betray, will not hurt or allow pain to fall upon me.

For all the pain that David endures in this betrayal, this truly is a psalm of trust—and, unfortunately, it's also a reminder for us that the only One we can really trust is God. I don't want to be cynical, but there is more than a grain of truth to that. If he can, Satan will use any and all relationships to harm us. If it works to his benefit, Satan will harm, confuse, abuse, mislead, lie, and work hard to break down people. Unfortunately, that means that you and I and everyone else will fall victim. And if we've taken anything from Genesis 3, you and I are broken and sinful and tend to break relationships, too.

Does this mean that we give up on relationships? Does it mean we hold closely any and all sensitive information and never share anything with anyone else? Not at all. I think we need relationships—that's how God created us; he wants us to relate to him and to each other. What this does challenge me to do is understand that none of us are perfect. We will have friends fall to hurtful betrayal, just as we do, and there *has* to be some room for forgiveness in those times and spaces. But there also has to be room for the feelings we have—the honest feelings that come with the betrayal of a close friend. And, ultimately, we must find comfort and peace knowing that God hears us, knows us, and will comfort us.

Does this psalm give us hope in those times? Probably not—but it's not supposed to anyway. What it's *supposed* to do is remind us of the wholesome, sacrificial, and loving relationship we have with God—and that though all other relationships may fail, God is ever faithful.

THREE QUESTIONS FOR YOU TO CHEW ON:

1. What in this psalm speaks to you? At what point are you drawn in? Why?
2. Have you ever betrayed someone? How did it feel? Have you ever been betrayed? Did you ever find the place of forgiveness?
3. Which hurts more, the betrayal or the fact that you lost a close friendship?

A PSALM OF
FEAR AND LONELINESS

urn with me to Psalm 56.

Scholars place this psalm in connection not only with Psalm 34 but also with 1 Samuel 21:10–15, when David was in Gath before the Philistine king and pretended to be insane. David, fearing for his life, started drooling and writing on the walls in the hope of throwing off the Philistine captors. It may seem like an odd text to reflect on, but this isn't the psalm of a drooling, crazed, wall-writing man. David has moved on from his time in front of the king of Gath, has been freed because of his act—and yet he still fears for his life. David is reflecting on where he so recently was, what he has just experienced, and (as I picture it) is sitting there watching his hands shake and feeling his nerves to be on edge.

I cannot fathom the emotions David must have been feeling—and yet I can assume that my response would have been the same. He needs to survive this situation—so he does the first thing that comes to mind! In some cases, when we feel imminent danger, our instincts kick in and we engage in what is called "fight or flight response" (also known as hyperarousal). We either fight our way out of the danger, or we flee from it. Either is a completely natural and physical response to a perceived harm. Simply put: it's a survival technique. David, in his own way, is doing exactly this by acting in this unhinged manner. And it works. The king sees this, "loses" his own mind at this lunatic before him (the king of Gath probably assumes that this man will either harm him or infect him in some way), and dismisses David.

So here we find David—*post* lunatic—reflecting on what just happened and where he now finds himself. He's alone and feeling like a dove that has returned to a long-lost place (hence the tune he has this psalm sung to). He has no support system where he is, no friends to lean on or help him recover from this scary moment. The fear of many has now been replaced by the fear of nobody. So, what does he do? He sings of God's devotion and love. I like what Matthew Henry writes about this: "Even in times of the greatest trouble and distress David never hung his harp upon the willow-trees, never unstrung it or laid it by; but that when his dangers and fears were greatest he was still in tune for singing God's praises.[2]"

These are two completely different responses to fear and stress that David experiences. Lunatic in one scene, then singer in the next. And while I cannot relate to the madman—I *can* to the vocalist.

When most people are in distress, we do things that bring us comfort—things that lift our spirits and bring us joy, . . . but I also think (this hasn't to my knowledge been scientifically proven) that we do things that are *natural* to us. I absolutely love music and singing, and so I frequently find myself singing songs in my head, singing out loud, or engaging in other music-related activities. Maybe you draw or bake when you find yourself here—the reactions and actions of people are unlimited and unique—and yet we all respond in *some* manner. Maybe you shut down, or maybe you lash out. Again, these are all natural responses to life's dangers. *But how many of our actions are healthy responses?*

The place I am drawn with David and his response to this fear and stress is something I hope and pray I will find, too—because my response in times of fear and stress doesn't always lean first and foremost upon God. It seems as though when I am at my lowest, then my natural response *is* to go to God—but if I haven't yet hit rock-bottom, my fight response kicks in instead of my prayer response.

Maybe this psalm needs to remind us that in our lowest of moments, when we are full of fear and stress and loneliness and feel as though we cannot go any lower, we simply need to reach out to God. Maybe, as we read David's psalm, we will see that David, while confident in the Lord's work in his life, still feels some hesitation. Then again, maybe David isn't too different from me.

I've said this numerous times—the psalms reflect honest relationships between people and their Creator. It brings me comfort to read that even David struggled, . . . and that in his struggle he clung to hope, too.

---

2   Henry, Matthew. *Matthew Henry's Commentary on the Whole Bible: Complete and Unabridged in One Volume.* Peabody: Hendrickson, 1994. Print.

THREE QUESTIONS FOR YOU TO CHEW ON:

1. What is there in this psalm that speaks to you? Where are you drawn? Why?
2. What do you do when you are stressed, worried, or uneasy?
3. What is it about that activity that you find soothing and calming?

A PSALM DECLARING THE FAITHFULNESS OF GOD

Take a few moments with me to read through Psalm 57.

Our psalm today has continuity with the previous one in that David has run from Saul and is found to be hiding in a cave—somewhere. He's tired of running, tired of hiding, tired of having to avoid trap after trap—so David goes to a place where he can not only hide but, should someone come after him, they wouldn't be able to get to him except by coming through the entrance. This is the kind of defensive position one assumes when one is scared, exhausted, and otherwise out of options.

This psalm goes from a crying out in pain and anguish to hope and goodness, back to anxiety and fear, and then back to more joy—it's as though David is pumping himself up with all this praise of God while danger looms before him. David, seeing the darkness, seeing the traps, seeing the disaster that has been chasing him, is not only crying out to God to save him but declaring that God *will* do so. And because of that his heart is steadfast, his level of joy is high, and he simply praises. David is praising God in his distress.

I remember when my wife was in delivery for our oldest son. We had a "plan" of what this delivery was going to look like, but it just wasn't working out that way; it was becoming glaringly clear that the further we progressed from the place we were, the more dangerous things were becoming. With every contraction and push my son's heart rate dropped drastically lower. So, we had to go to plan B—not a plan at all, since we had never considered needing an alternative.

Plan A: easy, pre-charted coarse. Plan B: unknown. And what made it worse for me was that not only was I unable to do anything to help my wife or my child, but I wasn't able to be in the room when she was delivering because my son's heart rate was getting too low. The situation had become an emergency—and a big enough emergency that I could hear the doctors and nurses giving and receiving orders in hurried fashion. I was terrified. Nearly in tears, I dropped in prayer—because that was the only thing I could do. Everything was out of my hands, and fear had taken over—so I followed my natural instincts and prayed. To be honest, I didn't pray like David here. I prayed for God to intervene and take over and deliver my son and wife from this and have them be healthy—but I never uttered words of praise during this time.

I'm utterly amazed that David had the ability to praise God in the midst of fear. And it was more than a habitual, everyday kind of praise. David praises God with this faithful expectation that the wicked will be snared, the pits will be filled, the nets tossed aside, and the ravenous beasts removed. I have never prayed and praised that way.

I'm challenged by David's words. Challenged by his steadfastness to praise God while danger looms, while fear fills him; he simply replaces that fear with joy. Maybe it's hard for me because I've never been in a situation like David's. Maybe it was easier for David because time and time again he had experienced fear and thus time and time again he had experienced God's deliverance. So, maybe by now, even while the fear and loneliness were deep, he was able to praise God through the chaos because this had become natural to him. But I'm not sure I want to experience so much pain and chaos and fear in my life that praising God in the midst of it becomes my instinctual, go-to response. The one stint I had with the fear for my son was more than plenty for me!

Ultimately, I think our lesson here is that God *is* faithful. That God had a plan for this man he anointed king and that nothing can thwart it. That God is merciful and will make the chaos relent. I think you and I need to come to a place of understanding, as David has, of our relationship with God. That he protects, guides, and watches over his children. That not even the deepest cave can keep God out—and not even the darkest cave should stop our praise and thankfulness. We, too, can praise God from the deepest of pits, for David declared that God will be exalted over *all* the earth. Pits, caves, deepest oceans, highest mountains, and hospital emergency rooms. It doesn't matter where we find ourselves—God, in his faithfulness, is present and worthy to be praised.

THREE QUESTIONS FOR YOU TO CHEW ON:

1. What in this psalm speaks to you? To what words/verses are you drawn? Why?
2. Have you ever been in a situation where you had to drop to your knees because the only conceivable response was to pray? Did you, like David, praise God in that moment?
3. If we state that God is in control—and that is something I do state— then we should never fear but always simply trust. In such moments, *should* we even drop to our knees in prayer? What is the benefit of the prayer? *Who* is the real beneficiary of the prayer when we declare that God already knows, has answered, and is working through the situation?

A PSALM OF SOCIAL INTERACTION

Open your Bible and read with me Psalm 58.

I love the contrasting imagery and the feeling we get from said imagery. Judges who don't judge justly (v. 2), wickedness from birth (as opposed to the presumed innocence of a child) (v. 3), fangless lions (v. 6), water flowing in an opposite direction (v. 7), arrows that are blunt and don't fly (v. 7)—all of these images are amazingly vivid and yet hard to comprehend. And yet, if you were to experience any one of these, the pain would still be real. Blunt arrows still can leave damage and pain. The jaw power of a lion, even a toothless one, can crush bones. Standing before a judge who rules unjustly? Well, you're still going to be punished, and it's still not going to be fun. But there is something else here: you're still alive. You may be broken and bruised, you may be sitting in prison, you may be hiding because you've been struck by arrows that didn't pierce but didn't feel good either—but you're still alive.

David is using this imagery like an allegory. These images, these different injustices, these pictures of evil, all speak of the horribleness of people who abuse and misuse their power to hurt others and wield personal gain. While much of this psalm is focused on the *opposite* of these evil things—they all speak to the last two verses (vv. 10–11) in the sense that God will redeem and avenge the righteous. Wherever David was when he penned this, whatever he was experiencing, because he faithfully followed God and trusted in God's ultimate deliverance—God would step up and take care of the situation. The Judge who judges the earth (v. 11) also judges those upon the earth.

What we need to understand is that this is not a psalm *about* David. Well it is—but it's not. It's really a psalm about those who are placed in powerful positions of authority over other people. Think of a governor, or, even higher—a president. These are people who have been entrusted with the power they have been given. They are to lead and govern and make rules and laws that benefit others, not first of all themselves. They are supposed to think of their constituents, the people they represent, and make decisions that are for *their* good—not decisions that might hurt them, belittle them, or sacrifice them so that the one in power can succeed.

Michael Wilcock observes, "This then is a psalm with a **social conscience**. It is concerned with the kind of wickedness in high places which has not only bungled or neglected those things which it ought to have done, but has also done those things which it ought not to have done—indeed, planned and perpetrated them with ruthless care."[3]

This psalm is a reminder for us in a couple of ways. One: we are watched over and cared for by God—even when we are trampled on and run over by those we put trust in to protect and lead us.

The second is that the God who holds the universe in his hands also has all within the universe stand before him in judgment. Paul writes in 2 Corinthians 5:10, "For we must all appear before the judgment seat of Christ, so that each of us may receive what is due us for the things done while in the body, whether good or bad."

But, alas, there is a third thing here that we cannot ignore. I think that frequently, when we are attacked and hurt, we become that wounded animal that seeks to destroy and repay. You wound me, and I wound you in return. But life is not supposed to work that way. What good comes of it when I repay you for the harm you did? I've fallen into that trap way too many times, and all it does is leave me more deeply wounded. I'm ashamed, I'm angry, I'm bitter, and it never makes me feel any better. I haven't been restored to what I was before you hurt me—I actually look and feel worse.

Peter writes that we are not to repay evil with evil or insult with insult. Evil is supposed to be repaid with blessings (1 Peter 3:9). Paul writes similar words in Romans 12:17, reminding us that we need to do what is right. If we are seeking to have *others* do the right thing, we have to hold ourselves to the same standard.

---

3   Ellsworth, Roger. *Opening up Psalms*. Leominster: Day One Publications, 2006. Print. Opening Up Commentary.

Ultimately, if we believe in a God who restores, if we proclaim that God will place all things under his feet—then we need to allow God to deal with the things God deals with. Our job in this world is not to be revenge seekers. We are to be lights in the darkness (Matthew 5:14; Ephesians 5:7–14), salt of the earth (Matthew 5:13), cities on a hill (Matthew 5:14).

Be salt, light, and a beacon of hope in the midst of a dark world, and, ultimately, put your trust in the Lord and rejoice in the One who redeems, restores, and judges all people based on the type of person, leader, and follower they are.

THREE QUESTIONS FOR YOU TO CHEW ON:

1. What is there in this psalm that speaks to you? Where are you drawn? Why?
2. Why do we often return harm to those who harm you? Is this the easiest reaction? Does it feel better, at least initially? We know it doesn't heal, so why do we still do it?
3. How do we take 1 Peter 3:9 to heart? How do we repay evil with goodness? A follow-up question: How do we make this response more natural than the harm reaction?

A PSALM OF PROTECTION

I invite you to turn with me to Psalm 59 and read it through.

Our psalm today is very similar to Psalms 57–58, where there is a request/ petition to be delivered from some type of enemy. While we don't know who the enemy is, many speculate that it is some foreign adversary. We need to go back and look at the title and the bit of information it provides. Upon closer inspection, what we get in this reflection on 1 Samuel 19:11–18 is a picture of Saul sending some men to David's house to watch it and kill David when he emerges in the morning. However, Michal, Saul's daughter and David's wife, gets wind and tips off her husband and helps him escape. In response to all of this, we get Psalm 59, a psalm of reflection, anger, dismay, but also hope and security.

There are quite a few of these psalms to which it is really hard for you and me to relate, simply because life is very different for us. But then again, there are some people who *can* relate because of the places they live and the environment that surrounds them. The fact of the matter is that there are evil people out there who conspire to hurt others; while we may not be able to understand the feelings and the anxiety that befalls people in those situations, you and I *can* declare that evil exists and that it is out to harm the people who love God. But here's also the thing, and this is more important than relating to a psalm: the trust that David professes in God—a hope common to believers that traverses time and space.

Think of all those times when you were scared, distraught, and feeling lost. Not knowing what to do or where to go, you simply turned to God, knowing that he watches over you. Yeah, that's where David's at. Think of all those times when there was nowhere to turn to, except to lift up your prayers unto God. Yeah—that's where David's at.

But I don't think we want to skip over a really important lesson that David teaches us here. In verse 11 we get this plea from David to *spare* these men who want to kill him (a theme that is constant throughout the life and writings of David—especially when it comes to Saul). The reason? He wants the Lord's name to be glorified and known throughout the earth, and he wants his own people to know and declare that the Lord is their shield. While he *does* want them severely punished—even "consumed"—a hope for their demise is simply not there. David wants God to do what is best for God.

When we combine all of these thoughts and ideas and insights, we get a psalm of declaration of the work of God. A declaration that God protects, leads, guides, and is over all things. That evil and hatred will be dealt with in God's own way—and that you and I, David, and Michal are all under God's divine hand. Even when the dogs continue to snarl at David, God is still watching, guiding, and protecting.

I think that's something interesting to recognize and profess. The "dogs" in this text never stop snarling and snapping, yet while that may be scary, there is no bite from them. The harm that *could* come doesn't. The fear is real, the situation is real, but the outcome of the situation doesn't sit with the enemies—it remains with God. Matthew 5:11 reminds us that these types of situations *are* real, but that in them we will be blessed. That is, you and I will be watched over and protected from all types of harm.

We believe in a God who watches, guides, and protects, and this is something that brings us comfort, not only when we are in propitious situations but also when we are in the midst of snapping and snarling evil—and the comfort we profess is that, even in those situations, it is God who still is over all. Watching, guiding, leading, and protecting—God is still in control, and he will not allow the final harm that could happen to *actually* happen. Now, obviously, we may get bit, and flames may lick at our skin and singe us—but death will not have the final say. By God's grace, by Jesus Christ's blood—God surely does watch over and protect his people (something David consistently professes) now and forever.

THREE QUESTIONS FOR YOU TO CHEW ON:

1. What in this psalm hits home for you? Where are you drawn? Why?
2. Have you ever asked God to not only stop the pain someone was causing you but to pray *for* the person who was harming you? For them to not only stop but to see their wicked ways and change?
3. What does it mean to be blessed in these situations? It sounds almost as though God is allowing these events to happen in order that we may feel blessed—but does he work that way?

A PSALM OF PROVIDENCE

Turn with me to Psalm 60 and read it.

In our text today we see that David has given us a teaching psalm based on his military battles over the Syrians at the Valley of Salt (2 Samuel 8:13). This psalm states that David struck down "thousands," but we see from 2 Samuel 8:13 that it was actually 18,000, . . .and David became famous for this exploit. This, to the Israelites, was a victory worthy of praise.

But what 2 Samuel does not tell us, and Psalm 60 does, is that there was loss for Israel, too. While we may not know the extent of the physical loss of life and/or of injuries suffered, we get the feeling that the emotional toll was devastating. While David praises God (vv. 9–12), the other eight verses consist of a sad lament (vv. 1–3) and a plea for salvation (vv. 4–8). That means that two-thirds of this psalm pictures David in distress.

This psalm opens up for us what exactly it was David was seeing and experiencing as he was in battle. Just as there are these three different types of prayer in the psalm, so too we get invited to see that three different waves of emotions have befallen him.

Seeing his troops initially overrun, David would have felt rejected by God in this moment. Knowing and declaring, however, that God is in the victories as well as the losses, the psalmist reflects in the opening verses that the people would have been lamenting that they had done something against God to make him angry and thereby allow them to be overtaken by their enemies. And so, in this moment of watching his men die and possibly calling them to fall back to stave off the wave of the charging army of Edomites before they are overrun, David acknowledges the sin of himself and his people.

But it is also in this moment that David declares that his relationship with God is still solid (vv. 4–8). In this moment of near loss, David reaches out to God to save them. God, he knows, will raise his banner, unite his warriors, encourage them, and lead them to victory. All the loot and land taken will be at the hands of God.

The final wave (vv. 9–12) is simply the victory cry. Think of it as an "It's now or never!" shout as the army of God digs in and begins to advance against the enemy. It's a reminder that God is not only their hope and victory but also their strength and the only enabler for them to stand. *All of this means that God's hand is not only in the victories and losses, but everywhere else, too.*

This psalm is fraught with imagery that reflects exactly how God is at work. We have images of the land moving and being healed, as well as of what too much wine does to a person and how that affects their ability to function. We have an understanding of banners being waved in war and of the emotional toll that takes, not only for the army that holds them but also for the foe that sees them. Lands and places are listed that were given to the people of God, and we read of military gear worn during battle, sandals, a washbasin, and a scepter. All of these images would have made perfect sense to David and his people. All of these are listed with the understanding that they were given to Israel not based on what *they* had done but on what God has done.

What this psalm does for you and me is reflect on just how intimately God is involved in our lives, too. From the smallest of things to the grandiose—all of them reflect God's hand in our lives. From the beginning of time God has walked and talked with his people and expressed his desires for them. From the beginning of our time *after* the fall, we also see how God was working to move and secure, restore and bring hope to his people. We see in all of this what God had done to lead, guide, encourage, and uplift his people. And throughout all of it—throughout all the human interactions and relationship breakdowns with God, he has always asked for one simple thing: a relationship with him. Regardless of our acknowledgement of him, he's still at work. It's what we call the providence of God (the workings of God's hand in all of creation). Regardless of our consistent work against him, we could never have stopped him from asking his Son, Jesus Christ, to enter into our lives and help us overcome the enemy.

While this psalm teaches us that God is in all things, David's words also convict us to reflect on God's work in *our* lives and *then to give thanks for it.* From the little to the large, give thanks; find, and then declare, that hope is in God and God alone. Simply put, *find a reason to praise God.*

It's not hard—his fingerprints are all over your day.

I get it—it *can* be really hard to worship God when you've just lost your job, when your loved one is dying, when you're mourning the loss of a friend, or your family is going through a divorce. Those are really, really tough times to "give thanks"—but even in those dark times we believe and affirm that God is not only present but that his will is still at work. That this dark and lonely place is not where we will end up, nor is it where God wants us to be. If that were true, he never would have sent Christ or the Holy Spirit. The providence of God reminds is that hope is still before us, light is still breaking through the darkness, and nothing on earth—nor princes or principalities or evil and darkness—will be able to undo that which God does. It is not darkness that puts out light but light that breaks forth and cuts the darkness.

So, praise God—in all times and all situations—for he is in all things. Praise him.

THREE QUESTIONS FOR YOU TO CHEW ON:

1. What in this psalm speaks directly to you? To what are you drawn? Why?
1. Oftentimes in war we see an "us vs. them" mentality—and yet both sides always suffer. Why is it easier to lament on one side than it is to see, or empathize with, the lament from the other?
1. What is there about the things that are ahead of us that makes it hard for us to see them? Perhaps it's that, when we're in grief and distress, it can be hard to see God because the event stands so prominently before us. Why is that?

AN ELEVENTH-HOUR
PSALM

Turn with me in your Bible to Psalm 61.

Many, if not most, of us take comfort and joy in knowing that there is no place we cannot go that would bring us *out* of God's presence. If I were to climb the highest mountain or swim into the deepest of caverns, I simply could not get away from God's presence, love, and knowledge. We proclaim and affirm that God is above and beyond all that we see and experience—as the Creator of all things, he simply *is* everywhere.

But what might that have looked like to a people who believed that God was *outside* their time? What might that have looked like to a people who proclaimed God's sovereignty, strength, and might and yet believed that God dwelled in a specific place? More specifically, what might that kind of paradigm have looked and felt like when one was in distress?

There are a lot of assumptions with regard to this psalm about where David might have been and what issues were before him. While we can continue to speculate, it really doesn't do us any good—and I am of the thinking that getting the most out of this psalm simply doesn't require it. We don't need to know exactly where David was or whom it was he had fled from or why he found himself where he did, because you and I can still relate.

David is evidently somewhere far, far away. Now, obviously, this is relative because the known world back then wasn't nearly what we understand it to be today, but David was so far away that he felt as though one simply couldn't get any further from God. He starts off this psalm with a petition for God to hear his cry and prayer: "From the ends of the earth I call to you . . ."—from the furthest place one could be, God, I pray that my plea for help reaches you.

When we think about where God was said to have dwelled in those Old Testament days (when we try to adopt the image and mindset of David and those Israelites), we can visualize only that David is *somewhere* in the wilderness, away from Jerusalem, away from the temple of the Lord—away from the presence of God. And in this far distant location he feels himself to be without protection, food, and shelter. This psalm is a gut-wrenching physical, mental, and emotional crying out to God for help. So much is packed into two simple verses. But David doesn't end there. This is only his first request: to simply be heard. *And God, once you hear my voice, here is my request:* "Lead me to the rock that is higher than I." Remove me from where I am and put me up in a place of protection. Place me upon a rock that is high above so that I can see, and know, that I am protected from all angles, sides, and enemies. David is seeking protection and safety. Physical, mental, and spiritual.

The terrible thing about being in a low place, either physical or spiritual, is the vulnerability of it—at least it is for me. Everything feels raw, exposed, intense. Words hurt more, any physical discomfort seems to take more of a toll, and the whole presence and space begin to take turns attacking me mentally and spiritually. You begin to think that this is *it*—you're done for. You begin to convince yourself that since you are *still* in this space, then obviously God is too far off. Self-doubt, a sense of worthlessness, and despair all begin to chip away at what little objectivity you have left. We know this isn't what we believe—and yet we find ourselves here.

If you're anything like me, you toss up an eleventh-hour prayer to God in the hope of his hearing your faint, fading voice. Again, *why* we find ourselves here—God only knows. And *why* we find ourselves feeling this way about God, . . . well, it's probably a mixture of lack of self-worth or felt value, self-neglect, and the influence of Satan all mixed in with our inability to see further than what immediately surrounds us. We just are really good at making *ourselves* sink deeper than the situation really warrants. And Satan is really good at utilizing darkness and despair to chip away at our self-worth, perceived value, and understanding of God.

I think we need to take an example from something David says here. While David throws up his eleventh-hour prayer, his request is for God to place him upon a rock. For God to become his refuge and take him under his wings for protection. It's interesting how David goes from such distress and feeling so far away to proclaiming that God is *not* far away and that God *can* bring him to higher ground and shelter him from the pain.

How can God be so far off in terms of perceived reality, and yet in that same breath David can proclaim that he knows God has heard his prayer and vow? I can't answer that one for ya. But we do the exact same things when we are in those places and spaces. We feel lost and abandoned and ignored, and yet, if that were truly the case, why would we be crying out for help? Why would we seek God in prayer? Why would we even turn to him in the first place?

I think the only sure thing we *do* have in life is the knowledge that we are *not* far away from God. We know his love and dedication and work in our lives because we see them and experience them in our hearts. And we read psalms like David's here and see his request for a rock and we acknowledge, "Yes, Lord Jesus! Place me upon yourself, for you *are* my rock! While you may cause unbelievers to stumble, you raise up your children and protect them! You lift us up in our despair, you lift us up from our foe, you shelter us under your wings, and you *are* our strong tower!"

In truth, this psalm reaffirms for me all those beautiful images we have of Christ and the work of God in our lives. And what I find strangely beautiful is that these truth images come to us in the midst of our moments of despair *because* we know that God is everywhere and able to do—and does—all things on our behalf.

THREE QUESTIONS FOR YOU TO CHEW ON:

1. What in this psalm speaks to you? Where are you drawn? Why?
2. Have you ever tossed up an eleventh-hour prayer? What was it for? What was it about the situation that made the prayer needed at that moment more than a typical prayer for you?
3. How would you explain to a nonbeliever the inner (immanent) presence of God and yet the all-around (transcendent) presence of God as well (within and yet everywhere, including above)?

A CHALLENGING PSALM

Please open your Bible and read with me Psalm 62.
Many of the psalms pose some difficulty for us when we try to figure out the context—and this is one of them. Some scholars place it within the Absalom context and the pain David endures with that relationship—but only because there are some similar words and feelings—nothing concrete for us to go on. But the beauty of the psalm is that we can find in it meaning, challenges, reminders, and ultimate hope. So, context or no context, the words still hit their mark.

What I find really interesting in how this psalm is laid out is that it reminds me of a ping-pong volley. David goes back and forth between his proclamation of who God is and a declaration of his ultimate goodness and strength—and then he goes to the other side to lament over the problem with people—from the goodness of God to the assault of people on him with their lies. Then he goes *back* again to God and how God is his strength and tower, his peace in all times. Three times David declares God's goodness, and two times he declares the ugliness of humanity. Back and forth.

God, you are my rock and my salvation—my fortress; I will never be shaken. (vv. 1–2)

You people, you assault me and try to knock me off this fortress I'm on. You and your finding joy in lies and pain—trying to be kind while the whole time you are a fork-tongued snake! (vv. 3–4)

My soul rests in you, God, my Rock and my Salvation, my refuge in all times. I will simply trust in you in all times and all situations. (vv. 5–8)

It simply doesn't matter who one is or where one is from. Both high and low, big and tall, short and stout—all people are liars, cheaters, and self-lovers. (vv. 9–10)

We live in a world where people are all about themselves. Liars, cheaters, people who will say what you want to hear in front of your face and then turn around and speak differently about you to others—and I don't think I'm sharing anything new with you. I'm pretty sure you have been on the receiving end of hate, lies, and abuse—as have I. And while this psalm is a reminder of that kind of world, it should also put *us* in our place and challenge you and me to look in the mirror and reflect on the words *we've* delivered to people. We can nod our head in agreement with David—David was human and worldly, too. David proclaims at the end of this psalm that "power belongs to you, God," . . . but he sure used his power to get what *he* wanted (*ahem* . . . Bathsheba!)—and you and I have also used our words to lie, cheat, and harm others.

But, again—this is the world David lived in, and this is the world you and I live in as well. But that doesn't mean we are to fall and succumb to things of this world. It should be a challenge for you and me to acknowledge the ways of this world and consistently do a reality check as to where we fall in line with them. Do we proclaim David's words of lament in three of the five stanzas but then also proclaim that we really are the ones he's seeing and dealing with? Are we professing sanctuary in God and yet the ones spreading lies about others? Do we spread rumors about people and yet still find breath to sing their praises to their face? Do we bless with our lips but curse with our hearts? Unfortunately, I think I personally have found myself in all of these spaces—and probably too many times to count. I've been on the receiving and the giving end of all of that vitriol.

Paul's words in Romans 2:6, 3:4, and 1 Corinthians 3:8, as well as in 1 Corinthians 5:10, all speak of how we will be held accountable for what we say and do. My words have meaning, and they have value—and in the end that's going to be a conversation I have with God. Honestly, how can I profess God's love and grace and rule and safety in my life but then turn around and speak harshly to and about others? Maybe we should reflect on David's final words here, in that God "rewards everyone according to what they have done." There's a gut-check reminder!

So, take David's words to heart as you reflect on the workings of this world, as well as on your own workings and doings. Know your surroundings and people—but also know your own heart. Ultimately, find comfort and solace (as I do) in that, just as David has God's goodness bookending this psalm—God ultimately has the first and last say for us.

THREE QUESTIONS FOR YOU TO CHEW ON:

1. What in this psalm speaks to you? What draws you in? Why?
2. What are some things you have done to speak against your faith and reflect yourself as someone who loves God with their heart but doesn't speak of God with their lips and actions?
3. How do we learn to respond with love instead of hate? How do we make love our knee-jerk response instead of things that are harmful and hateful?

A PSALM OF
LONGING FOR GOD

Open your Bible with me and read the words of Psalm 63.

The opening eight verses of Psalm 63 are some of the richest pieces of biblical poetry we have. They are words of comfort, hope, and passion. They are words of life. Written by a man who knew of all the joys of life—and probably lived with quite a few of them—but here he makes a stand. What's beautiful and heart-wrenching is that every word penned here is in stark contrast to what life has given to him and what he sees. We see contrasts in the surroundings and in the needs indicated throughout these verses. But it is in the contrasts that the psalmist finds hope and the fulfillment of his longing for God. While I do not have space to write all that I want, I do want to point out some of the contrasts.

First off, we see him speaking of thirsting for God. What a powerful image! If your Bible is like mine, you probably find written under the title "A psalm of David. When he was in the Desert of Judah." So, you find this man in a dry and desolate place, where there isn't much life and there is absolutely no water above ground—only aquafers (according to Wikipedia, an aquafer is an underground layer of water bearing permeable rock, rock fractures, or unconsolidated material—I get the picture of "water, water, everywhere, but not a drop to drink"!). So, he speaks of thirsting for God. He doesn't in fact want water—he wants God. He doesn't *need* water—he needs God. Even in a dry, arid death trap of a land where one must have water to survive, water is not what is desired or wanted. God is.

But that's not all. He then laments the love that people often find outside of God. There are these "things" we all proclaim to need, . . . and yet we really don't. Not in the end, at least. Things that we crave that bring us love and joy—things we "desire"—but they are *not* God. David says that the love he receives from God is better than the richest of foods! Better than not only your favorite foods but any and *all* foods! In fact, God's love is so good, so full, so rich that it is better than life! So, here is this guy, who could very easily be on the brink of dehydration, if not starvation, a man who could have food and water at his disposal to reinvigorate himself and come back to life, . . . and he wants none of it. He says that God's love is better than the food that could strengthen him and the water that could save him.

And then I'm struck by something that comes to us halfway through verse 1: David says that his whole being *longs* for God. What a powerful word! It's about desiring something so strongly that the craving takes over you. It consumes your thoughts so that you can concentrate on nothing else. One author, Robert Hawker, states that this psalm contains the "devout breathings of the soul."

Longing for someone—in this case, longing for God—that is something that takes over your whole body. Nothing else matters, nothing else compares. David says that we need none of the cravings of this world because none of those sustain us, none of those truly feed us, none of those give us true life. When we look at the rest of this psalm, we see other understandings of human longings that just don't match up when we compare them to the longing we have for God—that we *should* have for God.

So, here is my question: Do you long for God? It's a simple question, really. And, if not, why not? What is going on in your life that is more important than him?

What are you able to do here on earth that literally gives you life? What person in your life are you more passionate about, more in love with, than God? What food or water are you able to consume that will sustain you forever? That doesn't require you to return time and time again to it to acquire and consume more? *Nothing!* Life comes to us only from its source—from heaven. When it's put into *that* perspective—then, yeah—nothing does compare to our longing and need for God.

In Paul's words in Colossians 3:2, "Set your minds above, not on earthly things." And Jesus says of himself in John 4:14 that whoever drinks the water he gives them shall never thirst again. Again in Matthew 5:6, Christ states in the Beatitudes, "Blessed are those who hunger and thirst for righteousness, for they shall be satisfied." That doesn't mean that we are to be satisfied with earthly things; our need is satisfied *only in Christ*.

Do you long for God? Do you desire with every ounce of who you are to be in his presence, to feel his loving embrace, to know that eternity awaits you in his glory, . . . or is this a declaration we simply listen to during Sunday's service? Something we tell our kids as we raise them and encourage them to believe and repeat, without our really practicing this ourselves? When push comes to shove, where exactly are *you* here? Because we can, and do, get caught up in things of this world—we all know it, and we all do it. It's understandable—it really is—but that doesn't make it right.

God longed for you so much that he sent his One and only Son. He longed so deeply for your love, your presence, and your relationship that he was willing to not only send his Son to die for your return but to willingly move forward with a sacrifice we would have viewed as unthinkable. Do you long for him? Truly *long* for God? Because he longs for you. The Bible contains 66 love letters to you that declare that love—and we just cracked open the smallest part of one of them in this psalm.

THREE QUESTIONS FOR YOU TO CHEW ON:

1. What in this psalm touches you? What draws you in? Why?
2. In the midst of life, could you give up everything and simply long for God? Does that sound wise or practical?
3. Do you long for God? What, in your understanding and context, does that mean?

A PSALM OF
PIERCING WORDS

B egin today's reading with Psalm 64.

As I read Psalm 64, I have to admit that the first thing that caught my attention was the ways of these wicked people who were somewhere around David and plotting against him. As for context, which is always important for us to consider, we do not have anything to go on from this text. We don't know where David is, what point in his life he is at (information that would provide markers in his life for us to pull from), or what enemies are surrounding him. So, what we're left with is David lamenting to God whatever it is that is happening and then pronouncing the work God will do against these foes who scheme and plot his downfall.

But what really struck me is that all of these laments, all of these fears David has, all the *actions* these evil people are taking against him, appear to equate simply to words. There appears to be no active hunting or pursuing of David going on. No beating down his door or chasing him out of town. David isn't needing to hide in the hills or the fields as he fears for his life, . . . because the issue appears to entail just rumors. David does fear for his life, and probably rightly so, but his fears are based on words overheard in dark spaces by dark people.

- "Hide me from the conspiracy." (v. 2)
- "They sharpen their tongues, aiming cruel words like arrows." (v. 3)
- "They shoot and ambush the innocent [by their words]." (v. 4)
- "They encourage each other in their evil plans; they talk about hiding their snares." (v. 5)
- "They plot injustice." (v. 6)

What does David fear? The unknown, the rumors, the words spoken, the evil plotted—and the *possibility* of something sinister being perpetrated against him at some point by someone. It appears to me that the fear that has overcome David is of spoken or threatened harm.

One thing we do *not* want to miss is the fact that these were real fears for him—even crippling fears. Simply because I think that words should/ would not cause me harm, I can't assume that this is where David is. David has lived with near constant, real fear throughout his whole adult life. I'm fully aware that, while these may seem like simple, and possible even harmless, words to me, David probably has seen such rumors materialize into action too many times to count. So, I cannot belittle his fear. But what I can do, what *we* can do, is think about how many times we, too, were struck with a lack of ability to function effectively due to the grip fear has had on us when *we, too*, have heard rumors and rumblings with regard to our own safety.

Words *can* hurt, words can strike fear, rumors can make us anxious and nervous, and the spreading of hate can grip us and render us immobilized. Even worse, for me, is the fact that rumors and people talking about me hurt. But where I'm really struck and challenged is that I have been on the *other* side. I have been the "plotter." I've said things about people, plotted stupid things to pay them back and hurt them for what they have done to me (not physically harming them—but hurting them nonetheless), . . . and so, as I write this, I'm put to shame.

I want to write about excuses and have you understand why I said the things about them that I did and why I wanted to do what *I wanted to do*, but those words are hollow because all I would be trying to do is sway you to understand my perspective. All I'd really be trying to do is justify my words and actions—but there is no justification for them. I sought the harm of someone else. It doesn't matter if they tried to harm me first or said something first. I'm held accountable for my own words, thoughts, and actions.

Matthew 12:36 states that we all will have to give an account on the Day of Judgment for all the empty words we've spoken. This also means that we will give an account of the harm our spoken words may have caused. Do I need more reminders? Romans 14:12 is a good one, too, as are Proverbs 27:17, Jeremiah 17:10, and 1 Thessalonians 5:11 (these last three focus on the way we *should* act).

The ending of this psalm is the arrow that pierces my heart because the truth is still the truth. God will *not* allow these things to happen. These words, actions, plots, evil, and hatred will not and are not part of his eternal kingdom—nor will the people who do these things find themselves there. I'm thankful for the redemption, forgiveness, and grace of God, that *my* words and actions will not ultimately keep me from that eternal joy because Christ's work is greater than mine—and I thank God that he knows my real heart and desires, even when I'm caught up in the moment and acting out of character. I know that we are held to a higher standard—and that God will engage us in conversation about those things we have done when we stand before him in judgment.

I'm thankful that God's arrows of love and grace are stronger and pierce more deeply into us than our plots against each other. As with many other psalms, I find myself thankful that God's work overshadows the pain and harm we often cause each other.

THREE QUESTIONS FOR YOU TO CHEW ON:

1. What in this psalm speaks to you? What draws you in? Why?
2. Why is it that words can do so much harm? They're only words, right?
3. When you stand before God in glory, and he reviews your life, what good thing will he cite? What harm will he bring up that you brought upon someone else?

A PSALM OF JOYFULNESS

Take the time to open your Bible and read the words of Psalm 65.

This is a beautiful celebration psalm of harvest joy. Some think that this may have been an annual song sung as a song of thanks for that first harvesting of crops (at the beginning of the barley harvest or general harvest). The Israelites gave thanks for the harvest because they believed that a bountiful harvest was in direct response to their faithfulness in following God's commands. That is, God blessed the harvest when they were good Israelites. The thinking went that the more you followed the Law, the more you prayed, the better Jew you were—and the blessings of God would be given to you *in* a good harvest.

We can think of harvest celebrations for God that take place throughout the year, but for me, as I write this shortly before the first Sunday of Advent, I can't help but think of this season of thankfulness, praise, and hope for the blessings of God that are celebrated and proclaimed because Jesus Christ left his throne on high and entered into humanity as an infant. The notion that humanity, so overwhelmed by sin, would be worthy enough for the Son of God to come and eventually atone for our transgressions would simply be unimaginable if we weren't so accustomed to the reality of the incarnation. This whole psalm is drenched with the love of God and the work of Christ in our lives. I've already mentioned some examples within the first three verses, but there are many more:

- "Answer us with awesome deeds of righteousness, O God our Savior." (v. 5)
- "the hope of all the ends of the earth and the farthest seas" (v. 5)
- "who formed the mountains by your power" (v. 6)
- "who stilled the roaring seas [waves and turmoil of the nations]" (v. 7)
- "calling forth songs of joy" (v. 8)

And these are just the ones that stick out to me!

And yet this whole text is about giving thanks for all things. For the land, the waters that flow, and the waves that roll, as well as for the rains that drench and the earth that soaks it all up. With all that said, this becomes an all-encompassing psalm of joy. Joy found in the gifts of God upon the earth (his direct blessings to the people), but also in the blessing that come upon the people because God forgives. For us—for Christians—Christ is our all-encompassing joy, because love, grace, hope, joy, and peace are found only in him.

What's really interesting (for me at least) is that when you look at this psalm and at additional texts that speak of this theme, the majority of them are not Advent but Lenten themed. Which means that I may or may not legitimately be influenced here by the time of the season that is upon us. However, we cannot have Lent without Advent—nor can we have Advent without Lent. And right there is where I am challenged. The hope and joy of Christ must be fully realized as both in life and death.

This is my challenge as I come into the Advent season, . . . and yet I do not want to overlay the joy of birth with the pain of death. So, where is that balance? I honestly do not know, because all the feelings of hope and joy evoked for me by the *birth* of Christ are also present in the *death* of Christ—which seems counterintuitive but is yet completely understandable. Again, one has to occur in order for the other to occur. Both are needed, both are imperative, and both evoke many of the same feelings—and at the same time completely different feelings as well.

I find that interesting and challenging. How can joy be joyful and yet also sad? How can hope be both an elation and a conviction? How can peace indeed feel peaceful in times of happiness and thankfulness, and yet humility and sorrow also find their place in our peace? I honestly don't know, but those are just a few of the emotions that overcome us—not only during those two seasons but in all the seasons of our lives.

This psalm of praise and hope from David is one that elicits emotions we experience every day of our lives. Just as we praise God in the birth of his Son as our Savior, we also praise God in the death of that very same Son, . . . again, as our Savior. That thankfulness and joy and hope and pain can be messy—as are the rest of the emotions in our lives. I think that's okay, because there have been times when sadness was with me during Advent due to the death of a family member, . . . and I know that sadness will wash over me again as others come in and out of my life. That's natural, that's expected, and it's definitely okay, because God's love doesn't come to us for only two distinct seasons of our lives—it's a love that wraps us up both before we are born and after we die and enter that final phase of our eternal life.

THREE QUESTIONS FOR YOU TO CHEW ON:

1. What in this psalm speaks to you? Where are you drawn in? Why?
2. Can you find joy in Good Friday? What does, or would, that look like?
3. What things, as you look out the window or step outside, are you thankful for?

A PSALM FOR
ME, YOU, AND US

Take the time to read with me Psalm 66.

Psalm 66 is a beautiful psalm of thanksgiving that invites the reader in a few different sections to worship God. I appreciate how these themes weave from the singular to the plural, as well as from the corporate to the individual. I picture the psalmist leading a group of people as he shares his own struggles and joys and encouraging all those present to not only join in but find their own responses to God's awesome deeds.

Isn't that what all of life is about? One constant invitation to praise and thanksgiving? One call to find and give thanks in our own lives and then share and encourage others to see and feel it, too?

One thing I've been told numerous times by fellow pastors is that people will eventually get tired of hearing sermons with my personal stories in them—so I should keep them limited. The idea is that it is better to find stories outside my own experience to share, while inviting people to join in and find themselves within *those* contexts instead of just my own. While I agree that I shouldn't use *only* personal stories, I'm not quite sure, either, that simply stopping the sharing of my own struggles and life experiences is the right path. I think people engage more when they can relate to the one speaking. People can be encouraged and challenged in many ways, and I know that this is helpful to me when I'm on the listening end; it helps me to find a connection with the pastor. Obviously, there is a balance here that is important to find—but I find a peace in knowing that the psalmist, while encouraging others to give thanks, acknowledges his amazing relationship with God through his personal, as well as the corporate, relationship.

There are so many rich nuggets of praise in this text that it's going to be really hard to draw them out in the limited space I've given myself—so I want to share something that may help us not only with this text but with the Bible as a whole.

First off, it's really easy for a Christian to read the Old Testament and say, "Yes, that is Jesus being spoken of!" While it is true that we should see Scripture as a story of the brokenness and frailty of humanity and of our own fallenness, it is even more important that we view it as a developing story that points to Jesus. When we look through this lens (I had a professor call it the "Jesus Lens"), we *do* proclaim that everything points to Christ—not only in *this* text, but in this text too, and this text and, . . . here . . . and here. All of this points to Jesus! I get it, but we do still have to allow the author(s) to speak to those to or of whom they were speaking, and most of the time they did *not* have Christ, the Messiah, in mind when they wrote the text (most scholars feel that there is only *one* Old Testament text that is Christ-specific, and that comes in Psalm 2). We do see this connection now—but they did not then. So, when we read verses like Psalm 66:3–5, 7, 9, and then 17–20, we have to allow the author to speak of God's amazing love, goodness, glory, and (in this case) redemption. We must allow *his* voice to be heard and not my own or our own. Find your voice *in* the text, but allow the text to speak for itself (a good reminder for every text).

With that said, the greater narrative of this text is exactly what we've already talked about; the author of this song is encouraging you to find, proclaim, and give thanks to the God who is mighty, powerful, strong, and the Lord of all things. To give thanks to the God who is above all things, has worked and is still working on your behalf, and is worthy alone to be praised. The psalmist has lived and experienced so much that he is inviting those in attendance to see what God has done for them and to find God in that space for them as well.

So, where and what has God done for you?

I think this is an important daily reflection for you and me. Just as the psalmist praises God during the good times but also during those times of struggle, so should you and I. Just as you have relished your time in that space in the personal sense, you should carry those thoughts and joys and praises to others and invite them to see God working in *their* lives, too. For me (and I'm probably thinking this way since we had Communion yesterday at church), I see this as a sacramental understanding. Just as we take the cup and the bread and reflect internally, and just as baptism reflects God's anointing upon the person being baptized, neither of the sacraments is about the individual or something done by ourselves. There should always be others involved, because it's not about *us*; it's about the body. Communion, while deeply personal, is not private. And baptism, while deeply personal, is also about the body present, and their witnessing the ceremony, as well as their promise to walk, encourage, and help the baptizee.

Our walk, our joy, our faith is bigger than ourselves and beyond us—so why wouldn't we share, invite, and encourage others to join in?

THREE QUESTIONS FOR YOU TO CHEW ON:

1. What in this psalm speaks to you? At what point are you drawn in? Why?
2. Does your worship of God change, or feel different, when you are by yourself, in a small group, or participating in a church service? Or is it always the same?
3. With the psalmist sharing with others about their belief and encouraging others to worship, this psalm almost becomes a missionary text. Do you ever share your faith to the point that you encourage others to do so, too? Or do you keep it to yourself?

A PETITIONAL PSALM
OF BLESSINGS

Take the time to read Psalm 67.

I love that this psalm is simple and to the point. It's a psalm of blessings that I can see giving to a friend as we part ways, a psalm of blessings that would work wonderfully to close out a worship service, because it's a psalm of hopeful praise and a simple psalm of thankfulness to God for his blessings.

When you read this, you may recognize the beginning verses as being very similar to those of Numbers 6:24–26. Used frequently as a closing blessing, the words from the book of Numbers constituted the blessings of the church as people departed. They constituted a request for the blessings of the Lord to watch and keep the congregation from all harm, an invitation for the attendees to feel the warmth and goodness of the Lord's face shining upon them as they went out—and, finally, a request for the peace that only the Lord can give to fall upon them.

Implicit in the psalm is an understanding that God is everywhere and in everything (this is important to remember, so hold on to it).

We don't know the context of this song. We simply know that it's a song and that songs should be sung. And this song simply asks that the blessings of God be received, so that his name can be known. And not only known to the people there, not only known to those gathered in worship, but also known to the ends of the earth. Twice we read the words "May the peoples praise you, God; may all the peoples praise you." When we see repeated words, especially when the text per se is so short, we should take notice. What we find here is really nothing complex: the author realizes that it is by God's blessings that goodness happens, and yet it is also by God's blessings that people will know him. And not only those in their immediate circle, but all people everywhere.

What I find truly fascinating is that the author ends this text with a request for blessings, so that people may "fear" God. Maybe it's just me, but "blessings" and "fear" don't seem to be two words that work well together. It just doesn't make sense to have a petition of goodness *for me* in the same breath as a petition for fear and anxiety *for others*.

Deuteronomy 10:12 includes a beautiful charge to Israel; the Lord asks them to fear him, walk in obedience with him, love and serve him, . . . and do so with all your heart. Those words have always been really interesting to me. Love *and* fear the Lord? Train your children up to love and fear the Lord (Psalm 34:11; Proverbs 22:6)—those pairings seem so odd. Right? Well—if we think of fear as being afraid of something, then, yeah, . . . this *is* odd. But when we think of fear as respect, honor, and an element of reverential fear, then it becomes more understandable. What we're aiming to understand here is that, with regard to God's authority, there are all these emotions—fear being one of those. There's a power in God that is unlimited and that must be respected—and feared.

When we take those intermingled feelings, what we are brought to is this *total and complete respect* for God. And not just total and complete, but the *highest* of respect. It's being 100% "all in" for who God is and what he does and is capable of doing. It's an ability to fully walk in obedience and respect and love and commitment to God because you know that there is *nothing* he isn't capable of doing. Now, that doesn't mean "capable" as in "We're not sure if God's going to go psycho on us today, . . . so beware!" That's not what this means. It's more like, "There simply is nothing that is outside of what God can do, for he is the Creator of all, the holder of all things, and is in complete control of everything. His power and abilities are limitless." We, as his created beings, find awe and fear in just how powerful God is. That's something that should be understood and feared, . . . but it's not about finding only fear in our hearts.

Now, with all of that said, and coming back to our psalm—the understanding from the psalmist is that everything and all blessings come from God . . . *and that because of that* all people, every tribe and tongue and nation, should praise him. All people should sing with joy and gladness for the blessings and goodness of God. All people should praise God, for he gives harvests to the lands, rules the peoples with equity (think of fairness), and leads and guides them in all they do.

The psalmist simply wants all the people of the world to know, believe, fear, and love the One who creates it all, sustains it all, guides it all, brings joy to all—and blesses all things. It's a prayer we offer every day—right? That people will come to know the Lord. That those who do not know God will come to realize the love and mercy and grace he rains upon us, and that there isn't a part of this world or beyond that doesn't have his stamp of "mine" on it. Yes, there is an element of fear based on just how amazing and powerful God is—and an awareness of how easily he could snuff us all out—and yet he doesn't, because that's not who he is.

Sometimes the simple and short psalms like this one are richly complex, challenging, and affirming all in the same breath.

THREE QUESTIONS FOR YOU TO CHEW ON:

1. What in this psalm speaks to you? At what point are you drawn in? Why?
2. Like the Hawaiian word *Aloha*, can you think of a word that can be used in multiple contexts that expresses your love in conjunction with other feelings (hint, if you need one: Think of what you've very recently read)?
3. What does it mean, to you, to fear the Lord?

A PROCESSIONAL PSALM
OF HOPE

P lease consider with me Psalm 68.

This is a song of praise and worship that is meant as encouragement. But what's really beautiful is that this encouraging psalm is not only given but also felt and seen. What I mean is that you get this feeling that the author had a bullhorn and was rousing up the worshipers to see, feel, and let loose in their worship of God. I picture the worship leaders standing on an extremely high platform and seeing this parade of worshipers coming down the street; as they see people coming, they are getting more excited because they see different tribes and people in this extremely long procession. As they see all of them, their emotions rise, their voices kick up a notch in volume and octave, and they simply are at awe. Picture the Thanksgiving Day Macy's Parade with the cameramen and reporters with their cameras all over, able to watch, share, encourage, and find joy. The joy of this psalm, of course, is not during the American Thanksgiving, or with Macy's, or in New York, for that matter. Horrible analogy!

Here's what we know. If we believe the superscript (those words after the title of the psalm that say, "For the director of music. Of David. A psalm. A song."), then this could be a song after a victory, on the way to war/battle, or in conjunction with some other massive processional that would have brought all the people together (maybe even God's ark being returned to its home base in Jerusalem). It's really hard to drum up a historical setting when we aren't given much detail, so scholars are all over the place in terms of tying this processional to a specific context. But a praise song it is. A song of shouted encouragement. It speaks of the actions of God throughout time and history and declares that all the kingdoms of earth are to sing of God's praises.

As I type this, I keep coming back to wanting to see and experience the setting, today—and yet there has never been anything like this that I have ever seen. I've seen plenty of parades, either in person or on TV (my sister is still slightly obsessed with the Macy's Thanksgiving Day parade), and I've even been in quite a few small ones in junior and senior high, as well as in a big one my freshman year of college (Pasadena's Rose Bowl Parade). While the Rose Bowl Parade to some degree drummed up for me that feeling that David experienced here, it wasn't quite the same. Our parade celebrated people, events, businesses, college football teams, . . . and lots of lots of money. This one, the one David speaks of, celebrates God.

Can you imagine being in a massive processional that simply celebrates God? I imagine it would be like participating in a portable (moving) worship service, the whole experience of which would allow you (and everyone else present) to lose your shackles of shame and pain and let go of your personal struggles over caring what others thought of you while you worshiped—of being set free. What an amazing, invigorating, tear*ful* and freeing parade of worship that would be! I'm getting excited just thinking about it! And yet, . . . I know that I will have to wait. We will have to wait until the entrance of the King. Wait until Christ comes again to establish his final reign over all things here in the New Earth. When that happens and all will be placed under his feet—the parade will start. The people will sing. Kingdoms and nations will gather in one place from every tribe, tongue, and nation.

Will there be giant helium balloon characters? Maybe. I'm not sure what they would portray, because seeing Snoopy might feel kind of awkward, . . . but you never know. I picture church musicians and worship leaders playing and marching and singing songs of joy, hope, and gladness. Songs of Advent, Christmas, Easter, Pentecost and all the other liturgical highlights of the year.

I picture a processional of joy and hope that would draw in, lift up, and gather in. Is there any other thing on God's green earth that sounds more appealing and joyful? It *will be* the greatest thing that has ever happened in history. And why? Because God is the Father of the fatherless and the defender of widows (v. 5). Because God gathers the lonely into families and sets the prisoners free *with singing* (v. 6). Because God watches over his people and land and gathers them in with his outstretched hands. And if we need anything else to praise him about—*he is our Savior.*

Yes—praise be to God!

THREE QUESTIONS FOR YOU TO CHEW ON:

1. What in this psalm speaks to you? Where are you drawn? Why?
2. What do you picture would be in this processional?
3. Celebrations around the work of God were a big thing (all were associated with him). Why have we discontinued that practice today? Outside of Palm Sunday—do we do this? Why not?

A PSALM OF
MISSED INTENTIONS

B egin today's reading with Psalm 69.

Commentators have no doubt that this is a psalm of David—but as to what was going on in his life that motivated him to put stylus to parchment, we aren't sure. We know he's in pain or affliction; we know he's been crying out to God for some time; we know that *he* knows that his pain and suffering are warranted (for whatever reason); he knows that there are people who are persecuting him, and he seeks God's judgment upon them; and he ends with joy and praise—knowing that these things, offered up to God, mean more to God than anything else.

Here is something I picked up on as I read this psalm, a point to which I am drawn: the things we do *mean* something in life. As a parent, I quickly realized that my children watch what I do and respond to it. The comments I make to my wife or kids, the way I treat them, as well as the way I give and serve my community. All of these things are taken in and observed and responded to, in one way or another, by others. They learn from them, they respond to them, they emulate them, and—most importantly—their relationship with God is impacted because of them. Think about that for a second. If our words and actions mean something for others, then they most definitely mean something to God, because he desires us to love and serve others as he has done. And so, if Christ loved and served and sacrificed himself for others, we must emulate that relationship.

I'm really struck by David's words of guilt and confession, starting at verse 6. His prayer for others and for their relationship with God is striking. Understanding and knowing that he may have done something to hurt someone else's relationship with God is powerful and hits me hard. Early on in my time as a pastor, I remember having a conversation with someone who was new to the faith and was struggling in some areas. I approached that relationship with him in the same way I would have with someone who had a strong relationship with God and with me, . . . and it didn't turn out very well. I hurt him. And while I humbled myself and apologized for the things I had said (even though they were absolutely true, he just wasn't in a place to understand and hear them), the last thing I wanted to do was ruin his relationship with God based on the things I said. What's really difficult for me is knowing that, while he accepted my apology and admitted that he was really angry with me, I never saw or heard from him again. I don't know whether he's attending a church someplace else or whether because of our encounter he has tossed God to the side. I pray that my misplaced words, intended as comfort and encouragement toward faith, did not push him further away, in conjunction with the pain he already bore.

Again, our words and actions *mean* something. That shouldn't surprise us. From the get-go God created us to be relational, as he is relational. Loving, serving, building up, and creating—all verbs that have us doing things for each other and creation. But we broke that link when we sought to serve self. And we have been paying the price ever since. God sought to right that wrong by sending Jesus Christ, the ultimate self-sacrificing person, to walk the earth. And, while we thankfully affirm that because of this ultimate act of sacrifice we are brought back into the fold, back into love and grace and forgiveness—this doesn't mean that what we say and do doesn't still affect those who love us, observe us, and learn from us.

Ultimately, while I am still pained over what I have done, I find comfort in knowing that, though my words and actions missed the mark, in the end it isn't my words and actions that make or break someone else and their relationship with God. God is in control here—not me. And he has done everything in *his* power to make sure that *my words* and actions never override or undermine his own. While we are held accountable for the things we've done and the words from our mouth, it can never be said that he cannot undo the pain someone else endured based on our misguided or ineffective efforts.

So be challenged and reminded that people are watching, learning, observing, and taking in your words and actions. If you are a Christian and profess your love of God, then all that you say and do will be put under a microscope by the world, . . . especially by the ones you love and care for and have entrusted you with their spiritual care. Your words and actions mean something, . . . because *you* mean something to others.

THREE QUESTIONS FOR YOU TO CHEW ON:

1. What in this psalm speaks to your heart? To what in it are you drawn? Why?

2. If you could take the time to preview the words you were about to speak, and foresee the impact they might have, would you want to verbalize them? Or would you withhold speaking in certain situations because you saw what your words might do—even when they were truthful and coming from a place of good intentions?

3. Should *my own* words to that new believer have impacted *me* as much as they did? What soothing words would you give someone who felt bad about words they had spoken, who had apologized for them, and yet who still lived with the pain?

A PSALM FOR SHAME

B egin today by reading Psalm 70.
Sometimes those really short psalms are the ones that pack the most punch for us. This one may be one that hits the mark for you. Then again, it may not. Either way, David has some good words and reminders for us.

Psalm 70 and Psalm 40 are quite similar in nature, with similar petitions for help, so much to that many people feel that they were possibly combined at one point—but later separated for a liturgical reason. Whatever the background, this psalm's terse punchiness feels almost tangible. David, wherever he is and whatever he is going through, is in need of God's saving, God's work, God's deliverance.

What I find really interesting is that three different times we read either the word "shame" or "disgrace." Three different times David is seeking the God who delivers to bring dishonor and humiliation on those who seek to harm him and his friends.

Honor and shame were a big thing back in the day—and still are in many cultures around the world. Your name, the value of your word, the actions you took or didn't take all contributed toward making your community either function or fail to function effectively. For David and for those with whom he surrounded himself, this was all based on God and what God expected of his people. David fully understood that it is *only* in God that goodness, integrity, and a sound reputation are found.

This may seem counterintuitive, but I would propose that we've *lost the value* found in shame and humiliation. If you think about it—under what circumstances have you felt ashamed? Outside of a sporting event at which you got creamed and humiliated (usually humiliation happens in sports events when you're overconfident and expected to win and instead are simply slaughtered), when was the last time you felt a dose of dishonor?

More importantly—when did that dishonor and shame do more than affect your comfort level in the immediate moment? In many cultures shame and dishonor last long after the initial incident; they affect your family and all those you associate with, sometimes for the long term. David, for whatever reason, is seeking for God to not only turn away those who want to hurt him but to utterly and publicly destroy them. Obliterate them. Make it so that nobody will want to be around those people, nobody will want to be associated with them, and their whole family will cut them off. In essence, he wants them to have nothing, nobody, and zilch in the way of public face. To me, this feels like probably the second worst thing that could happen to you (with death being the worst).

I think we also have to remember that these cultures, and many today, depend on the community and body as a whole. To be shamed is to be shunned. To be shunned is to be, in effect, sentenced to death. Maybe this is even slightly worse than death—because in death you are physically removed. In shame and dishonor, you are seen but considered dead.

I want to consider this seeking theme we read here—because I think it's a good reminder of shame and dishonor. David, in verse 4, asks, "May all who seek you rejoice and be glad in you; may those who long for our saving help always say, 'The LORD is great!'" What I find interesting is that this "seeking" of the Lord is in contrast to those who *seek the psalmist*. David asks that those who seek him may not find him—whereas he asks that those who seek God may rejoice and be glad. Not only that, but that those who need God and his saving work may always proclaim that the Lord is great. To me, this also means that, when we seek God and find that he doesn't answer in a way we desire, we still must proclaim that he is great!

Here, then, is the challenge for you and me: even those who seek to humiliate and harm us should have the opportunity to turn to God and praise his name. Even in their experience of being shunned, even in their removal from society, even in their dishonored state, God still wants to be their refuge if they will seek him. While you and I easily know and proclaim this, it's a harder pill to swallow when we've been harmed by others.

We proclaim that God is a god of love and grace—quick to remove his punishment, even quicker to love, and quickest to forgive with his unimaginable grace. That is the same God who forgives you and me when we bring shame upon others and seek to harm others with our words and actions. The same God in whom you rejoice is the God in whom all the world can rejoice—should people desire to turn and seek his face.

This psalm, in its generalness, is a good reminder that in times of need we should not seek our own desires for retribution and harm but simply seek God. Dishonor and shame happen only when we take things into our own hands because we feel we've been slighted or want to harm someone—and thus it backfires on us. No shame and honor can happen when we simply go to God and allow him to respond, allow him to save, allow him to deliver us from our troubles. No shame can be found when God is working and we are thankful.

THREE QUESTIONS FOR YOU TO CHEW ON:

1. What in this psalm hits the target for you? To what aspects are you drawn? Why?
2. Have you ever felt shame or dishonor? How did you respond? How did you work past the situation?
3. When someone does harm and then finally turns to God, why do we tend to hold them in suspicion? Why is it harder to accept someone's repentance and conversion than it is not to do so?

A PSALM OF AFFLICTIONS

Begin today's reflection by reading Psalm 71.

Hope is an ever-present theme throughout the psalms. Hope for peace in the midst of trial, hope in the joy of a new day; hope for the relenting of sin and darkness; hope in the forgiveness of sins; and the simple hope in a God who knows, works, relents, draws in, and protects. Today's psalm is a psalm of hope that is weaved throughout the 24 verses as the psalmist struggles with his own afflictions. And as the psalmist deals with his own circumstances, as he struggles with those around him, *because* of his hope he finds a sense of peace. It's a hope in a God who responds, but more so in a God who always was.

Psalm 71 in some ways seems like a combination of numerous other psalms (which is absolutely understandable; How many times can you cry out to God in some "new" way that you haven't used before?) but needs to be understood on its own as well—since it constitutes a single unit of thought, a distinct expression of hope. From the beginning we see that the author is up in years (v. 18) and is still dealing with the harm others have caused him. There is still pain from the words of others, their actions against his life, still vestiges of the torment he has suffered throughout his life. But he is also struggling with the frailties that come as one gets older. It's almost as though he is struggling with something that always was (people and their desire to harm him) but now struggles as well with something new (old age and the body's slow deterioration). And yet throughout all of this, even though the trouble appears to be an ever-present reality of his life, . . . so is God. *That* is his hope.

What I find truly fascinating and convicting is the fact that so often we find ourselves dwelling on the constant pain that is a part of our lives—which is easy to do. When we have pain in our lives, it can become that constant against which we hold up everything else. Because of the pain, because of the associated feelings, because of the ever-present _____ (insert affliction here), that suffering becomes the *first* thing we think of, . . . as well as, oftentimes, the *last* thing in the day. It almost becomes our litmus test in life. Since it is an ever-present affliction, it always seems to find its way into our conversation, thoughts—and very being. But what about the ever-present joy that is also ours? What about the fact that God has also been present throughout it all? What about the proclamation that no matter where we go or where we've been, so too has God? Where is *that* litmus test?

Some of my readers know that I struggle with a health condition that will never be fixed. That it's a daily struggle for me that I *have* to deal with—there simply is no way around it. And, yes, there are times when it's really bad and I am frustrated and annoyed to the point of feeling lost in that feeling. Yes, there are times when this condition drains me, and I do not want to do anything but stay in bed. What can be really consuming is that in those moments it's really easy to focus on that and nothing else. Because of the pain, because of my frustrations, because of my annoyance, I can feel consumed and push away all the blessings that *I could find* in that moment but have a hard time doing or choose not to do. The pain has this amazing ability to take over and push aside all thoughts and feelings of joy, blessing, and hope.

My experience, as our psalmist understands and declares, reminds me that God is faithful in all times. The God who knitted me in my mother's womb (Psalm 139:13) and knows (even going so far as to count!) all the hairs on my head knows and understands my pain and affliction(s). As we get older, as we get weaker, as our bodies begin to break down, it's going to become even more apparent that God has always been with us as our guide. That even though our bodies have changed or we have struggled with _____ , the true consistency in all of it has been God. Hope has always been in our lives, and grace (as Paul reminds us in Galatians 1:15) had been bestowed upon us before we took our first breath.

May we all be reminded not of our afflictions, not of our pains and struggles, but of the work of our Lord and Savior. May we remember that his grace was placed upon us long before our condition or disability ever was.

THREE QUESTIONS FOR YOU TO CHEW ON:

1. What in this psalm speaks directly to you? To what in it are you drawn? Why?

2. Why is it easier to dwell on the pain we have than it is on the God who restores?

3. How can you support someone who is struggling with an affliction, as well as encourage them to see that, even before the onset of their condition, God had already redeemed it and set them free? How does one lovingly, caringly, and with compassion and truth encourage them to recognize even through their affliction the truth and hope that are in God?

A PSALM OF CHRISTLIKENESS

Join me in reading Psalm 72.

Well, we're at the end of Book 2 of the psalms (42–72). Most of the psalms in this section have had this "call to deliverance" feel about them—which is why many consider this portion the "exodus" of the psalms. Our last psalm in this division is absolutely fitting as a "closer."

Many of us picture Solomon based on the story from 1 Kings 3:16–28 in which he, in his wisdom, discovers the true mother of a child claimed by two women. But before that account we read of Solomon's simple request of God: for wisdom. Solomon, in his prayer to God as he looks ahead toward all that lies before him and the job he will have to do with God's people, seeks God to bless him with wisdom, the knowledge of right and wrong, and the ability to make the right choices. Our psalm today is a continuation of that theme of Solomon's hope and desire. Commentators differ as to whether this is a psalm *of* Solomon or *for* Solomon. That is—who the author was is up for debate (was this penned by David as he was dying or by Solomon as he stood at the gates of kingship?), but the intended person who is in view, as well as the hope, is still the same. We could even argue that this is a "Christ" psalm—but we'll get there.

Whomever we attribute this to—either David or Solomon—has one request of God: rain down your glorious attributes upon this man. Give him the wisdom you have for him to rule and make wise decisions and choices for his people. Give him passion and love for the oppressed and poor, so that he may defend those who cannot defend themselves and share with all the Giver of these gifts. Finally—make his reign be from shore to shore, sea to mountain, and land to land. What helps us understand all of these requests is the reminder that they reiterate the terms of a promise of God made to David back in 2 Samuel 7 and spoken of as the Davidic Covenant. It's really a plea for God to remember the promise he made to David and his descendants—that God would bless David and put him on the throne for his people, and then after David that his line would continue. This line, if you will recall, eventually comes to Jesus Christ. The request in Psalm 72 is that God would hold to his covenant with David.

This psalm is one of those that points its readers to the hope that David had in the continuation of his family line; it's a psalm that declares the type of people God's children should be, as well as the hope of the king to come—a look ahead to the type of king Jesus Christ is. It is in accordance with these last two understandings that Christians find their connection to the psalm. Knowing Christ, knowing the type of King and leader he was, are *we* emulating *his* attributes? Just as David was asking for God's wisdom and love and justice—we too should seek those causes.

As a parent of two children myself, I'm struck by David's request to God with regard to his son. David asked that he might be wise, compassionate, and a defender of the defenseless. So often we as parents talk about the qualities we want for our children, and yet we may find ourselves secretly wanting something else for them. We know that David was *not* the best father or leader or even the best person to emulate as a young person got older, but in his brokenness and humility God still worked with him, molded him, and valued his passion and zeal. I'm pretty sure David struggled to find balance between the things of God and the things of this world in terms of what he wanted for his children, and yet he had a deeply rooted understanding of what the issues were. My wife and I have had numerous conversations with a good friend about our kids, who are kind and compassionate toward others. We are convinced that their being kind and "good" is more valuable than their excelling in sports, winning awards, or earning good grades. David's hope for his son, a hope that was built on who God is, is a good reminder that, while I love the fact that my kids love music and get good grades and excel in their own sports (tennis or swimming), in the end that does not matter to me. My deepest desire for my kids? That they be kind and compassionate— full of grace, mercy, and kindness. That they *be* love to people and show them what love looks like.

And why do I want this? Because this is really what makes the world go around. This is the only thing that will fight against the hate and evil that are so prevalent in our society. Emulating and living a life as Christ lived for us is what really makes each day worth living, fighting, and dying for. David may not have had the Messiah on his lips when he voiced this prayer, but deep down that *had* to have been part of his hope, because David believed in the God who *is* all of these things for his people.

THREE QUESTIONS FOR YOU TO CHEW ON:

1. What is it in this psalm that hits the mark for you? Where are you drawn? Why?
2. How are you emulating the actions of Christ in your work, play, school, home, and neighborhood?
3. If you could have inscribed on your tombstone one phrase that described you—one thing, besides your name, on your tombstone that captured the essence of *you*—what would it be?

A PSALM OF WHY?

Begin today's reading with Psalm 73.

We are in a new book of the psalms. Book 3 is considered Levitical in nature, as most of the psalms (73–89) are considered to have been written by Levitical priests (the priests who were descendants of the tribe of Levi, as well as of Moses and Aaron, who were responsible for temple worship, sacrifices, and the like). We, the readers, will come away with the principle that *because* God is holy and *because* we come before him, *we too* should be holy and should remember our place.

Psalm 73 works beautifully with the book of Proverbs. It simply does not make sense to us when the wicked prosper. It simply does not make sense when people who are not godly and who abuse the poor and downtrodden prosper and grow "fat and happy" (or strong and lean). What can really begin to hurt us is that, when we see these people prospering while we are suffering, we can begin to wonder how much God actually cares: *I pray every day, I tithe, I give to the poor financially and physically, I donate, I sacrifice, I give! give! give! and yet why does* _____ *happen to me! Why do I have this* _____? *Why?*

This is the struggle of Job. This is the struggle of people who want to believe and yet cannot fathom why God does what he does—or why he doesn't do what people profess he does (love, act, restore, etc.) when hurt, famine, death, corruption, and affliction happen. How do we, how *can* we, profess to knowing God while those things are happening? This is the eternal struggle for *all* people (okay, that's a general statement, but I don't think it's too far off).

But life is all about perspective, isn't it? Simply because we see the person who has prospered by climbing the backs of others doesn't mean that she is truly prosperous in any way that counts, right? She may *look* so now, she may *seem* so on the outside, but eternally and internally the reality may look different. I think we have to keep *that* perspective.

There also needs to be a conversation about falling trap to the victim mentality, as well as to the "ways of this world" (as the psalmist realizes in v. 21). Bitterness, envy, lust, anger—those are all foolish ways of this earth. Those are things that are not even close to the wisdom of God's love that works not only in our lives but in his kingdom. And then there's the whole other conversation and reality that we too could have those things, . . . if only we would sacrifice what we know and feel of God and seek the things of this world instead of the things from above. The truth is that you cannot have one along with the other. James 4:4 is a good reminder that we cannot be friends of this world and a friend of God at the same time.

Finally, there is the truth that simply because bad people thrive in this world doesn't mean they are living and acting outside God's purview. God is faithful, true, and in complete control, and we trust in him and his work.

But here is where I *really* appreciate this psalm. For all the "yeah, I wonder and feel that too" that I read here, I sure do appreciate the grace extended in verses 23 to the end. For all my foolish thought, for all my anger, for all my pride, for all my arrogance, for all my claims of "wanting that too" ("stuff," money, etc.)—I still belong to and am loved by God. Even when I succumb to the thoughts of this world, I am still in God's thoughts. I may lose my focus on him, but he does not lose focus on me.

This is precisely the point at which we are encouraged to seek and ask. Are the things of this world that which we seek? Are you and I willing to seek the world and lose God—or might we consider seeking God and losing the world (Philippians 3:8)? Really, if we have God as our focus, are we losing anything at all? While the world would say yes, I would argue *not at all*. We are gaining eternity . . . and so much more.

THREE QUESTIONS FOR YOU TO CHEW ON:

1. What is there in this psalm that speaks to you? To what are you drawn? Why?
2. How do you navigate the world that says you can have it all—if you just conform to its ways?
3. How *do* you justify, or work through, the question of bad people getting more while good people seem to get less? Do you struggle with God in those situations? Is it okay to struggle with him over these issues?

A PSALM OF CONFUSION

Open your Bible with me and consider Psalm 74.

Psalm 74 is unique, . . . and yet not really all that unique in terms of what we've read thus far in the psalms. It matches quite a few different psalms in terms of its content, in its crying out to God to be saved and for God to remember his people, but what makes this psalm so different is that it never comes around to joyful praise. The psalmist, from verse 1 all the way through verse 23, simply begs God to remember his people. Here are 23 verses focusing on the unknown, despair, and confusion.

The truth of the matter is that sometimes, when we're in deep despair and darkness, we don't want to praise God with the accustomed words of hope. If we're totally honest with ourselves, sometimes our darkness remains dark and the furthest thing from our minds is praising God or even promising to praise him *soon*. Sometimes our complaints and feelings of despair simply beg, and need, to remain in that space.

This poem, or song, of Asaph is one that allows the singer to be in his own space. Asaph, as he looks around his beloved city, sees that everything that means something to his people is in ruins. And as he takes in their surroundings, the only thing that comes to mind in terms of *why* this could have happened is that God was angry and had rejected his covenantal people. The only reason any of this could have happened, the only reason God's sanctuary could have been so abused, the only reason the city of Jerusalem could have been ransacked as it has, is that God has allowed it. As he looks around, he just wants to know why. None of it makes sense to him.

One thing that is really hard for me (as a husband/father/friend/pastor/male) is to allow pain, despair, and grief to stand alone, unmitigated by opposing, more positive realities. So often I want to bring comfort to people by listening to them and then trying to offer words of encouragement and hope. So often we want to encourage the one in despair to find the "bright" side or remember the fact that God is good and working all things out. I want to assure people that, no matter where we are or what we are going through, God will not abandon or forsake us, and his grace will never relent. So often I just want to fix the problem, because I'm a male and we like to fix things. The problem is that those words of assurance are realities the other person knows already and doesn't need me to remind them of. Sometimes the person simply needs to lament without a theological diagnosis, a fix, or an explanation of their problems and observations.

I could easily write a few pages about *why* we we're uncomfortable with this "space" of lament. I think it's uncomfortable for us to see others there, to "help," only to have our attempts come across as a reflection of our own discomfort. I think we are uncomfortable with unresolved lament, with questioning God and his motives or reasons—and a whole myriad of other concerns—but I also known that, for me, I'm simply uncomfortable with the "why?" questions when it pertains to people being in pain or suffering. I don't know why God allows starvation or destruction. I don't know why a loving God allows things of this world to go the way they do, and so sitting with someone who is asking those exact questions makes me want to move them out from there and into a place of praise. But I think that this is precisely my issue. We've allowed lament to become *un*praise (another of my personal non-words), . . . which is absolutely wrong.

Psalm 74 is an honest psalm that reminds those who are in a relationship with God that *this* relationship will have its ups and downs—its questions and answers. Sometimes we are in a good place, . . . and sometimes we are not. Sometimes those situations overlap, and we can dig out a piece of our darkness and still find grace and hope—other times we cannot. And all of this is okay and natural. We don't know what is going on and why God is doing what God is doing. But even more, we need to remember that, not only is God big enough for our praises, but he's definitely big enough for our frustrations, questions, pain, and even anger. It's called a relationship for a reason—and we see that here.

The psalmist, even though he is confused and unsure of what is going on or why God is evidently so angry, still lifts up his concerns, his questions about the unknowns, his confusion, and his despair to God. He doesn't promise that he'll "praise him again when God restores the temple because he knows God will do so eventually . . ."—that's not the point of the psalm or the place he's in or even anything remotely close to what he is saying. He's confused, he's angry, and he's hurting, and that space simply needs to be that space. We're the ones who are uncomfortable with not moving the phraseology to a praise that makes us feel good—but here's the thing: *this is still praise.* He's still reaching out to God. He still recognizes and honors the relationship, and he *definitely* still knows and declares that God is in complete control, not only of the city but of the people (read the psalm again if you don't believe me).

I think we do a disservice to our own faith, our relationship with God, and our relationship with others when we try to take our pain and discomfort into a place where it simply is not ready to go. Sometimes we need to work through the darkness in order to fully understand the light. Sometimes asking "why?" simply needs to stand at that: asking without the need of working it through.

THREE QUESTIONS FOR YOU TO CHEW ON:

1. What in this psalm speaks to you? Where are you drawn in? Why?
2. How does your despair feel when you allow it to remain in that space, declining to forcibly let it "go" (so to speak) and move on? Is there a duration to the length of time we should allow things to sit before moving on?
3. How comfortable are you with other people lamenting? Are you by nature a solver? Do you let others speak while you just listen? Do you draw upon empathy or sympathy? Is your response natural or a sign of your discomfort?

A PSALM OF
GOD'S SOVEREIGNTY

Open your Bible with me and read Psalm 75.

As with many psalms, we have the writer seeing or experiencing and responding. I see foes coming at me? I turn to God in a plea of hope for deliverance. We're on our way up to Jerusalem? Then we sing songs and write psalms of praise and joy. What we're experiencing and where we are going or how we are feeling? We lift it all up to God and praise him.

The psalmist today is experiencing something from someone—or groups of someones—and is responding to it. Verse 1 ascribes praise of God, and then verse 2 gives us a hint that the psalmist sees the wicked doing something, . . . but we're more or less left there. Verses 3–8 are a proclamation of sorts that is given to the wicked and proud in terms of how they should act, because, ultimately, God will deal with them (a theme we consistently see throughout the psalms), for the Lord himself is in complete control (again, a running theme). Then in the end the psalmist closes with a proclamation of joy and praise because of God's goodness and complete holding of all things (aka, his "sovereignty"). So, where is the psalmist? What is going on?

The details of this psalm (writer, location, reason, etc.) are not clear. Our subscript states that it was penned by Asaph, possibly *for* David, but as to the context commentators are split. In one way this psalm suggests a connection to Elijah and the prophets of Baal on Mount Carmel (1 Kings 18), where we see the man of God in a match with people who are against God, but on the other hand we feel as though the psalmist is walking the streets and seeing all these ungodly people doing ungodly things to each other—and God—and is fed up with it. Yet neither of these scenarios really feels to me like the probable setting. To me it feels as though the psalmist is reflecting on how *he* has spoken into the lives of those who do not act justly, rightly, humbly, and in ways that God calls them to. It even feels a little like two friends who have come together, and one of the friends is explaining to the other what they have seen and how *they personally* have responded, how they have tried to get these proud and wicked people to stop doing what they were doing and see the errors of their ways.

No matter where the psalmist is at or who he is speaking to, the conviction to speak out when things are happening that are against God is duly noted. We are called to be stewards of God's creation (Genesis 2:15). We are called to be fishers of men/women (Matthew 4:19). We are called to be bringers of grace (Colossians 4:6) and truth (Ephesians 4:15). We are called to baptize and bring forth the Good News of Jesus Christ (Matthew 28:18–20. We are called to speak into, and respond to, evil (Ephesians 5:11). But how often do we really do that? How often do we do what the psalmist here has done and warn people when they are boasting and being proud? How often do we speak against the wicked *to* the wicked?

We're good about talking to each other or posting things on Facebook or other social media sites—but those are indirect ways of speaking, without confronting the person and correcting them. We may notice something someone does or says and tweet a response, but again, that's not correcting. That's not speaking into someone's life about the errors of their ways. It's simply back channel paths of nonconfrontational confrontation. And let's be clear here, . . . the psalmist's words speak of someone who is doing these evil things in *direct*, purposeful defiance. It's like the person who proclaims to be a Christian and yet doesn't act the way they *know* they should—and all this with a defiant attitude. I'm honestly not sure whether there is a more culpable person. To know you're do things openly against God and still go about doing them? Ouch.

But here's the thing—not that the two I'm going to contrast here are of equal harm: when *we* don't speak to our brothers and sisters when they do harm and go against God, . . . when we use back channels to speak of what they have done without confronting them face to face (in love and the hope of reconciliation), *we too are in defiance of God*. We are called to love. We are called to help each other. We are called to speak into each other's lives and bring correcting when correcting needs to be brought—and again, to do so in love (Matthew 18:15–17; Galatians 6:1; 2 Thessalonians 3:15, etc.).

I think that sometimes we need a good reminder that, just as the psalmist proclaims, God will have the wicked stand before him in judgment, as will his faithful followers. We will all be asked why we loved and/or didn't love.

Why we acted and/or didn't act. How we showed grace and forgiveness or didn't, . . . how we spoke to correct those who were acting unrighteously (and how we went *about* it)—and how we didn't. Let's not get so hung up on other people and what *they* are doing that we don't fully look within ourselves at what *we* are doing first.

THREE QUESTIONS FOR YOU TO CHEW ON:

1. What in this psalm speaks to you? Where are you drawn in? Why?
2. Have you ever had to correct a friend who was doing harm? How did it go? Was it easy or complicated? Why was it that way?
3. Are we more concerned with people and their feelings or with God and his commands of us?

A PSALM OF VICTORY

Before today's reflection, please read and consider Psalm 76.
For me, Psalm 76 as a manly man's psalm. It's a psalm of victory that speaks of flashing arrows, shields, and swords of war. It speaks of majestic mountains rich with game (not "game" as in animals to hunt—but of *people* to fight), where strong men lie sleeping their last sleep and unable to lift their hands because they're dead. This psalm is a psalm of war, of battle, . . . and of the power and praise of the almighty God, who destroys his foes by his wrath and strength, his power and might with which Judah is well familiar. Yes, this is a warrior's psalm (I can hear Tim the "Toolman" Taylor doing his grunt right about now)! But truthfully? This isn't a psalm of war at all. This is a psalm about the *end* of war. This is a psalm of the mighty strength of God and the proclamation of what he has done in overcoming his foes.

We don't know the exact details of this psalm; what we do know is that it was a song and that Asaph had a part to play in it (he was apparently a pretty good singer). But as we read it, we get the feeling that Asaph was asked to write and sing a song based on some victorious battle. It feels as though the mighty warriors of Judah have returned, and all the land is preparing a feast like none other for this day. The grill masters are running the grills hot and smoky, awaiting the various brined and rubbed meats to be placed over the coals. The harvesters have come in with the choicest bounty of veggies and fruits and grains that will be divvied up to various bakers and cooks who will prepare pastries, breads, salads, and various other delectable foods. The wine is flowing, and the invitations are out for the whole city to join in. This party will be like none other! And what party would be complete without a singer with stringed instruments to entertain and share what was seen on the battlefield? In his room sits Asaph with quill and paper. What words to write? What odes to sing? What victories to proclaim? Which battle highlights to share? Which mighty warriors to speak of? There is only one: God.

Most commentators feel that we need to read Psalm 76 with the previous psalm because they speak of the same battle, the same joy, the same proclamation and song. That where Psalm 75 speaks of the battle *to come*, the power and strength of God that will come down and defend his people, Psalm 76 is the aftermath. God has been victorious, and the results can be seen by the numerous dead people on the other side, while God's people stand, living—able to sleep another sleep and wake to another day. But where I am drawn today is the work of Asaph and the song he writes and sings concerning the work of God.

On the one hand I am encouraged to think about the song *I* would write of the God I know, but what is challenging is that, while Asaph writes of a God *he* understands in *his* time (a time of war, of defeating other nations), that is not the God I know in my life. Just as we have to allow the voice of the psalmist to be what it is (in that victorious battle style, in this case) and find the truth and goodness in it, we are encouraged to find our own voices, too. Do I know the God of victorious battles, with casualties strewn as a tribute to God's wrath? Only through the Scriptures—but I *do* know him; I just haven't experienced that side personally. Do I know the God who strikes fear into those who do not know him, who choose to profane him, and who are willing to do everything against him? Only in the Scriptures—but I *do* know him; I just haven't experienced that side personally. Do I know the God who breaks the spirits of rulers and should be feared by kings of the earth? I do know him—though, unfortunately, many do not, . . . and yet they will.

The God I know, concerning whom I *do* write and sing, is a God who teaches and gives love. The God I know is the God who serves and tells his people to serve as well. The God I know is the God who sees the dead and dying and offers his life in return. The God I know is patient, kind, and humble and requires his people to be the same. The God I know, sing about, write about, and share is a God of ultimate and true grace. *Is this the same God? Absolutely. Has God changed? Not a chance.*

It is really hard for some people to reconcile the God of the Old Testament with the God of the New Testament. We see war and famine and death and destruction and have a really hard time finding in these accounts that same God who sends his Son to die for us. The truth of all of this is that God's wrath still was poured out in the New Testament—we just see it all poured out upon Christ. As a living sacrifice for our sins, Christ took to the cross to experience not only its pain, suffering, and anguish, but to draw in all of God's wrath that had previously been directed toward his sinful people. Again, God hasn't changed.

So then, why do we see God differently in his actions from Old Testament to New Testament? That's a really good question, and one that I look forward to talking to God about—but at the very least it's a problem with *us* and *our* vision—not God. God's love has always been and always will be. God's work in the lives of those who love and fear him has always been and always will be—that concept may be hard to work through, but we take comfort in knowing that God is the only consistent and good thing that ever was or ever will be.

As we read this psalm, we too should find pen and paper (or computer and Word document) and write of the God we know and the celebratory joy we, too, find in his work. In his work in our lives today, but also in his victorious work upon the cross and the ultimate closing battle that will end all battles, when Christ returns and reestablishes his reign over all the earth. *That* is when *all kings* of the earth will know and declare his name.

THREE QUESTIONS FOR YOU TO CHEW ON:

1. What in this psalm speaks to you? What draws you in? Why?
2. What song of God would you sing? What actions, as you have observed in your life, would describe the God you know to those around you?
3. How would you explain to someone who believed that the God of the Old Testament was different from the God of the New Testament that they are one and the same? What consistencies do you see in the two?

A PSALM OF PATIENCE

Begin your reading today with Psalm 77.

Twice we get this image of outstretched hands. Once from the writer Asaph (in v. 2) and the other time from Asaph's remembrance of God's outstretched hands in the past (v. 10)—and to me that struck a chord. As you read this psalm, you encounter this emotional plea of someone in distress, frustration, and internal confusion. This person is shouting out to God to listen to their pleas of help. All night long they cry out to God, all night long they pray to God, and all night long they continuously lift their "untiring hands" to the heavens for God to respond. But nothing has been happening. For whatever reason, while their past was filled with rest, joy, singing, and love—those are now but a fleeting memory.

We don't have a lot of information about Asaph and where he is in this psalm, but we *can* recognize his feelings as a recurring theme throughout the exodus journey and what was happening at that time—thus, the psalm leads many scholars to surmise that this is a corporate lament, a crying out that points us back to the feelings the whole nation had as it wandered in the desert. What had God done in the past when his people were in distress and lamenting? He had responded with food and protection; he had given them rest. It is that knowledge that keeps Asaph in pain. The question he's asking: "Where is *my* rest?"

So, why does he feel so sad and distressed? If someone has seen the wondrous responses and love of a God of the past as he has helped those in need (and knows that this has happened time and time again), why would he feel so far away from him now, so deep in the pit, so rejected? Well, *that's* the point exactly. If God had responded time and time again to his people after they had rejected him, tested him, built false idols to replace him, and done so many other profane things, what has *Asaph* done that was so bad that God won't respond to him now? Asaph is so deep in darkness that he feels that God must proclaim that his place is further removed from himself than the Israelites have ever been. The present is so much deeper in darkness than the past that God must have cast him off forever.

What a dark, sad, and lonely place to be in—I would love to know more about where Asaph was at in his thinking. Because his struggle feels so real and painfully vivid. As he remembers God, he groans. He meditates, and his spirit grows faint. He can't sleep, and he can't even talk about it! I don't know whether he's ashamed, angered, or simply exhausted—but no words will come out of his mouth, . . . so forget reaching out to friends for help. And don't even get me started about the stark contrast in his words about God's "unfailing love" that has now somehow "vanished." And yet through all of this, there is a fine string he still holds to: the miracles of God of long ago: "I will remember your miracles of long ago. I will consider all your works and meditate on all your mighty deeds" (vv. 11–12).

I appreciate the statement of one author, Roger Ellsworth, that Asaph realizes that in his woe and distress he has been looking at all of this wrongly. Instead of looking at the past of a God who has responded and yet doesn't seem to be responding now, he realizes that he should be looking at the simple fact that God *did respond*. Asaph was allowing the glory of the past to depress him instead of bless him.

We see all the beauty and truth of the glory of God, and how he time and time again saved his people while they struggled to even remain faithful to him, and then we see where *we* are and wonder where *that* God is now. I never profane his name (at least not directly), I never construct idols (okay, I know we all do that one in various ways), I've never demanded things from God as other people have (Wait—I think I'm doing that now). Still, I *am so much better* than they are (shoot—I think I'm doing something bad there, too)! So, where are you, God? Why will you not take this pain away? Why will you not give me peace and rest from my distress? Why will you not respond and remove me from this place to one of peace and rest?

Oftentimes we struggle with looking at the love and glory of the God of the past when we're stuck in the pains and darkness of the present. And what that can do is taint our view of the very same God who pronounces glorious blessings on his people for their future. Our future, while we know it will be glorious and hopeful, seems too far off for us. Or maybe that's just me. Still, I sure would like a response in the *immediate* or *near* future rather than having to wait for the glorious future that is seemingly too far away (actually, I'd like both). *Isn't five seconds from now the future? You can take my pain away then, Lord . . . I'll be okay with that.*

But it's not about me, and I have absolutely no clue what God is doing and when it will come to fruition. I have to be patient with that (something I'm slowly working through, but my patience needs patience)—even patient during the pain and struggles. And we must always remember that the God of the past is the same as the God of the present and the future. And the God of all of those has moved mountains to bless us now and to crown our future (both immediate and beyond) with a glorious eternity in his New Creation.

I want to end with a powerful challenge that I read—a challenge for me and hopefully one for you too (it comes again from Roger Ellsworth): "When we are satisfied with God as he is, we will find ourselves no longer troubled by what he does."

THREE QUESTIONS FOR YOU TO CHEW ON:

1. What in this psalm speaks to you? What draws you in? Why?
2. Do you ever wonder why the God of the past seems to act differently today—and why he isn't stepping into *your* life right now, as he has so many times with others? How do you navigate that space?
3. Does Roger Ellsworth's statement at the end of this reflection ring true for you? Is it that simple? Or is there something else we need to work through?

A PSALM OF HISTORY

Turn in your Bible with me to Psalm 78.

Reading and watching history have always been something I've enjoyed. I love hearing stories about events and people that shaped nations, countries, places, and people. I love hearing stories about what *really* happened in history, because they not only share with us our past but help us frame our present. Knowing where people have come from and knowing the past of the country I live in helps me understand the people, the tensions, and the feelings surrounding where we are today. Psalm 78 is doing what TV and books did for me back in the day when there was no History Channel or internet.

The historical ways of things, way back in the day, was to orally share one's history. To illuminate the past so that you not only knew of your history but would also be challenged and encouraged for the future. From a Hebrew standpoint, this was all framed around who God is, what he had done, and the people's consistent response (both good and bad). Psalm 78 is known as a "historical psalm" for a reason. But this psalm isn't a history lesson given because people like history; this is a historical psalm that is meant to remind, challenge, and instruct the people of God who not only had no history books but also needed constant reminders to be faithful to God.

This psalm is broken up into only two sections—and they are not weighed evenly. Verses 1–18 are introductory in nature in that they prepare the reader/audience for what they're about to read or hear. Picture the psalmist (Asaph) saying, "What I'm about to tell you comes from old and has been passed down from generation to generation, stories given to me and stories I expect you to pass along as well, . . . but these aren't just stories. What you are about to hear are stories with instructions because the path our forefathers took is a path that we, too, could take. The mistakes they made are the very ones I see us making as well. So, let's learn from our past so we can be shaped in our present and future." What follows in the next verses (vv. 9–72) are all the instructions on their historical past from Moses to David. Instructions that speak of events of their sinful past and God's response to the sin of his people, as well his unfailing love.

It seems fairly easy to focus on the sins of the people (because, let's be honest, . . . they were consistent in their misbehavior), but that's not really the point. While that *is* part of the background for this psalm, it never should be *our* focus, either. The Bible isn't a book about the sins of God's people—it's a historical account of the persistent love of God. Yes, lessons need to be learned from our misbehaving past—but that backstory isn't the point.

It's really easy to read psalms like this, as well as the rest of the Bible, and get caught up in what *those people* were doing, all the while failing to see what *you* are doing. It's really easy to read history and walk away without making personal application. Lessons need to be learned because we are really good at repeating the sins of the past. It's also a whole lot easier saying, "I am *not* like them because I would never do _____!" without realizing that *they* would never have done _____ , which is what I do day in and day out. With all of Scripture there is always a consistent theme of grace and hope—a theme we should never ignore. So, while biblical history must be seen and learned from, the proclamation of God's ever-present love should remain front and center.

For all the persistent sin of the people, God's persistent love was greater. For all the anger of God we see due to the consistent turning away of his own people—God's love was still greater. No matter what they did, God would not leave, abandon, forsake, or ignore their pleas. There was nothing these people could ever have done that would have driven his love away. He most definitely punished, but his love always had the last word. Because however far our sin travels, however deep the destruction our sin creates, God's love supersedes. As I write this, an old hymn (old to me, at least) that I have always loved comes floating into my soul. I think I'll close with the words to the first verse and the refrain/chorus:

> The love of God is greater far
> Than tongue or pen can ever tell;
> It goes beyond the highest star,
> And reaches to the lowest hell;
> The guilty pair, bowed down with care,
> God gave His Son to win;
> His erring child He reconciled,
> And pardoned from his sin.

Refrain:
Oh, love of God, how rich and pure!
How measureless and strong!
It shall forevermore endure—
The saints' and angels' song.

THREE QUESTIONS FOR YOU TO CHEW ON:

1. What in this psalm speaks most poignantly to you? At what point are you drawn in? Why?
2. Is it easy or difficult to place yourself within the different stories of the Bible? Do you see yourself in David, in Moses, in Martha, . . . or Paul, . . . or Chloe? In another biblical character?
3. How can you see the love of God while in the midst of punishment?

A PSALM FOR HELP

Our reading for today begins with Psalm 79.

Much like Psalm 74, this is a psalm that speaks of the Babylonian conquest and the feelings of the psalmist as he looks around at his beloved, but now destroyed city. As we read and see, this psalm is broken up into two distinct sections: a reflection on what he sees and a petition for God to act (with the latter taking most of his attention).

If you were to think about all the things you've held dear and imagine that they were no more, how would you feel? You'd probably feel the same way the psalmist does and find yourself asking God to move, act, and seek vengeance on the people who perpetrated this. Your sacred place of worship has been demolished, your pastors and priests—the very people who've facilitated your worship—have been killed, and everyone you know has been put to shame. To a culture and nation that valued and thrived upon name and reputation, prestige, strength, might, and the ability to strike fear in others—this was an absolute blow (all cultures and nations and people around this time valued namesake). In short, to what extent is life worth living when you are under the rule of others and nobody fears you? What quality of life is left when you can't even worship your God?

The complaints laid out by the psalmist are straightforward: we've been invaded, and your temple and city (*your* home, Lord) have been sacked, the dead bodies of your servants are scattered all around and have become food for the animals, and there is nobody left even to bury the dead. We can't worship God, we can't offer proper burial, and we simply cannot live like this! Everyone around us mocks us, and we bow our heads in shame. How long, Lord?

What's difficult for these people is that everything they hold dear is gone, and God doesn't seem in any way to be acting. How can that be?

"There must have been something we *did—so God, please relent in your anger toward us and pay back these people who destroy all that is yours and profane your name!"*

When I read this text, I can't help but get the feeling that the psalmist is trying to incite God to move, all the while trying to pull on the Lord's heart-strings and remind him of his covenantal promises to his own. They are his people, his *holy* people. This is his sacred temple and place of worship. There are no others who worship him, who have this relationship with him, . . . so God *must* act. Right? Shouldn't he?

It is certainly true that God has a covenant with his people and will not break it—no matter what. That is the grace of the work of God: that no matter what we do or have done, there is nothing that will break the bond or negate the promise he has made. Maybe his people did do something forbidden, maybe they profaned his name one too many times (one time is too many!), and maybe God did allow their city to be sacked and overrun— but trying to incite God to move or act is an interesting way to go about trying to rectify the situation.

And yet, who are we to say they were wrong? This was the way of Job, this was the way of numerous Israelites throughout the ages, and this is a consistent mode of communication that we find in the psalms. The people depended on God, knew that without God they couldn't do anything—and so, when in need, they ask for divine help. Asked in a way they understood, asked in a way that made sense to them, asked in a way they had been taught and through which they had seen God's earlier responses in history, asked in their own way.

I cannot imagine praying to God the way these Israelites did, and yet in my own way I *do* pray this very type of prayer. When I'm hurting and angry, I get this feeling of having been left and tossed aside, and so I play the guilt card in the hope that I will hear God saying, "Yes, Kelly, I love you and have not abandoned you. No, you *are* important to me. No, I have *not* caused this pain in you because you have angered me. Kelly, . . . I just said, 'No, I am not angry with you'—so why are you asking again? Do you not trust me?" Is this prayer wrong? Maybe—or maybe not. Does it reflect my love and hope that God will restore me and effect the solution? Does it declare that I cannot do anything on my own and depend fully on him? Absolutely.

Relationships with God look very different for different people in different life phases and times. We all communicate with God differently— and yet all relationships with God understand one basic, hopeful truth: God is the only restorer. The psalmist understood it, his Israelite brothers and sisters understood it, . . . and you and I understand it, too. The beauty of the psalms is that they allow this truthful and honest relationship with God to develop. That reality may or may not speak to you right now—but that doesn't mean it's less than authentic. This implicit understanding we have simply means that the relationship is real. Maybe we too often find ourselves trying to tell people how they should feel about God and the way they should pray to him. Maybe we need to spend more time encouraging others to simply let it all out and cast it all upon his shoulders—in whatever way that helps them to understand that God has not abandoned them and will work all things out.

THREE QUESTIONS FOR YOU TO CHEW ON:

1. What in this psalm speaks directly to you? At what point are you drawn in? Why?
2. As you read this, where are you? Do you have the freedom to worship God openly and without harm? If you do—what might it look like if you couldn't? How would you feel? If you currently *cannot* worship God openly without fear of harm—how would it feel, and what would it look like, to be given that freedom and openness?
3. When you pray, what are you looking for? A response? An affirmation? Anything at all? If God *were* to clearly respond, would your prayer life change at all?

A REFLECTIVE PSALM OF GOD'S LOVE

The next psalm in our lineup is Psalm 80.

Why do bad things sometimes happen when everything seems to have been going well? How is it that God can show so much favor and give so much hope to a people, only to allow the carpet to be pulled out from under them, to ostensibly remove his hand and pull back his presence? Why is it that we can at times see all that is good and right and then feel as though it is being knocked down and we are being run over and feeling abandoned? Those are the questions and feelings Asaph is working through. Abandonment, destruction, chaos. Why has God allowed this? And where exactly *are* you, God? Nothing new in these questions; we've seen them a lot and asked them a lot ourselves.

As to the time and place that Asaph wrote this, we aren't too sure. Pre-Babylonian exile? Post exile? Commentators are split in their opinions, but, regardless of where we land on what may have been happening, it's abundantly clear that, as Asaph looks around, he sees nothing but destruction—and he's at a loss. Are the Israelites not God's chosen people? Is Israel not the flock of the living God? Why have they been abandoned? Why has the temple been destroyed? Where is their Shepherd?

I love the imagery we get in this psalm—notice that these are images we see throughout Scripture. The vine, being Israel, harkens back (or looks ahead) to Isaiah (5:1–7), Jeremiah (2:21), and Hosea (10:1–2). The glory of the Lord shining on his people gives us a beautiful reminder of God's glorious presence shining upon Moses when he came down the mountain after spending time with God (Exodus 34:29). The saving work of the Lord—well, that appears throughout the whole book of Psalms. Feeding his people—this time not with manna (as he did during those forty years in the desert), but with tears—these are all words and images we've read before, images the Israelites knew then and we know today. All of this imagery Asaph uses was written into the DNA of the Hebrew people. The stories of God from past generations are not only "stories of old" but stories that pointed the people forward and still bring peace today—because they reaffirm who God was and is. The God of old, who provided manna for past generations, will continue to provide food for today and tomorrow. But it was also a "litmus test," as the experiences of the people could be held up against what they knew of God. So, if something bad were happening, they would/could look *back* and know whether or not this was from God. The consistency of God will always remain—and that was and is a comfort.

Maybe it's odd that I love the imagery of the hope that *was* that is now being used as aloe upon the pain that *is*—but I don't know how else to explain it. The hope of God's Old Testament people was built on the God who was and who is and on the promises he gave. He cut his people out from all the other nations and set them apart. He protected them time and time again, not only from demise at the hands of others but from their own hands, too. To a people who lived out of their past, the gruesome present just didn't make sense—and so the only way to cry out in lament was to do so while reflecting on their past. Words of old, stories of old, understandings of God's love were being interwoven with their present pain. But let us not forget that they knew why the destruction had happened. They had been warned time and time again that they needed to remain God's people and to follow him with every fiber of their being. They had been warned time and again how to be in this relationship—warned that if they didn't remain faithful to God, then God would pull back his protection and allow them to fully realize the pain that was out there. God hadn't caused the destruction, but he would provide his protection. The people of Israel had long enjoyed God's love and favor . . . and had taken it for granted. Instead of working on that relationship, following those rules, loving to full capacity—they had turned away from working on the relationship. They had been repeatedly warned but hadn't heeded those warnings. God's warning was to obey and follow him . . . or else succumb to the bitter consequences.

We need to understand the reality not only of their situation but of ours as well. That outside of God there is no life. Outside of God there is only destruction and evil. When we revert back to our selves, we push away from love, goodness, and hope—because love, goodness, and hope come only from God. People are inherently evil due to sin running rampant through our lives. We read throughout Scripture that, due to sin, we cannot do any good on our own (Genesis 6:4; Job 14:4; Isaiah 53:6; John 3:3–5), and thus, left to our own devices, we revert back to sin. It is only by God's work, grace, and love that we can live, love, and be loved. It is only because of God that we can be in a relationship with him and each other.

So, what can we learn from this psalm? When I read Scripture, and particularly the psalms, I look to learn and grow through the experiences of other people in their relationship with God, allowing the authenticity of *their* relationship to come out. But here, in this psalm, I'm reminded of my true nature and of all that God *had* done for his people and *has* now done for his New Testament people through Christ and the Holy Spirit. I'm reminded of what could have happened to us if we had been left to our own devices; there can be no doubt that we would have lived like these Israelites did. Were it not for the work of Christ, that hand of protection, that saving work, we would not have been released from the grip of sin. When I read of the hope Asaph had in God's willingness to rectify his people's situation at the time of the exile, I revel in the reality that, based on the work of Christ, even when *we* turn away, God doesn't. When we turn, God is not caught off guard and isn't trying to turn with us and play catch up. God, knowing all and in his grace, has already turned before us and stands with us face-to-face. We may turn, but when we do we still see the grace of God.

THREE QUESTIONS FOR YOU TO CHEW ON:

1. What in this psalm speaks to you? Where are you drawn? Why?
2. How does knowing that it is only by the love and work of God in our lives that we can have loving relationships change how you see other people and interact with them?
3. Where would *you* be without God? For me that's hard to say, since I always knew him and grew up in the church—but not everyone has that background. What about you?

A PSALM OF
PAST, PRESENT,
AND FUTURE HOPE

Please turn with me to Psalm 81.

One thing that I absolutely appreciate and cherish about the psalms is that they give me insight and a fresh view of God. So often we focus on God in the New Testament and neglect God's movement and his people's responses as seen in the Old Testament. We like the New Testament because it gives us Jesus and his teachings, along with tangible understandings of the kingdom of God. Qualities like love, grace, hope, forgiveness, justice, and compassion. These qualities seem to find their true meaning when seen in the Gospels and the epistles. But if we were to read only the New Testament, we'd lose the history, poetry, and prophetic voice, as seen and read only in the Old Testament. If we were to ignore the Old Testament, we'd lose the *richness* of God's love, the *depth* of God's grace, the *extent* of hope, the *completeness* of God's forgiveness, the *reason* for justice, and the *truth* of compassion. We may *think* these realities come to fruition only in the New Testament, but the truth is that they were all in place before the world began.

What does all of this have to do with Psalm 81? Not a lot, really—and yet quite a bit. If we want to understand a text, we have to understand the people, their relationship with God, their past and present, and their hope to come. Our psalm today is a call to sing of God's love and of his covenant with a people who were cut out by his hand and separated from all others. Our psalm today is a song of historical remembrance, as well as joyful celebration, that draws the reader into understanding the heart of God's people long ago.

If you were of the Jewish tradition, then come September or October you would begin to celebrate the Feast of Tabernacles, a sacred holiday that encouraged you to give thanks to God. It was/is a sacred holiday that encouraged you to remember God's endless bounty at the end of harvest, how he provided for you also while your people were in the wilderness, and how he watched over you in Egypt and delivered you from Pharaoh's hand. Just as God provides for you now (with crops, grains, water, food, shelter, etc.), he provided for you when you had no crops to till, no seeds to plant, and when there was no water in sight. For while your people were in the wilderness, God was there, too. But even before that God was already with you. While you were slaves in Egypt, toiling under the fierce arm of your slave masters—God was there. Always watching, always protecting, always providing.

So, why is this important for us today? Because we wouldn't celebrate the Feast of Tabernacles, would we? We don't—but perhaps we should. We may not be Jewish or have any Hebrew blood in our veins, but these early people of God are still our people, this is still our past, and this is all about the hope and love still given to us by God.

The Feast of Tabernacles is about understanding the work of God and his constant love. This holiday is about proclaiming God's covenantal love, as seen, experienced, and received so long ago. This feast and holiday are about remembering just how dedicated God was, and how undedicated his people have been, . . . and yet throughout the ages God has been providing and continues to provide. We can only sing of that joy, remember his work, and live into those truths today.

Psalm 81 is a song of historical hope that sings of what *was* and is *still* to come, as given by God, seen, and experienced by his people so long ago. But this is also a psalm that encourages readers *today* to not only remember the past and see God's hand through it all but to also sing of the future, as God's hand is still moving, providing, and protecting. While our Jewish brothers and sisters are still waiting for the *messianic* hope to deliver them and usher in God's final authority, we proclaim that he (Jesus Christ) has already come, already saved, already delivered, and even now firmly holds us in the hands of the Father. All the love, grace, hope, forgiveness, justice, and compassion are given, received, and find their fulfillment in Jesus Christ.

So read historical psalms, drink from the well of their past and historical present, all the while giving thanks for God's work through Christ—back then, today, and in the future. Understanding and living into our past allows us to be in hope today and to experience the everlasting hope to come tomorrow.

THREE QUESTIONS FOR YOU TO CHEW ON:

1. What in this psalm speaks to you? To what are you drawn? Why?
2. As you read, and come to know, the Old Testament, how does that knowledge affect you and your walk with God?
3. If you wished to celebrate the constant love of God, what would that look like? Christmas includes presents (just as Christ was a present), and Easter is celebrated with a bunny and colorful eggs (yeah, not sure why; sounds more like a celebration of springtime), but what would a celebration feast of God's constant love look like for you?

A PSALM OF
UNIVERSAL JUDGMENT
AND JUSTICE

Begin your devotional reading today with Psalm 82.

Our psalm today begins and ends with *judgment*. When I think of judgment, I think of a ruler or someone in a position of power who enacts punishments upon those who break laws. As a judge would hand down a judgment (a punishment), so too would a committee or group of people who investigated and handed down their findings. Judgment in our thinking is usually about the handing down of findings and their consequences upon someone. Now this isn't wrong; it is simply what we (or I) understand this word to mean. While this isn't necessarily incorrect in terms of the Hebrew understanding, it isn't fully correct or complete, either. The nuances of meaning for the Hebrew word are more complex than that. And so, in order for us to understand our text, we need to understand the word and the theme that flow throughout the Old Testament Scripture.

The Hebrew word for "judge" (שׁפט) is rich and diverse, and yet extremely focused in its meaning. For Asaph and his readers, to judge meant to hand down punishments (just as we understand the term), but it also entailed defending, leading, guiding, settling disputes, making decisions, and acting as a ruler. To function as a judge or to find judgment was all about doing those things a leader does (this may help us to understand why the book of Judges isn't all about *judging* but includes *leading* and defending God's people). So, when Asaph cries out to God to render judgment (v. 1) and then to judge the earth (v. 8), this was literally a call for God to act, to do the very thing those in positions of authority (the judges) weren't doing.

We see God as the overarching judge (vv. 1 and 8), and then in middle section (vv. 2–7) Asaph calls upon the lower judges to not only judge but to *bring*, show, and enact justice. To do the very things that they should have been doing but have not.

Justice, like judgment, is a very interesting word; the two actually come from the same root (so they are of the same essence). While I won't go into all the ramifications of its nuanced meanings, I do think we all would agree that justice is good. Justice implies that right is happening and that wrong is ending or being curtailed. Justice renders this idea that good is overcoming evil, that wrongs are being addressed, and that all things are being restored to their rightful place and order. *Justice* is a word that pulls on the heartstrings of a man (Asaph) who is tired of seeing the recklessness and abuse all around him.

Asaph isn't calling out for *God* to *act*—he's calling on those human leaders who are responsible to judge to show justice, to act the way they are *supposed* to act and judge the way they are supposed to judge. And if they don't? If they refuse to act justly and render decisions wisely— then the ultimate Judge will do so *upon them*. Judges are supposed to be people who seek the heart of God. Who are morally above reproach; who don't take bribes; who defend the meek and broken; who don't side with the wicked; who come alongside and lift up the fatherless, the poor, and the oppressed. Being a judge in the ideal sense of the term means that one is functioning as a true, effective, and good leader in every sense; such a leader can show justice only if he, himself, is good and true. Think of this psalm as a challenge and encouragement to current judges, magistrates, leaders, kings, and all others in authority to hold true to their duty and calling.

Let's take a step back further and wider and draw you and me into the conversation (finding our own context today). Who are our judges? They include pastors, community leaders, mayors, elected officials (governors, senators, presidents, etc.). And we could easily add more to this list. Asaph would argue, as would both the Jewish and the Christian believer, that *all* leaders should lead from a place of godliness. It's not about you, it's not about your desires, it's not about what you want or don't want—it's simply about leading from a place of following God. *Your* actions must be reflective of God's heart. *Your* role as a leader in the community must be about making sure those who need help are helped, those who are hungry are fed, and those who need hope are given it. It's not about pandering to those who will give the most support to you, the community, or the church.

And it's not about doing what those who donate more money or more of anything else want, either. It must simply be about being God's hands and feet, his voice and heart, to those who need it.

Does this mean we are *not* to consider others—those outside those groups with specific and special needs? Do we ignore those who *are* fed and who don't need shelter because they already have it? Not at all, . . . but Christ's mission was to help the very people who needed it most but couldn't get it—and part of his commission to his disciples and followers was to do likewise. To show love and give hope to those who have been cast aside. Judgment and justice are about righting the wrongs that society has created, restoring that which sin has destroyed, and mending broken relationships. They are about ushering in peace and hope to a hopeless person and society.

And guess what: *you* are a bringer of that kind of shalom as well. You may not be a "judge" in the literal sense of the word, but you can hold judges accountable. You may not be a leader of an organized group of people, but you *are* a leader. And while *you* are held accountable as a Christian, you too should hold others accountable—even when they aren't Christians— because it's not about being a Christian or a Jew. I would argue that all religions have this sense of helping others. And ultimately, while God is the final Judge who will bring his justice once and for all—you and I have the difficult and yet hopeful job of being bringers of God's justice (both in mercy and in correction) in our day.

THREE QUESTIONS FOR YOU TO CHEW ON:

1. What in this psalm speaks to you? At what point are you drawn in? Why?
2. How are you using your voice for good?
3. What are the justice needs in your community right now? How can you speak into them?

A PSALM OF
ACTION IN THE MIDST
OF EVIL

Open your Bible with me to Psalm 83.

As I read through this psalm, I'm struck by the long list of nations allied against the psalmist (vv. 5–11). Seven verses delineate nation after nation that the psalmist sees conspiring against him, but then we read of a whole host of *other* nations that have conspired at one time but endured the wrath of God as he defended his people. To me, this type of psalm is one of the hardest to read, because while such psalms come from a place where war and battles were a matter of survival, it's still really hard for me to read a text—a *biblical* text—that seeks or rejoices in the destruction of a people (even if they were not God's chosen people).

Scripture is hard to read when we not only don't like what we read but also lack the context to understand it. Psalm 83 is one of those psalms about which, even if scholars don't fully agree on the context, all can agree in terms of the way of life back then.

Life was certainly hard in ancient Israel. From the long list of enemies that the psalmist enumerates, we are reminded that the principle of survival meant kill or be killed, fight or be taken over. You either defended, proactively attacked, and killed people, or all those things would happen to you—if you didn't take the offensive, there would be no "you" any longer. Not only would there be no you, but there would be no more of your friends and family, relatives, neighbors, or nation as a whole. But the psalmist isn't only lamenting and entreating God to destroy the nations around—he is doing so from a paradigm of chaos and war. These Old Testament warriors were not like me, sitting at this moment in my office peacefully watching the snow fall—they found themselves in the midst of war and contemplating possible future destruction. *More* destruction . . .

The reality is that, just because I don't "get it" doesn't mean this didn't, and doesn't, happen. There are a lot of wars going on between nations in our world today, and I don't get those, either. But simply because I don't get it doesn't make these conflicts less destructive or real. I'm looking at the headlines here in my office and am overwhelmed by all the violence, hate, anger, and injustice that affect every country around the world. Each and every day we seem to discriminate more, hate more, and love less. And this is just scratching the surface. We hate to admit this, but people are intrinsically evil, mean, and self-serving. As much as we would like to think that all people are naturally "good," that's simply not true. Reading psalms like this, or a few chapters from Lamentations, reminds us of just how bad things were and are. Looking at our world and how hateful it is today, *coupled with* what things were like back in ancient Israel and later on throughout humanity's often bleak history, is a good reminder of just how *necessary God is*.

So, what is one to do? Well, if you're a believer like me, you turn to the only source of resolution you can: God. Asaph, as he looks around at all this hate, anger, and animosity, reaches out to God with a plea for him to speak, act, and respond, . . . because the psalmist realizes that's all he *can* do. God must act and respond. God must defend his goodness and stamp out evil and its wicked works.

This, for me, provokes some really good questions:

- How often am I praying to God to speak, act, and respond to the hatred, animosity, and killings in this world?
- Do I turn a blind eye to the reality of war, famine, and the massive refugee crisis the world is experiencing? I acknowledge these evils—but do I daily pray for hope? It's a daily reality for the people directly affected. Why not for me?
- How often do we feel as though the only response is more war?
- How often do we feel that the only way to deal with anger, hatred, and death is to show just how powerful *we* are?

Maybe I'm going off on a tangent here, but I can't help but wonder whether we're absolutely missing what people really need—and that is God. Part of that reflection, part of that conversation has to entail more love from you and me. I say that because, while we believe that God is full of love and hope and grace and that it is only by his hand that war, death, famine, and destruction will end, he says that you and I are to *be conduits of hope* for others. So, while we embrace the reality, as Asaph does in verse 18, that God is the Most High over all the earth and that when Christ comes again he will stomp out all evil, war, hatred, famine, and anger and usher in love, peace, hope, and comfort, until that day comes we, you and I, are to be bringers of love, peace, hope, and comfort. We are to live into the reality of the realms of heaven and the New Earth *today*.

While we may not be able to stop the wars, the injustices, or the killings, fully understanding that those are things that only God can do, I think we *can* do a few things. Here's my short list (in no particular order):

1. Pray for, and seek, peace. (Hebrews 12:14)
2. Give love. (John 13:34; 1 Corinthians 16:14)
3. Bring hope. (1 Thessalonians 5:11)
4. Serve others. (Philippians 2:4)
5. Share Christ. (Matthew 28:19; Mark 13:10; Acts 1:8)
6. Do not be ignorant—evil is real. (1 John 5:19)

This list is not exhaustive, nor will doing these things stop wars and make all people happy. Only God can do those things, and we believe he will after Christ's return, . . . but we aren't simply supposed to stand still and look to the heavens, waiting for that day. Let's get on it. Let's *be* the people of Christ to a world in pain.

THREE QUESTIONS FOR YOU TO CHEW ON:

1. What in this psalm speaks to you? What draws you in? Why?
2. When you read the headlines today, what is your reaction to all the harm? Do you shake your head? Do you respond with, "Glad that's over there and not here!" Or are you moved to act?
3. In your own locality, how can you be a bringer of God's love and grace? How can you use your hands locally to help usher in hope and peace?

A PSALM OF ANTICIPATORY, JOYFUL WORSHIP

Take a few moments to read with me the words of Psalm 84.

Our psalm today is considered a companion to Psalms 82 and 83; these three psalms reflect a desire to worship God in his place and space. And yet all three psalms are uniquely different in their "worshipness" (again, one of my own "coined" words) and focus.

We don't know the author of our psalm today, but we get a vision of it being sung as the people are traveling *to* God's holy temple. As they journey along the path, they encounter sights and sounds that inspire their hope and continuously build upon it. I picture them walking down this path and seeing a sparrow and a swallow in their nests and being filled with the joy and hope of what "home" means. It's a place of rest, security, joy, comfort, and peace.

And as they see these birds in their homes, they are drawn to find an analogy in the house of God. The birds become a tether for the people to the priests and all others who minister in the temple rooms of God's house. "How glorious would it be to be in the presence of the living God day and night? How glorious would it be to have a home with God in his place? Oh, how I long for that!"

The psalmist goes on to say that, while that may not be the case, for they may not dwell there, they will spend one single day there (v. 10). And one day in the temple courts is better than thousands elsewhere. One single day in the presence of God is better than countless days never getting to be near him. "If my job were to be as lowly as that of opening and closing the doors for others as they came to God, I would choose that. Whatever the job, whatever the duty assigned in the temple of the living God, I would be happy and fulfilled." Why? Because God is the sun and the shield, the giver of life and love. He is the protector, guard, and bestower of all good things.

I'm struck by this reflection on worship and the joy found therein. To the pilgriming author, the understanding of worship is simply being in the presence of God. To be in the temple, to be in the space where God lives, is to worship him. But it's more a joy, because the psalmist is also yearning for it and consumed by his anticipation. We read in verse 2 that his soul "faints" to be in the worship and the presence of God! Can you sense the anticipation? The hope and joy? Have you ever felt that longing for worship? When Sunday morning comes and you are on your way to church, do you feel as though this is the happiest day of your life? Probably not. And I say that because I'm there as well. I love church, but my heart doesn't faint with anticipation as I travel there.

I'm challenged by one author's words that "the greater God is in our eyes, the greater will be our desire to worship him."[4] It's an understanding that our worship of God is tethered to our view of him. If God is your everything, then worship becomes your everything, too, and it's hard to argue against it. What's difficult is that I know too many people who proclaim that God is everything and yet do not make church a priority in their lives.

> Read the Bible?
> Pray daily?
> Go to church on Christmas and Easter
>   (we call them "Chreaster" Christians)?
> Go to church on Sundays? Uhhh . . . as in *weekly*?

Think about this: if the Church is the Bride of Christ—the one he died for—how can we not yearn to be with her in our worship of him? It is in this very house of worship that we are fed, nourished, and sent forth in the grace and glory of God. It is in this very house of worship that we are met head-on with the truth of kingdom living. It is in this very house of God that we are gathered, challenged, fed, poured into, and equipped to be the hands and feet of our Lord and Savior.

---

4   Ellsworth, Roger. *Opening up Psalms*. Leominster: Day One Publications, 2006. Print. Opening Up Commentary.

You and I need to imitate the psalmist and re-find the joy of worship. What's striking is that we aren't even reading about the joy of actually *being* there! This is all in the journey and anticipation of what will come! I can't imagine what's going to happen to these pilgrims when they actually *enter* the temple! I picture Agnes from *Despicable Me* getting that giant stuffed unicorn at the fair and screaming with delight, "*It's so fluffy!!*" That should be our response to entering church (minus the "fluffy" part)! Our hearts should burst with emotion, our voices should scream in delight, and we should be consumed in pure, radiating joy at where we are and what we get to do! I'm sitting on a plane as I write this, and I want to go to church! *Right now!*

Be challenged by our psalmist's joy. Draw upon his hope and anticipation of worship and church, and live into it in your own life. If you find that you're checking off all those "good Christian" things but not going to church, . . . then *go to church!* If you find that you are not finding joy in the anticipation of church, then I challenge you to look deep down inside and ask why? What is it that is holding you back from this joyful anticipation? What is holding you back from a near-fainting heart that yearns to worship God with your brothers and sisters? Because I guarantee you that it's not church that is holding you back from these joyous feelings—it's you.

THREE QUESTIONS FOR YOU TO CHEW ON:

1. Do you ever look at worship in the same way the psalmist does here? If not, why not?
2. How does attending church feel for you? Are you excited to go, or does it feel like work (a duty) to you?
3. How great is God in your eyes? Does that compel you to worship him differently than you otherwise might?

A PSALM OF
GOD'S UNFAILING LOVE

B egin your reading today with Psalm 85.

This psalm, as is the case with all of them, is a reflection on life. Understanding who and where you are; where God is in the midst of it all; and what you proclaim, and know, that he will do.

Whose life is perfect? Who has no problems, no issues, no rough patches, no questions about how "good" and faithful a worshiper they are—or are you following as faithfully as you could? Who here feels that they are somewhere along Lollipop Lane, where candy mountains and chocolate fountains are all of life? Many of us are not only dealing with problems now but have been for years. Many of us have given up on asking *"When will it end?"* and have resigned ourselves to saying, *"Just give me the strength for today."* Well, this psalm is for you.

This psalm was written by someone who was in the midst of life. And they've written it in three stanzas, or sections. The first three verses speak of the past—what the psalmist knows of the Lord through experiences, but also through oral traditions that have been passed down from generation to generation. Stories of God's past works and goodness. We see how the Lord showed favor, which means that he demonstrated grace and mercy; we read how the psalmist knows that the Lord forgave his people of long ago and covered their sins and how he knows that any anger God has had at any point he now sets aside. Then verses 4–7 delineate the pains that are now present due to the sins that have been committed. These verses cry out the psalmist's pleas, his needs, his understandings of his present condition and of how and why he got there. Finally, verses 8–13 come full circle *back* to who God was and is. It's verses 1–3 over again, but even stronger. It's the understanding of the *past* that becomes the present and the future. *Because* God was and is love and faithfulness and righteousness, he shows favor to his people and restores them. *Because* of his faithfulness, his people's sins will always be covered and his wrath *will always* be set aside.

As I read this text, I'm drawn to the middle four verses (vv. 4–7). These verses are about a need to be restored *now*. They are pleas to God to restore and return favor . . . now and not later. What's interesting is that there is this back and forth with the author—almost as though he is pulling on different emotional strings. "Restore us" and "put away your displeasure" are matched with "God our Savior." Verses 5 and 6 speak from an understanding that God is angry over something the psalmist has done, but in the same breath the psalmist requests revival from him, so that he can rejoice once again. The question that struck me is *Why?* Why would anyone want a relationship with someone who has all this power? The power to hurt and harm you, to knock you down and *keep* you down, whose anger can last forever and affect people not only now but in future generations as well.

This is the God many people see. A God who appears to be angry every single day. A God who could very easily snap you in half if he wanted to. A God whose anger appears to last from Genesis onward, finally relenting in Matthew but then hitting hard once again in Revelation. A God who, when he doesn't get his way, sends plagues, kills women and children, and even orders his followers to do the same. This doesn't sound like the loving, compassionate, kind-hearted God whom Christians worship! This doesn't sound like a God who is slow to anger, who teaches about loving and serving one another. This doesn't sound *anything* like what is preached. So, either this God doesn't exist and the God of the Bible is simply made up, or God has somehow changed and gone from mean and angry to loving and kind.

Our answer, of course, is in the text. This answer appears not only in verses 1–3 and 8–13 but also in those four verses in the middle. The psalmist knows, understands, and declares that God's anger does not come because he is hateful and murderous or because he's on some power trip. What the psalmist does declare is that God covers sin. And not just the psalmist's sin, but ours, too. The reason for God's anger and disappointment is sin, but God doesn't stay angry and stew in our sin—he does something about it. He actually covers that sin so that we are forgiven. You, and I, even though we as Christians are no longer *prone to* sin (Galatians 2:20)—find ourselves *in* it every day. And God comes in and covers us and atones for it. He restores us and makes us right again. He revives us, as the psalmist says in verse 6. He puts breath back into our lungs. If you've ever seen someone performing CPR, either by chest compressions, via mouth to mouth, or when they actually have to physically pump the heart, . . . that is what God does! He gives us *back* life. Verse 7 says that his love is "unfailing"—so, even when he is sad and disappointed in how we've acted and treated him and others, his love does not cease—it does not fail.

I asked the *Why?* question earlier. *Why* would anyone want to be in a relationship with someone who is like that? We, just like the psalmist, understand that what God has done has always been in response to what we have done—but his actions have always come from a place of love. God *is* love. Everything he has ever done is because of his love. Then and now. Love is our framework, love is what we receive, love is what he has given to us, . . . and what he asks of us. Toward him and each other. Above all other things, though, the greatest is *his* love to us. Psalm 85 is a psalm of love and a response by God to his people who fail at love.

THREE QUESTIONS FOR YOU TO CHEW ON:

1. What in this psalm speaks to you? Where do you find yourself drawn in? Why?
2. Are we drawn to relationships in which there is equal power/control or to ones in which the scale is tipped in your direction? Why is that so?
3. When it comes to parental (or church) discipline, which is ideally motivated by love and administered in the hope of reconciliation, why can love too easily look like anger when seen through the eyes of the one on the receiving end?

A CHAOTIC PSALM OF PRAYER TO GOD

Open your Bible and turn with me to Psalm 86.

As we read this psalm, it may appear to be one of randomness. Most psalms are very focused in their petition. If the psalmist is in need because he is hurting, then all his words focus around the pain and the need of the salve from God. If he is in hiding and fear that he may die because his foes are closing in, then the prayer to God is for him to drive them away, keep him hidden, and be his comfort in this time of need. But this one? This one is scattered with needs.

- Petition to guard my life (v. 2)
- Have mercy on me (v. 3)
- Bring me joy (v. 4)
- Bring forgiveness (v. 5)
- Back to mercy (v. 6)
- In need of saving (v. 7)
- I need teaching (v. 11)
- Back to mercy (v. 16)
- Back to saving (v. 16)
- Show me where you are (v. 17)
- Put my enemies to shame (v. 17)
- Comfort me (v. 17)

And then, in the midst of all this, we have verse 14 that seems *extremely* out of place. But that's not all, because we also have two random verses that proclaim the goodness and saving work of God. So, in 17 verses the psalmist appears to be trying to hit all the possibilities and needs one could have in life.

Psalm 86 is one of those psalms on which we don't have much information. We can assume, based on the subscript, that this is a psalm of David, but that's about where we end. We don't know where he is, what he is doing, or where he is going. We know that he's in need of God (from the sounds of it, he has *many* needs), but that's where our information ends. As I read this psalm and see how scattered his prayer is, I cannot help but get this image that David is overwhelmed with all that is happening. In response to that overwhelmedness (yup, *my* "word" again), he throws it all up in the air in a gesture of hope and shouts out, "There! Take all of these, God!"

Can any of us relate to David here? I'm sure many of us have felt so overwhelmed by our needs that our prayer to God began to feel like a grocery list scattered here or there with a praise. If you were to sit and reflect about all the things you do and need each day, you'd realize that God has in fact given us a very balanced life system. But what happens if it gets unbalanced? What happens if a foundational beam in our life gets yanked out from under the structure or something gets even slightly unbalanced? The whole edifice comes crashing down. It's now not just one thing we need from God—it's many. Now we are completely overwhelmed. And in desperation, we toss it all up into the air and plead for God to respond, restack, rebalance, and restore. Life is like the game Jenga at times. But instead of trying to remove pieces for fun, we're trying to keep it all stacked while riding alongside it on a rollercoaster, . . . blindfolded.

As is the case with many psalms, at least for me, I'm drawn to how the writer chooses to close out his prayer and petition. We have, in verse 17, David proclaiming that God has helped him and comforted him. Is this a declaration that God has helped him *in the past*? Or is it a proclamation that God has already helped, even though he has just lifted up his prayer and listed his needs? Or might this even reflect a moment of hopeful waiting? Yes. Absolutely *yes* to all three. David prays to God because he knows God and has a history with him. He knows that his prayers have been heard because God has been faithful all throughout his life. But he also knows that because God is who he is, his needs in this chaotic prayer of petition have already been heard. The peace, for David, is in the knowledge of who God is and what he does. That, in desperate times of need, even before a resolution is presented, is a very real form of peace.

The comfort, for David (as well as for you and me), is that, even in our messy lives, even in the balancing act of each day with all our needs and actions, we may stumble and fall—but God does not. While we cannot save ourselves or reassemble the intricate pieces of each day, God can, does, and has.

THREE QUESTIONS FOR YOU TO CHEW ON:

1. What in this psalm speaks to you? At what point are you drawn in? Why?
2. Is there another game, besides Jenga, that can serve as a good example of life?
3. Does God ask us to hold it all together? To keep the game pieces from toppling over? If he doesn't, then why do we continue to try?

A PSALM OF
GOD'S WIDE EMBRACE

et's begin today by reading Psalm 87.
Our psalm today is short and somewhat obscure, but most commentators harken back to psalm 86:9 in that someday *all* the nations will worship the Lord. When we read in verse 4 that God will one day "record Rahab and _____" (Rahab in this context is not the woman but the nation of Egypt), this means that the inhabitants of these lands will be listed on God's "register" (v. 6) as people who recognize him as the Lord. This is the hope we all have and the mission of the church, as well as the message of evangelism. And yet how much of this do we actually ingest?

How many times don't we witness a believer proclaiming that the reign of God is over all people, . . . and then observe that same person discriminate, hate, and spew vitriol about other people, nations, and cultures? How often don't we see and read the truth in the Word of God and yet put caveats on that same truth when speaking to others? Since this psalm speaks of other nations, how often do we close *our doors* to people of other beliefs because they believe differently? Does this psalm not declare that all people will be on God's register and under his name? Did Christ not come to open God's covenant to you and me and the rest of the Gentiles, the non-Jews? Was not the Great Commission to be proclaimed to all nations, all people, and all corners of the earth? Will not the New Jerusalem (New Earth) that comes down from heaven have its gates open for all people? How often do we allow hate, anger, fear, and self-preservation to dictate *whom* it is we will love? And how often do we allow what *we* feel about people to trump God's proclamation that all will stand before *him* (not before us)?

Maybe we should keep it even simpler: When we think of others, are our thoughts God's thoughts? Are the hopes we have the hopes of God? Does our love match God's love? If we answer "no" to any of those questions, then we need to spend a little more time with Scripture. If we answer "no" to any one of them, than we will be in for a huge surprise. While nobody expects you or me to be God or to have his complete and full heart toward others, we are called to still try.

Maybe this will help. The Lord declares that he will "register" and "record" those other tribes (Rahab, Babylon, Philistia, Tyre, and Cush). Who were they? They were the enemies of the Israelites. Rahab, once again, is synonymous with Egypt. Babylon? Philistia? Tyre? Cush? All enemies against whom the Israelites consistently battled—and to whom they lost loved ones. What does the psalmist declare? That even these enemies will speak of the splendor of God. That even these non-covenantal people will be with God, enjoy his presence, and drink in his love.

We need to remember that God's love is bigger than ourselves and that God declares in one simple breath that all things are his. *His* world, his creation, his work, his grace, and his redemption by his Son. You and I need to move past any and all issues we may have with other people and embrace the simple hope of Christ. Embrace the simple love of God. Drink in the covenant of the blood of Christ that was poured out for all who declare his name. Oh, and remember: it's not about you—it's about God. It's about God's story of redemption, God's story of love, God's story of Christ and his opening the gates and inviting people in. The beauty of the New Jerusalem is that we will rejoice with people of all nations, tribes, tongues, colors, and cultures.

THREE QUESTIONS FOR YOU TO CHEW ON:

1. What in this psalm speaks to you? Where are you drawn? Why?
2. Why is it often harder to push our enemies out of the way of God's grace than it is to sit with the fact that his grace is bigger than ourselves?
3. How does remembering God's "wide embrace" help us in our daily lives? How does it help us in our daily walk with our neighbors, fellow students, or people within the community?

AN HONEST PSALM OF DESPAIR

Let's begin by reading together Psalm 88.

Psalm 88 is a gut-wrenching prayer of anguish. No wonder it's considered the saddest of all the psalms! The psalmist, Heman the Ezrahite, from the looks of it doesn't offer up any hope of God restoring him. It doesn't appear that he will sing of God's hand relenting from the pain and suffering he is inflicting on him. Never once does he find peace and comfort, for in his eyes there *is* no peace or comfort! His whole life has been full of suffering, terror, and the wrath of God. As you read this psalm, you're hit with just how sad this man is. He's had friends but feels as though God has taken them away and turned them against him. He calls out to God all day long with outspread arms and hands—but nothing happens. It is in this feeling of forsakenness, this depth of despair and grief, that he begins to wonder:

- God, is your love in the grave? (v. 11)
- Is your faithfulness destruction? (v. 11)
- Do you work in the darkness of evil? (v. 12)
- What have I done to be rejected by you? (v. 14)
- What have I done to deserve your wrath? (v. 16)

Psalms like this are really hard to navigate through. On the one hand, we simply don't know anything about Heman (we see his name mentioned only in 1 Kings 4:31), except that he was wise and obviously in a lot of pain and anguish. We could try to assume things, but that gets us nowhere. All we know is that this psalm is personal and full of anguish—painful even to read (at least for me). I have never felt abandoned or forsaken or so lonely and full of grief that I tossed it all up at God and blamed him. I have never been in a dark place where all of my being cried out in lament to God over where I was and what was happening to me. As we read this psalm, our thoughts may harken back to Job, as Job and Heman the Ezrahite were in the same kind of space. They are afflicted, tormented, . . . and they blame God. Maybe God *is* to blame . . . or maybe he isn't. But is it fair or right for us to try to correct Heman?

There are two things I think we need to see when we read texts like this. First, and I've said this a few times already, we need to allow any writer to be himself (or herself, depending on the writer). If she is feeling as though God has forsaken and abandoned her, then we need to allow her words and perspective to stand. I am not Heman the Ezrahite, so no matter how much I want to yell and shout that God doesn't forsake, God doesn't abandon, God's wonders are not in the darkness, he doesn't consign us to the grave, and his faithfulness does not end in destruction, it's not my place to say this. This is Heman's psalm—not Kelly's. We must allow the writer to voice his authentic lament to God.

This leads into the second point: *because* this is Heman's lament, we need to observe what he says and pick up on his cues. What I mean is that, for all the despair and grief we read here, there is also hope. We read in verse 1 that he calls out to God as his "salvation" and his hope. He knows that God is his hope, that God is his salvation, and that his prayer will come to God and be before him. So, for all the pain and anguish, for all the despair and grief, for all the loneliness and questioning as to why this all is happening to him, he still declares that God can save. He still cries out *to* God. God *is* the One who saves him. Listen to verse 1: "God of my *salvation*." This is an active, hopeful word. Which means that the psalmist trusts in what God is ultimately doing and hopes for that salvation to one day fall upon him.

Oftentimes our present condition (afflictions included) weighs heavy upon our hearts, seeming to consume every ounce of us. This is especially so when physical, mental, and spiritual strains are present in our lives. We don't know what's going on or why. We don't know what God is doing, and all we can think about is this moment, this pain, these feelings. What's interesting is that we oftentimes blame God or cry out to God in wonder as to why he is allowing this to happen to us—and yet it is in that same space that we know that God saves us. I'm not going to belittle what Heman was going through because I cannot empathize or sympathize with him. I'm sure there are people who are reading this who can understand his space of anger, grief, lament, pain, and suffering, . . . but I can't. What I can do, though, is wholeheartedly agree that these feelings are real (I've talked to enough people in this space to know that it is a reality for some), and I can wholeheartedly agree that it is God who saves. So, while I cannot feel what he feels, I can agree with him.

The peace of our relationship with God is that, while we know we can be as authentic in our relationship with him as we need to be, we also know that, regardless of where we are, our salvation is held firmly in *his* hands. "Saving" doesn't happen because we deserve it; it happens because we need it. Saving doesn't come upon us only when we say nice words or gaze dreamily to the heavens and always have a smile for God. We don't have to painfully smile through our suffering, hold back our tears, or push aside our anguish and questioning of God and his work. Our relationship with God, our prayers to God, can be all over the place, . . . and even should be. We can be angry, we can be hopeful, we can be joyful, and we can question what he's doing. Regardless of the place we are in or the season of our emotions—God listens to our needs and responds.

Why God does what he does and allows what he allows, . . . those questions will be answered in his own time. But until then we take comfort in knowing that, no matter where we are or what we are going through, we can share those feelings with God—that he in fact *welcomes* them. Psalm 88 is a beautiful reminder for you and me to be authentic with God in how we feel and our expressions of what we need. It's called a relationship for a reason.

THREE QUESTIONS FOR YOU TO CHEW ON:

1. What is there in this psalm that speaks to you? Where are you drawn in? Why?
2. How does it make you feel that the psalmist ends on such a somber note? Do you want to finish his prayer on a high note, or are you okay with what you read?
3. If we affirm that God knows all, why is it that we try to hide our true feelings from him—as though he could be offended or harmed by our expressions of pain?

A COVENANTAL PSALM OF COMPLAINT

Please read with me Psalm 89.

Psalm 89 caps off the group of psalms that fall under Book 3. These psalms have covered a wide spectrum of feelings from authors who encourage us to stand in awe before the presence of God. And this last one in this section is no different.

At first glance, we may notice one word that we see repeatedly in the psalm: *covenant* (four times, to be exact). As we go through this psalm, we see this constant ping-ponging between hope and action: God's keeping the covenant and his people breaking it. But what is *really* interesting for me is that, while the psalmist declares God's goodness in keeping his covenant, while he declares that people are horrible at keeping *their* end of it, and while he cries out to God to remember them and hold to said covenant, . . . that's not enough. He wants *God to act—now!*

We don't know much about what was going on when Ethan the Ezrahite wrote this. Suggestions have been made that the people may have been in the midst of some military defeat, that they were in exile, or maybe that the psalmist was simply reflecting on all that he had seen and heard. But regardless of where he's been, there is this sense that he is not where he *wants* to be. I appreciate the observation of one author, H. D. M. Spence, that at first sight it appears that this is a psalm of praise, but in reality it is one of complaint. The psalmist praises God consistently for his love and the covenant he has made with David, but he seemingly does so as a way to encourage God to restore his people. Then again, he's not exactly *encouraging* God (at least he isn't approaching God in an encouraging tone); he truly is complaining and demanding:

- "God, you have done all these things, said you would do all these other things and never waver [vv. 19–37], but now you reject us? Now you spurn us? Now you are angry with the very one you established your covenant with? Why, God? Why is our crown in the dust? Why are our walls crumbled and our homes plundered? Why have we become a laughingstock to our neighbors and foes? [vv. 38–45]."
- "How long will you abandon us, forsake us, ignore us, hide from us, and pour out your wrath upon us? When will your love return, life come back, and faithfulness to the house of David be restored? [vv. 46–52]."

As with many of the psalms of complaint, as well as in all our lives, we frequently find ourselves caught up in where we are while wanting to be somewhere else. But what we often fail to realize is that so often our current place is where we are because of what *we* have done. The psalmist cries out and complains to God because of his surroundings, . . . and yet where is his apology for the sins he has committed against God and others? Where is the self-reflection? The repentance? Where is the remembrance not only of God's covenant (which he is quick to point out) but of the *people's* holding to their end of it? Where is the reflection on their *failing* to keep said covenant? Where is the request for God's love to return *and for* the people's promise to do better, be better, and act better? Where is the seeking of forgiveness?

The reality is that it is much easier to complain than it is to self-reflect and make any necessary changes in our life. It is much easier to ask God to move mountains than for me to take one small step in the right direction. It's less painful for me to declare the love and forgiveness of God than it is to take personal accountability for my sins. I'm really good at deflecting and pointing fingers at others—but not so good at looking in the mirror. But this isn't a psalm about the psalmist or about me; this is a psalm about a covenantal God.

Six times we read the word "love" in this psalm (vv. 1–2, 14, 24, 28, 33, 49), and five times we read about God's faithfulness (vv. 1–2, 5, 8, 33, 49). While the psalmist uses those terms in an attempt to motivate God to move, he does so because he knows these words are fitting and true of God. While I may not agree with his method, I 100% agree with the truthfulness of what he says.

The reason the psalmist can complain, the reason he has the voice to speak, the reason he isn't completely taken over (along with the rest of the people) is precisely the fact that God is faithful and loving and holds to his eternal covenant. And the reality for you and me is that we know how this story, this lament, this complaint will end: in the coming of Jesus Christ. It doesn't end because God remembers his Davidic Covenant; it ends because he offers a new, wider and better, *eternal* covenant for his people. One in which we don't need to worry about a fleeting life (v. 47) or escaping the grave (v. 48) . . . because we have died and been raised to life with Christ (Romans 6:4).

I do think that this psalm does a wonderful job of reminding us of God's covenant, but I also think we have something to learn from the lack of self-reflection that is going on here. We should never be complacent about being held accountable when we don't love and serve others. We should never blame God for where we are, when, oftentimes, it's our own choices that put us there. So, yes, hold to the love, forgiveness, and mercy of God, but do some self-reflecting as well. I suspect that all of our lives could be slightly easier if we were only to spend a little more time reflecting and a lot less time blaming.

THREE QUESTIONS FOR YOU TO CHEW ON:

1. What in this psalm hits home for you? Where are you drawn? Why?
2. Why is it easier to point fingers and blame others than to look within and maybe find our own faults (think of Jesus's words from Matthew 7:5 to the effect that we need to see and address the plank in our own eye before looking at the speck in other people's)?
3. How can we look at where we are, even when it's not where we want to be, and find the truth that this may just be where we *need* to be?

A PSALM OF PUNISHMENT AND HOPE

Open your Bible with me and turn to Psalm 90.

Psalms 90 to 106 are considered the "numbers psalms," in that they speak of the kingdom of Israel in relation to her neighbors. Hopefully, one theme you'll see throughout these 17 psalms is that of the blessings of God *toward* his people—as well as his steadfastness and faithfulness.

The common belief is that this psalm, as the subscript says in our Bibles, is a prayer of Moses. If that is the case, this is the oldest psalm in the psalter. As we read this text, we get the feeling that something is going on between God and his people that is causing them pain. While there is praise for just how mighty God is, just how far above all things, there is also the reality that this truth doesn't sit well with Moses. In numerous instances we see a reference to God being above time; thus, seventy years of a human life are really nothing in comparison to God's "time" (or lack thereof, time being a construct he established for our benefit). So, where does that leave us? Enter Canaan (Numbers 13–14). Scratch that. Go way *back* to the desert.

This psalm, this prayer, this reflection by Moses is in response to the failure of God's chosen people to enter the promised land the first time they had an opportunity to do so (after the exodus from Egypt). *Because* they did not obey, because they feared the people instead of God, because they doubted the strength God was giving to them (and then doubting God himself), they were being punished. Wanderings in the desert, reflections on the frailty of life and the hope of one day seeing that promised land— are all but pipe dreams to most of them. Now, because of their blatant disobedience (all except for Caleb, that is), they deal with the punishment handed down by God.

I don't think any of us ever likes to be punished. For me as a kid, *the worst* punishment was to be sent to my room. Endless hours of sitting there and having to be by myself—the *worst*. I recall even asking to be spanked just so I wouldn't have to play by myself (it may sound weird to desire corporal punishment over solitary confinement, but I think I'd take that to this day). It wasn't fair, either, because my sister would get punished and be sent to her room, and she'd thrive! Playing with her toys and using her imagination was something she was good at. I was good at that, too—but only when it involved other people playing with me (in full disclosure, I can recall only a handful of times my sister was sent to her room because she had done something bad. In most cases it was me who had done something, or at least it felt that way because the solitude was excruciating, . . . and, apparently, scarring!).

I don't know what it is about being punished—but whatever it is, in that moment the world seems to stop. *Anything* is better than that moment. Maybe it was the reflections that took place about what had put me there. Maybe it was the swimming in my own sadness or certainty that the punishment didn't fit the crime. There was definitely the feeling that this punishment would never end.

Moses realizes the mistake the people have made: they didn't trust God. God told them what to do and where to go. He constantly watched over them, fought for them, encouraged and protected them, . . . right up until this moment, and yet they got scared and took their eyes off God and placed them on the very large and intimidating people who were already in the territory. Instead of listening, focusing, and following the Almighty, they flat-out disobeyed, disrespected, rebelled, and ignored him. So, here they sit, in their room, by themselves, wanting God to take it all away. "Come, tell me I can leave my room and go play with my friends! Spank me so this punishment will be over—*please!* I've been in here *forever*, thinking about what I've done, . . . and I'm sorry."

We know how this story plays out because we have the whole rest of the Bible at our fingertips. We know that, while God *is* above time and space, and our lifetime is but a breath of a breath in his, he does relent of his anger. The people wander for a while and then find rest. They disobey lots of other times, too, but God never is what Moses feels God is in this moment. Numerous times in this text we get the sense that Moses feels that God is *very* angry. That he yells out, "Return to dust, you mortals!" (v. 3) and that then his anger consumes and brings terror upon the people (v. 7). While these are realities (we do return to dust and should legitimately be terrified of God's anger), never does God allow those things to get the best of us. We know this because, again, *we know the story and have the rest of the Bible at our fingertips!* God's love doesn't relent. God's forgiveness never wanes. While it's true that God is outside of our time, he steps *into* our time. Both Jesus Christ and the Holy Spirit step into our time and bring peace, love, harmony, joy, hope, and life. While it's true that our days may come to "seventy years, or eighty, if our strength endures," because of God's love, because of God's covenant, because of his redeeming our sinful lives, our story doesn't end there. Yes, we toil and struggle and endure pain during those seventy to eighty years on this earth, but our earthly lifespan is but a breath in comparison to the life to come! Since God is outside of time, that becomes *our* reality, too; as redeemed children of God we are also his heirs. Through what Christ has done, we are granted eternity with him in the New Heaven and the New Earth. God does not allow us to stay locked up in our rooms for eternity because of the sins we commit. And in truth? The punishment we receive *does not* match the sins we commit—because we are actually given hope and life when we deserve death and destruction, . . . but that's a whole other discussion.

Psalm 90 is a timeless psalm that draws me to a place of hope, a place of restoration, a place of love. Maybe it's just me, but I'm reminded of all that God could do—and that I deserve—and yet I'm brought to peace by what he has done, continues to do, and gives me anyway.

THREE QUESTIONS FOR YOU TO CHEW ON:

1. What in this psalm speaks to you? To what are you drawn? Why?
2. How do you handle punishment? What constitutes punishment for you?
3. Was the forty-year consequence a punishment or a means for getting lessons learned? Couldn't the Israelites have learned their lessons, and relied upon God, in *less* than forty years?

A PSALM OF PROTECTION

I invite you to turn with me to Psalm 91.

What do you do when fear strikes you? What do you do when terror sinks into your bones and any sight and sound makes you jump? What do you do when life is throwing everything at you and every corner brings a new terror? If you are this psalmist, then you reflect, remember, and tell yourself just how strong and mighty the Lord is. If you're this psalmist, then you remind yourself that there is nothing around that corner that will take you down. There is nothing that is unknown to you that is not known to God. And, ultimately, there is nothing that will remove you from his security.

We don't know much about this psalm except for the simple encouragement the author gives himself as he experiences terrors. Some attribute this text to Moses, and others to David, but this is all speculation. For you and me it simply is what it is: a psalm of encouragement in the midst of life. It's a psalm that is penned to build up the author as he observes and feels terror. It's a psalm that is written to remind him that God will protect him today, tomorrow, and for eternity to come.

Our psalm is broken up into four different chunks, with verses 1–2 comprising the theme of this text. Verses 3–8 speak of all the harm that *could* happen but that, due to the Lord's protection, will not; verses 9–13 speak of just how protected we are in God; and verses 14–16 provide the reason we will not fall to ultimate harm.

As I read this psalm I want to protest, "But wait! You *may* die—and eventually all of us *will*. People will fall into the "fowler's snare," or pestilence and plague will take some down (think Covid-19!). So, how does this psalm make sense?" The psalmist declares that God will keep his own from all these horrible things, but the reality is that people die from these and other causes every single day! So, how does this psalm ring true? God surely does *not* keep all people, perhaps especially those who believe, from danger and harm. And last I checked, I haven't heard or read a story of God's angels being commanded to guard anyone except for Christ. So, are we supposed to take this psalm as literal? Figurative? A generalization? What are we supposed to do with this material? Let's be honest here: verse 7 cries out that ten thousand people may die next to me but that I'll be safe, . . . but what if one of those ten thousand people declares the same truth I do? Will *they* die? This hope the psalmist has—is it false, . . . because I see holes all over the place!

As with most of the psalms, they are applicable first to the writer, and then, secondarily, you and I are encouraged to find the truth and hope in them as well. We need to remember that we can always find holes in things if we are looking for them and wanting to find them (I can punch a hole in any argument if I want to). And if you are anything like me, you easily can ask, "But wait, what about _____?" if you want to. That doesn't mean we should, though. This psalm isn't meant to be an end-all with regard to all things. The psalmist was experiencing fear in *his* life and needed a reminder of God's protection. So, let's allow it to be that for *him*. But let's *not* toss it aside, because ultimately there *is* truth in this whole text that we need to be reminded of. We need to ask whether this text is speaking of protecting *our* life right now or whether it is looking ahead to our ultimate protection for eternity to come. My answer? Yes . . . to both.

In terms of our day-to-day understanding, we need to remember that if we trust in the Lord, if we live by his ways and rules and not society's or Satan's, then more often than not we will be protected. It is when we live by sin, anger, hatred, or recklessness that we are likely to experience negative consequences. It's when we harm others that we are harmed. When we trample upon others and abuse them, we in turn often see wickedness and abuse brought to bear upon us. It is only when we live by God's Law of love, sacrifice, service, and hope that we are kept from many of the harms that happen when we live lives outside these protective parameters. It is only when we live lives *as* Christ, dedicated to him and filled by the Holy Spirit, that we experience God's love and guiding, protective hand.

Ultimately, when we live Christian lives—when we love God with all our heart and soul and mind and strength and put our trust in him—we are rescued, protected, delivered from trouble, and given eternal life with him. It's only then that we experience that *ultimate* protection with him in the New Heaven and the New Earth. So, there is a daily protection given on the basis of our living godly lives, as well as eternal protection from any conceivable evil that we worry might separate us from God.

The intention of the author is to remind *himself* that God protects him today and tomorrow and for eternity to come. His intention is not to say that he will never die or that he will never experience any kind of pain and suffering *ever*; we see that clearly in verse 15, where he acknowledges that God will be with him in times of trouble. What he *does* intend is to simply remind himself, in times of trouble, that he is watched over, guided, protected, and cared for. *That* is our ultimate peace.

THREE QUESTIONS FOR YOU TO CHEW ON:

1. What in this psalm speaks to you? To what are you drawn? Why?
2. In a way, the psalmist is giving himself (and us) a pep talk on the subject of God. Do you ever do this? Why? What is it about internal pep talks that seems powerful?
3. Does living by God's way of love protect us from harm? If yes—how? If no, then why do we do it?

A SABBATH SONG-PSALM

I invite you to turn with me to Psalm 92.

As you can tell from the get-go, this is a psalm that is meant to be sung on the Sabbath day, the Lord's Day. But what is really cool, at least for me, is that this psalm is built around verse 8, moving outward from there, both forward and backward, in concentric circles (vv. 6–7 relate to v. 9, vv. 4–5 to vv. 10–11, and vv. 1–3 to vv. 12–15). Here's how the scheme looks and works:

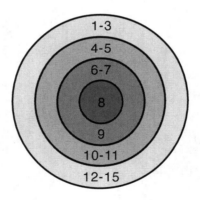

Each one of these circles relates one verse or group of verses to its matching verse or verses. So, where one side (e.g., vv. 1–3) speaks of what worship looks like, the matching verses (in this case 12–15) finish the thought by sharing with us what joy and happiness look like for the believer. Verses 4–5 and 10–11 speak of continuing joy followed by examples of such joy, and verses 6–7 match up with verse 9 in speaking of those outside the Lord and their folly. Finally, the center of this concentric circle proclaims that God will *always* be exalted. Why? Because the author realizes that goodness, flourishing, and life happen when we exalt God. You want to be happy? You want to live a long life? You want to flourish and grow like a cedar? You want to be glad? Then worship God. It's that simple.

Most of my psalm reflections try to encourage and draw out what is going on for the writer, but here we have something very different. This psalm it's not a reflection but simply a statement. The Lord is exalted forever because he is above all things, and he, himself, is never-ending. That's it. There isn't anything else to talk about. And so, because of who God is and what he has done, because of his goodness, we praise him. One of the beautiful ramifications of who God is is that we, as believers, will live *forever* with him. The senseless and wicked people may flourish now, but that will not last. Eternity and forever are not offered up to them. Why not? Because they do not praise the Lord.

With that being said, the background point of this psalm is that it's to be sung on the Sabbath, the day or the Lord. As we gather on Sunday, we should do so as people centered on God and his holiness, on time spent understanding sin and destruction (right and wrong) and remembering what God has done for us. Our Sunday worship should focus on God; the brokenness and sins of this world; the work God has done; and, finally, the hope we have to come.

Psalm 92 is a beautiful psalm of worship—a song in which the believer is reminded to put God at her center.

THREE QUESTIONS FOR YOU TO CHEW ON:

1. What in this psalm speaks most powerfully to you? Where are you drawn? Why?
2. How do you exalt God in your context and place?
3. What does it look like to make God the center of your worship when away from church or on a day other than the Sabbath? How does one do that while playing sports or meeting with friends?

A PSALM OF ENTHRONEMENT AND AWE

Today's reading begins with Psalm 93.

Our psalm today is one of the six "enthronement psalms" (47, 93, 96, 97, 98, 99) that are simple in nature. Their words are not of lament or sorrow. Their reflections are not of despair or full of chaotic scenery. They are declarative praise psalms, expressing hope in the God who is over all and in all things. These psalms are meant to be used in and to encourage worship, . . . and yet they reflect a future as well.

As I look at our psalm today, I'm struck by its simplicity and yet its grandeur. The psalmist declares that the Lord reigns and is mighty and above all things; because of his might and reign, the seas sing unto him. If you thought the seas were strong and powerful, the psalmist suggests, wait till you see *God himself!* There are two aspects of the seas that we can draw out from this psalm. First, their power.

I grew up in the Pacific Northwest, where on a stormy day you can see just how powerful the ocean is. Take a walk along the shoreline, and you can see just how much erosion the waves cause upon the rocks. I've watched surfers in Hawaii and California, and one doesn't have to watch too long before seeing the power of the surf toss a person around like a rag doll. If you've never seen the ocean or the power of the sea, take a moment to do a Google search on its destructive power. The images are breathtaking. And that's not even talking about hurricanes! Simply put, the sea, the oceans, and even large lakes are strong, relentless, and unbiased.

If they are foaming, frothing, and building up strength, . . . you'd best be somewhere else.

But beyond the seas' power, Old Testament peoples believed that their chaotic strength made them a place of fear. This is where massive beasts of epic proportions were said to have lived (Job 41). This is where sailors would meet their doom, and yet this is where fish congregated and food was provided. There was a dread of these unknown bodies of water, the surfaces of which could go from glassy to restless to uncontrolled danger, just like that. The ancient Hebrews were land people, and while they ventured into the sea for some reasons, it wasn't a place they were comfortable being.

When we consider those two pervasive feelings about the sea in ancient times, we begin to understand why the psalmist would be drawn to this imagery in this short psalm of praise. This also helps us understand Mark 4:35–41 a little bit better, to get why it was the disciples were so "blown away" when Jesus spoke to the raging storm that they asked each other, "Who is this that even the wind and the waves obey him!" To them, there was only one person who could speak and control this mysterious, powerful, and fearful thing: God. And there was only one person the sea would lift up and bow to: God.

Given our different context and mindset, many of us as we read Scripture fail to understand some of what the authors were trying to convey. The image of a powerful sea that is unknown and fearful just doesn't work for us. To us, it's just the sea. We know that it's the wind that builds up and throws the waters into their chaotic frenzy. We know that changes in temperature and vapor cause hurricanes and their destruction—not the sea itself. So, how do we relate to the terror of the ancients? Well, I'm not sure we *have* to relate per se. I think, instead, that we're *invited* to relate or to find our *own* source of praise.

Picture the most powerful force you can think of. Now put *that* into perspective in terms of the One who created it. For the psalmist it was the seas, but for you it might be an erupting volcano, a towering tsunami, or an F5 tornado. Regardless of where we land, the truth remains: God created it, and because he is Creator, he is even stronger than this fearsome force. It is in this understanding that we find our awe and fear and come to understand the majestic beauty and power of God. It's in the tangible wonders that we know and see that we begin to understand the power of God. And it is in those things that we also begin to understand that God, who is infinitely stronger and mightier than those, is *enthroned* above them.

Personally, I land somewhere else than I think the psalmist intends, and that's okay. While I affirm the strength and beauty and majestic power of God and his ability to control those forces that I fear, I'm simply floored that he created *you and me*. To move from such strength and power "down" to intimate care and love for you and me, . . . now *that* blows me away. *That* leads me to want to praise God.

THREE QUESTIONS FOR YOU TO CHEW ON:

1. What in this psalm speaks to you? To what images are you drawn? Why?
2. What do you fear? What is it about it that you fear?
3. How does one see beauty in the power of some of those events we refer to as natural disasters—like tornados, cyclones, hurricanes, and eruptions?

A PSALM OF . . . (WAIT FOR IT . . . ARE YOU STILL WAITING??) PATIENCE!

Open your Bible to the book of Psalms and read with me Psalm 94.

Our psalm is one of patience in the midst of life. Patience with others and patience with God. It's a psalm that speaks to me personally because I struggle with both of these. With that being said, it's time for me to get real with you. I have two real struggles in life: other people . . . and God. Am I alone in this? Probably not.

I suspect that all of us struggle with other people because, . . . well, they're not us. They don't think like me, act like me, talk like me, nor can I get them to do what I want them to do. While I can say that I'd hate to be surrounded by multitudes of other "Kellys"—in one sense it sure would be easier! I'd understand you better because you *were me—or something like a clone of me*. I'd have more patience with you because I'd know what was rolling around in your head that made you do as you did—because, well, . . . we'd be the same. But yet I'd also have *less* patience with you *because I'd know what was rolling around in your head to make you do what you just did!*

Even more than this, we would be on common ground because we would look at life through the same Christ lens. I would know how deep and strong your belief and faith in God are. I would know that you, too, are annoyed with so much of the way people respond to life in this world because I would know that you, too, are motivated by love, convinced that love is the answer to all of life's problems. We are told to love God and love others. Not only because those are the two "tablets" in the law of God (Mark 12:28–34) and the very law Christ lived by in all he did, but because you've realized how much smoother and better life is when those two rules govern all your actions. So, yes, it is absolutely trying for me to deal with life and other people because we are not the same, nor do we see all things in the same way.

Now for God. I struggle because I basically stink at doing life by his terms and conditions, and I get really frustrated by his law to love others above myself. But even more than this is the fact that I *really* stink at being *patient* with him. The reality of all of this is that I know what God wants of me, and yet I still find excuses to not do those things. Living a life by God's requests and standards is simple, . . . and yet I complicate it. Loving him above all else means knowing him and abiding by his commands, both now and always. While I know him and do my best to abide in him, it is still a struggle because I want him to work in *my* time (amongst other conditions). I want him to respond *how* I want him to. Trust me when I say that I know this is a contradiction. But it is what it is.

Our psalm today takes both of my struggles and smooshes them together. To me this psalm could be an ad in the paper:

> *Do you have problems with other people? Are people being stupid and bad around you? Do you want them to know God and respond to life with him in mind? Do you KNOW God, and yet you are struggling with wanting to act yourself, even as you wait for him to act? If so, . . . then have we got something for you! Patience! If you act now, we'll give you two for the price of one!*

ARRRRGGGG! The one thing I stink at even *more* in life rears its vicious head. If I were to look up "patience" in the dictionary, I imagine I would see: "Patience—Kelly's Achilles' Heel in life."

Our psalmist sees the arrogant evil doers doing life in their way, and it frustrates them. How can people do these things, act this way, and hurt others? How can they not know what they do or not care how they do it or about those they hurt? The psalmist's heart cries out for vengeance against the oppressors, and he also has tears for the oppressed. There is this internal struggle with all that is going on, as he realizes that God will deal with these oppressors in *his* time and in *his* own way. Having patience with

God is a struggle in and of itself, but having patience *with God* as he deals with others? That very prospect requires the psalmist to encourage himself. And yet throughout all of this the psalmist still appeals to God to act. How much of a struggle it had to have been for the psalmist to not only have patience with people and God but then to find the inner voice to encourage *himself* to have patience! "I'm so lacking here that I need patience in my patience!"

I appreciate what Matthew Henry writes about this psalm: that "it looks out to the oppressors with holy indignation, looks to the oppressed with holy compassion; but, at the same time it looks upwards to the righteous Judge with an entire satisfaction, and looks forward to the end of all these things with a pleasing hope."[5]

For the believer, all of life is about others and about God—and both of those are messy. And yet simply because they are messy doesn't mean we don't enter into them. The reality is that God has given us the charge to speak in and through the lives of others *and* to do all things in *his* way, with him at the helm. As we know, this doesn't always work out the way we want it to. And all of this comes back to patience.

We need encouragement to have patience while God works in his way because, well, . . . he's God, and he's way better at this than any of us. Patience allows you and me to interact with each other even when we don't see things the same way. And, in the end, we have to realize that with patience there is hope. Hope for today, hope for tomorrow, and hope for eternity to come. So, let us be patient with each other and with God. Oh, . . . and let's let love lead. Please, for all of humanity, let's have patience and love and let others—very much including God—lead us.

THREE QUESTIONS FOR YOU TO CHEW ON:

1. What in this psalm speaks to you? At what point are you drawn in? Why?
2. Do you have any close friends who are "eerily" similar to yourself? If so, what makes your friendship work? If not, what is it about your differences that makes your friendship work?
3. What do you do when you find that your patience (with God and others) is fleeting?

---

5   Henry, Matthew. *Matthew Henry's Commentary on the Whole Bible: Complete and Unabridged in One Volume.* Peabody: Hendrickson, 1994. Print.

A PSALM OF
FEARING THE LORD

Please read with me Psalm 95.

As with Psalms 47, 93, and 96–99, this is a "psalm of enthronement." That is, this is a psalm that declares God as the great King above all other gods. And not only does the author declare it, but he *encourages* the reader/ worshiper (the person who breathes any air at all) to acknowledge it and declare it as well. And so, what we get is seven verses of encouragement to worship and then four verses of encouragement *not* to do what the psalmist's ancestors have done in the past. Hebrews 3:7—4:11 is a really good breakdown of what this psalm is doing. When it's all said and done, this is a psalm of obedience in worship. And not only in worship, but in all facets of life.

As I reflect on this psalm, I'm struck by the psalmist's use of "fear" as a reason to worship God. To me, that is not something that works. Maybe it's just something that has never worked for me in my personal walk. Maybe it's that I've never met anyone who continued to believe and worship purely because they *feared* the alternative. Does that work? Maybe. I'm sure there are some people out there who lean heavily upon the fear and wrath of God. The psalmist sure thought so. Or maybe I am using my personal view of "fear" to override the biblical understanding.

"The fear of the Lord" is a major theme throughout Scripture. It's part of the Wisdom Literature of Proverbs (see Proverbs 9:10 for an example), and we see it in the rules and laws of the human relationship with God (throughout the books of Leviticus and Deuteronomy). The reality is that, while it may not be part of my discipleship style, there is validity to fear. And not only truth—but comfort, too. Why comfort? Because I think we probably have been looking at "fearing God" in the wrong way.

The psalmist wants people to worship God and be obedient to what he desires of his people. And in order to be obedient, one must *know* God. We must know that he is the King of kings and the Lord of lords. We must know that he is the Creator and sustainer of all things. We must know all that he has done and *why* he has done it. From his grace to his punishment and from his anger to his love. We spend time in those aspects of his nature and of his Word that allow us to know him. He gave us Scripture, . . . so we must read it as our gateway to understanding not only the path of God's people and where they have gone in the past but also the constant work God has had in their lives (and ours, too).

The problem we've had is that we've taken the word "fear" and associated it with being "scared"—but that's not what it means from a scriptural context. To "fear" the Lord means to know him, . . . and that includes all aspects of him. To fear the Lord means that we learn, grow, and are enriched by who God is. To fear the Lord means that we seek to know God and be led by him; never does it mean that we are to cower and shrink in his presence because we are frightened. I don't think it means, either, that we are to worship him because we fear the alternative. Yes, being scared (or at least reverently respectful) has to be part of that knowledge and understanding of God, but even that shouldn't be the motivation for worship.

The problem we frequently have, as believers, is that we tend to take a very narrow view of things and to apply our Western thinking and view to Scripture. We *may not* do that. We need to take our personal views and thoughts out of the conversation in order to understand the intentionality of what we read in Scripture. Once we understand what is going on and being said, *then, and only then*, can we can properly understand and apply it to our own lives.

What we need to remember is that verses like Psalm 95:8–11 can instill within us a sense of peace. Yes, we should heed the advice of the psalmist, but we should also recognize that, while God was angry with his people, and while he punished them for their disobedience, he still held to his covenant. He didn't walk away from them, nor did he wipe them off the face of the earth. And we need to understand *more* that the text doesn't state. Those forty years involved God feeding them constantly. Those forty years of punishment still saw God clothing them. Those forty years of punishment had God protecting them from outside invaders. Those forty years of punishment had God with them, leading and guiding them.

Helping them understand who he is, what this relationship was to look like, and why "fear" means *knowing* him but not cowering at the mention of his name. Again, God's judgment and wrath were present with his Old Testament people, but his grace, love, forgiveness, and mercy were *above* them as a shelter. The overarching theme of Scripture isn't God's anger. Yes, we see it, and, yes, we must acknowledge it, but from Genesis 1:1 to the final "Amen" in Revelation 22:21, it's all about Jesus. It's about hope, love, redemption, grace, and peace. It's not about cowering (which is what Adam and Eve did after discovering their nakedness) but about awe and joy.

So, yes, fear the Lord. Fear the Lord, for his anger and wrath are mighty, and there is nothing that compares to it. But "fear" the Lord also by marveling at his great love and grace and the hope they bring.

THREE QUESTIONS FOR YOU TO CHEW ON:

1. What in this psalm speaks to you? Where are you drawn? Why?
2. What, to you, does it mean to "fear God"?
3. How do you find awe and peace in your fear of God?

A PSALM FOR
SINGING A NEW SONG

Moving along in the book of Psalms, we arrive today at Psalm 96. We don't know a whole lot about this psalm, but the feeling it conveys is that it is "ark-worthy" (again, my own word) in nature. What I mean is that this psalm might have been sung while David was returning the ark of God (the ark of the covenant) to the city of David following its capture by the Philistines and sojourn in Philistia. While the ark was being carried and the people were being encouraged to sing, dance, and worship God. As the psalm progresses, we catch hints, little affirmations, that this psalm *could* be tied to the ark since the ark in that day literally housed the very presence of God. While the Israelites had the ark in their possession and obeyed God, they couldn't be stopped. No nation or people or "god" could stand before the Lord. This was something they knew, a realization that gave them confidence.

I'm challenged by the opening verse: "Sing to the LORD a new song; sing to the LORD, all the earth." What, exactly, *is* a "new" song? What's wrong with my current song? Well, this isn't about singing to God something that hasn't been sung before; it's more of an encouragement to remember that you have a *new reason* to sing each day. Just as each day granted to us is a new day—so, too, should our thanks to God be new—fresh, current, and specific. This is about singing a new song as, in each new day, we realize new manifestations of God and his love. To state it in a different way: God's love doesn't change each day, but our realizations of it do. The further we go through life, the more people we encounter and the more things we see and do, the greater and more complete the revelation of God's love. So, sing *that* song.

This is all about perspective and choice. Each day we wake up and are faced with the simple decision of whether we are going to go through the day giving thanks to God or ignoring or overlooking God's involvement. Do you see God in the everyday, and even in the mundane? *That*, to me, is the hardest part.

My day, for the most part, is all about routines. The challenge we get from the psalmist is that we are to find a *new* reason to praise God in our everydayness. I think the problem many of us have is that we fail to get into a mindset of thanks for each day. I know that I definitely fail to give thanks in my normal routines—but the fact that I *have* a routine and have things to do should in itself move me to give thanks. The fact that God is and was and always *will be* should move me to give thanks. The fact that he has asked me to be his hands and feet for one more day should move me to thanks. The fact that I am one day closer to seeing his face should move me to joy. The fact that we are one day closer to Christ's return should bring me to joyful tears.

Here's the second challenge of the psalm for me: praise him gladly. And not just gladly, but we are to proclaim, sing, praise, and rejoice. And not only ourselves, but we are to join the heavens, the seas, the fields, the forests, and all of creation! Habakkuk 2:11 and Luke 19:40 both state that even the rocks and stones will cry out God's praise. So, if those unmoving, nonliving rocks praise God each and every day, . . . what's our excuse?

Finally, as we look over this psalm, we should see its messianic declaration. That is, Christ and his victory over all nations and people, all creation, and all evil should be crystal clear. This is the hope that was given and may be seen in Christ. He will judge the whole earth in his righteousness and the people in his faithfulness.

Again, I ask—if even the rocks cry out in jubilee (and what do *they* have to sing about?), then what are *you* singing on this new day?

THREE QUESTIONS FOR YOU TO CHEW ON:

1. What in this psalm speaks to you? What draws you in? Why?
2. What does it look like to sing a new song to God in *your* context? If your schedule is pretty much the same each day, how can you get a fresh perspective for a new song?
3. Maybe singing isn't your thing—so how can you _____ a new _____ to God today? Paint a new picture? Hum a new tune?

A PSALM OF INSTRUCTION

Open your Bible and read with me Psalm 97.

If you recall the introduction to this book, you'll remember that this fourth "Book" of the psalms is all about the Israelites and their relationship to their neighbors. Not so much about "how to be a nice neighbor" (we really don't see a lot of that in the Old Testament), but more about how to be the children of God and follow him, . . . and how *that* doesn't play well with your neighbors in ancient Israel. Why? Because they don't follow him or abide by his Law.

This psalm is considered a "didactic psalm," a psalm that teaches or instructs. There are quite a few of these throughout the book of Psalms, and they are needed and helpful for various reasons:

- We all need instructions in life (Paul includes a good statement on that in Romans 7:7).
- We all tend to stray and need correcting from time to time (we see *that* theme frequently in the Bible . . . and while looking in the mirror each day).
- We need to be reminded of who God is and how our relationship with him looks (we wouldn't know what that looks like or how it is supposed to work without God's instructions).
- We need to understand *who* God is (in terms both of his judgment and of his mercy)—and Scripture helps us there.
- It is only by God and his Word, teachings, and Spirit that we are prevented from falling trap to the things and the ways of this world.
- We need reminders on why we should rejoice in life.

Before God cut a covenant with Israel and marked them as his—long before his people even *were* Israelites—they were worldly people, no different from the Amalekites, Babylonians, or inhabitants of any other nation of this world. They worshiped multiple gods, made idols, and lived life for themselves; it wasn't until God chose them and started instructing them in his ways that they started to *be* the people of God. They lived by evil and wickedness, stole and murdered, and did whatever pleased them. Instructions? Yeah, they needed them. And if God hadn't stepped in? If God hadn't marked them as his own, then they'd have been in the same boat as all the other nations and people. They'd have been on the side of God's judgment, experiencing the fire of his wrath instead of judgment with mercy.

I've written quite a bit concerning judgment in these reflections, and that's because people are judged on the basis of their actions—a theme we see in numerous psalms. Even the Israelites were judged, and they were the very people of God. God judges because of *who he is*. God judges because there is a way to *be* people of God. The reality is that, not only does God hold his covenantal people to his standards, but he also requires others to abide by them. We all are called to love. We all are to be kind and good, and we all must worship him and him alone. We may find it unfair for God to hold those same expectations for others who don't believe in him—but that's on them, not him.

The reality is that, while we may find it uncomfortable and even unfair for God to expect others to worship him and hold to his standards even though they don't believe in him, it would be a completely different conversation if God were to require us to do weird or even horrible things to each other. But the truth is that God *hates* evil and wickedness and calls *all* people to be good, loving, kind, and merciful in life. All people are held to *that* standard, and *all* people are going to be judged according to it. This is all about personal moral culpability. My actions are my actions. The right things I do bring *me* honor, and the bad things I do bring *me* shame. And God holds me accountable for all I do. Whether or not I proclaim God as my Lord and Savior, judgment will come for what I choose to do or not to do.

I am personally scattered when it comes to where I am being drawn in this psalm. I am pulled to the "instruction" and the need of it from the Word of God, but I am also pulled toward the joy of God's mercy, *as seen in his judgment*. A judgment that declared sin must be held accountable, all the while thrusting judgment *through God's grace in Christ* into our lives. I am challenged by the reminder that I am no better than anyone else in this world and that simply because I proclaim God as my Lord and Savior doesn't mean I don't fall prey to the "ways of this world," to its constant beckoning and pull on my life. I am personally challenged in my hope that all people will play by God's rules, and I tend to find myself angry when they don't, and yet I find myself constantly saying that I cannot expect others to live by godly rules when they don't acknowledge God as God. Is that last one a cop-out? I don't know, because I *should* expect others to worship God and live by his standards. And I *should* proclaim that his Word and Law *should* be in all hearts and minds.

Maybe it's me being scattered (which is frequently the case), but I find peace in all of this with the two bookend verses and the theme we see in them (vv. 1 and 12): we *should rejoice*. All that God has done, and all that God asks of us, should move us toward rejoicing. Rejoicing for God marking us as his; rejoicing for God instructing us on how to be good and loving people; rejoicing in God, who hands down judgment *with* mercy; and rejoicing because no matter what goes on in this world, no matter how many errors I make in terms of being a "godly man"—God offers mercy in his judgment. In the end, no matter what you or I do, God still reigns. We may need constant correcting, we all may fail at being loving and kind, we may fail to heed God's instructions each and every day, but in the end it's not about what *we* do—it's about what *he* does. So rejoice, all you people. As we read in Philippians 4:4, "Rejoice in the Lord always; again I will say, rejoice."

THREE QUESTIONS FOR YOU TO CHEW ON:

1. What in this psalm speaks to you? What points or ideas draw you in? Why?
2. Have you ever imagined what your life would be like without Jesus? What might it look like?
3. Do believers put themselves on a pedestal above non-believers? Do we tend to judge ourselves more leniently, or more harshly, than we do others? In essence, how do we view ourselves when we look at non-believers?

A PSALM OF HOPEFUL JOY

Turn with me for today's reading to Psalm 98.

Psalm 98 is a psalm of joy and praise. It's a psalm that encourages not only the believer to praise, worship, and sing to the Lord, but all of creation to join in. This psalm includes beautiful, descriptive words whereby we hear the seas resound, the rivers "clap" their hands, and the mountains sing together (vv. 7–8). Everything about this psalm is one massive natural song of joy. So, why do I feel so sad?

For me as a believer, this psalm warms my heart. As a musician and leader in the church, I want nothing more than to experience this joy of singing each and every day. As a steward of creation, a role to which we all have been ordained, I proclaim "Yes!" as we acknowledge the world's praise of our King. Mountains, rivers, trees, earth, and rocks all singing to God? Absolutely! But, as a person who also lives in a broken world, today I witness anything but singing.

We live in a world that, while God created it to praise him, too often doesn't. People harm the earth by polluting the waters and taking more from nature than what they need. We cut down too many trees, fail to replant as much as we take, and dispose of things we could very easily recycle. Our drills pull out precious ores and metals from the earth at an astronomical rate, and we continue to pollute our waters and natural resources. We burn things we shouldn't, take over habitats and drive out animals, and are constantly trying to improve ourselves and our lot while destroying things all around us. Stewards of creation? Caretakers of this earth? Nope—not us. How can the mountains sing of *joy* when we've blasted and hollowed them out? How can the rivers clap their hands while they are carrying trash and layered in oil? We have become abusers instead of stewards, as has from the beginning been our assignment from God.

And then there's the reality that people are broken and have been given the choice to love or to ignore God. While that is the way God created us to be, it still breaks my heart knowing that my neighbor doesn't know God. It hurts me to know that so many choose to ignore God, to deny our Savior, and to push away the Holy Spirit. I want them to know pure and holy love. I want them to know that Someone values them to the extent of putting them above himself. I want them to know that God loves them so much that he sacrificed himself for them. What else in this world could possibly mean more than that? Nothing.

And don't get me started about the fact that even we Christians hurt people, ignore the poor, close our doors to the immigrant, shut out the widow, and look away from the broken. The more I read this psalm that *should* be encouraging joy and praise in me, the more I lament at just how far we have fallen from joy. But sometimes it is *in* our lament that we remember the hope and joy we have.

This psalmist again invites the reader to sing a "new" song to the Lord. Why? Not because of the height from which we have fallen, and not because of the harm we have caused throughout creation. Joy *is present*, even in the midst of lament, because of what the *Lord* has done: provided *salvation*. That word alone is everything to us.

To have experienced salvation means to have been "rescued," "saved," "delivered." As we read this psalm, we see that this delivery is not only for Israel but that the "ends of the earth have seen the salvation of our God" (v. 3). Which means not only that God saved Israel and the people beyond its borders but that *all of creation* has been rescued.

Paul writes in Romans 3:25–26 that God gave us salvation through Christ. That it was by his sacrifice that he atoned for our sins. To "atone" means to pay; Christ offered up his life as a payment *for our brokenness*. But let us not stop there. We affirm that, when Christ comes again, he will not only put a full stop to, will not only *remove* all sin and destruction from people, but will restore the earth to that which it was. We read in Ephesians 1:10 that all things will be restored when Christ returns (Acts 3:21 reflects this also). So, why do the mountains sing, even while they stand hollow and abused? Why do the rivers, polluted though they may be, still clap? They, too, proclaim the goodness of God now, as well as the restoration to come.

I think it's really easy to see the joy and hope in Scripture and cling to the promises we have, all the while lamenting the reality of this broken world. It's as though hope and joy are intertwined with sadness and grief. Is this okay? I think so, because it reminds us that this is neither the way it's supposed to be nor what will be. But I think it also should challenge us to be better today because of the promise of God's restorative hope tomorrow. We long for restoration. We long for pure joy. We long for all people to feel God's love—and to know that they don't do so now is heartrending. It really makes me wonder how fine that line is between joy and lament (there's a discussion all on its own there!).

Joy in the midst of pain, suffering, and brokenness? Yes, but not based upon what we have done or continue to do but only on what God has done. Salvation, righteousness, faithfulness, and joy: the very blessings that are *in* and *given by* God—and the gifts of which the whole world will sing one day.

THREE QUESTIONS FOR YOU TO CHEW ON:

1. What in this psalm speaks to you? To what imagery or ideas are you drawn? Why?
2. How do you find hope in the midst of all that is going on in this world (the evil that even we Christians participate in)?
3. How can we be better today knowing that God will come again and restore our tomorrow?

A PSALM OF WORSHIP

Open your Bibles, and let's read together Psalm 99.

Our psalm today is one that encourages the reader to praise and worship God, and the writer begins by establishing who God is. By saying that he reigns and that all the nations tremble is to proclaim that God is higher, mightier, and stronger than all the other gods. All the nations should fear him because they can't fight against him. The statement that he "sits enthroned between the cherubim" (a comment concerning the ark of the covenant) acknowledges God's presence in this world.

After establishing who God is and his power over all things (vv. 1–3), the psalmist goes into a few attributes of God and what he desires of his people. The mention of God's loving "justice" and of his establishing "equity" is a call to the worshiper to follow suit. It seems odd to have to mention that we should be just and upright in this world, but that should remind the reader (and the worshiper) that those traits were *not* common in the psalmist's day (and what about our own?). This reminds the reader/worshiper that they should develop and exhibit those traits.

The closing verses (vv. 6–9) are a reminder that these words weren't pulled out of this air, that this call to worship God is real. By naming Moses, Aaron, and Samuel, the writer is pointing backward into history, but also demonstrating that God interacts with his people. We see God speaking and are reminded that he was present in that pillar of cloud when he led his people out of Egypt (v. 7). We read in verse 8 that he "answers them," which means that he interacts with and responds when they come to him. We can even hark back to verses 5 and 1 with the mention of the "footstool" and "cherubim," the places on earth that housed God's "presence." The reference is to the place/space for the people of God to *be* in his presence.

So, while God reigns on high, he dwelt down below in a very real sense for his people. All of this is about God's work, presence, and place here on earth. *So, what does all of this mean for you and me?*

On the one hand, this is a beautiful reminder to worship God. A reminder not only that the Lord is real, not only that he is above all the nations and the earth itself, but that he is good, right, and just. And that we have justice and righteousness and goodness not because we generated them but because God gives them. And yet this is also a proclamation of the hope and work of Christ.

Everything about this psalm looks to the future Messiah. Why do all the nations tremble? Because Jesus Christ reigns above all. The picture of his sitting between the cherubim is an indication that the presence of God is upon his people. And who is it who sits there? Jesus. Who is it who not only establishes justice and equity but loves it, lives it, and fulfills it for us? Jesus Christ. We read that Moses and Aaron and Samuel called upon God, but we can expand that and say that many, many others have called upon God, too—up to and through the present day. And how did God answer? By sending Jesus Christ. How did God forgive not only Israel but also the rest of the world for their misdeeds? Through Jesus Christ. *The answer to all of life's questions? Jesus Christ, the Son of God, the second Person of the Trinity.*

Ancient Israel was experiencing a time of chaos and fear. There was war and then peace . . . and then more war. Nations attacked other nations, kings overthrew other kings, and even families fought internally for power— and Israel was no exception. Even though this was going on, Israel still was encouraged to worship God. And simply because this was the world's reality didn't negate the fact that God's people were still called to worship.

We don't know the backstory of this psalm. This could have been penned while the city was under attack. This could have been written while the men were off fighting some nation or defending their territory. There could have been a lull in faith among the people, and so writing this psalm could have been a reminder and an act of encouragement. We don't know the history, and yet the psalmist tells us that the hope and answer to all of life's problems is God.

To worship God is to know your past, present, and future. To worship God is to know that he reigns over all things, that when people call on him, he answers (v. 6). To worship God is to acknowledge that God doesn't simply sit up in heaven but speaks and guides us in his ways (vv. 7–8). It's to proclaim that God forgives sins (v. 8). To worship God is to know that everything God has ever done has pointed to the Messiah, Jesus Christ. *The answer to all life's questions? Jesus Christ, the Son of God and the second Person of the Trinity.*

As you read this psalm, I encourage you to remember that everything in life is about Christ—and that Christ created everything about you. One day there will be a massive trembling among the nations, for when Christ comes again the earth will shake and sin and evil will be no more. He will do this to firmly establish justice, equity, and righteousness overall, but he will also do this *for you*. This psalm calls us to worship, and we must do just that. Worship God. Remember all that he has ever done, what Christ has done for you, and what Christ promises to do in the time to come.

As you look at the world today, as you reflect on who God is and the hope you have in him, . . . the psalmist encourages you to worship God. So, worship him. Exalt him, approach his throne of mercy with hope, and give thanks for his complete forgiveness.

Worship God.

THREE QUESTIONS FOR YOU TO CHEW ON:

1. What in this psalm calls out to you? To what are you drawn? Why?
2. How does what you experienced yesterday or already today reveal Jesus and his love for you?
3. As you look at the world today, how are you encouraged to worship God?

A PSALM OF SIMPLE PRAISE

Turn with me to Psalm 100, and let's consider it together.

Our psalm today is short, punchy, and simple. We are to shout for joy, worship with gladness, and give thanks to God. Why? Because God made us, and we are his sheep. As our Creator and Great Shepherd, he loves us with a love that endures through eternity. It literally is *that* simple. We should need no other reason to worship God than those two: because he is the Creator and our Shepherd.

Psalm 100 comes right off the heels of five psalms that are under the banner of "enthronement psalms." Psalms 95–99, as we have discussed, were sung to coronate the new king and to remind him of not only the place he had as king of Israel but that he must worship the King who was over him. He was to recite and sing those five psalms and then sing and celebrate this one. For me personally, as I read this psalm, there are numerous other songs that come to mind, songs I grew up singing in church. Songs that would help the congregation open our worship, songs that would encourage us to shout for joy, and songs that reminded us of the joy we have now and of the eternal joy to come. As sheep of the Great Shepherd, we long to be in his presence. And as our Great Shepherd, he has promised to bring us to lush meadows and the greenest pastures.

There isn't a whole lot to this psalm. We have only five verses here, and a total of 79 words. This isn't the shortest psalm out there (that distinction belongs to Psalm 117), but by my estimation it appears that this psalm is #5 on the ranking of the shortest psalms. Does this mean anything? Not really, but I am challenged by the punch it packs despite its brevity.

I appreciate how this psalm brings the enthronement psalms to a fitting close. What a beautiful reminder to those who have been placed in a high position to understand that, while they have this power over people, there is One who has infinitely more power than they do—including power *over* them. As such, they must bow down to him. As the conclusion of the enthronement psalms, this psalm reminds those in power that they must give thanks to the One they serve and remember that they serve *him* and not themselves.

As I type these words, I'm wondering just how beautiful this world would be if all men and women in power were to acknowledge the Lord as their King and serve him as such. Think of the hope we would have. Think of the love we would feel. Think about the goodness that could be accomplished if all the men and women in power all around the world were to acknowledge, serve, love, and live out their positions of power with God on their hearts! No, the world would not be perfect (we need Christ to return before that can happen), and obviously there would still be many things wrong due to sin and brokenness—but think of the many hands and feet, hearts and minds that would come together to love, serve, encourage, and build up the people under their leadership. Think of the wars that would be prevented, the nuclear arms that would be dismantled, and the starving people who would be fed.

But you and I know this will not happen. We can speak of free will and can reflect on sin, but deep down we acknowledge that we, humanity as a whole, fell from God's original, loving intent. Because of this there will continue to be sin, brokenness, and self-serving power all over this world that has run amok. We know this not only by what we see and read today, not only based on our current leaders, many of whom claim to be Christian but fail to live up to their proclamation, but also by our knowledge of leaders and kings of long ago who sang this very song and had this very hope! David sang this psalm, believed in God, and probably heard this text, and yet he was a broken king. And he isn't alone. All the kings before him and all the kings after him: broken. They did some good, and they did some bad. That's the reality of the sinful world we live in.

But this isn't just a psalm for kings—this is a psalm for all people. We all "lead" and interact with others, just as we all are sheep of the Great Shepherd. We need to swing wide this net to include not only kings—not only presidents, governors, senators, judges, and other people in power—but you and me, too. Maybe that's why this psalm is so short. *Maybe we all need a simple, basic reminder and encouragement to sing of our hope and joy and thanks to God.* Maybe we complicate things too easily, and thus keeping it simple and to the point is where we need to begin. Maybe, even though this is the capstone to the enthronement psalms intended for kings, the singing needs to start with you and me.

Maybe? I think *probably*.

THREE QUESTIONS FOR YOU TO CHEW ON:

1. What in this psalm speaks to you? To what are you drawn? Why?
2. How would our world change if all leaders were to acknowledge, and live into, Jesus and his teachings?
3. How would that change your life and how you live it? Or would it? Should it?

A PSALM OF "BESTNESS"

O pen your Bible and read with me Psalm 101.

As with all Scripture, if there is a word that keeps popping up, or a theme that keeps finding its way into a writer's voice, then we should probably look into it. Today's text not only focuses on doing what is right in the eyes of God, but three times we see the word "blameless" used:

- "I will be careful to lead a blameless life." (v. 2a)
- "I will conduct the affairs of my house with a blameless heart." (v. 2b)
- "The one whose walk is blameless will minister to me." (v. 6)

But what does "blameless" mean in this context? Does it mean that anyone who talks with the psalmist or watches him walks away never finding any fault with David? Because to be "blameless," at least in our definition, means exactly that. Perfect, right, and complete. Not only do we know that David did *not* live a blameless life in that sense, but we also know that none of us can do that, either!

So, what exactly is David stating he'll do?

David isn't saying he's perfect, nor that he will *ever* succeed at being perfect. He's making a vow, a promise, to God to do his best. He pledges that he will be "careful" to be as faithful to God as possible. He will work hard at living a life focused on God and will make sure that those who council him try to walk that same path. It's a vow he's making from a personal standpoint, but also as king, in terms of how he will govern his people and of his expectations of them.

I have *extremely* high expectations of myself—especially when it comes to my relationship with God. Maybe it's because I grew up in the church. Maybe it's because I was surrounded by love and hope and goodness my whole life—or maybe it's simply because I'm a pastor. For me, my "best" for God is expected without question. But I also carry within myself thoughts of what *you* expect of me—both spoken and assumed). So, we have a potential clash in terms of criteria in terms of expectations for "my best" (internal and external)! I say this not to place any guilt upon my readers and congregation but because this is truly what we do. We place our own expectations for what one's "best" should look like upon ourselves and upon each other, some assumed and some expressed. We *definitely* have done this to David! And if we fail at meeting all of these expectations (some of which, it goes without saying, may clash!), then our expectations, thoughts, and feelings tank for ourselves and others. A question I want to pose, and with which I am personally wrestling, is whether these expectations are good or even healthy.

Jesus says in John 14:23 that if anyone loves him, they will keep his word. How often do we keep God's word? Are we giving it our *best*? Are we "blameless" in this endeavor? Paul writes in 1 Corinthians 5:11 that we are not to associate with anyone who has been guilty of sexual immorality, greed, idolatry, or drunkenness. We aren't even supposed to eat with them! Paul isn't, of course, talking here about hanging out with such people—that is precisely what both Jesus and Paul advocated and practiced—but about participating with them in their evil deeds, about allowing ourselves to be influenced by them. How many of us have botched that one? (my hand is raised). How many of us *are* those people!? (my hand is raised yet again).

"Best?" You've got to be kidding! My best is not even close! If I truly were to give it my best shot, I'd write notes for myself each and every morning reminding me of what I may and may not do, as well as what I should and should not say. If I were truly giving God my "best," then (in the spirit of Paul's comment, above) I might need to surround myself with only people who went to church, prayed every single morning/noon/night, and never had any bad things to say about anyone else.

But if I were to surround myself only with people who were living like that, they wouldn't be around me. If I surrounded myself with people like that then I would be lonely. And let's remember that Jewish people *did* "carry" notes and warnings in their life like that—it's called the "Torah" or the "Law" (think of the Ten Commandments and then add like 600 more rules and regulations). And good Jewish boys, girls, men and women, had to live by them. Daily! And if you were *really* good, you kept these notes in a phylactery (a small leather pouch) tied around your forehead to remind you of how you're daily bound to the Law.

The truth is that my "best" is broken—as was David's, . . . and as *is yours*. We stink at being covenantal children of God, which is exactly why God holds to the covenant even while *we* break it. When Jesus states, "I am the good shepherd. I know my own and my own know me" (John 10:14), he is declaring just that. He knows us completely. He knows that our best isn't up to *his* best, and yet that is okay. It's not great—he expects more— but those expectations aren't deal breakers. And why not? Because God's standards, though expected of *us*, are held and completed in *him*.

Paul writes in Romans 8:3–4 that that law we had, that covenantal law that we were given by God to hold to and do our "best" at keeping—was "weakened by the flesh" but that we have been given "righteousness" *in it* anyway. How so? Because of Jesus Christ, who died for us and took our sins away. In simple terms, our promise to give God our "best" could never be fulfilled because we are completely broken people. That is why God sent his Son, Jesus Christ (who took on human flesh), to atone for us (die and make our payment for sins) so that our "best" wouldn't be required. We became "blameless" because he is blameless (Philippians 2:15).

The saving grace of Christ is not a matter of "best" any longer, since we have been made blameless in God's sight on the basis of Christ's sacrifice. This doesn't mean that we don't try or give God our "best"—it simply means that though we try hard, struggle, and fail, we don't hold it against ourselves because our future is secured in him and not in ourselves. Our future is in God's hands, based on what *Christ has done*. So, we can rest, assured that, though our "best" is neither perfect nor good enough, God still accepts it. God deserves our *best attempts at bestness*.

THREE QUESTIONS FOR YOU TO CHEW ON:

1. What in this psalm speaks to you? What in particular catches your attention? Why?
2. How do you struggle with the expectations God has for you and yet your knowledge that your "best" can never be enough? Or *is* it good enough in God's eyes? How do you work through that tension?
3. How do you work through someone else's failure, hold them accountable, desire more from them, and yet not hold their failures against them?

A PSALM OF
LAMENT AND HOPE

Take out your Bible and open with me to Psalm 102.

Does it seem weird to say that I "love" the psalmist's imagery here? I don't *love* the pain he is in, but the descriptive words he uses in this prayer help us understand his plight, his pain, and his feelings, which he describes so vividly! Days vanishing like smoke and a heart withered like grass in a desert. The loneliness he feels, the taunting of enemies, and even eating ashes because it's the only food he has. I simply am drawn in to this depiction of his pain and suffering. Amidst all that is going on, knowing that God will hear and restore him, . . . he lifts his private prayer to God.

As for context, we don't know who (or where) the author is. He appears to be in exile, struggling with his current condition and space. And while this appears to be a very private prayer between the lamenter and God, as the psalmist speaks of his own problems, he does find hope in God's restoration of his *people*. So, the prayer is private, but the restoration he seeks is corporate (see verses 13 thru 22 and verse 28, where he speaks of Zion and generations, as well as of stones and servants).

The challenge we get from this psalm comes to us in the contrasts between the lament and the hope. It's almost as though we feel a grayness in the *lament*, followed by a full-on brightness with beautiful, spiraling color, in the *hope*. I picture the psalmist, as he is lamenting to God, with his words and prayer coming out in these very dark black/gray scale words and images. Nothing about his lot is bright and colorful. It's depressing and sad. And yet, in this dirge of lament, God's compassion, work, love, and "infiniteness" skyrocket down from heaven and invade those dark words, suffusing the scene with beautiful reds, purples, greens, blues, and yellows.

The words of lament don't change; they are still painful, and the psalmist is still in this place of pain, but the hope and joy of God and his covenantal love overpower what had seemed to be the finality of the sadness.

What's tough about laments is that, while our hope is in God and the peace he brings, this doesn't alter the pain we are in. We are given the hope we need, but the hope (as is the case with all hope) is for the future. Don't get me wrong, if it weren't for the love of God, the sacrifice of Christ, and the indwelling of the Holy Spirit we would all be sunk! If it weren't for God, we would have no future. But let's be honest and real for a second: until we see Christ descending from heaven and feel ourselves ascending to join him as he comes to usher in his victory over sin and death, our lives will still be tough. We may lose our house because we've lost our job and can't pay the mortgage. We may struggle to put food on the table day in and day out. If it weren't for the kindness of strangers, the support of the church, and programs in our community that donate clothing and food, our children might go poorly clothed or hungry! We still see anger and hatred and death in our communities, state, country, and world. These things still exist, even though our hope is in the Lord and the fact that he has overcome these very things *for* us!

The psalmist declares that his heart is withered and that he is lonely. He is in distress and being taunted. There is no food for his belly, and the only fluids he seems to be able to consume or even procure come to him from his own tears. These things are daily occurrences for him, and his situation isn't getting any better! And yet his hope remains, even in the midst of his pain.

What I truly appreciate about this psalm is that we are able to see in it hope in the midst of pain. We are able to understand that we cry out to God *because* we know that his grace and love run to meet us and give us the very thing we need: hope. I really like imagining that I'm sending up my needs and prayers to God and seeing his compassion, work, love, and "infiniteness" shooting down and hitting my words—not to change them, but to instill in me purpose, peace, and hope. A hope for eternity in God's presence, where the blacks and grays of life are no more.

THREE QUESTIONS FOR YOU TO CHEW ON:

1. What is it in this psalm that hits home for you? To what imagery or encouragement are you drawn? Why?
2. Have you ever been truly in need? How did you hold on to hope while in the midst of the pain?
3. How do you find hope in the midst of pain without diminishing the pain in your mind or making it less than it is?

A PSALM OF "COVENANTNESS"

I invite you to read and consider with me the words of Psalm 103.

Psalm 103 is a favorite for many people—and it's not hard to figure out why. Going from individual praise (vv. 1–5) to corporate praise (vv. 6–18) and finally to encouraging creation to praise the Lord (vv. 19–22) it's uplifting, hopeful, and full of life.

As to context and voice? Your Bible is probably like mine in that it states that this is a psalm "of David," and there is no reason not to ascribe authorship to him—but that's about where our information ends. Psalm 103 doesn't appear to be a psalm in response to anything in particular or a crying out because of a need. It simply *is*. I get the feeling this psalm should be read with Psalm 104, which is a lengthy psalm that continues on with this vibe—but there are others who feel that this psalm is a response to Psalm 102, which, as we have seen, is a psalm of lament. I appreciate one commentator's statement that this isn't a psalm of exposition (breaking down, moving in different directions, and deciphering what is being said). It is a psalm of praise—and one for just general use. You don't need to be in a special place or at a special function. You don't need to be in the right mindset or in a "happy place" to praise God. You simply need to praise him. From your soul and outward. It is that simple.

I appreciate that this psalm covers pretty much all of life. We sin, and yet from there we praise because we have the knowledge that we won't be treated as our sins deserve. We experience the depths of life, and yet we praise because that pit isn't where we will stay. We experience justice for the oppressed, compassion for those who are harmed, and *love, love, love!* And we praise God because he is the giver, restorer, and bringer of all those things.

One theme that runs a string throughout this text is *covenant*. The word may not be stated outside of verse 18, but it is definitely implied! If we skip verses 1 and 2, which delineate the reasons we should praise God, we get this beautiful treatise concerning the covenant-making nature of God. Why is your life freed from the pit, and why are you crowned with love and compassion? Why do we receive righteousness and justice? Why does the Lord bestow his compassion and grace, and why, after all the wrong we've done to him (time and time again) is God slow to anger and abounding in love? Why does God's anger relent and our sins are treated with a softer hand? Because God holds to his covenant. It's that simple.

God established a covenant, a promise, with Moses and the people of Israel—and he held to it. Later on, God sent his one and only Son, Jesus Christ, to come and spread his love wider. Instead of just with Israel, God's covenant was opened up to every tribe, tongue, and nation. So that, should you believe in him; should you call on the name of Jesus Christ; should you join the heavens, the earth, and the chorus of praises from east and west; should you join the heavenly hosts and angels in praising Jesus Christ and his work, then you, too, become a beneficiary of God's covenant.

As the one commentator has put it, this psalm doesn't need some great expository work to draw out its purpose. It is meant to encourage you to praise God and to remember why you are doing so. It's a psalm that puts your place and God's in perspective and gives thanks because of it. Oh, and one more thing, maybe it's just me, but it blows my mind when I think about the fact that, when I stop and praise God, . . . millions upon millions of people are doing the same thing around the globe at that very moment. And not only humans, but heavenly hosts and angels are doing it too. I wish I had the ability to hear all those voices singing and praising God. One day, . . . one day we will.

THREE QUESTIONS FOR YOU TO CHEW ON:

1. What in this psalm speaks to you? What draws you in? Why?
2. Does our praise of God need to be some huge, 4th of July-type celebration? What does quiet, intimate praise look like for you? How jubilant do you get in your full-on praise?
3. How can you praise God while at school, work, or in some other public setting?

A PSALM OF
CREATION PRAISE

I invite you to read with me Psalm 104.

This psalm is considered a companion to Psalm 103. As both begin with the same words ("Praise the LORD, my soul"), they both invoke praise for who God is. But where Psalm 103 is about the God of the covenant and his love of his people, this one is about creation and its splendor. We are encouraged to praise the Lord because of all the mighty wonders and works God has done in this world! From his glorious splendor to its perfect functionality for living creatures.

As we read this psalm, we should be instantly pulled back to the very beginning, not only of Scripture (Genesis 1:3–31) but of time itself, when God spoke things into existence. As I look at the creation account, and this psalm specifically, I'm drawn to the intentionality of creation. Creation doesn't exist just as a place for you and me to stand. Instead, there is an intricate natural balance, with all things having both meaning and function. "God said, 'Let the water under the sky be gathered to one place and let dry ground appear.' And it was so" (Genesis 1:9). In verse 5 of our psalm we read, "He set the earth on its foundations; it can never be moved." And this is only one part of Genesis that matches with Psalm 104. In our psalm we also read that God makes grass grow for cattle and plants for people to cultivate. The Lord gives birds trees and nests, and the wild goats have mountains, while the crags are there for refuge for the hyrax. All that we see the Lord created—and he did so for a reason (except for the mosquito—those have to be pointless. I'm sure birds and frogs could find something else to eat . . .).

When was the last time you looked at the tree outside your window? I mean, *really looked* at it and reflected upon all that it does and gives? From its function to its potential—it's limitless! Trees help make oxygen, prevent erosion, provide shade, offer up homes to various animals, and give shelter. And that's just the living trees. If you were to cut down a tree, you could build homes, make paper, create mulch, provide fire, build things for your home, and slow burn the wood to coax out wonderful flavor in foods. You can carve glorious works of art and whittle beautiful sounding instruments. You can use it to help frame photos and memories, as well as to create new memories as you climb it or use its broken-off limbs to have sword fights. The potential joy of the tree is limitless! And that's just a tree! Now, imagine all the other things in creation that God has made and all the wonderful articles and memories you make with them. From mountains to valleys to streams to giant rocks. As well as animals that fly, swim, or gallop!

Now, imagine that you didn't have all of those natural things. What if there were no trees to climb? What if we were to drill into all the mountains and extract all their precious metals and lay bare all that God had created? What if we were to take away the homes of the mountain goat, hyrax, and birds, and to poison the streams of the fish to the point that they couldn't survive? What if we were to look at the marvelous and "many works" of God (v. 24) and then contrast them against the "many works of man" that are doing more harm than good? What if we were to look at this world and realize that, while God created a perfect balance, so that all animals were provided with food in their habitats, there was no longer a perfect balance because we, the very ones entrusted to care for creation, cared more about ourselves than the natural order and failed to worship God when viewing his created world?

I'm not going to get into a discussion here about global warming and disasters happening in creation, but I am going to remind us of the fact that God gave us a command to "take care of" his creation (Genesis 2:15). He commanded, after his perfect garden was created, to care for it and then asked Adam to name the animals, which also implied taking care of them. God called Adam, you, and me to be stewards of his beautiful creation.

We all need to realize, too, that we were not only asked to take care of the things of this earth, but we are to worship God and praise him when we do those very things. We need to go beyond looking out only for ourselves and the things we want in life. This world, this cosmos, is about more than me or you. The care God took in creating humans didn't stop there—and let's not forget that, though we are the crowning jewel of God's creation, we were not created first. Yes, we need to realize that we are vastly more valuable than the birds of the air (Matthew 6:26), but that doesn't mean we may neglect, cut down, or destroy God's created beauty or that he doesn't love the birds. We are worth more in part because he asks us to be caretakers of his creation. We are worth more in part because we can do more, help more, love more, serve more, and make sure that the birds do have nests, trees, and food. Most importantly, we are worth more because we are created in God's very own image.

I appreciate what the psalmist encourages himself to do in his praise to God for the beauty of his creation. I appreciate it because it is easy to look at the created things of this world and take them for granted, to miss their beauty, splendor, and true function. It's easy to look at the grandeur of the mountains or the glorious depths of the Grand Canyon—but hard to do the same thing in response to a dandelion. And yet God made them all—each for its distinctive purpose(s). I don't think God is saying not to cut down trees or use the streams to better humanity—but I *do* think we need to work harder and be better stewards of creation. We need to plant more trees, drill less, and be more creative in terms of functioning in this world without harming the ecosystem.

I think we need to take a step back and use our stewardship, our earthly caretaking work, to praise God a little more and to find more beauty—with possibly a little less personal function—in what we've been given.

THREE QUESTIONS FOR YOU TO CHEW ON:

1. What is it in this psalm that most speaks to you? Where are you drawn? Why?
2. Take a moment to think about trees. If we were to remove them all, how would that affect your life?
3. How does appreciating the world, and what is in it, change the way you live today?

A PSALM OF
HISTORICAL PRAISE

Turn with me to Psalm 105 and take the time to read and reflect on it. The 104 psalms we have already considered have covered much ground, some of it the same or very similar, but this praise psalm really strikes me in terms of its masterful storytelling. As the psalmist reflects on his people's past, he praises God. As he traces their history from the patriarchs to the exodus, he praises God. As he reflects on God's Word and covenant, he praises God.

Who is this psalmist who sings of praise and recalls a long timeline in the history of God's covenantal work in his people's lives? We're not sure. We don't know much of anything about authorship, time, point in history, or reason for writing. Was the psalmist sitting in bed, unable to sleep, before moving to his table and beginning to write? Maybe. Had he returned home from a long day of work and slid into his tub to soak, reflecting during his bath on God and the praises due him? Why not? Maybe he was leading a worship service, and this constituted the "call to worship" for the people. Possibly. Or maybe he and his family were sitting around the dinner table, and each person was given an opportunity to share a historical praise? Could be.

There are numerous psalms for which we don't have background information—and we have to be satisfied with that. It's not that it doesn't matter, it's just that if we dwell upon and argue about what we don't known, we fail to look at what we *do* have. In this case we have an encouragement to praise God through recalling events of the past. It's not as though the psalmist is dwelling on the past; he is simply reflecting on God's work from the vantage point of a very specific time period. With that being said, is there a story *you* would use as your "historical praise"?

What's interesting to me is that the psalmist doesn't use a personal narrative, doesn't use a story from his own past—but instead draws upon the community and work of God in and through all his people. We oftentimes are so inwardly focused, so individually driven, that we fail to see the realities outside our limited scope. But let us remember that life is not primarily about us—especially in God's wide redemptive plan. We are part of it, yes—but so are billions of others. The story of God's plan may have started with one person, but that one person quickly multiplied into a small group of people, who went on to open up their doors to become the Church worldwide. No longer was it all about Abraham or all about the Jews. Christ's Church now includes people from every tribe, tongue, culture, nation, and place (Revelation 7:9), all of whom will gather as redeemed people under the banner of Jesus Christ and his atoning blood.

So, I ask again: What is your historical praise story? Do you go back to the exodus and tell of God's work, as our psalmist does? Do you go to the story of David and Saul and God's workings from that first Israelite king through his relationship with David? Or to a story that isn't about Saul, isn't about David, but *is* about God's covenant, the establishment of his kingdom, and his protection of his people through David's genealogy? Do you share the news that a "seed" was promised to David who would lead, guide, save, and endure forever (1 Samuel 7)?

Maybe you would hark back to something more current. I don't know. But, in truth, this is where I'm stuck. I may be *struck* by the notion of using a non-personal story and challenged to find on—but I'm *stuck* on that very point. Maybe I feel too far removed from David and Saul. Maybe their story simply doesn't feel enough like my story.

Maybe we feel that our story doesn't find its place in the exodus or, even further back, in the history of the patriarchs (people like Abraham, Isaac, and Jacob). But that's misleading. The Bible, while it speaks from Genesis through Revelation of *God's* story and the revelation of Jesus Christ, is still *my* story, as you and I are an intrinsic part of it. Simply because I *feel* removed doesn't mean that I am. The beauty of the Bible is that it not only speaks of a sacrificial, atoning love for us but pulls us into a greater story that speaks directly to us. Words of encouragement, hope, peace, grace, mercy, and love jump off each page as we remember all that God has done for us. It may not be my direct history, . . . but it is still part of my story. Of *our* story. *God's story.*

God's story is one of love, sacrifice, heartache, joy, praise, lament, forgiveness, hope, and so much more, and *we, you and I*, are part of it. It's a story that is not finished, is still being carved out and unfolded. Each day we have an opportunity to praise God—because *yesterday* is now part of our collective past. And tomorrow? We'll be able to praise God for today. Maybe that's part of this challenge. A year from now, five years and even ten years from now, we'll be encouraged to reflect and praise God for his past workings in and through his people. What are your eyes open to seeing *today* in terms of what God is doing with you and your brothers and sisters that will bring you to praise him tomorrow, next year, or ten years from now?

THREE QUESTIONS FOR YOU TO CHEW ON:

1. What in this psalm jumps out you? What draws you in? Why?
2. What story would *you* use as your historical praise story?
3. What can we do to help us understand, see, and tell the exodus as part of our story?

A PSALM OF
PRAISING CONFESSION

P lease read with me Palm 106.

We've made it to the end of Book 4—a section of psalms that have mirrored the Old Testament book of Numbers, a grouping of psalms that focused on praise and hope and God's kingdom rule over all. We went through highs and lows in terms of emotion, and now we come to the doxology—the closer. And we end with a beautiful "hallelujah chorus" of "Amen! Praise the LORD."

Psalm 106 is considered a "sister" of psalm 105, as they both encourage the listeners (or the writer themselves) to "praise the LORD." But what sets the two apart is that, while Psalm 105 encourages praise, it does so from a mainly positive voice, at least positive from the standpoint of the Israelites. Psalm 106 still sounds that voice of praise, but it does so with a sadder voice. Psalm 105: joy. Psalm 106: confession of sins.

We read in this psalm about the blessings God bestowed, but this is in conjunction with a recitation of the many sins of the people. Praise God? Yup—but praise him because he is patient and kind and has not wiped us off the face of the earth as we definitely deserve! Praise God for saving us? Yup, but realize that he did so because of his namesake and not because we're good or worthy of salvation (v. 8). We are to praise God for his relentless love for us, even though we have not reciprocated that love.

For all the praise that this psalm encourages, it's kind of a bummer of a psalm! This psalm reads more like a constant reflection on the failures of God's chosen people than it does on God's relentless, pursuing love! And yet this is still a praise psalm. Why? Because confession and praise go hand-in-hand. At least in my mind they do.

What does it mean to confess to God? It means that we acknowledge our sins, faults, and crimes—right? And we do so because we concede not only what we've done but the fact that we've done it *against him*. To confess our sins and our wrongs to God acknowledges a hierarchy, a power, and a place in which God is above and we are below. Confession proclaims that God is high and mighty, good and true, . . . and I am not. And because I am not, I seek forgiveness, restoration, and a place of betterment. I confess because I realize, acknowledge, and know that God is the only One who can bring me from where I am to where I need to go.

Now, what about praise? What does it mean to praise God? It means that we acknowledge God's power and strength, his hierarchy and place above, right? To reiterate, praise proclaims that God is high and mighty, good and true, and I am not. And because of his place above all things, we praise him. We acknowledge the beauty, experience the "ahh," and accede to the truth of who God is. We give him thanks, sing to him our joys, and proclaim that it is he alone who has brought us, or brings us, to hope.

Did you notice the difference between confession and praise? Though the two may seem diametrically opposed, the difference—or the distance between the two—isn't all that great. God's place, in both of them, is the same, and because of that we respond. Through confession and praise, we acknowledge the same truths and beauties, as well as a hope in God. And then there's the reality that *when* we confess, we are actually praising God because *in* confession we not only seek forgiveness but find hope and joy. Every ounce of confession is wrapped up in praise. Every time I try to break down what it means to confess our sins, I come back to praise.

Maybe our issue with confession is that we have a faulty understanding of it. Maybe our problem with confession is that it seems so negative that we feel it's on the opposite end of the relationship spectrum we have with God. Maybe, . . . but we'd be incorrect in that kind of thinking. Confession and praise work together to bring us closer to God. As author Matthew Henry writes, "Our badness makes his goodness appear the more illustrious, as his goodness makes our badness the more heinous and scandalous."

THREE QUESTIONS FOR YOU TO CHEW ON:

1. What in this psalm speaks your name? At what point are you drawn in? Why?
2. Does your church take time for confession during your worship service? Why is that important, both individually and corporately?
3. What about *confessing* our praise? Confession in this context is frequently used as a synonym for profession, but are there connections between the two uses of the term?

A PSALM OF
ENDURING LOVE

Today's reading begins with Psalm 107.

We have reached the last section of the five Books of Psalms." Psalms 107–150 are considered "thanksgiving psalms," as they weave back and forth through thoughts, prayers, and experiences of the people connected with the giving of thanks.

This psalm encourages the reader to offer thanks for God's enduring love through a redemption story. But this redemption story is extremely inclusive. Maybe I have a flawed short-term memory, but, prior to my engaging with it just now, I did not recall a psalm or Old Testament story with a redemption history that included people going out onto the sea in ships (v. 23). I did not recall a history of God's people in which a good number of them were facing death upon (let's make that "under") the waves and cried out to God, after he calmed the sea to a *whisper* (v. 29). I remember Jonah, but that was one man. In Noah's case, it was just himself and his family—no merchants, and no sea-calming divine voice. I recall Jesus calming the sea in Mark 4:35–41, but that's in the New Testament. What's going on here?

As we engage this psalm, we read of people doing things we have never heard about in any other format in the Old Testament. We should recognize that this psalm is inviting *all* of God's people, in whatever situation they find themselves. to realize his saving grace. As we read in verse 2, "Let the redeemed of the LORD tell their story." So, what's your story of God's love, his redemption, his hand of protection?

Verses 3–9 reflect the period of the exodus and picture the people of God wandering in desert wastelands (v. 4). Have you ever been wandering and in need? We read of a time when God's people were hungry and thirsty and God gave them manna and quail (Exodus 16). We read of God leading them into the promised land, a land flowing with milk and honey, in the book of Joshua. Have you ever found yourself crying out to God to provide and bring you food when you had no money to buy it? I know many people have. I've heard numerous stories of people on their last loaf of bread, when the next day, by the grace of God, food was delivered, money was found, or people came through with brotherly/sisterly love.

Verses 10–16 speak of the books of Judges, Kings, and Lamentations. This was a time when the people consistently rebelled against God and his desires for his people. Time and time again they pushed against him, worshiped other gods, ignored his commands, and chose to do something different. So, they were punished. Their land was taken over, and they were brought into captivity. While captives in a foreign land they cried out, acknowledging their sins, . . . and God delivered. How many of us have chosen to walk away from God's desires for us, only to find that his ways were right? Disregarding his plans and commands for us brings us to chaos, hopelessness, and a destructive path. But, even while we're going down that road, we cry out to God for restoration . . . and are brought back into goodness, hope, and love.

Verses 17–22 reflect those who were foolish and chose to keep being rebellious. Knowing that they needed to turn to God, knowing that calling out would bring restoration, their ignorance, stubbornness, and self-righteousness pushed them to near death. And it was only there, as they stared death directly in the face, that they fell to their knees and repented. It is precisely here that God's unfailing love (v. 21) still finds them. While I've never stared death down, I have been foolish numerous times.

Verses 23–32 provide a beautiful declaration of God's sovereignty over the depths of the ocean. But more than that, we hear God's voice over the chaos and presumed evil. There was a common belief in Old Testament times that the sea was full of monsters and that this was where evil reigned and worked. While people ventured into the sea to get food, they were taking a risk in going there. And so, for God to still a storm "to a whisper," to hush the waves, declares that when life is a storm, a churning chaos completely outside *our* control, it is not outside *his* control. How often has *your* life been in chaos, and not only did God calm it but then guided you home (v. 30)? Maybe you haven't been in a raging sea, but I'm sure your life has been calmed by his voice, presence, and love.

Verses 33–38 reflect God's ability to change a desert oasis that is full of abundant life into a deserted, dry, and thirsty area—but then back again for the sake of his people. And, finally, verses 39–42 speak of what happened to the Israelite people after they were taken over by the Babylonians and forced into captivity (Jeremiah 29:1–14). This was a time of chaos and heartache, of feeling as though there was nothing left for them—and yet God told them to dig in, plant vineyards, and have their children married.

Simply put, God has always been and will always be there to save his people. And why? Because his love endures, his hand moves, his grace abounds, and he will not allow his people to be abandoned. And so, as verse 43 encourages, as you read these things, as you ponder God's enduring hand, as you reflect on your life and what he has done for you, take the time to ponder his love. How vast, deep, great, and abundant it is!

THREE QUESTIONS FOR YOU TO CHEW ON:

1. What in this psalm speaks to you? To what images are you drawn? Why?
2. Can you relate to any of these images through your life and what you've experienced?
3. If we declare that God is always there to save his people—what does it mean, or look like, to *not* be saved from my current space? We declare that our ultimate saving is with him—but what about right now, in the place in which I find myself and the need I have? How do we wrestle and find peace with that?

A PSALM OF VICTORY

I invite you to turn with me to Psalm 108.

Our psalm today is pieced together from two different psalms of David. Verses 1–5 are nearly identical to Psalm 57:7–11, and verses 6–13 very nearly match Psalm 60:5–12. Why would David borrow from his other psalms? Not sure—and, in truth, there is no way for us to know. Some people feel that psalm 108 was possibly written by someone else *for* David, and so they took a couple of "oldies but goodies" and smooshed them together. Regardless of the reason it was penned, or even who penned it, the results are the same. This is a psalm of *victory*.

As I read this psalm, I can picture why David would sing praises about those victories God had given him and his people. During a time when you either attacked or prepared to *be* attacked, a time when war was frequent, you praised God for defeating your enemies. War was a way of the world and a reality David faced. But what about me? What about today? I always say that we should allow Scripture to speak . . . and to speak for the author who is writing it, but the beauty of Scripture is that it's God's living and breathing Word. Its voice gives us rest, assurance, and hope, as seen through God's constant love and dedication toward his people. We not only get to see what God has done but how that matches with what God is doing right now. So, what is God doing now? What victory is in my life that I can sing about, praise him for, and take comfort in?

That's the challenge. I'm not at war. I don't have people trying to take a kingdom from me or snuff me out. My victory each day is that I made it home safely, my family got fed, and I didn't accidentally kill anyone who had been entrusted to me. Not that I would, . . . but, really, those are my goals as a parent and husband. Put everyone to bed safely, and if we all wake up tomorrow—get everyone back to bed safely the next day too. Wet, lather, rinse, and repeat.

So, maybe I'm not to look to victories in my life but to simply take joy and comfort in the knowledge that *if* there were a battle, *if* there were a confrontation, *if* there were a need like that, . . . God would provide. But we shouldn't just stop there with this psalm. There's more here than simply victory, because this psalm is a call to worship (vv. 1–5), a prayer psalm (v. 6), a psalm of praise (vv. 7–12), and a psalm of joy (v. 13)—and all with words that have been used before.

If you're anything like me, you've probably used the same prayer multiple times. Maybe you've used it time and time again and it's simply your go-to prayer. And if you're anything like me, then you've kind of felt bad about that. "Am I not creative enough to pray something different?" is a question I've asked. But let us not get hung up over saying the same words, praying the same prayer, or anything of the sort. Just as prayer doesn't have to be eloquent or sound as though it were written by a speechwriter (if that were the case, then *most* of us wouldn't pray)—it doesn't matter if we rehash previous prayers. A need is a need, a praise is a praise, and a prayer is a prayer. If you have a recurring need, then why wouldn't you continue to make the same petition? If you've experienced an answered prayer, then why wouldn't you ask again, should a similar situation come up? And if you're still waiting on God to answer a prayer, why wouldn't you ask again and again? There is no wrong way to pray, nor is there an incorrect way to give glory to God.

In truth, Christ prayed the words of Psalm 22 as he hung on the cross. And frequently you and I sing psalms ourselves, even though we didn't write them. Psalm 23 is a text I frequently use in funerals, and those aren't my words, either—and yet they *are* mine because many of us, including me, have made them ours. A voice from long ago still speaks today, particularly when the subject matter is timeless and universal. The basic, core needs of long ago are still the needs of today. And the God who gave victories long ago is still the God who gives us victories today. Even as "little" as making sure I don't kill my kids today.

THREE QUESTIONS FOR YOU TO CHEW ON:

1. What in this psalm speaks to you? To what are you drawn? Why?
2. Is there a psalm or other text that is a favorite of yours? What about it speaks to you, and how does it comfort you?
3. What victory has God given in your life lately (doesn't have to be big—a victory is a victory)?

A PSALM OF ANGER

L et's turn together to Psalm 109 and read it.

If we remember that the psalms were written by people in *their* time and with their own need(s) in mind (which we should always do), then when we come to psalms like this one, it takes the sting out. When we *fail* to allow the writer's voice to be heard, then we find texts like to be a struggle. Wishing that someone's days may be few (v. 8), that their children may be without a father or a husband to their mom (v. 9)? Asking God to make their children wandering beggars (v. 10) who are never shown kindness (v. 12)? What's the deal!? Well, again, . . . we must allow the voice of the writer to stand. So, let's let it stand. But let's not end there. Let's go deeper. Let's remember that this is about God and not about you.

The psalms are a collection of hopes, dreams, expressions of thankfulness, prayers, petitions, and sorrow. We encounter theological ideas and a messianic hope, and throughout it all we see God's hand moving. When we read this psalm specifically, we must recognize that the psalmist declares God's sovereign rule to be over all. Declares that God is holy, good, pure, and righteous. And because he is those things, he doesn't stand for sin, corruption, pain, or anything that people do to harm others. So, what happens when the author, being a good follower of God, comes across evil, anger, and people who wish to harm God's people? He prays for God's holy and righteous hand to snuff out and remove evil. He prays for the reality he envisions. In other words: God deals with sin . . . So, God— come deal with *this* sin!

This is the prayer we get in Psalm 109. A prayer for the reality and truth of God to go against the wicked who are persecuting, hunting, and causing pain to David. Is it severe? We assume so. Are David's words severe? Absolutely. But, again, these are David's thoughts—not mine or yours. And, ultimately, we must remember that everything David is asking God to do, . . . God *will* do. Evil will not win, succeed, be prosperous, or continue on. And I think all of us know that. The struggle is that we find it uncomfortable to ask for the destruction or suffering of others. We squirm in our seat when someone expresses a wish for others to fall. And, especially in cases like this psalm, we get uncomfortable when the requests get specific and vivid. We begin to feel as though David is going over the top. Why else would he be so specific?

So, what do we do? First off, we don't ignore psalms like this one. We don't ignore psalms like 137:9, either (this verse declares, "Happy is the one who seizes your infants and dashes them against the rocks") or any other psalms that seem, sound, and *are* disturbing. Listen to the psalm, hear the words, and seek to understand what the psalmist is going through, the pain he is experiencing, and the hope he clings to in the God who listens and responds. Then take a step back and look at the bigger picture. Take in who God is, what we declare of him, and who Scripture reveals. In *this* case, while the words may be vivid, painful, and uncomfortable, we see the hope and declaration of Christ throughout these 31 verses.

Will God remain silent (v. 1)? No. Christ comes as the physical response to evil, pain, and suffering.

Will evil itself oppose our enemies (v. 6)? Yes. Evil is all consuming—even self-consuming. So, evil doesn't "lift up evil"; it will consume it, as it has no moral compass, nor will it play nice very long with other evils. They may be allied today, but at some point one will seek to overtake the other. Someone has to win. If you think *you're* bad, . . . know that there's someone worse than you who will seek to destroy *you* so *they* can succeed. We read stories of God allowing evil to *appear* to succeed in order to punish other evil doers (read Lamentations or Habakkuk).

Verses 8–15 simply ask that the sinful not succeed—and they won't. God will not allow that to happen. It may not be in this lifetime, but their downfall will come.

Want deliverance from oppression (vv. 21–25)? Jesus Christ is your answer.

What about crying out to be saved, according to God's unfailing love? (v. 26). Once again, go to Jesus Christ—love incarnate.

The challenge in this psalm needs to not only be about allowing the voice of God's people to speak authentic feelings in prayers, but to allow the psalm to declare God's stance against sin and evil, regardless of how we may feel. We need to remember that it all points to Christ. Christ is the revealed response to the needs of people, the direct response to evil. Christ is the final stamp assuring us that evil will not move forward, take root, and prosper. Christ is the incarnate, physical love of God.

So, let's not skip over the psalms we are uncomfortable with. Instead, let us realize the truth they speak—even when it feels painful or uncomfortable to read them. Because, ultimately, while this may be the most painful of the psalms, it clearly speaks the truth and hope of the gospel.

THREE QUESTIONS FOR YOU TO CHEW ON:

1. What in this psalm speaks to you? To what are you drawn? Why?
2. Do you find that you avoid uncomfortable psalms like this? What lessons can you learn from them? Are there lessons we can learn here to help us *avoid* certain actions or thoughts?
3. Is it wrong to ask God to deal with sin when it seems so embedded in a person? Are we asking God to harm *the* people . . . or to deal with the sin?

A PSALM OF
OUR KING AND PRIEST

Before reading today's reflection, take the time to engage with Psalm 110. What greater words would a king want to hear from his prophet? That the battle and war that loom before him will be victorious. That troops upon troops are ready to fight. Like dew upon the morning grass (v. 3), they will be so numerous that no one can count them. What more encouraging words than to hear that the Lord will go before you and make all your enemies your footstool? What better words than to hear that the Lord is on your side and that he will fight and win for you? David could not have heard more reassuring words.

We don't know much about this psalm except for the words we see on the page. There is no context (beyond war), and there are no words that lead us to a time and place. But here's what we *do* know:

1. This is the *most quoted psalm* in the New Testament. Verse 1 is quoted in Matthew 22; Acts 2; 1 Corinthians 15; Ephesians 1; Philippians 2; and Hebrews 1, 10, and 13.
2. It's Davidic *and* messianic in that it speaks of the promise to David *and* to its fulfillment in Jesus Christ.

This psalm is broken up into two short stanzas (vv. 1–3 and 4–7). Verses 1–3 speak of what the Lord says and does for the king, and then verses 4–7 speak of what the Lord does, as *priest*, for *himself* against the other nations and people. For David it would have been reassuring to know that the Lord was blessing him with fighters (vv. 1–3), as well as the fact that the Lord promised to defeat all the other nations. For you and me as Christian readers, we cannot help but see the gospel in this psalm.

Who sits at the Lord's right hand and has all enemies as his footstool? Jesus (Acts 7:55–56)

Who rules in the midst of enemies? Jesus (1 Corinthians 15:25)

Who is both priest and king in the order of Melchizedek? Jesus (Hebrews 6:20—7:28)

Who crushes all kings and judges all nations? Jesus (1 Timothy 6:15)

So, here's my question: Why does this psalm matter? Why does it matter to you and me, and why does this psalm matter as a whole?

Most commentators agree that, while this is a psalm "*of* David," it is not a psalm composed *by* David. This is a promise *to* David about God's work. And, while the prophet made this declaration to his "lord" (David), the psalm isn't *about* David but about the Messiah, Jesus Christ. And *that* is why it matters. David may have been a king, but he was not the perfect Priest-King. That distinction belongs to Jesus Christ. This psalm may have been given to David, but it is clearly about the Messiah and his return (Zechariah 14:1–15; Revelation 19:11–21).

So, why does this matter? Because everything we do is for our King. Because our whole lives are lived in response to his commands and the fact that he reigns over all things. Because all of our hope lies in his lap; it all depends on the throne he rules from, the scepter he holds, the crown he wears, the judgment he brings, and the destruction of death by the life that he gives. This psalm is everything to us because it reminds us that everything is in and upon him.

THREE QUESTIONS FOR YOU TO CHEW ON:

1. What in this psalm speaks to you? By what are you drawn in? Why?
2. Outside of what I said, why does this psalm matter to you?
3. How do you live in to the truth, reality, and *life* of this psalm in your context?

A PSALM OF LOVING FEAR

B egin today's reading with Psalm 111.

Now that you've read Psalm 111, please go ahead and read Proverbs 1:7. The reason we read the Proverbs text is that this psalm is *that* type of declaration. To know the Lord is to fear him. God is great, and we are not. God is mighty and strong, while we are weak and frail. God is forever, while our earthly sojourn will come to an end. Are we to fear God based on these realities? Yes, . . . but no. *Yes* in that he could snuff us out with only a thought, but *no* because those who love God and obey him have nothing to fear. Just as God is above all and in all, just as God is *the* only One who is above all else, the *no* comes to us as a reminder that his love knows no bounds and his grace endures forever.

I remember when I was a kid that when I scraped a knee the first thing I would do (after crying) is go to a parent. I knew that, with my mom or dad there, I would receive love and encouraging words, as well as benefit from the expertise of a person who could stop the bleeding and address the wound. Inevitably, though, after those soothing words of comfort and to get me to stop crying, my mom would take me to the bathroom sink, rinse off the wound, . . . and then the torture triplet would appear: *hydrogen peroxide*, a wad of TP, and a washcloth. The wound had to be disinfected (which always stung) and then scrubbed (which hurt even worse). Not patted, not just cleaned around it, but scrubbed. The dirt, the rocks, and any other foreign object present in the wound had to be removed so infection wouldn't set in and healing could begin.

I think that *fear* and *love* for the believer work like that. We fear what is painful, and yet we know it's the best thing for us. We know what God expects, and we fear we won't measure up to those standards. We experience fear over how God is feeling about our failed love, our harsh words, our faulty grace, and our inability to simply be the salt of the earth and a source of hope for many. When we understand those realities, I think we can begin to feel what the psalmist declares and what is repeated throughout the Old Testament in a plethora of texts (like the Proverbs text mentioned above, as well as Psalm 33:8 and Proverbs 14:26–27).

We *fear* that which is scary—which is ordinarily in our best interest—but let's not fail to understand and remember that fear is also a kind of *knowledge*. To "fear" God is to *know* God. How could you believe in God, know God, or understand his works if you didn't fear him? Because if you don't know God, then you don't know that you *should* fear him. And if you don't have a reverential fear of the holy God, then you obviously don't know him. This is circular—and confusing—but it's the truth.

Everything we are is based on God's love and on his imparting wisdom and truth into our lives. We love and serve others not only because of his love and service to us, but because he reveals and bestows those blessings upon us, . . . and he does that because we know him, worship him, adore him, and believe in him. So, what happens when I break a law of his? What happens if I commit adultery, murder my neighbor, or abuse my wife? In any situation involving sin, we are allowing Satan and his work to take precedence over and cloud our relationship with God. In those situations, we are not allowing the *knowledge* of God to come through. We are focused on sin instead of on him, and we consequently fail to receive any knowledge *from him. Fearing the Lord* allows knowledge and grace from God to pass through what would otherwise be a sin barrier.

I apologize up front for what is to follow: a really interesting, though quite possibly flawed, analogy that makes sense in *my* head (as though that will help you at all). Think of a drain and a faucet. If the drain is not taken care of and maintained, if we don't watch what goes down it and how much of it gets through (other than liquids), it can get clogged and fail to allow much water from the faucet to make its way through. We need a chemical drain cleaner to be poured down and allowed to loosen the clog. Fear of the Lord is like that (can we call it "Drano of the Lord?"—probably not). In order for us to receive knowledge from God (from the faucet), there has to be a clean path into our minds and heart (through the drain); that doesn't happen when we're living in so much sin that we are refusing to get to know and follow God (clogged drain). Receiving the goodness of God cannot happen when you're so clogged that you cannot receive the living water he gives. So, enter Drano—think fear—that allows you to take in all of who he is and what he offers.

So, do you fear the Lord? Do you fear the power and expectations he has for you, and the consequences of your failure to follow through? Do you fear just how beautiful his grace and love are and how completely they overpower our sins? Do you fear his provision of his covenant promise (v. 5) that was poured out for you in Christ? Well, you can't fear them if you don't know them, and you can't know them if you do not fear him. So *fear* away!

THREE QUESTIONS FOR YOU TO CHEW ON:

1. What in this psalm speaks most impactfully to you? Where are you drawn in? Why?
2. Would we know what love was without some aspect of fear in it?
3. How can we fear God if we believe that our fear has been wrapped up and taken with Christ? Does fear even mean anything today?

A PSALM OF ETERNAL PRAISE

The next psalm in Book 5 is Psalm 112. Please take a moment with me to read it.

This psalm works well with the previous psalm in that they are both acrostic in format (each line, at least in the Hebrew, begins with the next letter of the Hebrew alphabet), and both speak of the "fear of the Lord." But, really, this psalm is seen as a continuation of Psalm 111, a response to Psalm 111:10. The biggest difference, however, is that this text is considered a "wisdom psalm," as it encourages the reader/hearer by offering guidance for praise along with reasons for praising God. So, whatever you have been given and in *all* of life: praise God.

As we read this psalm, we notice that verses 1–9 are very positive for the believer, while verse 10 speaks of those who do *not* believe and of their envy of the believer. So, believe, worship, and fear the Lord, and you will have wealth, riches, and a plethora of goodness in your life, . . . while the nonbeliever will get annoyed, confused, and long for your lot in life but will walk away with nothing. Why? Because *longing* and *desiring* bring you nothing. It is only God who gives, delivers, and hands down his blessings to his believing children who walk and delight in his commands (v. 1).

Is that how life works for you? I know that, for me, many of these words hit their mark, . . . though not all of them, and some of them I don't even know what to do with.

- "Mighty in the land" (v. 2)—I'm not sure what that even means in my context.

- "Wealth and riches in their houses" (v. 3)—Can we redefine "wealth" and "riches," please? I'm a pastor, and my wife works for the local school; while we are absolutely blessed to have what we have—and we have plenty—"wealth" and "riches" are *not* building up our bank accounts.
- "Surely the righteous will never be shaken" (v. 6a)—I'm not even sure where to go with that one. My *faith* hasn't been shaken, . . . yet (and I'm not sure whether that should be a statement or a question), but I know some God-fearing, faithful Christians who have had their lives shaken in many different ways.
- "They will be remembered forever" (v. 6b)—Why does that even matter?
- "They will have no fear of bad news" (v. 7)—Uhh, . . . clearly this psalmist has either never had bad news delivered, or his tolerance for bad news is *really* high because he has been through a ton in his life!
- "In the end they will look in triumph on their foes" (v. 8b)—I'm not sure I have any "foes," . . . nor do I ever use that word.
- "The wicked will see and be vexed . . . The longings of the wicked will come to nothing." (v. 10)—Yeah, this whole verse leaves me confused, as all I see here is the wicked prospering, getting what they want, longing and receiving all they desire. While it's true that in the end they will "waste away," he knows that already.

So, what are we supposed to do with all of this?

First, we must always remember context and voice. There simply was a different way of life back then. People sought different things, desired different things, and understood things differently than today. Wealth and prosperity looked and felt different. Having your name "remembered" was important, as was the reality of "foes" and having dignity amongst the people. So, while we may not be able to understand the psalmist's perspective, we *can* understand his hope and comfort. And it is there that we can find our own voice. So, if we go back to the intention of this psalm (in that it is a response to the very last line of the previous psalm), then we can find our own encouragement to give God "eternal praise" (Psalm 111:10).

For the psalmist, that "eternal praise" brings to the fore all the blessedness he sees and experiences in life. Children and namesake, wealth and riches, light in darkness, conducting affairs with justice, good news and bad news . . . All of life calls forth one giant eruption of praise. One nuance I think we may easily overlook is that the psalmist declares we should praise God "eternally." That is, we should break forth in praise without end. This is the kind of praise that encompasses all of our lives and then moves beyond that and beyond the beyond.

I desire to *eternally praise* God because I do enjoy "wealth and riches." I may not be able to add much to my bank account after each paycheck, but I have plenty, and we are able to do things as a family and support our kids in their desires. We have a wealth and a richness of laughter, joy, hope, and comfort in our house. We are able to have enough so that we can have people over and feed them and do life with them, too. Am I rich financially? No, although "rich" in that sense is such a relative term, . . . but I am abundantly wealthy in what I've been given.

To be honest, there are a lot of other things in this text that I'm still personally working through, but that doesn't mean I won't praise God for what he has given to me or for the promises he has delivered (those fulfilled and those waiting to be fulfilled). That's where I think we need to land. Eternal praise doesn't mean praise only when things are good or even more praise more when things are bad—it simply means never ceasing, never ending, . . . always praising. Because regardless of where I am or what is happening, God still *is*. And because God *is*, he will always bestow blessings upon his children.

THREE QUESTIONS FOR YOU TO CHEW ON:

1. What in this psalm speaks to you? At what point are you drawn in? Why?
2. What does eternal praise look like for you?
3. Praising God when things are "bad"—do we do that as an expression of *hope* or as a form of internal encouragement? Do we do that because *we need it*? We know that our praise doesn't encourage *God* to act in our lives—so why praise him during the hard things?

A PSALM OF PRAISE

I invite you today to turn with me to Psalm 113.

This psalm doesn't have much backstory to it, but it does kick off the set of psalms (113–118) that are considered the "*Hallel* psalms" (a collection of psalms that were sung during certain Israelite festivals), with this one and Psalm 114 specifically being sung *before* the celebration meal (others were sung between drinks, after meals, or at other points). As we see from the opening words (and a total of six times in this text), this song once again encourages the people to "praise the LORD." From morning till night and in all places of life: praise the Lord.

What strikes me about this psalm is the "high" and "low" imagery we see throughout these short nine verses.

- Verse 1: Lord and servants (high to low)
- Verse 3: Rising sun to wherever it sets (low to high and back to low)
- Verse 4: The Lord is exalted over the nations, and his glory is above the heavens (high to higher)
- Verses 5–6: God is enthroned on high and stoops down to look upon earth below (high to low)
- Verse 7: Poor and needy are raised (low to high)
- Verse 8: Poor set to the height of princes (low to high)
- Verse 9: Childless women are made happy (*feelings* are brought from low to high)

It's no wonder that Psalm 113 is used in conjunction with the Magnificat of Mary (Luke 1:46–55) and thus tethered to Jesus Christ. It's no wonder that we see and feel these images of the *high* brought *low* and the *low* brought *high* and think of Jesus and how he left his throne on high to come to earth below. How he humbled himself by taking on human form and enduring our pain and torment so that we, who are low, can be brought to him on high (this is literally in his name: Immanuel, God with Us). So, praise God? I know I shall.

But there is also something else here that strikes a chord with me. While there is encouragement to praise God all day and every day, there is also encouragement to do so even for that which is beyond the range of the psalmist's knowledge or experience. In verse 3 there is an encouragement to praise God from the "rising of the sun to the place where it sets." Where *does* it set? What really struck me as I read this psalm is that there was so much that wasn't known by people back then, and yet all that they saw, even the mysterious or unexplained things, still brought them to praise God and give thanks for who he is and what he has done.

What about me? With all that I do know, with all the knowledge I have access to, am I still praising God for it? Do we seek answers that are "outside" God, or do we still see God even in those things that can be or have now been explained? Are there phenomena in this world that cannot (or cannot yet) be explained and understood, and do *those things* bring us/you to praise God? *How much of what we don't know and don't see is God working and deserving our praise? All of it!*

As children who declare that every square inch of this world is God's (a reality famously voiced by Abraham Kuyper), we need to also remember that this includes *all* things, both seen and unseen. In today's world with its technology and scientific knowledge, we like to think that we can explain away all things and find answers to all questions—which is fine by me. I have no problem with the marrying up of faith and science. I do have an issue with science telling me how the world was created, though. I'm okay with explosions and movements of solar systems that are expanding, along with all those other explanations of natural "behaviors" that I do not fully grasp. And I fully accept the notion of God and science playing perfectly together, because for me everything comes *back* to God. Everything comes back to his touch, his voice, his work, his world. We can delve deeper and deeper into what causes this or that and state that this came from a _____ event, . . . but there is always going to be *one more step, one more link,* one more explanation for said event/result/action/thing. And for me there will always be one more beyond that one, . . . *until* we work our way smack-dab into God, the Creator and Sustainer of all.

So, what does all of this have to do with Psalm 113? Just as the psalmist didn't know the exact workings of the sun, we, too, lack comprehension of the extent of all things in this life, . . . and yet we know *God does*—because it all comes back to him. And so, we praise him. We praise him for what is known and unknown. We praise him because he is above all and in all. From his place on high to our place below, we praise him. And I'm okay with that. Scratch that—I'm overjoyed with that!

THREE QUESTIONS FOR YOU TO CHEW ON:

1. What in this psalm moves you? Where are you drawn in? Why?
2. How do you work through the conundrum of feeling the need for answers to explain things while faithfully declaring that, just because we don't know the explanation for something, or even know at this point *of its existence*, doesn't mean that God did not create it?
3. How can you dialogue, in a good way, with people who do not see God as the Creator about some event or *thing* that (may have) caused it? How do you affirm their feelings and yet live into your faith, even when you cannot explain *how* God created something?

A PSALM OF REMINISCING ENCOURAGEMENT

Turn with me in the book of Psalms to Psalm 114.

If you were to think about a major event in the history of God's people, what would it be (outside of Christ's coming or crucifixion, that is)? What event stands out more than anything else and speaks of God's dedication, love, and presence? Many people would probably say the exodus. Most Christians would point to God's stepping in and leading his people (Israel) out of Egypt, parting the sea, safely bringing them across, and then pummeling their foes as they sought to return them to slave labor. Well—that's what we have here. We have a short expression of praise to God for the exodus and his deliverance of his people. It's a psalm that gets right to the point. It encourages Passover praise (from Exodus 12) and earthly awe as mountain, hill, and sea respond to his might.

As we read this psalm, we see that it's broken up into three poetic sections. The first one speaks of the event, verses 3–6 the response to this event, and the last section (vv. 7–8) offers encouragement to praise for the work of the Lord. God caused the Red Sea, the Jordan, mountains, and hills all to move in ways that were not natural. Because all of creation is affected when God works.

This is a psalm of encouragement, reminiscence, and hopeful reflection.

Oftentimes we get stuck on the past and fail to find in it hope for the future. I know I do this. I often talk with people about how wonderful it would be to see God's mighty hand moving, as it once had. But while these conversations are honest and make a good point, we need to be careful not get stuck in dwelling on the past work of God and then simply remaining there. We must never sit and reminisce in wistful nostalgia, while failing to breathe in the hope of God's promised work to come. Yes, God did mighty things in the past, but never should we fail to expect God's mighty work to come. We think the exodus was something amazing? Wait till we see full earthly restoration! But those are the *big* things—what about the small ones? The individual, daily acts of God?

Oftentimes the big things in life overshadow the little things—but isn't God in both? We read about Moses's conversations with God and his delivering that message to the people and wish we could say that dynamic at work today. We want to know God's will, God's plans, God's directions in our lives, and sometimes we want a direct line from him, telling us those very things. And then we're sad when life doesn't unfold in the manner we desire. But doesn't he do this already? Isn't the promise of the Holy Spirit, who dwells within, that very thing? Isn't God's presence in leading, guiding, directing, nudging, and prodding the very thing we long for? We may not have a person in our life who comes down from a mountaintop experience, radiating with God's presence as Moses did, but God still puts people in our lives who speak with his authority. The question we need to ask—the question I'm asking—is whether you are listening to them! Are you looking at them and seeing that person and hearing *their* voice—or are you seeing God and hearing his voice as the Holy Spirit uses them to bring you a message?

I think one of the biggest issues Christians have is that we get very nostalgic in thinking back on what once was and fail to see what still is. Scripture is breathed to give us a glimpse of God, to declare the Son, and to show us how his Spirit directs us today. It's about the *complete* redemptive work of God. We fail to fully understand Scripture when we see it only as an account of God and his people and ignore the prophetic voice that still rings true today. Scripture is the revealed truth of God, not a former truth that no longer applies. That voice, that truth, carries into today and eternally beyond.

So, here's our challenge from this psalm. Are we singing of the work of God in the past and *wishing* God were still active today, as he was so long ago? Or are we singing of the activity of God as he *still works today*? Are we seeing how all of creation leaps and jumps—or do we believe that this has stopped, never to happen again?

Hope isn't hope when it's stuck on/in the past. Hope speaks of a future that was promised. Hope puts a stamp on what is to come because the future is tethered to the past; what is to come is revealed in what has been. Big and small—all are in God's hands. And if God can make the sea flee and turn back, . . . if God can make mountains and hill skip, . . . think of what he can, and does already do, in your life!

THREE QUESTIONS FOR YOU TO CHEW ON:

1. What in this psalm speaks to you? At what point does it draw you in? Why?

2. Do you have a person in your life who speaks wisdom to you? Do you see them as a "Moses" type person, or not? Are you reminded by your mentor of another Bible character?

3. How do you respond to people who say that the Bible was good for its time but doesn't speak today? Or others who say that this text/message is for _____ but not for them?

A CHALLENGING PSALM OF PRAISE AND HOPE

I invite you to open your Bible with me and read Psalm 115.

Once again, we have a psalm without available context. Some commentators feel that this is a psalm that would have been sung by a choir in a worship service, while others set it as a prayer for the people. While we may not know the intention or place for this psalm in the wider corpus of the psalms, or how or when it would have been used, we do feel its intentionality within the people of God. This psalm is meant to encourage the believer to continue to worship the only living God, and nothing or anyone else. Regardless of what else may be going on around you or whom/what others are worshiping, nothing and no one else compares to God.

It's no surprise to the reader of Scripture that pagan worship was running amok in the days of the psalmist, nor should it be any surprise that the Israelites and their ancestors had been among those pagan worshipers before God made them his covenant people. I don't have the time and space (or the knowledge) of why people have created idols of gold and silver and worshiped them. I don't know why people would make something themselves, only to turn around and bow to it, sing to it, speak to it, and seek its voice and direction in their lives. That doesn't make sense to me. But people all around the world have done it—and still do it today.

We are forbidden to create physical idols (although there are religions that do this still to today), but this psalm *does* challenge us in times of persecution. When the Christian is challenged by another religion, when the believer is mocked and attacked by people with different beliefs, do we crumble or stand strong? Do we fear them and their gods, or do we stand firm in *the* one true God? This psalm is meant to encourage the believer in those times of fear, when persecution is near at hand. This psalm is meant to remind the believer of the living Lord, even when all those around her worship dead idols they have created with their own two hands.

In truth, this psalm means a lot to me, and yet I struggle to put my feelings down in words—I think that is because this type of idol worship is not rampant today, as it was in ancient times. While we still do have many religions in this world, with many of them bowing to manmade sculptures and idols, I'm struggling with the effect of this reality on me. Am I simply clueless? Am I oblivious? Do I have on blinders, or am I unwilling to look at the idol worship of various kinds in my own surroundings, and even in my own life? I don't know. Yes, people worship money and their jobs and their homes and other people. Yes, people create false gods and lure vulnerable people into their religions, though we don't see or hear much of that. Maybe it's hidden, maybe this is all about blissful ignorance on my part and others', or maybe it's just that we have become so desensitized, so tolerant of other people that we simply look the other way, allowing them to "do whatever they want as long as it doesn't bother me."

Outside of verses 9–11 (that speak of protection and help), most of this psalm is simply declarative. Which suggests to me that nothing "bad" was going with regard to the people and that this psalm was just an encouraging reminder not to fall or to be ignorant to what was going on around them. Maybe this psalm was meant to challenge the believer to speak up against idol worship. Maybe this psalm is challenging me personally to not only continue to place my confidence in God but also to open up my eyes to the harm others are doing as they worship anything that is *not* God.

I think that one of the biggest blessings—and sources of harm—we experience is the idea that people have the right to believe and do whatever it is they want (within reason, obviously). While this freedom is foundational here in the USA, and while this has been a blessing, it has also been a curse. No longer do we share with conviction the grace of Jesus. No longer do we push against man-made religions for fear of violating that sacred American "freedom of religion" we so love.

Maybe this psalm is a challenge for me to shake my head at idol worship and false religions and to remember the living God, whom I love and who died for me. Maybe this is a challenge for me in times of trouble to follow verses 9–11 and trust in God and nothing else. Or maybe this psalm is a challenge for me today to share the grace of the living Jesus with those who put their trust and hope in something or someone else, rather than worrying about stepping on toes or making someone else uncomfortable. *All* people need to know of true hope, love, sacrifice, and eternal blessings that come from the One and only God. All people need to know the destructive path idol worship of any kind takes. All people need to know the forgiveness, hope, and love of Jesus and the fact that he died for them. All people need to know that every idol/relationship/house/job/possession that you worship and put your trust in will fall away, while only God and his love stand for eternity.

THREE QUESTIONS FOR YOU TO CHEW ON:

1. What in this psalm speaks to you? By what are you convicted? Why?
2. Why is it so difficult to focus on worshiping God when the rest of the world seems to be collapsing around us? How do you stay focused on him in such times?
3. Do you tend to find yourself quietly believing and letting your actions show your faith, or are you one who actively (verbally) shares Jesus with others? Is one approach right or wrong over the other? Can it be that both are necessary and equally important?

A PERSONAL THANKSGIVING PSALM

I invite you today to read with me Psalm 116.

Whereas Psalm 115 was more congregational, this one is deeply personal. As for background and context, we don't have any, as this psalm is anonymous. Here's what we do know (through gleaning information from the text): the psalmist gives thanks; speaks of his love for the Lord for all that he has done; and knows that, no matter where he is, no matter what happens to him, God will deliver him from death, as he has done countless times before. So, why am I so stuck on verse 7 ("Return to your rest, my soul, for the LORD has been good to you.")?

Bear with me here. This feels weird to say, but I have been *set aside* since day one. I came from a fully intact, loving home, and my parents are still together and still love each other (not that they've never had their problems—but they've seen them through). I know too many people who have come from broken and/or abusive homes, or even homes in which Mom and Dad were together but their love for either each other or their kids wasn't demonstrated or received. I also came from a home with parents who taught me the love, grace, forgiveness, and fear of the Lord. I was raised going to church; at different points my parents served as either elders or deacons. I've simply always known God. This is why I feel that I have been "set aside" since day one. My upbringing could have been broken—as so many are—but by God's grace I have never known that pain or the accompanying uncertainty. I have never known extreme chaos, familial heartache and brokenness, or anything else *but* God. And for that I give thanks. *So, why am I so stuck on verse 7?*

The psalmist clearly has been through quite a bit in his life. Verse 1 speaks of a crying out, of a felt need of mercy and of seeing God deliver. Verse 3 speaks of death entangling him and anguish overcoming him (we find very similar words in Jonah 2:5), and then verse 8 speaks of death, tears, and stumbling, . . . and all along God delivered. Every single time. The psalmist's response to all that God has done? Praise, thanks, and vows of love and service. Why? Because every time God delivered. It didn't matter what the author had gone through or experienced. God always provided, cared for, watched over, protected, and delivered. So, why *wouldn't* he praise him? Why *wouldn't* he give thanks! I would do the same.

When I read verse 7, I'm challenged and convicted by the "return" and "has been" that I read in it. The psalmist appears to be telling his own soul that God has always been good, that God has always protected him—followed by a call for that soul to *return* to rest. Which to me implies that his soul isn't already at rest at this point. For whatever reason, his soul is uneasy, restless, and wavering. Which gives me comfort (which is awkward to admit).

For all the protection God has provided throughout my life, for all the hard things that *could* have happened to me, for all the guidance God has given—there are times when my soul is not at rest. There are times when I still struggle with wondering whether I'm going to make it through whatever given circumstance confronts me. There are still times when I doubt that God really is going to continue to protect me. And why? He has never failed, though I'm not the best follower and truster (that's not *exactly* a word—but it fits).

I think that most of our lives are sprinkled with seasons of doubt. I suspect that most of us experience times during which, while we know God and continue to declare his love and grace, we wonder whether we're going to pull through and whether God is still going to watch over us. While this psalm doesn't speak of sin and forgiveness, I know that many of us, when we experience doubt and fear, wonder whether that very doubt will make God question his protection of us. *That* is why I'm stuck on verse 7. For all that God has done, there are still times when my soul is restless. Even though God has always come through, even though the Lord has consistently been *more than good* to me—more so than I have even deserved—I still experience those seasons of unrest in my soul.

I suspect that all of us go through those seasons when we need to remember not only that God *does* always come through (I would challenge you to point to a promise that he has broken or failed to deliver on) but that this kind of experience is not only okay but also common. We are all broken. We all doubt. We all are struck with fear, and we all wonder about God's love and grace. This is normal. It's normal because, again, *we're broken*. Sin has ravaged every inch of our lives, penetrating every fiber of our body and corrupting every space in our head. So, first off, we all need to remember that this is not unusual.

Second, Christ came to redeem the broken, the doubter, and the fearful soul. God did not send his Son to die for the perfect or the "always-at-peace" person. You and I and everyone else are included in this. So, remember that Christ died for you—and that includes *every aspect of you*, including your brokenness.

Finally (and more importantly), God's love and grace *always are*. God's protection will always be. His deliverance is final and complete. None of these are dependent on my faithfulness, my completeness, nor the ability of my soul to stay strong and focused on him. Grace, forgiveness, deliverance—simply *are*. They're based on him and his love, his work and its completion upon the cross. Why? Because, while Christ was fully human, he was also fully God, and his faithfulness to the Father is 100% pure and complete. The joy and hope we have may well include the reality that *our* times of faithlessness don't hold water in comparison to what he has done. While our souls might not be at rest at this or that point in time, this doesn't undue what he has done. Our unrest doesn't undo our deliverance.

So, yes, "return, O my soul, to rest, for the LORD has been good to you"—even though you are not always good to him or deserving of his goodness.

THREE QUESTIONS FOR YOU TO CHEW ON:

1. What in this psalm speaks your name? To what are you drawn? Why?
2. Does God *keep* us from certain painful experiences? Or is our lot in life simply varied and seemingly almost random?
3. Why do we struggle with working through our honest emotions of doubt, despair, and frustration with God? Are we afraid that God cannot handle them?

A SHORT PSALM OF IMMENSE PRAISE

Take a moment to read through Psalm 117.

Did that take long to read? Probably not. This psalm is the shortest psalm in all of Scripture. And on top of that, if you were to add up all the different chapters of the Bible (from Genesis through Revelation) and then find its very center, this psalm would fall precisely where you'd land. This psalm is short, to the point, and simply about *praise*. We begin with praise and end with praise, . . . and the middle gives the reason: because God's love is immensely great, and his faithfulness endures forever. It's as though we have here a praise Oreo.

We don't know who wrote this short expression of praise, but it's part of the "Hallel psalms" (again, Psalms 113–118). These psalms are meant to be sung by the readers or singers in a worship service, acclaiming God's faithful love and enduring presence. The Hallel psalms praise God for his vast and unending work (Psalm 113), as well as for his salvation (Psalm 114), his dedication and protection (Psalm 115), his mercy and compassion (Psalm 116), his love (our psalm today), and his enduring work (Psalm 118). When Jesus was about to depart to the Mount of Olives on that final Passover night of his life, Matthew (26:30) states that he and his disciples sang a hymn, and most commentators feel that this hymn would likely have been one of these Hallel psalms. While we don't know whether it was *this* one specifically, many commentators agree that Psalm 117 appears to have been the most fitting in terms of its relation to who Christ is, what he spoke of, and what he was doing. Even Paul quotes this psalm (in summary) in Romans 15:7–13 to proclaim who Christ is and what he came to do. *So, for all its brevity, this psalm is heavy in its association with Christ.* Psalm 117 is a psalm of hope, love, mercy, forgiveness, joy, anticipation, and grace. It's a psalm of God's enduring love.

As I write this, we are in the season of Advent. What does your praise look like during this time? I'm caught between two different praise styles. On the one hand, I'm moved by the angels and their pronouncement to the shepherds in Luke 2:8–20. A praise with light, and sound, and singing, and clearly one of pomp and circumstance. I love to praise God in that manner and look forward to spending eternity praising him like that in the company of vast choirs. And yet, I'm also moved by the song "Silent Night" and its unelaborated declaration that "all is calm, all is bright." While I picture that night as having been anything *but* calm and silent (have you ever been to, or through, a delivery? Yeah, even there in the stable it probably wasn't all that calm). I do feel that the earth and all of creation took a deep breath . . . and then exhaled a sigh of relief—for that night brought the Savior into the world. Jesus's birth was the ultimate declaration of God's faithful and enduring love for all the nations and all of creation. The "calm" and "silent" adjectives might describe that exhalation of relief, for the earth and all creation had been waiting and yearning for God's redemption. So, yeah, . . . my "praise" of God right now is kind of all over the map! And yet it's the same praise, in terms of content, no matter what the style. I praise God for his love, his compassion, his dedication to his people, his covenant faithfulness. I praise him for the Holy Spirit and his work, as still to this day he is drawing us close to the One who loves us with an unending love, and for my Lord and Savior, who came to earth as a baby so that he could take away my sins.

Where and what is your praise on this day? What does it look like? Silent? Blazingly glorious? Raucous and ecstatic? Maybe it's even the "fall-to-my-knees" in tears variety and style. All of these approaches are right and true—because all of them constitute a response to God's great and faithful love.

THREE QUESTIONS FOR YOU TO CHEW ON:

1. What in this psalm speaks to you? What draws you in? Why?
2. Does your praise of God change depending on the season, time, location, and place? If so—how and why?
3. In this season (wherever it falls on the calendar year), how are you encouraged to praise God?

A PSALM OF
GOD'S ENDURING LOVE

Today's reading begins with Psalm 118.

This psalm, for me, is littered with New Testament images and bits of other Scripture. Why? Because it is quoted throughout the New Testament. This psalm was a typical song that was sung during Old Testament Israelite/ Jewish festivals (it ends our series of "Hallel" songs that began with Psalm 113). When Jesus triumphantly rode into Jerusalem on a donkey during that Passion week, this song was sung (Matthew 21:9). As is clearly stated in the opening four verses, as well as repeatedly throughout the psalm and then in the final verse as well, it is about the *enduring love of God*.

What does it mean for a love to "endure" forever? It means that it doesn't end, . . . and yet, in this case, it never *began*, either. It simply always has been (even before time) and always will be. In this case, God's love eternally exists, and that alone should give us pause and imbue us with hope. But let us not stop there. Because if God's love eternally exists, if God's love really does endure forever, then there are some massive implications we must understand:

1. God's love cannot, and will not, dwindle. *No matter what.* Because if it always *was*, then it always *will be.*
2. God's love will not be removed or changed. Even as we read in this psalm that the Lord "chastened" the psalmist severely for something he had done (v. 18), God's wrath did not cause God to put him to death. On the contrary, God's love provided salvation (v. 21), as well as opening up the door of righteousness. No matter what we do, God's love doesn't change direction away from us. I cannot push God's love from me. I may not *feel* loved, but that's only my emotion speaking and not the reality.

3. God's love responds. If God's love has always been—then God's love was present already in creation, as well as in his response to the sins of his people. There simply is no way to separate God from his love. No wonder we see it throughout the New Testament! Christ *is* the living love of God because Christ came *because of* God's love for his people.

The struggle we often experience is that we want to put caveats on God's love. If we are to proclaim that God's love endures forever, then we must realize that this is a love that is bigger and wider and longer and deeper than ourselves. The psalmist encourages Israel to declare this (v. 2), calls out that the "house of Aaron" needs to declare it (v. 3), and then proclaims that "all those who fear the LORD" must declare it as well (v. 4). So, we begin large, with God's chosen people (the Israelites); narrow the focus of God's love embrace to a smaller group, the priests; and finally burst forth in the opposite direction, moving back through the chosen people and the priests to unrestricted inclusivity, encouraging anyone and everyone who fears the Lord to declare his enduring love. The clear implication is that God's love is bigger than me, bigger than my church, bigger than my community, bigger than my state, bigger than my country, bigger than my continent, bigger even than this world—encompassing all of us, as well as any aliens (Who is to say?) who might live in other galaxies and earth-like planets (if there are any). I do not have an exclusive hold of God's enduring love. Neither does my church or my denomination or tradition—and definitely not the United States, where I live—or any other national entity that might lay claim to God's favor.

We need to stop putting a cap or lid on God's love. We need to stop insisting that *this or that sin* keeps people away from God. We need to stop ranking sins, ranking people, or judging anyone and everyone based on who they are or what they've done. Because it's not *about* us. It's about God. It's about what he has done, will do, and continues to do. It's about him and his work, his love, his life-giving, salvation-granting, righteousness-imbuing work. Once again, we see this beautifully expressed in verses 18 and 19. The psalmist declares that he has done something atrocious and horrible and that the Lord has punished him (he has been visited with consequences for his actions), but the Lord hasn't snuffed out his life because of this. Not only has God not taken out his life, but God has opened up the door of righteousness for this sinner. This unrighteous person is able to walk *through* and *into* the gate of righteousness because of God. In fact, God himself opens that door and allows the sinner to enter.

Does that sound familiar? It should. The whole Old Testament reflects the constant life-saving work, patience, and love of God, and then the whole New Testament is one giant reflection of it. And it's all summed up in one person: Jesus. This psalm is about God and what he does for his people. It proclaims that, no matter what you have done, where you have been, or what you deserve, *love* is what you will receive. Salvation is granted unto you, righteousness is bestowed upon you, life is given to you, and it is the Lord who saves you.

The Lord's love endures forever? Absolutely. But that love is much more than enduring—it's all-powerful, all-consuming, and always forgiving. No wonder his Old Testament people sang about his love as a body of believers!

THREE QUESTIONS FOR YOU TO CHEW ON:

1. What in this psalm speaks to you? Where are you drawn? Why?
2. How have you seen the pursuing love of God at work in your life?
3. How do you comprehend the idea of "enduring love"? All we know in our human life is things that start and end—and yet God's isn't constrained by time (or space, for that matter). How does that even make sense? Or do we just have to accept it as true?

A PSALM OF TORAH

My challenge for you today is not simply to take a few moments to engage with a few verses but to commit yourself to reading through all 22 stanzas (each eight verses long) of this massive psalm, Psalm 119.

This skillfully executed masterpiece is arranged in an "acrostic" style (with each section, at least in the original Hebrew, beginning with the next consecutive letter of the Hebrew alphabet). The intention was that this clever pneumonic device would facilitate memorization of this very long piece by the follower of God and his Law. More impressive still, verses 1–8 make up the first collection/poem, and *each of the verses in this section* also begins with the same (in this case the first) Hebrew letter. Verses 9–16 follow suit, with each line beginning with the second Hebrew letter, and so on throughout the psalm.

All 22 stanzas of this giant psalm (the longest we have with its total of 176 verses) are about the *Law of God* (the *Torah*, which is actually synonymous with the first five books of the Old Testament in their entirety). This poem is about *knowing* the law, *following* the law, *obeying* the law, and *loving* the law (the Hebrew word translated "law" appears 25 times—more than any other single word in the psalm). But *why* was this done? On the one hand, as mentioned above, the psalm was written this way because it would have been easier for people with an oral tradition to memorize it. On the other hand, and more importantly, *the Law is everything*. It shows us how our relationships *should* work while revealing how broken we are in terms of keeping its precepts. The Law challenges us to live as godly people, and yet it also reveals God's truth, love, grace, and hope for his people.

So, let me ask: Do you love the law?

That may be hard to answer. Maybe we, as New Testament believers, have failed to remember just how important the Law is to us. We may think of it as an archaic, Old Testament (old covenant) set of regulations rendered obsolete by Christ's sacrificial death). We may view the Old Testament Law (roughly synonymous with the Ten Commandments, although there were some 600 additional rules that good Jewish boys and girls read and followed right on through adulthood). Since I'm not Jewish, may I assume that I don't need to know it, love it, or follow it? If that's our thinking, then maybe, just maybe, . . . we're wrong. Maybe we need a little "Torah 101" to help us.

- The Torah points to Jesus. In John 1:45 we hear Philip and Nathanael proclaim that, when they saw and met Jesus, they realized that he was the One whom Moses had spoken of and the Torah proclaims. Then in John 5:46–47 we find Jesus proclaiming that, if we know and believe in Moses, we should know and believe in Jesus because Moses spoke of him. So, we have hints of Jesus, proclamations of his coming, and hints of God's work through him (as seen in texts like Exodus 15:2).
- We need to stop thinking that the Law (Torah) is separate from Scripture. The Law is part of our Scripture—and all of Scripture is God-breathed and profitable for teaching, reproof, correction, instruction, and equipping" God's people to do good works (2 Timothy 3:16–17). This is why we don't read only the New Testament but the Old Testament as well. This is also why preachers must preach from both Testaments in their sermons.
- The Torah convicts our hearts and draws us closer to God because it reveals the truth of his Law, his commands, and the ways he wants us to live in this world with him and others (Deuteronomy 5:29).
- Jesus kept and taught the Torah. If it was good enough for Jesus to follow, abide in, teach, and read, . . . then don't you think it would be good enough for you and me? Yeah—probably. Oh, and you know what "Christian" means? It means "follower of Christ"—so, . . . we should probably follow the One we're called to follow. Just a thought. (First John 2:6 is a good verse here).
- Jesus proclaimed in Matthew 5:17–19 that, while he came to fulfill the Law, that doesn't mean he has abolished it. Torah still exists, and its precepts are still to be followed until his second coming takes place (Revelation 21:1–4).

- All the convicting, challenging, lifting up, encouraging, love, and work that the Holy Spirit does *enables us to keep the law and abide by God's precepts.* We need to see that, as Christians, we are called to walk in God's light, abide in his Word, follow his commands, love him and love others, serve him and serve others—and *all of that is part of the Law.* If the Holy Spirit, the third Person in the Trinity, is here to empower us, challenge us, and help us to feel God's presence, then he does so in a way that draws us *to his law.* Romans 8:5–7 proclaims that our sinful ways are hostile toward God and that, when we live according to the Spirit, we set our minds on the things of God. So, following his Law means that we draw closer to him as we love, serve, and think as he does.
- Finally, but certainly not least, Jesus came because of the Law and to fulfill its requirements. Romans 8:3–4 reminds us that the Law was, and is, still in place—and yet Christ came to die on our behalf in order to fulfill it.

Let us not neglect the law, disregard it, or tuck it away, thinking it has nothing to do with us, because in truth it has *everything* to do with us. The Law is what we need in order to know God, abide in him, and love him. It is through his Law that our eyes are opened to our sins. The big difference today from yesterday (New Testament vs. Old Testament times) is that by Jesus we are saved. As one author writes, "We don't keep Torah *to be saved*; we keep it *because we're saved!*" The Torah? Yeah, . . . kind of a big deal. No wonder people sang it, memorized it, and loved it. But do you?

THREE QUESTIONS FOR YOU TO CHEW ON:

1. What in this psalm speaks to you? To which section or theme do you find yourself drawn? Why?
2. How have you felt about the Law? Do you feel as though Christians may forget about it or think of it as something that was abolished by Christ's sacrifice and is hence obsolete today?
3. How can we make the Law of God more important to Christians?

PSALM 119: ALEPH

Before today's devotional reading, reread with me the first section of Psalm 119, verses 1–8.

The beginning of this psalm declares that one is "blessed" when they fully walk in obedience to the Law (the Torah). The psalmist claims that, when you keep God's statues, when you follow what God asks of you, when you seek him and his ways with all your heart, you not only are blessed, you not only recognize that you are blameless and perfect, but your obedience to God *is perfect*. He acknowledges that God's rules not only change you but are here to lead and guide you along a good and right path, a path that blesses you. But then there's the kick to the shin: after the psalmist declares all that good stuff, he looks at himself and declares, "That's not me. I wish it were—but it's not" (v. 5).

The psalmist's recognition of his own sins and failures doesn't comprise much of the psalm, only two verses, but that's enough to make us pause and wonder. What is it exactly that he has done? What "ways" is he speaking of that have not been steadfast? How has he not been obeying God's decrees? Clearly, he feels himself to have been "put to shame" by his actions, but *what*, *where*, and *why*? Where's the context?

The easiest thing for us to do is look at the end of verse 6 to get some understanding—but that's pretty much where it ends. While we may not know the gory details of the psalmist's failures, we do read that he was falling short in following the commands of God. Which ones? All of them. Commands like putting God above all else, not worshiping false gods, loving his neighbor, keeping the Sabbath holy, abstaining from certain foods, seeking to be cleansed when he consumed or touched unholy things, . . . and hundreds of other laws. The list is lengthy (613, to be exact), but the point is that the psalmist knows how he is *supposed* to act and simply has not. Has he chosen not to? We don't know. But this isn't about getting down on himself/ourselves for what he/we have failed to do. These eight verses are about recognizing what we *should* do, the goodness of those things (the laws), our failure in obeying them, and our moving forward in a healthy direction.

I think that we often approach our failures in the opposite manner from what we should. We tend to look at what we *haven't* done, what we have failed to do, and then chastise ourselves for those shortfalls. We look at each broken step we've taken, each wrong move we've made, and focus on *that*, instead of saying, "Okay, I failed—here's how I'm going to move forward." The difference? One focuses on the failures, while the other focuses on the healings and corrections. Ultimately, this is what I love about verses 7 and 8. The psalmist makes a stand that he is going to do better. He isn't going to focus on what he has done—because, well, what's done is done. Instead, he is going to praise God, focus on his righteous laws, and move forward. So, when the psalmist declares in verse 7 that he "will praise [God] with an upright heart," I get the image of a person standing up and making that declaration. He is not going to wallow in his failure but is declaring (this is the "standing" part) that from now on his praise and worship of God will be holy, blameless, and from a full—an all-in, thoroughly committed—heart. He will follow God's ways, walk along his paths, and fully obey the laws God has given (those laws declared in vv. 1–3).

I think that we too often focus on our missteps and failures. Too often we're so hard on ourselves that we feel it's impossible to get back on the right path. It's as though we tell ourselves that our trajectory along the wrong path somehow prevents us from re-tracing our steps and returning to the point at which we went astray; perhaps it even prevents us from leaping from where we are onto the *right* path. If that's a place you currently find yourself—let me tell you: that line of thinking is false. We do not believe in a God who tallies up our wrongs and lets us sit and stew right where we are—unable to right ourselves or get back on track. We do not believe in a God who says, "Once you've walked away you can never come back." We believe in a God who responds by forgiving our sins. One who speaks of forgiveness seventy times seven times [think infinity!] (Matthew 18:21–22). We believe in a God who sees his wayward child coming home and unabashedly runs toward her with arms outstretched. We need to recognize that this is *after* that ungrateful child has shouted in her father's face that she wishes he were dead . . . and treated him as such (Luke 15:11–32).

We believe in a God who forgave by giving his sinless Son's very life for us.

We believe in a God who holds to his covenantal word of love, no matter how many times we break his Law.

We believe in a God who allows us to take the paths we choose and yet declares that the path we take does not define us or have anything to do with where we will end up. That's because God's grace is above and beyond and *vastly* more powerful than any decision you or I could ever make.

We believe in a God who, through his Son, Jesus Christ, took our failures at keeping the Law and fulfilled that Law completely on our behalf and in our place.

We believe in a God of love who does not forsake.

So, I affirm wholeheartedly what the psalmist declares: that while he has failed miserably at holding to God's Word, that doesn't mean he is destined to be a failure for all eternity. We, too, can stand firm and upright; while the God of love, grace, and mercy *does* call us to be blameless and to walk according to his perfect Law and Word, he knows full well that we don't and can't.

THREE QUESTIONS FOR YOU TO CHEW ON:

1. Is there a part of this text that stands out for you? A part that speaks directly to you? Why is that?
2. Why does God call us to be blameless even though he knows we cannot? What's the point? If we are destined to fail, then why even try?
3. How do we praise God with an "upright heart"? What does that look like?

PSALM 119: BETH

Let's read together the next section of this lengthy psalm, Psalm 119:9–16. This portion of the psalm begins by asking a deceptively simple and yet complex, timeless question: How do I walk along the path of purity? Now for you and me, that may seem like an odd question—or maybe it's just me. The Hebrew word here means "proper" or "innocent," but even more than that it brings the connotation of a superior moral quality. For me—and again, this is me—I picture some hoity-toity person who never does the wrong thing, always makes the right choice, has never gotten a bad grade, has never defied her parents, and has never had to sneak into the house because she missed curfew—in general, someone who is *beyond* perfect. But is that what the psalmist is claiming to be?

No. He is asking a question—so, in case you've missed it (as I tend to do)—here it is again with some emphases that are really important (read it, even if just in your mind, using these inflections): "How *can* a young person *stay* on the *path* of purity?" David is declaring not only that he is *not* pure but that everything he does keeps knocking him off this path of purity, . . . and yet he wants to walk it. He wants to be of a high moral character. He wants to make himself pure (think of washing here), wants to be proper and proclaims to be innocent—but he just isn't. So, what is he to do now? How can someone who is walking down the wrong path get himself onto the right one?

We first need to clarify just what the wrong or the right path *is*—because, ultimately, this is about making the right choices in life. The psalmist doesn't delineate what those wrong choices might be, but we can find them "hidden" (or maybe not so hidden) in this set of verses:

- Verse 9b: Living according to God's Word
- Verse 10: Seeking God's heart and following his commands (this would be the Law, including for the Old Testament faithful those 613 additional commands the people were supposed to adhere to)
- Verse 11: Not sinning against God
- Verse 12: Learning God's decrees
- Verse 13: Speaking the Law rather than just knowing it
- Verse 14: Following the statues of God
- Verse 15: Reflecting on God's way and Word
- Verse 16: Seeing the beauty of God's Law, finding joy in it, and obeying the Word of God

This is the path the psalmist professes to *want* to be on. It's a path that leads to joy, happiness, and eventual purity. Yeah, that's what I *want*, too, but how attainable is it? Not so much. But is it a pipe dream? Is it some false reality that we try to achieve but know we never will? If that's the case, why even try? Because I know this is not going to be my reality. I will sin—a lot. I will *not* stay on that path of purity because I wander all over the place, and my attention span is like that of a dog who is walking along, doing great, and then sees a squirrel and takes off running!

I know I've said this quite a few times about the psalms, but I love the fact that they are not only timeless but also extremely honest. I love the way the psalmist, in this text, declares what he knows he needs to do, but in that same breath declares that it's going to be hard. Here are a few examples:

1. "Do not let me stray"—The psalmist is declaring that he *will* stray so needs God to hold him close. (v. 10)
2. "that I might not sin against you."—The psalmist recognizes that he *will* sin against God. He hopes he won't but knows otherwise. (v. 11)
3. "Teach me your decrees"—What I love about those four words is that the psalmist is saying, "I don't know what the right thing to do is, I'm probably doing the wrong thing, but I do know that your ways are right and true—so, teach me the right things so I can stop doing wrong." (v. 12)
4. "I recount all the laws that come *from your mouth*" (my emphasis added). I love this last phrase, because it implies that the laws that come from *our* mouths are not the laws of God. (v. 13)

These eight verses declare that the ways of God are good, and yet the young person knows that it is a struggle to walk his path. More than a struggle: it's impossible, and he needs God to lead, guide, uphold, and help him, . . . which is why I love that question in the opening verse: "How can a young person stay on the path of purity?" Answer, once again (in case we've forgotten already): we can't. Better answer/understanding: it's a path that *leads* to purity—it isn't about already *being pure* while we're on it!

You and I, because of God's grace through the redemption of Jesus Christ (Romans 3:24), understand that this is the very reason Christ came! I'll say it again: we know that the path we're on isn't *already* pure, but because of Christ our path *leads to* purity—because *he himself* is pure. We're called to walk that path and work toward purity (by following the laws, precepts, and decrees of God), all the while understanding that we cannot keep God's laws completely. This is a beautiful lesson for all of us broken sinners.

THREE QUESTIONS FOR YOU TO CHEW ON:

1. What does the path *of* (or perhaps we should say *to,* given our understanding, above) purity look like for you? Are you currently on it? What changes should/will you make?
2. Are you like me and have a vision of what someone "pure" looks like? If so, is that vision negative or positive? If negative—why? Why is "doing the right thing" so often seen as negatory?
3. Verse 14 seems to work completely against the ways of this world. How can we "rejoice" in the statues of God, just as, or more than, one rejoices in "great riches" (like money and "stuff")?

PSALM 119: GIMEL

The next section of Psalm 119 covers verses 17–24. I invite you to reread these verses to refresh your memory.

The psalmist here finds blessings in the Word of God—which is nothing new because that's what this whole psalm is about. We see that he wants to obey the Word of God while he lives (v. 17), that he wants to see the wonder of the Law (v. 18), and that his soul is literally "consumed with longing for [God's] laws" (v. 20). The psalmist goes into the fact that there are people in this world (rulers; the arrogant; and those who show "scorn and contempt" for God's and his laws, who want nothing to do with the Law and thus seek to distance themselves from him. Again, none of this is anything new—so, what is this passage saying? How are we challenged by this word?

First off, we need to recognize that the repetition here is deliberate, intended to reinforce the psalmist's point(s) in the minds most particularly of his *listeners*. This psalm is stating that there is so much richness, so much depth, so much hope, so much truth, so much *life* in the Law that he is seeing only the smallest part of it. His own eyes are only scratching the surface, but it is at this surface that he recognizes more and more layers of God's blessings in his Word. Yet the psalmist recognizes that the more he scratches that surface, the deeper he delves, the more he finds himself at odds with people of this world, . . . and the more he needs God's help.

So, what does that mean for you and me?

First off, we must recognize that God's Word is vast and deep and that there simply is no way for us to plumb its depths. It seems as though, for every step we move downward toward understanding those depths, twenty more steps are revealed. Should we be discouraged by this? Maybe—but only because many of us want to know everything. Sorry, that's impossible; the truth is, anyway, that God's Word wouldn't make sense to us unless the Holy Spirit revealed it to us. So, take hope in the fact that each time you "scratch" away at the Word of God, a beautiful new truth is revealed. Take the time in each instance to dwell in *that new truth*.

Second, do not allow yourself to get complacent with the Word of God. Don't just read it once, set it aside, and check this item off your bucket list. Continue to read because God continues to reveal. There are times when we just gloss over a given verse or passage, only to come back to it days, weeks, months, or years later and exclaim, "Where in world did *that* come from! I don't remember *ever* reading that before!" So, keep on reading. Keep on finding the truth and comfort in God's Word.

Third, and this goes back to the reason for Psalm 119, *know the Law.* The Law of God declares what it means to be holy, righteous, good, and just. As Paul proclaims in Romans 7:7, the Law of God shows us our brokenness, our sin, and opens our eyes to how bad we truly are. So, don't think of the Law as some collection of outdated commands of God. Remember that they are still pertinent today. Although Christ came to fulfill the Law on our behalf (Matthew 5:17–20), these requirements are absolutely current for disciples in our day.

Finally, we must understand that this broken world (broken until Christ returns and makes everything new) wants nothing to do with the goodness that people are able to accomplish when they follow the Law. You're gonna feel like a stranger at times, . . . maybe even *all the time.* Even worse: you're gonna be talked about, slandered, and hated upon; people may even try to cut you down. But never should you or I stray from what God calls us to be. We are not to repay evil with evil, slander with slander, or hate with hate. So, when the world is trying to cut you down—hold firm to the Word of God and the Law he has given.

THREE QUESTIONS FOR YOU TO CHEW ON:

1. What in this section speaks most pointedly to you? At what point are you drawn in? Why?
2. How are you doing in terms of your daily devotional time and reading of Scripture? I know that life can be busy and that I can easily neglect spending even five minutes each day reading. Make it a priority. If you have problems remembering, then *schedule* some time with God and his Word. It may sound weird, but I actually enter this into the calendar on my phone. It works for me—discover what works for you.
3. What gives you strength to keep on going each day when people around you aren't abiding by the goodness of God? How do you stay in his Word and continue living by his Law when it's so easy to conform to the ways of this world?

PSALM 119: DALETH

Today we will consider Psalm 119:25–32.

From the outset of this section, we can see that our writer is in a dark place—and not just physically. We see that his soul is emotionally weary (v. 28) and that he needs God to strengthen him. He has been reflecting on the wrongs he has committed (v. 29) to the point that, ultimately, he considers himself "dust" (v. 25); perhaps we could rephrase this as "near death."

I'm struck by verses 26 and 27. The psalmist is declaring that he has "given an account" of *his* ways. He has either explained and confessed to God what he has done, defended his actions to God, or come to the conclusion that his way of living has been atrocious. But now? Now he realizes that his way of doing life has also been harmful. That the actions he has taken have brought him down to the dust and that, in order to go on living, he needs to understand and follow God and his statues. There is a *right* way and a *wrong* way to live.

The wrong way: my way.

The right way: God's way.

For me as a parent, one of the very first things I learned is that my job entails preventing my kids from dying, keeping them fed, and teaching them to learn a degree of independence that will help them to become self-sustaining adults at some point. And yet it seems as though so much of their younger years was fraught with frustration on my part in that they insisted on trying to do everything on their own. The frustration didn't come from the mere fact that they felt the need to try to do everything without the guidance of their father; it was all about the simple truth that there is a right and a wrong way to do things. There's an easy way and a hard way, and it seemed as though my kids always preferred the hard way. Yes, I want them to try on their own, to fail, and then to get back up and try again, but at some point this just gets ridiculous. At some point, son and daughter of mine, you just need to stop and let me show you, correct you, and guide you (I like to tease them that their stubbornness comes from their mother—but that'd be a lie).

Our psalmist is at the point at which he has done things his way and now recognizes that his way has been wrong. His prayer here is to be drawn closer to God, to be taught *his* ways (the right way), and for God to strengthen him as he moves from the dust (from the lip of the grave) back into life. It is now that the psalmist declares that he desires to be faithful to the Word of God, to know it, to be strengthened by it, to be encouraged by it, and to gain hope from it. Why? Because he recognizes that his way has not only been wrong but also harmful.

So, where is the challenge here? Well, for me it's simple: How often don't I feel constricted by the Word of God? How often don't I feel that things would be easier *my way,* as opposed to *God's* way? Why is it that I *know* God's Word gives life (Proverbs 3:1–2) and is meant to help and not hinder (v. 50), and yet I still find that I'm trying to do it *my* way when I know *God's* way would in reality be *so much easier?* Slow learner? Yes. Yes, I am.

My brokenness, and yours, means that there are times when we feel we can do things better on our own. Our brokenness means that, while we know God's Word is there to help us, we still find that there are times we don't *want* any help. Just as with a little child, there are moments in our lives when "my way" takes over and "God's way" gets pushed to the side. And then, just like that child once we've realized we can't do it, we come running back to our parent, in tears, frustrated that it didn't work out the way we had planned/thought/desired.

If we pull back from this part of the psalm and begin to look at Scripture as a whole, we begin to get the *whole* story of God's "let-me-do-it-on-my-own" children. And within every story we see God's children failing and failing and failing again. But when we look at the whole picture of Scripture, we see an even *bigger* story than that of strong-willed, failed children. We see God's patience. We see God's correction. We see God's aid and assistance. We see God's embrace (following those times when we've push him away and growled, "Let *me* do it!"). Ultimately, we see God taking over of the situation, removing us from the dust and setting us back down into life. All of Scripture is about God's loving patience with his children and his work to correct them from their deceitful ways. All of Scripture is about Jesus Christ and his correcting us from our wrong ways and giving us right ways.

- Jesus restores us from dust into life. (v. 25)
- Jesus preserves our life, (v. 25)
- Jesus is God's "wonderful deed" on our behalf. (v. 27)
- Our souls go from "wear[iness] with sorrow" (v. 28) to joyful elation, as Christ has given us life in his death.

- By Christ's full adherence to and fulfillment of the Law (Romans 10:4), and by his taking us with him in his life and death, we too are kept from deceitful ways (this doesn't mean we won't do bad things—it simply means that we are ultimately forgiven through Christ).

Does this mean that we'll still keep trying to do things on our own? Yup. And it also means that we'll keep failing. But, hopefully, we'll continue to remember that God's way is not only the right way but the better and easier (let's make that "best" and "easiest"). It's a lesson from eternity . . . and a lesson we'll keep learning till the day we die.

THREE QUESTIONS FOR YOU TO CHEW ON:

1. What in this portion of Psalm 119 speaks to you? Where are you drawn in? Why?
2. Is there a particular lesson you keep failing to learn? Why is it so hard to learn this lesson and stop from repeating the same mistakes?
3. If God knows what's best for us, why do you think he even allows us to walk down the wrong path or make stupid mistakes at times? Wouldn't it be easier for all of us if God were to just keep us on the straight and narrow and/or impart into our minds via osmosis the right thing to do in certain situations?

PSALM 119: HE

I invite you today to read with me Psalm 119:33–40.

Faithfulness is an interesting and important word. It's the backbone of and the glue for marriage. It's what friendships cling to, employers ask for, and all of life's relationships desire. You remain faithful to me, and I remain faithful to you. But what about our relationship with God? Is there faithfulness there? Absolutely (no question, at least, from *his* side). As this caveat implies, that faithfulness is guaranteed to go in only one direction (spoiler alert: it's a top-down faithfulness we can count on; we aren't consistently faithful to God by any stretch. Sorry if that's news to you).

Faithfulness is a running theme throughout these eight verses of Psalm 119, and what we see here are two variations of it going on: God's complete faithfulness to his Word and then (yup, you've guessed it) the lack thereof on the part of the psalmist.

Here are the lack-of-faithfulness points made by the psalmist in the text. Just to be clear, and to pull this into our context, I'm switching from the psalmist, as our human representative, to us.

- Verse 33: "that I may follow. We simply aren't going to follow very closely, so this "may" is a request for God to work on our behalf.
- Verse 34: "that I may keep your law and obey it with all my heart." Here we see yet another failure coming up that we must acknowledge.
- Verse 35: "direct me in the path." We need God's guidance and direction because we aren't going to walk the right path on our own.
- Verse 36: "Turn my heart towards your statues." Left on our own, we'll turn toward our own selfish gains. Every . . . single . . . time.
- Verse 37: "Turn my eyes away from worthless things." Ditto the above.
- Verse 37: "preserve my life . . . according to your word." We cannot do life on our own; it is only God and *his* faithfulness (his *word*) that will preserve life for us.
- Verse 39: "take away the disgrace I dread." What would disgrace a believer? Disobeying God and his Word—which means that there is no faithfulness in our future (it's as though the psalmist is conceding that unfaithfulness will take place and that disgrace will befall him regardless, . . . so please God, just take away my disgrace *now!*)

That's a lot of unfaithfulness on our part. But what about God's side? What about God's loyalty and faithfulness to his children? We could work through this section line by line, as we did above, and point out the *opposite* of what God's *unfaithful* children do—but we don't need to because the undisputed reality is that God is faithful *despite* our unfaithfulness! *How much more faithful could God be?*

God is faithful despite the fact that we turn away from his decrees. God is faithful despite the fact that we know the Law of God and yet choose to avoid it, ignore it, work against it, and look away from it. God is faithful to his wayward children, who, instead of walking along the path of holiness and righteousness, still decide to veer off into la-la land and head toward destruction, . . . even when goodness, hope, love, grace, and mercy are strewn all along the path that he has clearly marked out for us. It would be a different conversation if God's laws, decrees, and precepts were horrible and harmful—but they aren't. He asks us to follow them *because* they are life-giving, joyful, holy, and good. And that promise from God we read about in verse 38? That promise of love, devotion, faithfulness, preservation, hope, and a future? It's a promise rooted and founded in God's covenant.

Our psalmist does a beautiful job of declaring the faithfulness of God while unpacking not only *his* (and *our*) unfaithfulness but our need for God's faithfulness. It's a beautiful reminder that we are nothing without God's faithfulness. For the Christian, is there anyone more beautiful and more faithful than Jesus Christ, God's covenant and faithfulness in the flesh? (the answer is "no"—there is *nothing* and *no one* more beautiful than Christ).

THREE QUESTIONS FOR YOU TO CHEW ON:

1. What in this section speaks to you? At what point in particular do you relate to the psalmist? Why?
2. Reread these verses through a "Jesus lens." Where do you see a response from God, by way of Jesus, in these verses? Here's an example: How are we taught God's decrees? Through Jesus's teachings and by his words, his actions, and his love.
3. A non-believer (or a "seeker" of God) might look at the last verse and its request for a "preserved life" and wonder what that means. How would you respond? Do we believe that once you've come to Jesus you will never grow old and die?

PSALM 119: WAW

Please turn with me to Psalm 119:41–48 and reread these verses with me. "Law" and "love" are our themes in these eight verses. Which leads me to a simple opening question: Do you love the Law (commands) of God? Clearly our psalmist does, and while this is his writing and reflection, it should still mean something to us. *We too* should love the Law of God. We *too* should understand why we should love it and be led by it.

I know that I've written about this before, but the commands of God, for Christians, don't always feel as though they equate to expressions of love. The Jews understand this connection. They get it. They fully grasp that the Law, given directly by God, isn't a set of *rules* to be feared. Instead, there are, in total, 613 guidelines for love. The Torah tells the people of God how they are to walk with him and with each other. How they are to serve him and each other. How they are to act toward him and each other. Remember, the Law wasn't given on the seventh day after God had created—the Law came after the people had broken covenant (Genesis 3); been kicked out of Eden; lived for quite a while as rebellious, nonloving people of God (who didn't always recognize him, . . . but that's a tangent!); but then eventually were brought back to God as he led them out of Egypt. You and I need to see, and understand, that the Law is part of God's love. The Law is a representation of God's love handed down to his people. Instead of allowing them to run amok, harming others, harming themselves, and destroying any relationship with him, God gave them instructions on how to love each other, along with declarations of how *he loves them*. Remember, the Law isn't some random set of instructions—it's all about ways to live and actions to take, and it proclaims and highlights the very characteristics of God himself.

Our psalmist completely understands that God's love, through his Law, is what *he needs*. He sees it as his motivation for each day, sees God saving through his Law, and is so moved by the loving Law of God that he wants to obey it day in and day out. And so he makes a promise to God to always "hope" in that Law (v. 43); to always "obey" it (v. 44); to "walk" in its *freedom* (v. 45) (yup, you read that right); to speak of it always before all people, no matter what they say or do against it (v. 46); and to meditate (or reflect) on these precepts daily (v. 48).

Maybe I'm a cynic, or maybe I'm just too Reformed in my belief (thus declaring that we are so broken and full of sin that we cannot fulfill any part of the Law), but while I appreciate the psalmist's words and promise, I see immediately that this is just not going to happen. Will God's people always obey the Law? Nope. Will they speak of it before all people? Certainly not always. We'll do it when convenient or if there is a willing ear, but more often than not we'll find our lips sewn shut when they should be speaking. We simply cannot hold to the Law of God each day. The invasion of sin into our lives doesn't allow it.

But *that* is exactly why God's law *is love.* Again, these are the very characteristics of God that he has given us to live by and abide in. He wants us to love and serve like him, so he gave us rules and regulations that not only help us love and serve *like* him but draw us closer *to* him. Every time we love as he loves, serve as he serves, and sacrifice as he sacrifices, we inhale a breath of who he is. And in the end? All of the Law points to Jesus. As believers in Jesus Christ, we affirm, believe, and hold to the fact that Jesus is not only God's love in the flesh (1 John 4:7–12) but the fulfillment of the Law (Matthew 5:17–20). Jesus, in how he loved, served, and showed compassion and mercy, not only showed us what the Law looks like but *received* it for us and *bestowed* it upon us.

If you're anything like me, you need to stop looking at the Law of God as a set of rules and regulations and view it as more of a "love list" from God. All of us need to see the Law as tethered in Christ. It's too easy, in our brokenness, to view it as a bunch of no-no's and do not's rather than as a path of holiness, righteousness, love, and mercy. So, let me ask again: Do you love the Law? You should, . . . because to love the Law reflects that you love the One who gave it, fulfilled it, and lived into it, both in his living and in his dying. David's request at the beginning of this text is for God's "unfailing love" to come to him—is that not embodied in Jesus?

THREE QUESTIONS FOR YOU TO CHEW ON:

1. What is there in this portion of the psalm that speaks your name? Why?
2. What does it mean to "hope" in God's laws (v. 43b)? What does that look like for you and me?
3. How does Romans 13:8 enhance your understanding of God's Law? Do you find this verse helpful? This can also be a difficult challenge for us. Which side is true for you, . . . or can you relate to aspects of both?

PSALM 119: ZAYIN

Begin your reading today with Psalm 119:49–56.

Hope is our theme here. We see it in the beginning of the text, as the psalmist claims the "word" of God is his hope; we see hope as his comfort in suffering, as well as his preservation in life. We see hope as comfort once again, this time in the "ancient laws" of God and in the remembrance of God's name; and, finally, we see it as the author practices God's Law. For him, hope is everywhere and everything.

I've always struggled with the definition and understanding of *hope*. So often we use the word as synonymous with a desire or emotion. We *hope* something will happen. In this case, it's a strong desire for something to take place: I can *hope* to eat ice cream soon. This doesn't mean I will . . . or that I won't. It's simply a willed anticipation that this or that will take place. In most cases, this is our definition. But when we use *hope* in terms of our relationship with God, the nuance of meaning changes. Hope, when placed in God, is still a desire or feeling, but there isn't a conversation around something happening or not happening. We don't hope in a God who may or may not come through, may or may not respond, may or may not love, may or may not teach and guide, or anything else. Hope, when placed in God, is a firm statement of fact, an anticipation of something positive we *know will happen*. Our positivity is justified in that there is no uncertainty about the outcome.

The psalmist declares that the Word of God, which has been given to him, is his hope. Why is this? Because God's Word is binding and true—it's called a "covenant" for a reason. The psalmist goes on to declare that in his suffering he is comforted, because his hope is built on the foundational promise of God. That promise, which was spelled out in the previous verse, is life-fulfilling. It's life-giving—which also means that it's life-preserving. What more could you or I hope for than to know that, despite our suffering, we will not ultimately die? Bringing this home to our own context, while this suffering may be a part of our life right now, it will not defeat us or gain the upper hand; we will make it through, whole and intact, to the other side. Then in verses 51–53 we glean comfort in the Law—in the reality that, regardless of the people around us, we will stand firm in the Law of God. It's a Law that tells us not only how to act and respond, but that also shows us (and others) the love of God and how *he* acts and responds.

Clearly, in this moment, the psalmist is going through a lot, and so he has paired hope with the things that are hard for him right now. His suffering is matched with concrete examples: the people who mock him, treat him badly, are arrogant, and are just generally wicked. And yet, through the attacks of his peers, through their verbal (and possibly physical) assaults, the psalmist is able to hold firm because his *hope* is in the God who restores, refuses to abandon, and never forsakes him. What about you? Where are you right now, and how does the hope of God bring *you* comfort?

THREE QUESTIONS FOR YOU TO CHEW ON:

1. What in this psalm hits home for you? To what language of the psalmist are you drawn? Why?
2. How would you distinguish the hope you have in your daily life and interactions from the hope you have in God? Can you think of a different word that better describes either one?
3. Verses 51–53, while still hopeful and focused on doing right, mention harsh feelings the psalmist experiences in response to harm from others. Is it okay to be indignant while at the same time hopeful in a God who is in control and will deal with sin on his own terms?

PSALM 119: HETH

Turn with me to Psalm 119:57–64 and refamiliarize yourself with these words of David.

The psalmist declares that *because* God is his "portion," he seeks his mercy. Because he has sought his Word, his Law, his face, and his commands, he desires God's relentless grace to flow down upon him. So, let me ask: Is God *your* portion? Maybe we need to clarify what a "portion" is all about.

Depending on what translation you're using, you may find an alternate translation of the term "portion," such as "source of security" (NET Bible). To say that the Lord is your *portion* means that he is your security, your peace, and your comfort. But this Hebrew word also has to do with *inheritance*. While it's frequently used in the Old Testament with regard to land holdings, it has other uses as well (especially in an Old Testament context).

Let me see if I can break this down in a way that makes sense:

- Who, ultimately, owns the land and everything in it The Lord, and he disperses it as he sees fit (see Genesis 1 and the creation account).
- The land given to the 12 tribes of Israel, which had not been theirs originally, was inherited by them from God (Joshua 13–21).
- The land was the covenant promise of God; thus, to *inherit* one's *portion* meant to be given what God had promised as one's possession. The receipt of this land comforted you, secured your future, gave you a feeling of security, and promised you a future (to have *nothing* was considered tantamount to having no future at all).

In Psalm 73:26 we read that, "My flesh and my heart may fail, but God is the strength of my heart and my portion forever." So, for the people in their relationship with God, *portion* took on a new, spiritualized understanding. If the land provided a future, if the land were one's safety, in that it was God who had given it to you—then *he himself became* your portion—your safety, your future, your comfort, and your peace. The implication of the word "portion" had moved from the physical (land, safety, inheritance) to the intangible and spiritual. The promise was made to Aaron and his sons in Numbers 18:20, the psalmist declares it also in Psalm 16:5, and the writer in Lamentations 3:24 finds comfort, even in his lament, in that God is his everything and that he will thus hope in him.

So, let me ask again: Is God your portion? Is God your everything? Is God your present and your future—your "prize"? If everything were to be taken away from you, if all that remained in your life were God's hand on your head, his name on your soul, his Word in your heart, and his promise of your *eternal* life, would that be enough for you? More than enough? This is the point the psalmist is at in his life. He seeks to follow, abide, and turn to God day and night. Should everything else be taken away, should the "wicked bind" him with ropes (v. 61), God's Law will still be on his lips, bringing him peace, comfort, and hope.

For me as an American, and a privileged one at that (I have an intact family, a secure and fulfilling job, a home, cars, money, and all my needs provided for), it's really hard to imagine a life without stuff—and yet it's harder still to imagine a life without God. The American way of life suggests that, even if God were to turn away, at least we would have our *stuff*, and that would provide us comfort today and tomorrow. But would it? Believers in God affirm that he is our everything and that life isn't life at all if he's not in it. I may be able to take some temporary comfort in my stuff, but when I die it will all fade away. That which I have on earth cannot go with me to God. We must realize the truth of the quip "He who dies with the most stuff . . . still dies." Ultimately, we as Christians declare that our portion *must* be God because without him *we have no future. No inheritance. No comfort.*

We need to go back to the Numbers 18:20 text to fully live into the truth that God is our portion. As God is talking to Aaron, his priest over the people, he's declaring to him that he as a priest won't have the riches and joys of this earth—instead, he will possess the riches and joys that are eternal: God himself. Why are we coming back to this text? Because this is the same promise handed down to believers in Jesus Christ. We must recognize that, in our inheritance of all eternity with God as his adopted children by the blood of Jesus (Ephesians 1:5), *we too* are made to be a kingdom of priests (1 Peter 2:9). *Our* inheritance is the very same one given to Aaron.

So, bring on God as my portion! I may struggle not to prioritize the things I have on earth, but I know that they will not last or give me peace and comfort. Only Christ will. Only God has.

THREE QUESTIONS FOR YOU TO CHEW ON:

1. What in this section of Psalm 119 speaks to you? Which words of David give you pause? Why?
2. What are the important *things* in your life—and how would you go on if all of this were taken away (think of Job, who was stripped of nearly everything except his life)?
3. It seems as though, when times are hard, we have a tendency to turn to God in a negative way (angrily and with an accusing tone). Can God be our *portion* and yet the focus of our anger?

PSALM 119: TETH

Turn with me today to Psalm 119:65–72.

Twice in these verses the psalmist refers to his affliction (whatever that was) and to how during the time before he was afflicted (v. 67) he had strayed and disregarded the Word of God. Now he recognizes that the affliction served a good purpose in that it brought him to a space of growth. The basic formula: before God he was not afflicted and did bad things; now he is a follower of God (or has returned to God) and finds himself afflicted. But he's okay with that because he has realized the value of the Law *because of* his affliction. Wow. He's *happy* to be afflicted? Sounds to me like some convoluted logic!

We don't know what the psalmist is afflicted by, or what he has done, but his understanding is that he has wronged God, violated his Law, disobeyed him, and lived a lifestyle that was against his Word. Because of that, he concludes, he is being disciplined. And it is in this discipline that he recognizes not only the wrongs he has committed but the goodness of God's Law. He fully recognizes that God's Law and goodness aren't being handed down as "rewards" but as the blueprint for a way of life. He sees the goodness of the law not out of fear, but in appreciation, hope, joy, peace, and love. What's really interesting is that, while he acknowledges his sins, he *also* acknowledges (v. 65) that what he has been given (his affliction/punishment) has been the appropriate response from God. Yikes. I'm pretty sure I have *never* felt that my punishment matched my crime (when I was a kid—not as an adult)! But that's me—and I'm not the psalmist here.

I am fully aware, as a son and a parent, that discipline is not only a learning experience but that it is handed down out of love. I'm fully aware that this isn't always the case, as some people come from broken homes with bad parents, . . . but my own parents disciplined me appropriately when I had done something wrong. In the same way, my wife and I discipline our children when they have done something wrong. The discipline doesn't take place out of spite or to relieve our own anger but to bring home the principle that actions have consequences. When you do something wrong, there will be a consequence handed down to help teach you, guide you, and help you. *That's* the context in which we need to understand David's "affliction" logic. Does affliction sound any better now? It does to me. But let's keep on going . . .

The Law of God is supposed to guide people into a right relationship in all facets of life—to the psalmist it is more than that: a complete *way of life*. So too with you, when you break that way of life and later come to your senses, you accept whatever consequence for your actions God has meted out to you (or allowed to happen to you as a natural consequence of what you have done). You accept the consequence not because you feel you necessarily deserve it but because you acknowledge that God loves you and wants you to be set right. You declare through your actions and attitude, if not your words, that his ways are right and true and that what he does, because of what you have done to him and others, is also right and true. However, I think there is something else we must recognize: "affliction" is not only meant to correct but also to encourage and help.

David's words here are very similar in nature those of John 15:2 and Hebrews 12:11. The intention of God, as expressed in all three places, is to help. To help not only to correct by way of some affliction, but to afflict as a way of helping. I think the problem here is that we often view affliction as a negative thing, . . . but let's not get stuck there. God "afflicts" sometimes as a way of pruning our dead leaves. When we prune a plant or cut back the limbs of a tree, we are encouraging growth. Pruning helps by removing damaged limbs, and it helps maintain the shape of a plant. You and I, too, need to be pruned. We need to be pruned to help us focus. We need to be pruned to help encourage growth—as well as to remove those things in our lives that are damaged, sick, and unhelpful. Affliction, based on this understanding, is exactly what we need. It may be less than comfortable, but it's what's best for us. Ultimately, this is why the psalmist is able to understand that, while God has afflicted him, all is still good.

It's hard to be in a "good" space when you're being punished, and I'm not sure I ever have been. But I am fully in agreement with the psalmist that all that God does, even in disciplining us, is for our good. While I have lived a relatively easy life, I know that what God does is always for my betterment; this is true of all that he has done, is currently doing, and will do. That's why he put the Law in place, that's why he sent his Son to earth, that's why his Son took on the weight of the Law and fulfilled it for us: so that we *wouldn't* keep failing to uphold it. And that's why, when Jesus left earth and returned to his throne on high, he sent his Holy Spirit to bring us peace and comfort and to direct us toward holy living.

Affliction can be difficult to understand and live into if you believe in an evil, self-serving God who is only out to punish. But, thankfully, that is *not* the God we worship or the God we love. How do we know this? The Bible tells us so.

THREE QUESTIONS FOR YOU TO CHEW ON:

1. Which of David's words here cut to the quick for you? How so?
2. Have you ever thought at the time of enduring a "consequence" that your punishment fit the crime and was for your good?
3. What does pruning look like in the lives of God's people?

PSALM 119: YODH

For today's reading, I invite you to turn with me to Psalm 119:73–80.

Our eight verses today piggyback on what we've just read in verses 65–72. The psalmist finds that his affliction is actually based on God's faithfulness. That in his love, in his mercy, in his desire to be in relationship with the psalmist, God has disciplined him for breaking his Law. We have here the declaration that God created David, along with *tons* of declarations about God's loyalty (vv. 74, 76, 79) and faithfulness to him (v. 75). A few of the words that speak here of these divine qualities include "devotion," "promise," and "commitment.

In the tradition of the Christian Church to which I belong (the Christian Reformed Church), we hold to a confession dating back to the Protestant Reformation and titled the Heidelberg Catechism. In this confession (set in question and answer format), the very first question we come to is "What is your only comfort in life and in death?" The answer, in short form, is that "I am not my own, but belong, body and soul, in life and in death, to my faithful Savior, Jesus Christ." It's a simple question with a *huge* answer. We are not our own. We belong to Christ. Why? Because he paid for us by his blood. Because, through his sacrifice, Jesus purchased us upon the cross (Romans 14:7–9; 1 Corinthians 3:23; 6:19–20, etc.). One thing our psalm touches upon that we don't get in Q&A #1 of the Heidelberg Catechism is that the very One who saved us is the same One who created us. *This* is why these eight verses speak of loyalty, faithfulness, devotion, promises, and commitment.

It can be a hard pill for us to swallow that God disciplines his own, but this makes absolute sense. While we have spoken of "affliction" as a kind of divine pruning, another point we see here is that God's affliction of us (his discipline) reflects his loyalty, faithfulness, devotion, and commitment to us. God could easily walk away when we disobey and abuse his Law—but he doesn't. Instead, he sticks around and corrects us. He wants us to get it right. He wants us to learn his "better way." He wants us to understand that his Law is here to love and help, lead and guide. He gave it to his people not only because his love (reflected, as we've seen, in his Law) is *who* he is, not only because we need it, but because that Law declares just how devoted, loyal, and faithful God is to his children (vv. 75–76). And in the end? They recognize God's faithfulness and love in their own affliction—and not only want to be consoled and brought close to God but to be an example to others as well (vv. 78–80). "So, use me, God—correct my wrongs and afflict me in any way you deem necessary, for I know you love me without end and that I deserve what I get. And, in the end, if my example stirs the hearts of others toward you? Then count me in." Once again, I'm reminded that this is both about God and about others (just as Jesus summarizes the Law in Matthew 22:36–40).

The verb "let" (or "may" in some translations) is another reoccurring word in this section. Verses 76–80 are all requests of the psalmist to God, and all use this construction: "May your love console me" (v. 76); "may I experience . . ." (v. 77); "may the arrogant . . ." (v. 78); "may your loyal followers . . ." (v. 79) and "may I be fully committed . . ." (v. 80). What is it about these requests that draw me? They are all questions, hopes, and desires—that simply hang there. They are petitions to God that do not find an answer in the text, and so they feel to me as though they hang there without answer. *However*, they *are* answered for the psalmist because, as he proclaims, God gave us his Law. God afflicts in order to correct, and he is faithful, just, loyal, and devoted to us. So, those instances of "may" or "let" *are* answered even if we don't see those answers in the text.

These eight verses should challenge us to see the faithful hand of God in our lives and to recognize and acknowledge that we have this beautiful relationship with him and with each other. The faithfulness of God is with us regardless of how we feel or what we are going through. This life is about more than me; it's about making me right with God and helping others in their relationship with him as well—because his Law, his Word, his living, and his dying upon the cross were not only for my benefit but for *our* benefit. Life is bigger than you and me, and these verses are a great reminder of that truth.

THREE QUESTIONS FOR YOU TO CHEW ON:

1. What is it in this section that speaks to you? To what are you drawn? Why?
2. When, if ever, was the last time you thought of a punishment you received as being helpful *to others* as well as to you? This does makes sense—doesn't it? One beauty of Scripture we may not recognize is that we can learn from others' mistakes. Can you name a few examples of biblical characters from whom you have learned a lesson?
3. How does the truth that God owns you, from your birth to your death and eternally beyond, help you in your faith journey?

PSALM 119: KAPH

Open your Bibles once again to Psalm 119 and reread verses 81–88.

I am not a patient person by any stretch of the imagination. I never have been. Just ask my wife or my sister or parents. Not only am I impatient when I see something and I want to buy it, but I'm not the most patient as I wait around for anything—and our psalmist seems to be in the same boat as me. His soul "faints" as he looks around but fails to find God's salvation (v. 81). His eyes fail as he looks but does not find his promise (v. 82). So, he begins asking "How long?" (v. 84). His enemies are prospering, and yet God's actions, his promise, his salvation, still do not appear to go forth. If I were David in this situation—and it's probably good that I'm not—I would have acted. I would have taken matters into my own hand. But the psalmist doesn't. It's as though he is holding on by a thread as he waits for God to act; though impatient, he waits.

These images are poignantly beautiful. A soul that longs for salvation is reminiscent of a similar image in Psalm 42, where the author describes his soul as panting for God like a deer for streams of water. Eyes that "fail" can be eyes that are going blind, or they can be so laser focused on one thing that they get blurry. To be like a "wineskin in the smoke" implies becoming shriveled and dried up. And through it all, the psalmist feels as though all that is happening to him is unjustified, that he is being "persecuted without cause." And so, his question is valid: "Where are you, God? How long must I wait for you? All that is happening is unjust and contrary to who you are. So, I ask again, *where* are you?" The struggle is that God's Law states one thing, and the psalmist knows that to be against the Law is a violation not only of God's Word but of who God is. He knows that God will deal with all those who corrupt his Law, his Word, his nature. When that happens, they expect God to work, to step in, to do something about it. And yet here they wait . . . and wait . . . and wait, . . . and nothing is happening. Scratch *thing*. *Things* are happening—but it's not God's actions that are taking place. The arrogant and the evil, the ones who are abusing God's nature—they are the active ones.

The psalmist's issues are our issues still to this day. We see the arrogant, the proud, and the self-loving prosper, while the loving, kind, and God-fearing people too often seem to get stepped on—and it doesn't make sense. If God's ways are true and right, and we follow them—shouldn't *we* be the ones advancing? Shouldn't *we* be the ones securing the better job, more money, and better lives? Shouldn't it be the wicked and proud who struggle and can't seem to make it work? Don't get me wrong: sometimes life works the way we think it should—but it sure seems as though more often than not it doesn't. What's striking here is that the psalmist isn't asking God to punish the evil-doors. The psalmist isn't asking God to make the righteous prosper and to bring all others low. He just wants to be comforted—and in the end he is.

What's really beautiful—and I almost missed it—is that as we look through these eight verses, we see human failings contrasted with God's unfailing nature and ways. Human souls fail (v. 81). Eyes and thoughts fail (v. 82). Bodies fail (v. 83). Patience fails (v. 84). Humans fail at holding to the Word of God (v. 85). God's command, in contrast, does *not* fail (v. 86). Life fails (v. 87), but, again, God's unfailing love does not (v. 88). The psalmist, as he takes stock of all that is going on around him, all that he is feeling and doing, recognizes the failure of his own life and yet acknowledges the unfailing hope coming from God. Even while he struggles, he knows that God's unshakable Word, love, and promise will save him, preserve him, and hold him fast. Why? Because humans are broken and God is not. Because God's love is true and good and will never fail.

The struggle we have throughout most of our lives is that we are faced with not only brokenness (ours and this world's) but a realization that we simply can't achieve what we want to in life. We cannot do things on our own, cannot accomplish most things on our own, cannot work effectively against many of the individuals and challenges that might harm us. The fact that 99% of that which surrounds us in this world is outside our control can be frustrating—and yet I'm not sure what I would do without the truth and comfort that everything *is* within God's control. While I don't necessarily know *when* he's moving or going to move, I am at peace knowing that he will move and has already done so. I may be impatient while I wait, and I may get grumpy, but I hold, as the psalmist does, to the reality that, while all that I do seems to fall short—God does not fail. My life may hang by a thread, but God's work, love, and strength are mightier than that thread, and he will see to my well-being. In the end we know that our salvation, God's unfailing love, and his promises are all held firmly in the One who gives us salvation. The One whose unfailing love went to the cross and died upon it. And whose promise to you as a believer is that, regardless of who or where you've been, paradise awaits you.

THREE QUESTIONS FOR YOU TO CHEW ON:

1. What in this psalm speaks to you? Where are you drawn? Why?
2. How do you move past impatience while you wait for God?
3. How do you reconcile the fact that we at times see evil prosper and goodness fail in this world?

PSALM 119: LAMEDH

I invite you to turn with me to Psalm 119:89–96.

David's theme for this portion of Psalm 119: time. Words like "eternal," "generations," "endures," "perish," "preserved," and "boundless" sprinkle these verses; with the exception of "perish," these words call to mind the timelessness of God and his Word. Why is that important? I'm glad you asked.

In many cultures, ancient Israel included, history mattered. Your namesake and the generations of your people that you could trace, life, and eternity—these all meant something. It meant you had a past. An individual had a lineage, and life had consistency, depth, and meaning. These things still mean something today. We trace our history, our lineage, through DNA tests, through genealogy, and in other ways. Being able to know where we were, where we came from, and the people who were involved along the line is encouraging and exciting. We feel a sense of pride if we can trace our ancestry further back than someone else. And here, in our text, the eternal Word of God is not only the comfort of the psalmist but, he recognizes, the comfort of his people—and all people—since the earliest times. The difference here is that it isn't about pride. Here it involves joy, peace, and comfort.

The psalmist not only recognizes the timelessness of God's Law but God's eternality; David declares that God's Word has been good since the beginning of time. But even more affirming is that in the middle of this passage we find the contrast between God's eternal changelessness and the constant state of flux in our world. Generations change. The march of days pushes onward. The earth moves. God's servants come and go. Life comes and goes. The greatest comfort we have comes back to the reality that, regardless of all that changes, God and his Word never do.

For you and me this means that God, and his love, have always been. This means that we can read the Old Testament, see all that went on, and yet always draw a line from those horrible events to God's love. Since the beginning of time itself God has sought us, loved us, and wanted the best from and for us. This means that, when we see Jesus through his love, his work, and his grace, we should also see the unchanging Father (John 14:9). It means that, when the psalmist asks God to "save me, for I am yours" (v. 94a), he isn't asking to be saved *because* he has sought out God's precepts (v. 94b) but because he has always been and always will be God's child.

What's *really* amazing is that, if God's Word is eternal and stands in the heavens, if God's faithfulness is through all generations and his "law endures to this day," then that Law, his Word, and his faithfulness are still evident today. Which means that we cannot read Scripture and say, "Well, that was written a long time ago and doesn't mean anything today." It means that we cannot pick and choose which laws and rules we want to hold to and which we do not. We cannot cherry-pick the "feel good" texts, pull them out of context, and accept those at the expense of passages that are for one reason or another less comfortable for us. If we declare that God's Word is eternal, then it has to remain eternal regardless of how *we* feel. So, if God tells me to love (and he does), then I am to love. If I am supposed to love my wife as Christ loved the Church (don't forget that he died for her), then that's what I'm to do—with an unconditional, undying love. It also means that, regardless of what I've done or *will do*—God's love will always endure and remain steadfast.

Praise be to God!

THREE QUESTIONS FOR YOU TO CHEW ON:

1. What in this portion of the psalm speaks to you? What insights draw you in? Why?
2. What does an "unchanging" God mean to you?
3. Are there any texts that make you uncomfortable to the point that you wonder whether they are still relevant today? How can you engage with these texts, come to understand their context and meaning, and find truth and relevance there?

PSALM 119: MEM

The next section of this acrostic psalm covers verses 97–104.

With age comes wisdom—or at least that's what people say. That the older we get, the more we experience, the more in life we do, the more wisdom we gain. Which is true in many ways. When we are younger, we don't yet understand the way the world works. It's only through experience and growing up that we learn more about ourselves, the world, and how to navigate it. And, clearly, the more we've been through, the more experiences we've had, the more our brain develops and the higher our wisdom quotient becomes. Does the psalmist agree? Maybe—but he writes here about a specific variety of wisdom that isn't gained by experience. He writes about a wisdom that is gained only through studying and drinking in God's Law. While the teaching of the Law would have been done by the rabbis, the psalmist is clearly stating that the Law per se, in its purity, is perfect and good. People can corrupt and change the Law, can misconstrue or misinterpret it, but the Law as it stands, as it has been given to us by God, is flawless.

Still today, we put a high value on teachers and what they've learned and are able to teach us. I personally have an undergrad degree, as well as a Master's degree. There is so much to learn, not only in this world but also in Scripture, and in order for me to teach wisely and honestly I need to continue to learn, study, and grow. But how much extra "truth" may we attribute to someone just because that person has gobs of degrees and letters behind their name? Certainly, we need people who have studied more, experienced more, and have thus acquired wisdom beyond that of most. They most likely have truth to share that we should listen to. But I appreciate that the psalmist is declaring that there is simplicity, truth, and honesty *in the Law itself*. One doesn't need endless schooling, more and more teachers, more interpretations, more _____ to know God, be led by him, or to understand his nature and love. You want to know God? You want to know what you're supposed to do? You want to be drawn close to him and understand how to live in this world? Spend time in his Word.

I own volumes of commentaries by men and women who are much smarter and better educated than myself—and I rely heavily on them when doing research for sermons and anything else having to do with the Bible.

Why? Because they are informed, have studied God's Word exhaustively in its original languages, and have done seemingly endless legwork to ensure that they understand context and meaning. They've conducted word studies, topical studies, and all kinds of other studies—and they know their subject inside and out. Again, I rely heavily on them—but only to a certain extent. What's even more important than their work? *My work* that I've done before I even look at what they've written. My work devoted to spending time with God, wrestling with the text, and hearing what *he* has to tell me. Am I on the same page as the psalmist with thinking that I'm *above* my teachers? No, that isn't my point. Is the psalmist arrogant in his comments that he has more insight and understanding than his rabbis? Maybe—but it's his voice speaking here and not mine. But there *are* some important, big truths in these eight verses. There is always an unbridgeable gap, an essential difference between what God says and what others say. There's a difference between God's revealed truth and a teacher's feeling that *their* truth, or their understanding of the truth, is "gospel" (so to speak). Does the psalmist really meditate on the statutes of God more than his teachers do, as he is suggesting? Maybe—maybe not. We just don't know. But our place is not to pick apart the words of this or any other biblical author. Our goal is to understand what the psalmist is saying. And what, at bottom, is David saying here? That God's Word alone gives one wisdom, truth, and insight into who God is.

Let's think about the implications here, as well as about what *we* tend to do to complicate God's Law/Word:

- God's Word is not complicated—*We're* the ones who complicate it.
- God's Word isn't fuzzy or difficult to understand or interpret—*We* fuzzy it up.
- God's Word isn't hidden—Our understanding is limited, and we need the Holy Spirit to open our mind and heart to its truth.
- God's truth is timeless—*We're* the ones who try to corral it into artificial time and space categories.

In the end, this psalm encourages us to just spend time in God's Word. To know his Law, understand its intention and reasons, and realize that the Law and the Word of God are the means by which we can draw closer to him. Don't shy away from teachers and really smart people—but don't neglect, either, the real importance of time alone with God allowing *him* to reveal himself to you.

THREE QUESTIONS FOR YOU TO CHEW ON:

1. What in this portion of Psalm 119 speaks to you? Where are you drawn? Why?

2. I've had many teachers who have been favorites of mine—and all of them for different reasons. Who were some of your favorite teachers, and why have you so appreciated them? What did they do, teach, or say that made them stand out as exceptional for you?

3. Have you ever reread a passage of Scripture and found yourself wondering, "Where did *that* come from? How have I missed that?" Or have you come across a text that speaks to you differently now than it did before? Why is that? Is this because you weren't paying attention before—or might God be instilling within you new insight you need in this very moment?

PSALM 119: NUN

Please read with me Psalm 119:105–112.

As I read this psalm, I'm struck by the understanding of life that has come to the psalmist in his walk with God and his Law. He has suffered much, and he declares that: God's Word will preserve his life (v. 107); though he constantly takes his life in his own hands, he will not forget God's Law (v. 109); snares have been set for his life (v. 110); the Law of God is his heritage forever and the joy of his heart (v. 111); and his heart is set, to the very end, on God's decrees (v. 112). Life . . . life . . . existence . . . and more life. The Law of God, for the psalmist, is both life-giving and life-preserving.

I have been a Christian my whole life; my parents raised me in the church, shared with me *their* love of Jesus Christ, and made sure that my sister and I knew him, feared him, loved him, and understood what we believed and why. I remember reading Scripture and a daily devotion as a family after dinner as we sat at the table. It was through this time, through Scripture reading and my family's conversations, that I grew to understand that the Word of God is more than just words on a page—that those words are life-giving. That the Word of God shapes every stage of life. That I am to turn to God not just in need but also in joy, happiness, sorrow, and grief. And that every word, on every page, gives me a glimpse into history, sin, redemption, love, restoration, and life. That the Law of God isn't something to be feared but something to be understood—a guide for living and a source of hope.

The psalmist fully understands that the love of God, and the life he gives, are poured out into us by his Law. That God didn't set up some rules and regulations just to mess with us but that there are hope and life and living *in* them. That's why the psalmist speaks of God's Word illuminating his path. He recognizes the pain he is in, the snares that have been set before him, and the constant jeopardy his life is in, but he realizes also that the remedy, the hope, the life are in God's righteous rules. Again, the Law of God has been given to save and protect. But does it end there? Is simply abiding by God's rules going to give us life? No, not in the way many expect.

God's Law is not a "fix-all" if our hope is for *it* to make our life better. If I'm looking for an immediate remedy for my turmoil, the "snares" in my life, and the harm that is before me, then my simply abiding by the Law of God is not going to make all the trouble disappear. I wish it would, but it doesn't. What the Law *does* do is *help* us today in our walk with God and each other. What the Law does do is guide us toward knowing what is right and wrong and help us step in the right directions. What the Law does do is help us recognize (as Paul declares in Romans 7:7–25) the sin in our lives. What the Law does do is help us understand that we cannot fight the sin in our lives and that we need the Law to not only illuminate our pathway and guide us but help us realize how dependent on God we really are. Ultimately, we recognize that we *cannot* keep/uphold/live out the Law as God commands us to; thus, we need Jesus—the One who fulfills the Law on our behalf (Matthew 5:17–20).

So, we're left reflecting on the words of the psalmist in his declaration of the life-giving, life-saving nature of the Law. Is God's Law *to you* what it was to David?

THREE QUESTIONS FOR YOU TO CHEW ON:

1. What in this portion speaks directly to you? What truth draws you in? Why?
2. If the Law of God is a "lamp" unto our feet—how does it light your path? How does it lead and guide you? Do you use it as a guide, or do you go back to it when you're stuck and not sure what to do or where to turn?
3. How would you respond to someone who claimed that the Word of God and the laws he gives are "recommendations" that you really don't need to follow?

PSALM 119: SAMEKH

L et's read together Psalm 119:113–120.

As I read this portion of the psalm, I'm struck that throughout the eight verses the psalmist recognizes, and speaks of, the fact that one cannot claim she loves God and abides by his Law while not actually abiding in it. Verse 113 speaks of people who say one thing and do another; verse 114 speaks of how the psalmist not only hears the Word of God but puts his hope completely in it (it's all-or-nothing); verses 116–117 continue on from verse 114 and share that the psalmist has gone all-in in terms of his hope in God's Word; and, finally, verses 118–119 recognize that God commands his followers to abide by his precepts and that, if they don't, he will reject them from his presence. Again, all of these verses recognize that God's Law isn't here to just be read and not ingested. God commands his children to live into his Law.

One of the biggest complaints non-believers have of believers is that we tend to live differently from what we preach and speak. That we speak of the Law, the Word of God, and their impact/truth in our lives, and yet as soon as we step away from church, as soon as we get into the "real" world, we fail to practice what we profess. I know that I'm guilty of that; I have fallen flat on my face too many times to count. I have fallen prey to other people's ways of living and begun marching in step with them. I have gone "toe-to-toe" with people in terms of my lack of love and care—all the while knowing that *this* is not how God called me to live and love. In the psalmist's eyes, I am just as guilty as the "double-minded" evil doers he speaks of. And many of us, yours truly included, have put our "hope in the world" instead of in God as we seek to impress, and respond to, people instead of him. We may declare God's restoration and our reconciliation in him by *his* work, but we seem to put a lot of stake in worldly actions and lifestyle.

So, where do we go from here? Verse 117 gives us a beautiful clue: "Uphold me, and I will be delivered."

The psalmist is declaring that he needs God's "upholding" to keep him close to him—but I think we can go deeper than this. To be "upheld" means that we cannot be let go. To be "upheld" means to be supported, encouraged, *held*, and kept. It's a being held not for the sake of comfort—the psalmist declares that it's so that he may be delivered. Delivered from his foes, from the naysayers, from the double-talkers. And I would argue that he, too, needs to be "upheld" and "kept" from his own sins, because no matter how much he speaks of the double-minded people around him, he, too, is part of that group. Sin runs deep in all of us, so let us not forget that we are no better than *they are*—because we *are* them.

In the end I am fully comforted in the hope the psalmist expresses here in God's upholding him, because he finishes off verse 117 with anticipation of an already-completed deliverance. Because of who God is, because of the truth of his Law and Word and because of his covenant (this is just a fancy word for "promise"), God, in his grace, has *already* held, kept, saved, and delivered us. This truth is what we have needed and hoped for and declare in our Father in heaven. The challenge that confronts us is that we have to recognize our double-minded actions and the reality that we can easily fall prey to the ways of this world. When we see that our feet are stepping off the path, we must repent, turn in the other direction, and seek our Lord and Savior.

THREE QUESTIONS FOR YOU TO CHEW ON:

1. What in this section of Psalm 119 do you find convicting? Where are you drawn in? Why?
2. Have you fallen prey to the ways and actions of this world? How did you move past this hurdle? I've had to humbly go before God—and the other person involved—and ask for forgiveness, . . . which wasn't fun but helped me to process the implications of my actions and move forward. What about you?
3. What are some things you can do to safeguard yourself from the worldly "call" to walk away from God's Word?

PSALM 119: AYIN

Our next segment of Psalm 119 covers verses 121 through 128. Please take a few moments to refresh your memory be rereading them now.

What do you do when you've done everything else you can? What do you do when, no matter what you do or say, people still oppress you, kick you down, and speak ill of you? When your words and actions have been "godly" and on par with him standards, and yet darkness continues to overwhelm you—what do you do? That is the question the psalmist is struggling with—and the situation has gotten to the point that he is not only fed up but is trying to motivate God to respond.

What's interesting here is that the psalmist feels it necessary to lay out his circumstances before God—as though God weren't already aware of where he is, what he has done, and the oppression he is facing. David declares that he has done what is "righteous and just" (v. 121); that he has upheld the Law of God (v. 126); and that he loves the commands of God more than any earthly riches (v. 127). He considers the Law of God to be pure, right, and good and anything that is against this Law to be evil and wrong. So, is it right for the psalmist to *demand* that God respond? Is it right for him, and us, to be so bold as to speak to God in this way? *Absolutely.*

As we read through this text, we notice that nowhere does David say anything like, "God, if you don't do _____ , then I'm done with you!" In contrast, he admits that he can't do anything on his own. That he needs God to step into his life and relieve him of the oppression that surrounds him. He needs God—because of his Word, his Law, and his love, the psalmist needs him to act. David needs God to stand between him and those who wish to harm him.

Countless times I have waited and waited, only to lose patience and take things into my own hands. Countless times I have needed something from God; then, when it didn't come, I resorted to taking my own measures. Are there times when God *wants us* to act? Absolutely. He gave us a brain to use and wise people with whom to surround ourselves, and we have the power of prayer with which to discern truth and wisdom—so, yes, we are to use these resources. Oftentimes our prayers seem to be going "unanswered" because we're looking for a direct "yes" or "no," but what can also happen in those moments is that we sense his implicit "yes" when we're looking for direction. Sometimes his "yes" is an affirmation that, no matter which step we decide to take in terms of a looming life decision, God will bless us. But when we're dealing with "oppression" (as the psalmist is) and sin that is impacting us from the outside, the situation becomes more complicated. We must remember that we cannot deal, or respond to, sin in any way *other than* by turning to God. We can love our oppressors, but that's only going to take us so far. We can pray for our oppressors, but that's only going to do so much. In the end, it's up to God and his hand to deliver us, save us, and restore us.

I'm challenged by the psalmist's last words, in which he declares that he loves God's precepts and commands more than he does gold. That he loves God's laws and seeks them more than anything in this world. *Which means* that he will respond to oppression by seeking out God and never through a worldly reaction. *That* is our challenge and reminder. To remember that God's ways are right and true; that he has put provisions in place to help us deal with sin and oppression, anger and hatred; and that we must allow *him*, and him alone, to deal with such issues.

THREE QUESTIONS FOR YOU TO CHEW ON:

1. What in this section hits home for you? At what point are you drawn in? Why?
2. People have tried to deal with oppression since the beginning of time. How does Scripture remind us of the failure of humans to deal with oppression? How has God ultimately dealt with it?
3. Can you imagine any scenario in which you would feel comfortable making demands of God?

PSALM 119: PE

Please turn with me to Psalm 119:129–136.

Confession time. Never in my 42 years of existence have I ever used the word "wonderful" to describe the Law and the Word of God. Should I? Maybe—probably? The word of God *is* wonderful in its truth, hope, joy, and love (there, I've just said it!), but "wonderful" is just not a word I would ordinarily use. I may use it to describe the amazing flavor of bacon, or my *terrific* wife—or maybe even to describe a movie—but the Word and Law of God? I haven't . . . until just now. The psalmist lays out the case for why he does, and I suspect we'll find out shortly why we should, too.

- The psalmist declares that the Law is wonderful because the "unfolding words" of God shed light into all human lives, so that even the young, the ignorant, and the inexperienced can fully comprehend God's call and message. (v. 130)
- The psalmist declares that the Law is wonderful because it nourishes, sustains, and strengthens us as water to our thirsty souls. (v. 131)
- The psalmist declares that the Law is wonderful because it reveals God's love and justice and thus reminds us that he is merciful, kind, and good. (v. 132)
- The psalmist declares that the Law is wonderful not only in that it shed lights (as stated earlier) but in that it directs us where we are to go and keeps sin away from us. (v. 133)

Wonderful? Well, when put in *that* light—absolutely. Taking this still further, everything God has done, continues to do, and plans to do is miraculous and wonderful—isn't it? Creation. Restoration of his people. Atonement for their sins. Virgin birth. Overcoming the grave. Miracles, healings, raising the dead—we could go on and on. And all of this is *played out in his Law!* The Law was established to lead us to something better and to *point* us to *Someone*—Jesus. As we look at the Law and its requirements, what we see is not only their fulfillment in Christ but their intentional placement there to point us to him. Maybe my issue, or our issue, is that we've untethered the Law of God from Jesus. Maybe we need to remember that John in his Gospel (John 1:1–5) declares that Jesus was not only incarnated, not only born a human, but that he *is* the Word. Isn't Jesus wonderful? Isaiah called him our "Wonderful Counselor" (Isaiah 9:6), a title that not only speaks of his life and actions but of how completely awesome he is.

The psalmist fully understands that the Law isn't just a set of rules but the life-giving, life-changing, holy, just, and good Word of God (Romans 7:12). As such, the Law is not only a light upon the path that helps us know where to step and which direction to take—it illuminates the darkness around us, the sin that is present, and the death and destruction that lurk in its dark presence. In the end, God's Law and his works hold his children close. How is this not wonderful?

THREE QUESTIONS FOR YOU TO CHEW ON:

1. What in this portion of the psalm speaks to you? To what expression of David are you drawn? Why?
2. Does "wonderful" come to mind for you when you think of God's Word and Law? If not, what one adjective best describes your feelings?
3. What does it mean to "pant" for God's word? Do you ever feel that way—thirsty for his Word and needing it to quench and fulfill your need?

PSALM 119: TSADHE

I invite you today to turn with me to Psalm 119:137–144 and take the time to reread this short section.

In these eight verses we see the word "righteous" (or a form of it) five different times—along with a few other words that support this concept and its meaning. What does this word mean? Because, as with so many other words we find in Scripture, we no longer use the term in our everyday speech (unless it's being used as Bill and Ted did in their *Excellent Adventure* (sorry—that's an old movie from 1989). How has it happened that good old English words still appearing in Bible translations, words like "righteous" and "awesome," have lost much their meaning, have been watered down and adopted during recent years to mean virtually nothing?

In Hebrew this word *righteous* pertains to something being better than or beyond "good"—just, right, true, and even guiltless or innocent. For the psalmist to say that *God* is "righteous" means that his Word, his Law, his actions, and his promises *are righteous, too*. You cannot separate the goodness of God's rules from the goodness of God. God's Law reflects his righteousness, though for us as sinful humans its call for such goodness can at times seem to bind us, to weigh heavily upon us, and to seem constraining and even unrighteous.

Just as God is righteous, just as his laws are righteous, his desire for us is righteous, too—He is perfect and good, his Law/Word is perfect and good, and his desire for us is perfect and good. We cannot separate them— even if we wanted to or tried. We cannot say that God is one thing and then go on to state that the will and work of God are outside that parameter. Since the beginning of time, both God's righteousness and his desire for us to be righteous have been in place. Since we were not righteous, he put forth a law that would help us walk in the way we should.

It is precisely here that we must land as believers: if God is righteous, then all those who want to be around him, with him, and near him must be righteous as well. That's why the Law was given (so that we would know what is righteous and what is not); ultimately, this is why our righteous Savior, Jesus Christ, came to earth. Once again, we cannot escape the righteousness of God, as his expectations for us are built into it, his Son is completely Righteous, and his righteous act upon the cross wraps us up in that righteousness. In the end, we are challenged by this psalm to recognize the righteousness of God and his righteous act of salvation for his unrighteous children. When we act righteously, we are walking in synch with our God.

THREE QUESTIONS FOR YOU TO CHEW ON:

1. What in this psalm speaks to you? At what point are you drawn in? Why?
2. Do you ever feel as though God's Law, and his Word, are a burden? A kill-joy?
3. How best can we walk in righteousness with our God and with each other?

PSALM 119: QOPH

Please open your Bible with me to the book of Psalms and read Psalm 119:145–152.

Once again, the psalmist repeats a word or words that should draw us in, and this time it's all about a "call," a "cry," and a "voice." The psalmist calls out to God, seeking for him to hear and respond. He cries out to God for help and seeks God's response to his voice. Why is he crying out? What need does he have that he cannot fill? We read in verse 150 that his enemies are scheming and making plans, plans we can assume are against David. That's why he cries out to God in fear. We read that he is staying up through the night and watching (v. 148), but we're not sure whether this is from a defensive posture or whether he is gazing out toward the hills for God's response to his crying. The psalmist appears to be in a very dark place.

We invariably lose some words in translation, and there are also words that don't impact us as they would have in David's time. When many of us read "whole heart" (v. 145), we think of something like "every ounce of us" or "from deep within," but to the psalmist, and to our Hebrew brothers and sisters, the "heart" was seen not only as the very core of the person, not only as the organ that pumps blood throughout one's body, but the core from which the mind, soul, spirit, and selfhood proceed. The heart was that place in which true thoughts were created, the place from which feelings went out and were understood. So, when the psalmist declares that "with my whole heart I cry," we should take the word "heart" as a reference to the deepest, most intimate and internal, most secure space within a person. Given this understanding, we now realize that everything the psalmist is about to say will come from the deepest inner recesses of his being.

- The psalmist isn't only "keeping" God's statues—he is ingesting them, living into them, breathing them, loving them, and abiding by them.
- His call for God to "save" him isn't just a surface level shout in the general direction of the sky—it's a low, bellowing, full-bodied call for saving.

- The psalmist isn't just calling periodically; we read that he is calling before dawn and still calling during the watches of the night—all because every ounce of him is entreating the only One who can save him.
- The psalmist knows with everything in him, with his whole heart and soul, that the Lord is near; that his commands are loving, good, and true; and that he *will* come to save him.

I have never been in a place where my whole being was poured out into . . . well, anything. I have never known war, destruction, pain, or suffering to the extent that every fiber of my being cried out to God. I'm thankful to have been spared that experience, . . . and yet I can't help but feel that I've somehow missed what might have been a beautiful opportunity for me to cry out for my Maker, Deliverer, and Savior in such an all-in manner. In the end, I have to be okay with this, because I cannot force myself into a situation like that. And yet we *can* train ourselves to be more in touch with our core, so that every facet of our being can work in tandem. *How?* We can pray.

Praying is a key part of our walk and of our faith journey, but so often our prayers seem to reach a conclusion just because it's "time" to do something else (eat, sleep, etc.). Either that, or the opposite extreme: those times when we are indeed "calling" out to God because we're in desperation. When we become more cognizant of the nature of our praying, more intentional about our calling/crying/communication with God, then we can become more in tune with our Creator, our own needs, and his voice. So, don't *just* pray; set aside time, clear your mind of any and all distractions, and not only mouth words to God but allow your heart, and your head, to work together. In time, I'm convinced, you and I will start to speak from our *hearts*—from a Hebrew understanding of "heart," that is, and not a Western one.

THREE QUESTIONS FOR YOU TO CHEW ON:

1. What in this portion of the psalm speaks to you? To what are you drawn? Why?
2. The psalmist seems to be in dire need, but is he being patient or not so patient? How do you go about your normal routines of the day when you are at the same time crying out to God in desperation and waiting for his answer?
3. How would you rate your prayer life? Do you tend to resort to "rote" (habitual and even memorized prayers) and to pray at specific, preset times, or do you try to set aside a more focused, "special" time for prayer?

PSALM 119: RESH

I invite you to turn with me today to Psalm 119:153–160 and to refresh your memory with David's words.

There is a love here of God's Law, a love that is seen and felt. The psalmist declares that he hasn't "forgotten" God's Law (v. 153), that he recognizes and declares God's promise (as seen in the Law) (v. 154), that seeking the decrees of the Law leads to salvation (v. 155), and that preservation happens because of God's Law and his love for those who abide in and obey him. While there are some things mentioned in this text that give me pause—I'll get to these—we need to bear in mind the voice, time, place, and context of the psalm.

The people of God in David's time were in a covenantal relationship with him, but this relationship was based on their Law-abiding actions. God had given them his Word, along with his requirement that they obey him and follow his commands, lest they find themselves being cut off and removed from him. It makes sense, then, that in David's time of need, when affliction is upon him (v. 153), when his cause and pressing need for God to step in and preserve his life are urgent and pressing, he reminds God how faithful to his Law he has been. David's need, as we know so well, is for rescue from the wicked, who do not abide by God's decrees and who are surrounding, persecuting, and oppressing David (vv. 154–155, 157). The dynamic for David, and other Old Testament Israelites, involved a relationship whereby the people of God lived into his Law, and in response God kept his promise of deliverance and life. But what about today? Is this still the way it works?

Many of us do still buy in to feeling and living as though what we do, how we respond, and the lifestyle we follow somehow prompt God to act, love, and keep to the promises of his Word. The idea is that, as we go through life, we will be blessed, loved, and ultimately *saved* based on what we do—as though it's *our actions* that usher in God's grace. The problem is that this is not scriptural. We believe in a God of grace. Grace is undeserved, unmerited, unearned, complete forgiveness. Grace is a free gift, given by God; it is not based on some form of *credit* we can build up with God, not on anything we can say, do, or ever deserve. We read in John 1:17 that the "law was given through Moses; grace and truth came through Jesus Christ."

And again, in Acts 15:11, we see that we are saved *only* through the grace of Jesus Christ. This is repeated in Romans 3:24; 4:16; 5:2, 15 and in countless other New Testament texts. Grace is the complete forgiveness and washing away of sins given by God through Jesus Christ. It's offered and received not on the basis of *our* work—or by God's looking into the future to *see* what we will do. It's a free, no-strings-attached gift of God by way of Jesus. So, what are *we* as new covenant (New Testament) Christians supposed to do with this text?

To begin with, we need to recognize as we engage this passage the way things were and the fact that Christ came because the Old Testament system simply didn't work. Nobody could have followed the Law well enough to overcome the sin barrier.

Second, this portion of Psalm 119 *screams* of Jesus Christ—and not only because of the issues surrounding fulfillment of the Law. The psalmist needs deliverance from his suffering, needs to be defended and redeemed, needs salvation from the wicked, needs to be saved from those who are persecuting him. The psalmist declares the compassion of God, as well as his preserving work and righteousness. Are not all these qualities and attributes seen in God; delivered through Jesus Christ, the Messiah; and given to his children? Yes . . . yes, they are.

This psalm is beautiful in how, historically, it reminds us of just how things were—and yet it leaps us forward to remind us of how badly we needed God to enter this world by sending his Son, Jesus Christ, to live into the Law and fulfill it for us.

THREE QUESTIONS FOR YOU TO CHEW ON:

1. What in this segment of Psalm 119 speaks to you? Which of David's words draw you in? Why?
2. *Grace* is a beautiful, and yet deeply complex, word and reality. Would life be easier if God were still working in the Old Testament way, . . . if our own works were what led us to justification and salvation? Wouldn't life be easier if we had a "works of the Law" meter on our arm that told us where we were at and whether we had "done enough" for God?
3. Should we look upon the "faithless with loathing" (v. 158)? Is that helpful? How should we perceive, and interact with, those who do not believe?

PSALM 119: SIN AND SHIN

We're nearing the end of this extensive reflection from David. I hope and trust that you've found it worthwhile sticking with it. Let's turn today to Psalm 119:161–168.

Whom do you fear? What in this world would give you great pause, make your knees buckle, or even make you slightly worried? The psalmist maintains that it's not about the persecution that's been happening to him or about the liars and cheats who surround him. What makes *him* worry? What puts the "fear of God" in him? It's God and his Word, right? And, ironically, it's *also* God and his Word that he considers the greatest gift and treasure in the world.

I, like David, absolutely love the Word of the Lord. But am I the perfect Christian? Not a chance. One temptation I need to avoid is taking these eight verses and putting myself in the sandals of the psalmist. I say that because that would be *really* easy to do. Have I been persecuted without cause? Absolutely, though certainly not in the way David has. But do I worry about what my detractors say or do? Yes, afraid so. The psalmist declares that what makes his heart tremble is God's Word—*not* the persecution. My own heart trembles at the persecution. Does that mean I don't love God's Law enough? "Seven times a day" the psalmist praises God—do I? Please allow me to clarify that this is *not* meant to be a numerical understanding of how often praise is, or was, to be offered. The number seven in the Bible symbolizes "wholeness," "completion," and even "perfection." The psalmist is saying that he never stops praising God; every step or breath he takes and every thought that comes to him are all about God, his Word, his promises, and his praise. Do I do that? One would think that a pastor would—but we don't. I try to be more and more cognizant of God and of my surroundings, but that does not mean that I'm perfect, consistent, or complete in my praise of him. Finally, I don't have "great peace," and I stumble left and right. Thus, I confess that I do *not* truly love the Law of God or his Word. Right? *Wrong.* Scripture is not here to give us a measuring stick or ranking in terms of the quality of our worship—perhaps, in fact, we could say that the psalms *in particular* do not do that. God's love for his children is based not on how often we pray or how fearful we are with regard to his Word—it's based solely on himself.

My wife and I have two kids, and they are completely different. One's a boy and one's a girl; one is four years older than the other; but the bigger differences have to do with their personalities, joys, gifts, talents, education, desires, hopes, fears—and even their walk with God. Very early on I realized that holding one against the other would never work. We required both of our kids to take piano lessons for two years. For two years my son exceled, . . . and then he voluntarily continued on for six more years. And to this day music is natural to him. My daughter? She took piano lessons for two years, and it was two years of tears, anger, unnecessary words, and more tears—most of which seemed to come from me. She just doesn't get music. Learning to play had seemed to take so little effort for my son. But I realized that I was expecting my daughter to be at ease with the piano, just as he was. This was a lesson *I* had to learn. My kids are different—and now that I recognize this, I am thankful for each of them in their own special way.

God does not love us or judge us based on a sliding scale, depending on where we are, the gifts we have, the things we say or do, or how we match up against others. If you pray "seven times a day," then good for you. If you can stand up to persecution and not falter or bat an eyelid because your foundation is the truth of Scripture and nothing else will shake you—then good for you. If you spend your first and last thirty minutes of each day in the Word, that's beautiful. But if you can carve out only fifteen minutes of your lunch break or have to schedule time in your calendar in order to pray each day because you consistently forget (I've done this), there's nothing wrong with that, either. We worship a God who wants to be in a relationship with us. Yes, he'd probably like us all to be in a deeper relationship with himself, but his grace, his love, and his Word don't come to us based on anything we do or on how "perfect" a follower we are.

In the end, this segment of the psalm reminds me that, even in my imperfect worship of God, I can still draw close to him. That somehow my broken worship is acceptable and pleasing to his ears.

THREE QUESTIONS FOR YOU TO CHEW ON:

1. What in this section of the psalm speaks to you? Where are you drawn? Why?
2. We tend to look at others and emulate them based on flattery or some other motive. Have you ever tried to copy someone else's spiritual habits? Sometimes another's example can be helpful in that we need some guidance—but sometimes this just doesn't work. If you have done this, how'd it go?
3. How is your daily walk with God? Perfect? A little less so? Just right? I suspect that all of us could be better in *some* way. How could you work to improve the quality of your prayer and devotional life?

PSALM 119: TAW

Please open your Bible once again (I could say "one last time," but my hope is that it won't be!) and read with me Psalm 119:169–176.

We have come to the final eight verses of this lengthy psalm on the Law. And the irony? The irony is that Psalm 119:1 declares that "blessed are those whose ways are blameless, who walk according to the law of the LORD," and yet here we find the psalmist declaring, "I have strayed like a lost sheep." David cries out to God because he doesn't understand his Word as he should. And the rest of the psalm, outside the hope he knows will come to fruition, is this supplication for God to help them sing of God's Word. The psalmist recognizes just how faulty he is, how in need of God he is to lead him, guide him, give him speech, and allow him to simply live. It's a humbling place to have such high hopes but then realize that you're lying flat on your face.

Years ago, I began this psalm-writing journey because I was blessed to serve a bunch of middle school and high school students in Iowa for a week during the summer. What we as counselors noticed was that during camp the kids were completely energized for Jesus. They were surrounded by nature and engulfed in their interactions with and support from other Christians, including those counselors who loved them. We worshiped together every morning; we had a speaker share the Word every day; we gave them "TAG" time (Time Alone with God), in which they reflected, wrote, and read Scripture based on the talk; and we conducted cabin devotions every night. When the kids left after their week with us and went back home, . . . they were on fire! It was wonderful. But then, two months later, nearly every person went back to her routines.

And so, as an encouragement, I started blogging the psalms each week. One psalm per week. The reason? We need help—all of us. We all, when surrounded with goodness and encouragement, prosper and flourish; life is easy and going well. All of us, including the counselors, had the best of intentions when we left, and yet nearly every one of us fell flat on our faces. It wasn't that we loved the Word of God any less, it wasn't that we just didn't want to—there were probably a ton of factors, but most of it came down to the fact that we had so many distractions in our lives that it was hard to continue on our course. We had competing activities and events that were pulling us in different directions. And so, even with our greatest intentions of praising God, studying his Word, and being in prayer "seven times" a day, we found that we were unable to follow through. These final eight verses of our psalm serve as a breath of fresh air for all of us who have tried and yet fallen short. But let's not let "failure" be the last word here, because we'd be missing what this text is really doing: it's *celebrating*.

This whole psalm, in fact, is a celebration of who God is and what he does. As the psalmist recognizes, we fail to uphold our side in this relationship with God—but our failure doesn't mean that God walks away.

- The psalmist cries out to God because he knows God listens.
- The psalmist declares that he doesn't understand God's Word, and yet he wants to—living this life is all about the *wisdom* we glean from engaging with God's Word, because the principles for how to live this life are based solely on that Word and come only from *him*. God doesn't want us to stay confused on how to live and love!
- The psalmist declares his need for deliverance, . . . and God brings it.
- The psalmist wants to praise God—and not only to praise him but to do so with "overflowing" lips! Even in his brokenness, in his lying flat on his face, he is still able to muster praise of God (I actually love that picture).
- The psalmist declares that God's hand is ready to help—which means that God doesn't abandon or forsake us.
- The psalmist longs for the salvation of God—which he knows will come because salvation is based on God and his love—nothing else.
- The psalmist recognizes that he is lost. That he has strayed—and yet that it is God who will find him and return him home.

We, thankfully, worship a God who doesn't love us only when we do good things. If that were the case, then God would have given up on us long ago. Instead, we worship a God who recognizes and accepts our broken worship of him, our inability to hold to his Law, and who in response to our sin and weakness has sent his One and only Son, Jesus Christ. So, never should we worry when we're lying flat on our face, for it precisely from this posture that we recognize just how much we need Jesus.

THREE QUESTIONS FOR YOU TO CHEW ON:

1. What in this entire psalm speaks most pointedly to you? At what point(s) are you drawn in? Why?
2. What helps or prompts do you have in place to help you stay focused on God and his Word each day?
3. There is something about being surrounded by other believers that energizes us. Why is that? What do you think all that energy will look like when we stand in God's glory?

PSALM 120

A PSALM OF
ASCENDING AMID
A SEA OF LIES

I invite you to read with me Psalm 120.

We are now at the beginning of the group of psalms under the category "song of ascents" (Psalms 120–134). These psalms would have been sung while Israelites were "ascending" to Jerusalem for some annual feasts (it is assumed that, no matter where you were, you "went up" to the city and into presence of God). In this very short psalm, we hear a crying out for mercy; a prayer for saving; a prayer for punishment; and then, finally, a statement of fact that differentiates the Israelite people from those who surround them.

As with many other psalms, there is limited information available. We don't know who the author is but recognize that he is *very* thankful that he doesn't live like the people in Meshek (which was near the Black Sea in Anatolia) or Kedar (which was located in Arabia). Why does he mention those cities? We aren't too sure, but these appear to be references to two locations he would have considered heathen cities full of pagan people. Maybe these were cities with which his own people had feuded, or maybe he had actually lived in these places and struggled against the lifestyle there while he himself sought a godly way of life. We simply don't know. But these do appear to have been cities that were considered the worst when it came to deceitful and lying tongues; in the author's mind, we surmise, to live there would have been to make his home in the most despicable place in the world.

So, what is this psalm saying? Psalm 120 proclaims that our words mean something. That lying lips and deceitful tongues (v. 2) have no place within the temple and the presence of God. But let's expand that even more: because we know that our tongues, our words, our lips can either say wonderful things or wreak horrible havoc (James 3:2–13). We can build people up or break them down. But our tongues and lips do more than that, because they not only can hurt others but hurt us. We read in verse 6b of James 3 that when our tongues function as "fire" and are creating evil, they corrupt our whole body. *Your* body. Yes, they can cause harm to you and to others—and you'd better believe they can "hurt" God. Who believes a liar? Hopefully nobody—unless a person is gullible or has no history with the liar. So, how can a liar share the gospel, share the Good News, proclaim Jesus, and live out the two commandments in Jesus's summary of the Law: to love God first and to love others as much as she loves herself? She can't. Lying and deceitful tongues do not build up but only break down; when we lie, we do so to protect ourselves—thus our concern is for *us* and not *them*. A liar may acknowledge Jesus as her Lord and Savior, but she surely will not live out this calling in her life.

One issue our text does *not* pick up on, but with which I have direct personal experience (as, I would assume, do you), is that living in a city like Meshek or Kedar would have been deeply challenging. Not only because of the ungodly way of life, but also because it is very easy for a resident to become that which he despises. Think about sayings like "When in Rome, do as the Romans do" and "If you can't beat 'em, join 'em!" We know that it is extremely hard to continue to fight against the things that are not of God when we are surrounded by those very things. We know that it can be challenging to function as that one solid example in a sea of depravity. I personally have fallen and succumbed to the sins of the people around me, . . . while in other cases I've managed to stand strong and eventually get out. At various times I have both "played the game" and "fought the good fight." Both were hard, but one allowed me to walk away with my head held high, while the other approach left me regretting my course in sorrow and shame.

This psalm challenges me with the fact that the psalmist is declaring truth to be a godly attribute and way of living, along with the reality that anything outside of that, especially lies and deceit, have no place in God's presence. While I want to cry out and point a finger at others and their lying lips, imploring God to do something to them, I cannot ignore my own tongue and my failure to use it in a God-pleasing way. Because I fail at times to use it properly, . . . do I deserve to ascend to God's presence? Will my lies keep me from ascending to God and being with him?

The short (and perhaps surprising) answer? Yes, they will. My sins are my own, and they keep me from rising up to God. However (and this is no doubt the answer you were expecting), because of God's grace, love, mercy, and forgiveness we no longer *need* to ascend to him. Why not? Because *he has already descended to us.* We don't rise up to him, not only because we can't but because he has lowered himself to us through Jesus's incarnation and crucifixion. Jesus descended. Jesus atoned for my sins. Jesus redeemed me by his blood upon the cross and *lifted me up* to himself. None of the work has been or will be my part—it has all been on him.

You and I are people of Meshek and Kedar. *We* are the very people who live pagan lives. Yes, we come to church on Sunday and praise God with our lips, . . . but then the other six days of the week (and even the other half of Sunday) are often marked by moments when our lips do not reflect the worship in which we have so recently participated. Maybe, just maybe, we're *even worse* than the pagans in Meshek and Kedar. At least they don't vacillate back and forth between truth and lies. At least they are consistently cold to God and his ways, while we can too often be *both* hot and cold (read about that with respect to the church of Laodicea, addressed by the risen Christ in Revelation 3:14–21). Which is worse!

Our takeaway? Pray to God for the people who surround you, those who challenge your faith, challenge your desire to live a godly life, and even challenge your attempts to do so. Seek the Holy Spirit's work in your life to give you the strength to hold fast while he purifies and sanctifies you. And praise God that, while our lying lips steer us in other directions than we desire (I appreciate James's description of our tongues being like a rudder on a ship)—our ship's navigation system remains right and true. While we may veer off course, our GPS is set to Jesus—and *that* is where we will set anchor.

THREE QUESTIONS FOR YOU TO CHEW ON:

1. What in this psalm speaks to you? What draws you in? Why?
2. When surrounded by non-believers, how do you act the way you have been called, as a follower of Jesus, rather than falling prey to their challenge to become what they are?
3. Mahatma Ghandi once said, "I love Christ. It's just that so many of you Christians are so unlike Christ." Do you find this to be a fair assessment of Christians? A convicting one, for certain!

A PSALM OF
COURAGE WHEN FEARFUL

Open your Bible and turn with me to Psalm 121.

Our psalm today is the second in a series of psalms of ascents that would have been sung or used as the people *ascended* through the hills and into the city of Jerusalem. It's a psalm that helps the singer find comfort as he remembers that God watches over his people at all times, no matter where they are or go. Whereas the Baal worshipers believed that it was necessary for adherents to wake up their gods, the God of all things, the all-seeing Yahweh, is always alert and watching. He doesn't rest, doesn't hunger or take breaks for lunch and dinner, doesn't sleep, and he never slows down, stops, or gets distracted. No vacations, no holidays—nothing but watching over his people and protecting them from all harm.

This psalm, while we don't know who the author is, is simple in its layout. Verses 1–2 are a declaration that in times of need it is only God whom we may call upon; verses 3–6 speak of harm that can befall during the day and night; and verses 7–8 close with the remembrance of God's promise to keep his children safe. In essence, this is a pilgrimage song of courage in the midst of fear.

Maybe it's because I listen to a *lot* of NPR, or maybe it's because, for whatever reason, *The Wizard of Oz* is being pushed as I write (I believe a new play will be coming out shortly), but all the sudden I can hear, playing in my head again and again, that all-too-familiar line "Lions, and tigers, and bears . . . Oh my!" As Dorothy, the tin man, and the scarecrow are walking through the dark forest, they begin to hear noises—and those noises infiltrate their hearts and minds and strike fear. What's out there in the forest? Who knows, but there are the sounds of animals that could harm them! And when you're in the *dark forest*, what *dark animals* with sinister ways and hungry mouths could possibly come out to eat you!? In this case, what brings the three comfort is singing this song (with Dorothy's memorable "Oh my!" after each repetition). What started as fear soon morphs into a dancing song of comfort, as their singing takes their minds off whatever it is they have imagined might be lurking in the shadows.

Our psalmist, and the Israelite pilgrims, like Dorothy and her friends (well, . . . not exactly), are heading to a place of hope and comfort. But along the way, outside the city of hope, the city of God, there are dangers, including wild animals, bandits, falls, and even heat strokes that could harm them, and thus their overactive imaginations are struck with fear. While we don't have a lot of information on this text, I'm personally led to believe that they sing *because* they are fully aware of the harm that could befall them. They've either experienced these perils before, seen them visited upon others, or heard rumors, . . . or they might simply need encouragement not to fear the unknown—which, as we so well know, can be a most alarming pitfall. And so, as darkness falls or as the blazing sun beats down upon their heads and backs, they find collective comfort in God. They most fear being left alone, . . . being abandoned by God and left to the whims of whatever it is that may harm them. And yet they *know* that he is always present, always watching, always protecting. Their singing of this psalm becomes an emotionally uplifting chant, raising their spirits as the path rises ever upward toward the city of God.

The people of God fear that he will abandon and leave them to the terrors of this world.

Dorothy, the tin man, and the scarecrow, on the other hand, fear those things they cannot see but can hear.

What are your fears? And how do you push past them? Do you take a page from *The Wizard of Oz* and find comfort in singing, with the hope of forgetting the very fears that initiated your song in the first place? Or do you, like the Israelites, lean into God and draw upon his strength and promises as you sing your praise?

Most of us, hopefully, launch into prayer. We reach out to God and draw upon his peace as we talk to him, lay out our fears and worries before him, and take comfort in knowing that he is not only intimately aware of our needs but is listening to our words, attuned to our heart and to our soul. Now that I think of it, there really isn't a great deal of difference between singing and praying. Just as many songs *are* prayers, so many prayers are songs.

Wherever it is we turn in times when we need an infusion of strength, we as believers find rest in the same God the Israelites declared in Psalm 121. Our help doesn't come from mountains or trees or rivers or caves—it comes from God. It comes from the very person *who created* those mountains, trees, rivers, and caves. Our peace and comfort come from the God who, unlike you and me, doesn't have to succumb to human necessities like rest, food, water, or shelter. No matter what might happen during the day or night, God maintains his ceaseless vigil—both now and forevermore.

So, sing, pray, or chant when you need strength! But remember that strength doesn't come from ourselves or from our forgetting our fears while we dance along a yellow brick road or otherwise distract ourselves from what we dread. Peace, strength, and comfort come from the only God, whose protective hands, eyes, and heart are all over our lives.

THREE QUESTIONS FOR YOU TO CHEW ON:

1. What in this short psalm speaks your name? What draws you in? Why?
2. What is your go-to response when you are scared or worried? What helps you to push away the fear or focus on something else?
3. How can that which we fear draw us closer to God?

A PSALM OF
UNIFIED REJOICING

I invite you to turn with me to Psalm 122. Let's read it together.
"Let us go to the house of the LORD." Those words strike me on this day.
I know I've written about the house of the Lord in other psalm reflections,
especially with regard to the joy we should have in going *to* church, but
today I'm reflecting on the divisions among the children of God. I'm
hopeful for the time to come when such divisions will no longer exist.

One of the most harmful separators of us as Christians is our tendency,
consciously or subconsciously, to envision God dwelling exclusively in a
house *in our neighborhood*. In the very building my church family and I
attend. We acknowledge other believers, churches, and denominations,
of course, but we remain divided in terms of what it looks and feels
like to worship in a different setting. "*You use wine!?*" "*You sprinkle for
baptisms? I just couldn't go to your church!*" While, clearly, things in the
larger Christian community aren't as they used to be, when people had
an allegiance to a particular denomination (we have since become serial
church daters), we still are divided when it comes to the proper way to
worship and receive the Sacraments, as well as on many other issues,
both practical and theological.

"Let us go to the house of the LORD." These words were an encouragement
for the believers to enter into the house and presence of God—*together*.
Not divided, not in exclusive groups separated by race/class/creed/
denomination, . . . but together. The place where God dwells, the place from
which he judges, the place in which believers are drawn into a physical
nearness to God was/is *for all people*. This song of ascents encourages all
singers, all worshipers, all people of God to enter in the the company of one

another into his presence, his peace, his courts, and his love. We read that *all tribes* are to do this. I think of Catholic, Protestant, Lutheran, Christian Reformed, Presbyterian, Methodist, RCA, PCA, PCUSA, Baptist, and so many others. The psalmist is declaring that *your denomination doesn't matter!* "For the sake of my family and friends, I will say, 'Peace be with you,'" he declares! Notice that he *doesn't* say "Let me and my friends" enter into the house of the Lord. Or "Let all those in my denomination" enter into the house of the Lord together. Not only is the psalmist saying that all those different "tribes" should enter together but that we should greet one another within God's house with "peace be with you."

In N. T. Wright's book *Surprised by Hope*, he talks about our having work to do in the kingdom of God—today. We don't live for *what's next* because that's already happening now, in anticipation of what is to come. So, if we declare that there are love, peace, goodness, and joy in the New Heaven and the New Earth (the kingdom to come), we also must declare that we are to live into those very things today. *Today* we must give and show love, peace, goodness, and joy. We must live it, seek it, proclaim it, and demonstrate it. We read in Revelation 7:9 that a great multitude of people enter into God's presence. And, guess what—we're not going to enter God's house and then disperse to separate rooms. We're not going to follow signs that say "Sprinklers Here" or "Dunkers Here." We're not going to attend separate worship services, where one gymnasium is filled with drums, guitars, and dancers, while the sanctuary next door features a pipe organ, and the auditorium next to that has no music at all. We are going to enter, together . . . and shout and sing our praises together.

So, let's stop dividing and enter God's house as one, in joy, worship, and hope. Let's *ascend* today, together, because tomorrow you and I could be standing before God, hand in hand, regardless of class/color/creed/nationality/worship style with one unified voice. Let's not wait for tomorrow to sing together, worship together, dance together, and praise together. As fellow believers, brothers and sisters in our Lord, let's engage today in what tomorrow may bring.

THREE QUESTIONS FOR YOU TO CHEW ON:

1. What in this psalm speaks to you? What draws you in? Why?
2. Why is it easier for us as Christians to identify our differences than it is to discover our similarities and find joy in them?
3. How can we overcome our differences? How can we approach someone who practices some traditions or accepts some beliefs that are different from ours?

A PSALM OF
GOD'S MERCY

J oin with me today in reading Psalm 123.

This psalm, to many of us, is going to feel somewhat odd. It starts off in a compelling and comforting manner: "I lift my eyes to you, to you who sit enthroned in heaven." In times of need, in distress, and in praise and joy, we lift our eyes and heads up to heaven toward God's mercy seat, his judgment seat, his presence, and his throne. We do this because we know he watches, protects, leads, and guides. We also do this because in all moments we know he responds to our needs. We understand that, when we cannot move, when we are stuck, when we are oppressed, the only One who can help is God.

But then we come to the next verse, and it may feel for us a little uncomfortable. Two different times we read the word "slave." Two different times we get the image of a master (in one case it's a "mistress"), and those words and concepts don't sit well with us. We don't know what to do with these words because we've always been taught that slavery is evil. That being a master over someone else is a bad thing. But that's on us and nobody else. Times have changed since the psalmist penned those words, and we must realize that the concept and practice of slavery in his time didn't have a negative connotation. The institution of slavery was intrinsic to the culture of the time, though it is certainly true that slaves were owned by their masters. A more apt understanding for us might substitute the image of a servant for that of a slave. We ourselves, as servants of God, wait for God, as our Master, and his hand to move, direct, and help us.

Combining verses 1 and 2 brings to our recognition that our eyes are set upon God and that we wait for him to move his hand. When God's hand moves, it's a sign of his will, desire, and action. And, as the end of verse 2 declares—moving us along into verses 3 and 4—God's movement on our behalf primarily has to do with his mercy and our need of him to help, save, and deliver us from contempt and ridicule.

When we take all of this in, we get the picture of a servant of God who understands his place and is in need of God's hand to save him, as the surrounding people who do not believe in God are hateful, neglectful, full of ridicule and scorn, and in complete defiance of God and his ways. When we understand all of that, we can begin to make sense of this psalm of God's mercy.

You and I, and the psalmist, are surrounded by people who do not live according to God and his Word. Our society loves self and pushes ideas and notions that are counter-God. When we try to live lives worthy of his calling, we are looked down upon and pushed aside. When we try to live as his worthy servants, we are too often stepped on and walked over. A sacrificial, godly life that puts others first oftentimes invites others to hurt us. So, it makes sense that we look up to God, acknowledging our need for his hand of mercy, because it's only by his hand that the ways of this world will be put down. And it's only through God's hand of mercy that we can endure this world while trying not to buy in to its lifestyle and value system.

That is where we are to find peace and comfort.

- You cannot endure any longer? Look to God.
- You don't have the strength to go on? Look to God.
- You need relief from the pain, suffering, and other difficult experiences of this world? Look to God.

God is the only One who can help and deliver us from a world of seemingly endless contempt. When the arrogant are oppressive and loud, we find peace and rest in our master, knowing that his hand delivers. And he *will* show us mercy. The second coming of Christ reminds us that contempt, arrogance, and pride will be put to an end. God's loving mercy will usher in his complete control and push sin and destruction out of the picture. But until then—keep looking up, knowing that our Master is in control.

THREE QUESTIONS FOR YOU TO CHEW ON:

1. What in this psalm hits home for you? What draws you in? Why?
2. How do you respond to people who feel as though we Christians worship a slave master and that we are at his beck and call?
3. In what ways does God treat us as anything but our master? What are some things he does that breaks that stereotype? Other than Master, what other words describe the relationship God has with you.

A PSALM OF "WHAT IF?"

et's open our Bibles and read Psalm 124 together.

Our psalm today continues with the psalms of ascents, as the people sing and move, proclaim, reflect, and cry out to God. What danger and chaos are they reflecting upon? We don't know. But that's not their goal. Maybe they assume that everyone already knows the historical situation. Or maybe it simply doesn't matter what event they are going through. Because in the end all tragedies are difficult. The bigger question? The more pressing issue? *What if the Lord hadn't been with us? What if the Lord had abandoned us?*

What if . . . ? What if . . . ? What if . . . ?

I hate What if? questions—always have. My wife and I have numerous conversations with our kids on this kind of issue, because they tend to hit us with those hypothetical What if? questions that really do not serve a purpose. Often when a person asks this kind of question, she is trying to accomplish one of two things: she's asking a question that either *cannot be answered* or simply doesn't matter because the worst-case scenario *hasn't* happened and very likely will not. "What if?" Is a worry question about the future, and we cannot control or see the unfolding of time ahead of us. It's a moot point. Not only is the future beyond our control, but it does no good worrying about often remote possibilities, . . . so don't even ask. But the big one we get from the kids seems more ridiculous still—it's the worry about what *could* have happened, even though it *didn't*. What you are doing is asking a What if? question as an alternative to what *has already happened—* differently from the hypothetical scenario. "Yes, we landed safely on the tarmac, . . . but what if we hadn't?" Who cares? It doesn't matter because it didn't happen and that's not the outcome we are forced to deal with. People who live in such scenarios fret and worry about everything—which can in itself be harmful.

But what is interesting here in our text is that *this* What if? is *not* an unanswerable question. The What if? we see in this text is actually a declaration—a praise—a statement. "What if the LORD weren't on our side? We would all be swallowed up. The inferno that blazed around us would have burnt us alive. The crashing waters would have consumed us—just as they did Pharaoh's army so long ago." Verse 6 speaks of those imagined calamities that aren't *going to happen . . . because they have happened.* The psalmist is declaring that *this was* happening to us. We *were* in the teeth of the beast and getting shredded. Far from avoiding the trap, we were *in it* and couldn't escape. The only reason we got out of the trap is that the Lord broke it. The only reason we were removed from the grip of those teeth is that the Lord did not let the one terrorizing us tear us apart. But remember this: we *were* torn up. We were ensnared, and we got soaked!

Those Old Testament days were tumultuous times for the Israelites—as well as almost all other people. Wars were common. Other nations, other peoples, were continuously trying to wipe out God's people. Trying to take their land and kill them. A "you have what I want" mentality was thriving in these lands. Greed flourished. People saw something, wanted it, and tried every means possible to get it. Our world, beginning so shortly after God gave all that was good to Adam and Eve, fell into a morass of pain, suffering, greed, hate, and envy. Still today, there are people who want what others have and will do whatever is necessary to grab it. There are people out there who hate others with every ounce of their being, who are willing even to die to bring harm to them. The sad reality is that, if people are willing and driven to harm, there isn't a whole lot you or I can do about it. Evil has strength and power on its side that neither you nor I can hinder or halt.

So, what if? What if God weren't on our side? What if he were to allow evil to win? What if God were to allow Satan to exert his power for eternity? What if God hadn't loved his children to the point of dying for them upon the cross? What if God hadn't held to his promises or delivered upon his Word? What if . . . ? What if . . . ? What if . . . ?

Paul says in Romans 8:31, "If God is for us, who can be against us?" The Lord watches over us and delivers us. He negates the finality of harm and, more importantly, has removed for his own the sting of death. From the day of our conception until the day we see the glory of God, our lives are bookended with his presence. His Spirit, whom he has sent *to be* his presence in our lives, the embodiment of his love and guidance until he comes again in all his glory—will never leave or abandon us. The Holy Spirit convicts us, reminds us, loves us, refreshes us, encourages us, and shows us hope.

From the moment God, in his triune self, decided to create the heavens and the earth—and to place man and woman upon the surface—to the time when Christ returns in all his glory, . . . we are watched over, protected, upheld, and held. There is no area of our lives, no place in history, that God has not bookended with his love and covenantal promise to never abandon or forsake. No matter what harm people may try to bring upon you—they cannot overcome the power of God. No matter the type of snare created to entrap you, it cannot keep God from snapping it with the flick of a finger. No matter the raging waters that may crash upon your head and try to sink you, they cannot overcome the voice that calms them. No matter what beast may come, no matter how sharp the teeth it bares—no matter, even, the amount of blood it draws from you—it cannot offset or counteract the blood of the Lamb that was shed for you.

We are a delivered people who need to remember the kinds of What ifs? in which the psalmist exults here, to make of them a praiseworthy, declarative statement and not a worrisome question that has no answer and that fears for the possible future—because we *do* have an answer, and his name is Jesus Christ.

THREE QUESTIONS FOR YOU TO CHEW ON:

1. What in this psalm speaks to you? To what are you drawn? Why?
2. Why do we ask What if _____ *had happened*? kinds of questions? Are we not satisfied with the outcome that *has* occurred? Why might we like to dwell on something that could have happened but didn't?
3. Can there be a benefit to What if . . . ? questions? Can they be helpful? I'm thinking of questions that promote thinking about our faith and its implications, questions like "What if Christ hadn't come?" (1 Corinthians 15:17). How can *that* question, and others like it, help us understand who we are?

A PSALM OF
ETERNAL HOPE

L et's read together Psalm 125.

As the people of Israel climb up to the Lord, they reflect on the goodness and security he provides. A frequent image we see throughout the psalms is Mount Zion, which is used as an image of stability, strength, and immovability. But what really stands out, at least for me, is the patience of the people. We read in verse 3 that "the scepter of the wicked will not remain over the land allotted to the righteous." Now, *that* is some patience! The psalmist is declaring that the wicked *are currently here* but that their power, strength, and governing rule will not always be present. Because at some point—whenever that is—the Lord will return and remove the wicked from their place.

But the psalmist doesn't end there. The second half of verse 3 declares that, should the wicked remain, those deemed righteous can/will use *their own* hands to do evil. The power and strength of evil is so strong that, should the Lord allow it to remain, all people will be corrupted. All will do evil. All will be shaken and turn from God. Sin runs deep. Even those who have the best intentions, the holiest of views and ways, and the godliest of desires are full of sin. In essence: people are broken. *All* people.

My wife and I try to do our best with our children, and we constantly tell them that we love them and that all we do and say is for their best. At this point our kids (ages 15 and 11) still think highly of us, even though we tell them that we are not perfect, that we are *all* full of sin and destruction. But at this point we've never done anything (that they can remember) that was wrong or harmful to them. But one day we may. One day we may *not* act in love. One day we may *not* do what's best for them but instead do what *we* want. Because no matter how strong our love, no matter how focused on God we are, . . . sin runs deep. The Old Testament people of God knew it. As they ascended to Jerusalem, to the city of God, they knew that the wicked were all around them. And I'm sure they had seen their close friends and family fall victim to sin's rule. But the people of God know something that evil doers do not: the scepter of evil will not remain. Not only will it not remain, but those in Jesus know that the scepter of evil has been broken.

When Christ died upon the cross and then arose three days later, he snapped the scepter of sin and death that had been ruling over the world. By his grace, love, and mercy, he removed the curse of death and sin that ran deep within us. Now, this doesn't mean that sin is no more; that tainted blood is still here today—but its rule is no longer. Its power is no more. This is why sin works in the shadows and darkness. Light has come—Christ has come—and so sin is now a wounded animal that hides, only to snap us up when we get too close.

This psalm also reminds me of how dependent I am on the scepter of the Lord, the protection of God, the love and mercy of Christ, and the work of the Holy Spirit to keep me close to God. Since sin runs deep within us all, we all fall into the temptation to do evil. We need to keep our focus on God and commit our lives to him—and yet that snapping of sin and temptation is around every corner. Scratch that—it isn't at every corner but is actually walking with us and speaking lies into our lives. But I'll say it once again: sin runs deep, and you and I tend to listen to those lies, obey those crooked ways, and allow sin to act. Which is why verse 5 stings so much . . . and yet gives us hope.

Verse 5 declares that all those who turn to crooked ways will be banished. Well, . . . I guess I'll see you in eternal damnation! But wait! While sin runs deep and eternal damnation is where we *should* go, let us go back a few paragraphs as we remember Christ! Because Christ came, because he broke the scepter of evil, we also know that Christ embraces and gives eternal life to all those whom the Father has given to him (John 17:2). Because even though we "turn to crooked ways," even though we have zero ability of our own volition to turn to Christ, God turns to face *us*, and the Holy Spirit lifts up our head so we can gaze directly into the eyes of hope, truth, love, grace, mercy, forgiveness, and all those factors that broke the scepter of wickedness. Because grace wins. Forgiveness rules the land. Love and hope have pushed sin into the shadows, and when Christ returns, when the King of kings and the Lord of lords makes his second appearance, *his* scepter will not only break and banish . . . but will completely remove all that is opposed to him.

So, hold fast, people of God! The wicked may be here now, and wickedness may run deep within each of us, . . . but God's truth and love run deeper and cleanse us from all our sins.

THREE QUESTIONS FOR YOU TO CHEW ON:

1. What in this psalm speaks to you? Where are you drawn? Why?
2. We all fall prey to doing wrong things because of the sin that is within and around us. How can we have patience when those around us succumb to the temptations of sin? How do you have grace in those moments— knowing full well that you, too, are just as broken?
3. Because "grace wins," what do we do with sin? Do we just say "Well, . . . it is what it is!" or do we work to do something about it?

A PSALM OF RESTORATION AND RENEWAL

I invite you today to turn with me to Psalm 126.

When things aren't going well, what do you, or we, tend to do? We reminisce on the one hand (look backward) and hope on the other (look ahead). *That's* where the people of God are in our text. They remember the time when things were really good and God restored all their fortunes. They remember the time when they dreamed beautiful dreams, laughed till their sides hurt, sang till their voices went hoarse, . . . and all that goodness spread across the nations. Why? Because God was good and blessed his people (this is covered in vv. 1–3). This was how the people of God reminisced.

But now? Now things aren't so good. There are no fortunes. There is no joy to sing and laugh about, . . . for now the people cry and weep. But it goes beyond that. The author is saying that the people "sow with tears." As they go out into the fields, their tears water the ground. This is some vivid imagery. The Hebrew word for "crying" refers to a short-term, immediate response, whereas weeping denotes a full-on, body-collapsing avalanche of tears. Yet in verses 4–6 the people assess their current situation, and though it hurts, they aren't going to remain in that pain. Those tears of sorrow aren't going to be the last word, because they know that God will restore. While they understand their current situation, it is their *future* that carries them each day.

It is really hard to look past our current lot in life. It's often difficult emotionally to dig out of our pit, past our current circumstances, to glimpse the hope to come. We even have a saying that "You cannot see past the tip of your nose." What that means is that you've got about an inch past your eyeballs that you can clearly see—and that's about it. Why? Because we tend to focus so hard on what's directly in front of us that we fail to see what's around us. And oftentimes when our focus is on our surroundings, those surroundings invade our emotions. The difficulty we have is that we simply do not know what's coming down the trail that's ahead of us.

I once heard an analogy that has been helpful for me both in my life and when talking with others. So often when darkness is closing in, we tend to run as fast as we can toward the setting sun and away from the darkness. The hope is that, if we can just get closer to the sun, the light will remain longer. That if we can get closer to the sun, we can outrun the darkness. The problem? No matter how fast or how far we run, the sun is still going to go down and darkness is still going to set in. What should we be doing? Running the opposite way. Running *into* the darkness. Now, that advice may seem strange, but when we run into the darkness (opposite the setting sun) we are actually running *into* the *rising* sun. So yes, darkness will surround us more quickly—but it won't last as long. This is the hope the psalmist speaks of. It's the encouragement to look past our current situation and look *to* the one that is coming, for *we know it will come.*

Just as running toward the sun means that we acknowledge that hope is coming and that the current reality, the current darkness, will not last, the psalmist is not stuck in his current place but is looking ahead toward the hope to come. Yes, he has tears—yes, he weeps—but his head is up and his eyes are set. That's another thing: *keep your head up.* When in turmoil and distress, when weeping and crying, don't look down. When we stare at the ground we cannot see, feel, or hope, because we are stuck right where we are. Hope looks up. Hope looks forward. Restoration and renewal come from in front of and above us, so we cannot see them when staring at our feet or the barren ground on which we stand.

But let's be clear: the psalmist isn't telling us not to cry or weep or be in pain right there where we find ourselves. On the contrary, he speaks of going out, sowing, and living his life. *While* crying! Yes, it sucks. Yes, it's painful. Yes, he longs for joy and hope, but he isn't sitting where he is, wallowing in his misery. He is moving on. No matter how painful it is, . . . move on. No matter how dark it is, . . . lift your head high. No matter how hard the tears flow, . . . don't stare at the ground.

One of my favorite movies is *The Shawshank Redemption.* In the movie Red has this line: "Get busy livin' or get busy dyin.'" How real is that!? This is a mantra we do well to live by, for our hope, just like the Israelites', is for what is to come—so, let's live for *that day.* Christ declared that he will return, . . .

and when he does he will make all things new. "He will wipe every tear from [our] eyes. There will be no more death or mourning or crying or pain, for the old order of things has passed away" (Revelation 21:4).

Part of the reality of all this is that we struggle when in darkness—and right now many are struggling. With that said, here are some things to remember:

- "Rejoice in hope, be patient in tribulation, be constant in prayer." (Romans 12:12)
- "And after you have suffered a little while, the God of all grace, who has called you to his eternal glory in Christ, will himself restore, confirm, strengthen, and establish you." (1 Peter 5:10)
- "May the God of hope fill you with all joy and peace in believing, so that by the power of the Holy Spirit you may abound in hope." (Romans 5:13)

Hope comes because Christ comes. So, while we may be in darkness now, while we may be weeping now, our tears *will* give way to joy and laughter. And our songs, once sung, will be sung again. But this time? The singing won't stop; only the weeping will.

THREE QUESTIONS FOR YOU TO CHEW ON:

1. What in this psalm hits home for you? What draws you in? Why?
2. What are some ways by which you can look *around* and *past* your nose, as opposed to just focusing on what is right in front of you?
3. What helps you look up when experiencing sadness, distress, or grief? Do you allow yourself time to grieve? If so—how long is an appropriate amount of time? Can we set a time limit?

A PSALM OF BLESSINGS

Today's reading begins with Psalm 127.

Everything we do the psalmist considers "vain" unless it is God who enables us to do it. You want to be "blessed" in life? Don't try to do things on your own. Allow God to work, lead, guide, and go before you. You want to build a house? You want to protect a city? That's fine, . . . but make sure God, not you, is the builder and protector. Simply stated: trust in God. Whether it's home, work, play, family, or friends, . . . give it all to God. I appreciate this short psalm—and yet it sure takes a jab at my feelings (I'll get to that).

Our psalm is broken up into two sections, and upon my initial reading it looks as though the psalmist is talking about two different things here. What do children have to do with house building or city-watching . . . or getting up early and staying up late due to your work?

- A house is a blessing, but your efforts to construct it are useless unless God builds it for you (v. 1). The understanding here is that your home is a blessing from God—so, let's see it that way.
- You cannot protect your house or your city, you cannot watch and see your enemies coming, unless God is your protector, watcher, and hope. Because what happens when your enemies come? You can fight and try to defend, . . . but holding strong against your attackers and watching over the city are in the hands of God alone (v. 1).
- What good is being a slave to your work when it is God who provides your goods? God will give you enough for today. What is needed today will be provided, so don't slave away for more than that (v. 2).

- Children are a blessing from God. Already in the ancient Middle East, it was understood that the blessing of little ankle-biters came from God. We see this throughout Scripture with Sarah, Hannah, Mary, Elizabeth, and countless other women (vv. 3–4).
- When your opponent takes you to court and you stand against him, if he has a family of eight and you have a family of twelve, you win. You outnumber your foe. And if all of the males in your family are big and strong? The advantage is *clearly* on your side (v. 5).

So, . . . why am I rubbed raw by this psalm? Well, in the order of the implications of the psalmist's declarations:

- If you don't have a home because you cannot afford it, . . . then you're not blessed.
- If you and your city are taken over, . . . then God isn't blessing you.
- If you cannot find work or get enough food, then you are not blessed. If your job entails working atrocious hours (or you're without a job), then you're not blessed. Or should you just be happy with the little you do have—even if it won't provide for your family.
- What if you cannot have kids? What if you never get married? What if you lose your kids—are you not blessed? Does God not love you?
- What if you're taken to court and lose the case? What if you have no support and yet know you're innocent—are you destined to lose because you have fewer people on your side?

We believe firmly that God is the author, director, and watcher-overer (another of my words) of every part of our lives—and of this world/ universe. His hand traces everything (except for sin). But we need to check our own feelings and thoughts . . . after we first understand the author's. The Israelites firmly believed that God was in all things, just as we Christians do today. God's ancient people believed that everything they were given, everything they received, and everything they did was not only a blessing from God but to the glory of God. Your crops were abundant this year? God blessed you, because while you sowed the seeds, he provided the rain, sun, and moon. You and your spouse had a boy? God blessed you (boys were considered more of a blessing than girls), because you had yet another child to help with the house; carry on the family name; and, eventually, give you grandkids. You have a house, food on the table, a field to work in, or a boat to fish from? Then God has indeed blessed you.

Do we feel any different today? Do we hold to any different conclusion about God's blessings? Not at all. You have a job, kids, a home; then you feel and declare that you are blessed. We all say it, and we all feel it. But what we need to remember is that simply because someone doesn't have kids, doesn't have a marriage, or doesn't have a job does not mean they are not blessed by God.

The reality and truth this psalm declares is that blessings are about what *God* is doing and not about what *you* are receiving. Nor are we to compare ourselves to what others have received and think that *they* are more blessed. Who grows the trees or compresses the rock that provides us with building materials? Is it you, . . . or God? Who watches over every city on earth? Who topples powers and prepares evil for their ultimate destruction? We may drop seed, but who provided that seed in the first place? Who brings the rain and sun? Who allows the seed to grow into a crop that sustains us? Who provides you with the energy to work? Who created your body, which is able to work hard and rest harder, so that tomorrow you will have the energy and ability to repeat the cycle? Who enables our bodies to have children?

So, wherever you are, whatever you "have" or don't have, . . . *really look* at your life and recognize the blessings God bestows. You may not feel as though you have much—and, in fact, you may *not* have much by our society's standards—but that doesn't mean God doesn't love you or want you to be blessed. The blessings God has bestowed on us include redemption, salvation, and life eternal. These ultimate blessings will be realized for us when Christ returns. But until that day comes, whatever you do—do it for the Lord.

THREE QUESTIONS FOR YOU TO CHEW ON:

1. What in this psalm touches your life most directly? Where are you drawn in? Why?
2. How can the psalms encourage and challenge us even while we recognize that they were not written for us, nor do they reflect our own exact feelings?
3. How would you define being "blessed" to someone who didn't understand the concept? And how would you lovingly encourage someone who doesn't *feel* blessed to recognize the blessings they have received?

A PSALM OF
FEAR AND BLESSINGS

P lease open the book of Psalms to Psalm 128 and read it with me.

Our psalm is a simple one. Its premise: all those who fear the Lord are blessed by him. We fear as we obediently follow, fear as we worship, fear as we learn from him, and fear as we receive from him. But what's really interesting is that all of the blessings mentioned by the psalmist fall into what we could consider *domestic* and *relational* categories. I know that we've pretty exhaustively covered blessings (think Psalm 127, which is probably still fresh in your mind), but none of those earlier psalms have to do with domestic relationships; in that area Psalm 128 stands somewhat alone.

I definitely count as blessings all that I have in life. I have a job I adore and serve a church and community I love tremendously. My wife and I have enough money coming in to be able to pay for our needs and even to tuck a little aside for fun events or unplanned expenses. I count my health as a blessing, no matter what struggles I have in this area, and it is certainly a blessing to love and serve in the ways I've been able to. But in truth? You could take my job away, and I'd still feel blessed. You could remove my ability to earn money and even to set some aside, and I'd still feel blessed. My health could tank, and I would still feel myself blessed by God. *But if my family or community of friends were to be removed?* Not having the support of my wife, my kids, my parents, my sister and her family, my in-laws, and/or all my friends? I could be the richest person in the world and still feel utterly lost without those relationships. In my case, I find the peace of Psalm 128 in the psalmist's declaration that to be blessed is to fear God—and then, in return, to be "blessed" *by God* with my family.

Our psalmist is encouraging people to understand what they truly have in relation to God. Does that mean that happiness for me depends primarily on my having a spouse and kids? Well, yes and no. Having a wonderful and fruitful marriage is always a blessing, and having kids and being around to see them grow . . . and then watching your own grandkids grow (I haven't gotten to that part yet): definitely blessings. The psalmist is not saying that these relationships are the *only* blessings that come upon us, but, still, he is all about community, family, and relationships. Our author declares that, from your wife to your kids to Jerusalem, . . . your life is all about the people in it. But hold up! What does his call to "fear the Lord" have to do with family, community, and relationships?

Here's where I'm led: when you have a right relationship with God (one based on "fear" and "obedience," according to the psalmist), then your relationships with others will be blessed because *they* take on a different feeling and meaning. Our relationship with God trickles down to affect all of our relationships.

I am a better husband when I understand Christ and his love, dedication, and sacrifice to the Church (his Bride). I love and serve my wife better, have a better relationship with her, and treat her better when I live as Christ with his Bride. I am a better father to my kids when I live a life of dependence upon, communication with, respect for, fear of, and love for God the Father. When I spend more time with God, when I pray to him more and understand him as my Father, then that relationship trickles down to my dealings with my own children, and I become a better father. I treat my own parents better when I see how Christ loved, respected, and cherished *his* Father. I treat the church better, my neighbors better, and my friends better when I try to live a Christ-like life of service, love, hospitality, dedication, appreciation, and hope in my interactions with all of them. When I think of how Jesus thought of us instead of himself, I begin to reflect that thought process in my own relationships. How can we not be affected by God when we are in a right relationship with him?

To "fear the Lord" isn't about cowering in the corner as far away as possible from a scary monster in the sky. To fear the Lord means to love, appreciate, understand, and be in a relationship with him. When we fear the Lord, we begin to experience his blessings upon our community-relational life because we begin to treat others as he treats us. Just as our triune God is relational (interacting within himself as Father, Son, and Holy Spirit), and just as he created us to be relational (we are created in his image), those blessings of God rain down upon us as we relate to one another. And when we do that? When we live a life focused on relationships and see the need for them in our life? Then we truly are blessed.

The challenge for you and me? We need to remember that our "family" is bigger than our closest family members. When we live that kind of life, when we understand family as being so much wider than we commonly view it, then we truly begin to live the life of Christ as we welcome the stranger, serve the hurting, mend wounds, and love every person on this beautiful earth, as God does.

THREE QUESTIONS FOR YOU TO CHEW ON:

1. What in this psalm speaks to you? What draws you in? Why?
2. What blessings in your life do you feel you could live without if you had to? What is there about those things that makes them blessings but not necessities?
3. How would your relationships change if God were not part of your life, if he were not intimately and intricately woven into the fabric of your relationships?

A PSALM OF
LOVING RESPONSES

L et's begin today's reflection by reading Psalm 129.
How does one push on *today* when yesterday was so rough? When we've gone through the fire, when oppression has sunk its teeth into us, when destruction and desolation know me by name—how do I respond? When I've been wounded since childhood, will I carry that sting (and possible damage) with me today? And when I see these abuses *still happening* to others, where will I stand? How will I respond? These are but a few of the questions that pop up in my mind as I read this psalm.

We don't know much about this psalm or the psalmist. The psalm appears in the "song of ascents" portion of the book, so we expect it to be reflective, praise affirming, and hopeful. By way of reminder, these song of ascents psalms would have been sung as the people climbed up toward Jerusalem from their homes (Jerusalem was located *up* from every direction), which is why they are hopeful, challenging, and reflective. They are meant to be songs of response, songs of hope, and songs of preparation for the people of God just before and as they enter God's presence.

As I read this psalm, I cannot help but feel the pain Israel has endured and of which it sings. Verse 2 begins not only with a reminder of oppression but of oppression that has lasted for as long as the author can remember. Verse 3 speaks of the plowman plowing the people's backs (What an image!) and making the furrows long. We understand from this that, not only have they been beaten, but their backs have been trenched deeply with long and deep cuts. While these recollections may be fresh in the people's minds, though, we may be surprised by their response. Oppression may have been occurring since their youth, but that doesn't mean that evil has been or will be victorious. My back may have been plowed and furrowed, but the righteous Lord has removed the whips and bindings of my oppressor. While the psalmist's hope is striking and challenging in its reflective nature, the *real* challenge for us comes in his *response* to his oppressors. Sin, anger, hatred, and evil have been perpetrated against them, . . . but has he responded, or will he respond, with that same sin? Does the anger the psalmist has for his oppressors find a voice in this psalm? Does he respond with evil, just as evil has been done to him? *No.* His response to all of this is that God will intervene, will disallow the evil from having its way. The psalmist is saying, in essence: do not allow evil the space to even begin to work.

Nearly every time evil has been perpetrated against me, there has been a welling up of evil within me that wants to respond. Many of those times I allowed it not only to fester but to boil over and out—this has never ended well. Oftentimes we allow the "an eye for an eye and a tooth for a tooth" reaction to take hold even while Christ's injunction to "love [our] enemies" is rolling around in the back of our heads. I picture the old cartoons where there is a good angel on one shoulder and the devil on the other, and both are trying to convince the person why their response to a situation would be best. While the angel is counseling, "Just turn away and forgive," the devil is whispering "Yeah, but payback feels sooooo much better!" Oftentimes we know we ought to forgive and ignore, and yet we find ourselves repaying evil with evil, anger with anger, and hatred with hatred. Yet here, in this praise of the people as they head up into the presence of God, what do they do? How do they respond to their oppression, slavery, and abuse? Their response is that it can simply crawl back to wherever it came from, never again to find food to feast on to give it strength and power.

Verse 8 is a really good challenge for me. The psalmist is asking not only that evil *not* prosper but that it *not be rewarded or encouraged*. Why? Because when it is rewarded or encouraged, it sinks its teeth in even deeper, prospers, and gains strength. Think about the time you responded to evil with more evil. Did it work? It hasn't for me. It only made things worse. And why? Because evil feeds off evil. Think about darkness and light. Does darkness push out darkness? No, only light does. Or think of two storms or tornadoes colliding. They don't knock each other out, as a boxer would. Instead, they merge and get stronger. They get bigger. Sin and evil work the same way.

Psalm 129 reminds us that sin and evil exist and that bad things do happen to people. But it also challenges us to respond not in the way we often find ourselves *wanting* to react or even the way we have in the past. Instead, we are called to respond in the way of love by not returning evil with evil. The psalmist's response to his own pain should challenge us to seek not revenge but God's action to remove the evil altogether. If we want a candle to burn out, we don't add more oxygen. Instead, we remove the oxygen and allow the flame to fizzle out. What is it that snuffs out evil more quickly than anything else? Love. Our challenge, then, is simply to love. In allowing love to respond in all situations, we force evil to consume itself because it has nothing to feed on. *That* is our challenge, and yet there is a reminder in this psalm too: evil will not win.

We read in 2 Corinthians 4:8–10 that we may be afflicted but are not crushed. We may be perplexed but will never be driven to despair. We may be persecuted but will never be forsaken. We may be struck down but will not be destroyed. Why? Because God wins. Because Jesus took on evil and won. He didn't do this with more evil—he did it with love. I cannot think of a better song to sing as we enter the presence of God.

THREE QUESTIONS FOR YOU TO CHEW ON:

1. What in this psalm speaks to you? At what point are you drawn in? Why?
2. What are some ways to keep your love in the forefront of your mind regardless of what is going on around you?
3. Is this a matter of remaining positive or of seeing a bigger picture?

A PSALM OF GRACE

I know, I know. "A psalm of grace" again? Haven't we considered a lot of those already? That's right, . . . but hold up! This "grace" is something different. Think of it as another "room" in the house of grace. Is your imagination piqued? We'll get there. But, first off, let's take the time to read together Psalm 130.

Our need for forgiveness runs deep. Oftentimes our request for forgiveness relates to something we have just done, but our sin runs deeper than that moment of sin. Our sin is physical, mental, and spiritual. But it's more than that, as sin encapsulates our relationships and physical place in time. Psalm 130 may not give us much detail, but the details we do have help us understand the depths of sin and the gratitude of our psalmist.

He begins his psalm by crying out to God from the "depths." Is this a reference to the depth of sin within him? Is it a space in the physical world—has his sin dug him into a pit? Is this not about sin per se but about harm? We simply do not know, for the psalmist doesn't share the sin he has committed or elaborate on the depths in which he finds himself—and yet we do have a hint as to where he *could* be. The Hebrew word translated "depths" in verse 1 is typically associated with the sea. And, as we know, the sea in ancient Israel was considered a dark and evil place, a place where monsters lurked and unknown evil lived. It was a place of chaos. So, was the psalmist calling out to God from the sea? Was there a storm on the water so loud that the psalmist feared God wouldn't hear his call for mercy over the crashing waves? Maybe. Or is he at home and surrounded by the sufferings brought about by his personal sins? Again, . . . maybe.

No matter what the circumstances, something has made the writer feel so far from God that he senses a space, a physical distance, between himself and God. Verse 2 voices the hope that his voice can cover the distance. That his crying will be heard. Which is interesting, because we in our day affirm God that is everywhere, that he is outside space and time. We affirm that God, while we use human terminology to help in our understanding of him, . . . *isn't us*. He took on "human form" in the sense of Christ coming to earth, but God is not a human being with human characteristics and physical traits. I find it fascinating how in our desperation, pain, and suffering we often "humanize" (personify) God by attributing to him human, physical characteristics. I get this, because I do it, too. The only way we can begin to understand spiritual things is by what *we* know, so we resort to our experience in an attempt to understand and communicate with God. But let's think about this for a second. Why *wouldn't* God hear us? Are we suggesting that God *can't* hear? Are we putting God in a box and limiting him and his powers? No, . . . but it sure feels as though my own intrinsic limitations can put an artificial limit on God's ability to draw near and save me; redeem me; and, most importantly, forgive me. So, where is this psalm taking us? What does it mean?

Martin Luther once wrote that this psalm (along with four others, which I won't specify here) is "Pauline" in nature. That is, they convey a feeling and have a focus very much like that of Paul's New Testament letters. For Luther, this psalm felt like one of Paul's letters in that it speaks of sin and our need of being saved. It speaks of a salvation from God that is not dependent on anything but God's mercy. It speaks of grace.

We may not know what depths the psalmist speaks of or finds within himself—but it was evidently very real, to the point that he felt far removed from God. We may not know the nature of the psalmist's sin, but we do know that this was neither the first nor the last instance of it. And we know that he is thankful that God keeps no tally. But it's not only that God doesn't keep records; it's that God uses his grace to allow the psalmist to stand before him, receive forgiveness, and be comforted in the knowledge of that forgiveness so that he can worship and praise God *today and tomorrow*. There is an aspect of grace that I had never thought about before (as promised, we're moving to the uniqueness of this psalmist's "take" on grace). Grace doesn't just completely forgive (without merit on the part of the one being forgiven), but grace allows us to live today and tomorrow in worship to God. Without grace, there would be no need to worship God today and tomorrow because my sins would have condemned me already. My sins would have put up a wall preventing God from attending to my cries. My sins would have forced God to turn his back on me and cast me down to where *I deserved* to go. But grace not only washes my slate clean, not only forgives and makes me white as snow, but gives me hope, a reason, and the ability to worship God *after the sin*. Not only because he forgives, but also because he doesn't condemn, destroy, or cast aside.

Go figure that, yet again, we have a new understanding, a new nuance, of grace. Go figure that grace has become not only more complex but complete. Go figure that grace not only gives us the hope of tomorrow but opens up a conduit for our praise today.

Forgiveness, redemption, mercy, and grace. Know these realities and their implications for us as Christians, because they're not only what you need for tomorrow but what you live on today.

THREE QUESTIONS FOR YOU TO CHEW ON:

1. What in this psalm convicts you? What draws you in? Why?
2. Is it harder to cry out to God from our internal depths (our sorrow over our sin) or from some external "depth" (disaster or outside problem)? Why is that?
3. I've had conversations with people who struggle with the concept of grace—and most of this is because they struggle with their own baggage. What is it about grace that can make it so powerful and yet so hard to accept?

A PSALM OF HOPE

I invite you to turn with me to Psalm 131.

Once again, we are reminded of how our lives, our faith, and our living must be "child-like" (similar to Jesus's point in Matthew 19:13–14)—which has often been a source of contention for adults. I've lost count on how many sermons I've heard over the years or references to this text, and the conclusions and applications have been scattered. For some reason I always wonder whether Jesus is including the little kid who is having a temper tantrum—or only the prim little lady who is on her best behavior . . . *at that moment.* But this text, as well as the above mentioned one, isn't about our emotional outbursts, about our tendency to act like children who don't get their way. The point is that we can learn from the little ones in terms of their unquestioned trust and hope in their parents.

This "song of ascents" is ascribed to David; while we don't know when or in what context he penned it, we do see that, while reflective, it is also challenging in nature. David speaks not of things he has never done but draws upon his lessons learned to encourage his fellow Israelites as they ascend toward Jerusalem. The psalm is about understanding and living into the hope and grace of God (v. 3). It's about humility and trust (v. 1). It's about patience and about leaning into, and upon, God. It's about remembering that we are children of God and dependent on all that he is. As we read this, we get the sense that at some point David has had to come to this realization himself. While he may *now* be "content," that probably wasn't always the case.

As you read through this psalm, you may or may not have picked up on the fact (I know it took me a few passes) that all of the issues David speaks of have to do with internal thoughts or expressions. Pride, haughtiness, and concern for great matters that are beyond the scope of one's knowledge or ability to resolve—those things are internal. The psalm is about trusting in ourselves, assuming that *we* can work through our problems and figure out the answers—and our response to our eventual realization of the outcome is usually internal as well. But *hope* (the last thing of which David speaks (v. 3)? While hope is internal, it's externally focused. It's an internal yearning, a reaching out from within, that focuses on and places or transfers trust *outside the self*. The hope about which we read is centered not on a storm within but on a *calm* from without.

Maybe it's just me, but being proud to the point of haughtiness, being overly concerned about things that are beyond my control, seems to always lead to storms within. When I've let go of these attitudes and concerns and resolved to simply put my trust and hope in God, all the weight and worry seem to lift; I'm free from concern and as calm as a glassy lake.

Our two kids are observant and pick up on things easily. The more my wife and I talk within their earshot, the more listening we can tell they're doing. Because of both our kids' kind hearts, they are always willing to help. But beyond that, they feed off adult concerns they should know nothing about (we clearly need to have more talks outside the home or when our kids are not around). Inevitably, if the conversation is financial in nature, one of them wants to offer money, or they ask questions about the situation and want to take the concerns upon themselves. Our response? "Don't worry about that. We'll take care of it." These worries are not meant for the shoulders of an 11- or 15-year-old. They're meant for the parents. The issue is *our* concern, our worry, and the resolution is dependent on our ability to work through it and figure it out. (I'm in no way suggesting that we aren't, as parents, going to take it to God. Just sayin . . . But, putting myself in the place of our kids, I can't help but see an analogy to our doing just that— passing the onus along to God, especially if the issue is something beyond the routine, one for which we see no immediate or practical answer.)

"Come to me, all you who are weary and burdened," says Jesus, "and I will give you rest. Take my yoke upon you and learn from me, for I am gentle and humble in heart, and you will find rest for your souls. For my yoke is easy and my burden is light." (Matthew 11:28–30).

David learned a lesson at some point in his life: that trying to take on the worries of God is neither healthy nor viable. Our lives are chaotic enough already, and the last thing we need to do is worry about challenges over which we have no control. And God? Well, he wants us to come to him with our supplications, needs, cries for help, joys, and anything else.

But more than anything else he wants us to see that we can trust him, lean upon him, and place every ounce of our hope in him. There are so many dilemmas in this world that could consume us if we were to allow them to. And there are so many problems in this life our minds and hearts yearn to *fix*, to resolve, even though they are outside our control. So, what do we do when life is what it is? We hope. Because our hope is in the God who has made (and who keeps) promises. Our hope is in the God of the cross, the One who paid for our sins and set us right with God. Our hope is in the God who saves the lost, holds the whole world in his hands, and doesn't allow anything in this world to happen without his knowledge and will. Our hope is in the Alpha and the Omega, the beginning and the end, who rights wrongs and resolves conflicts and conundrums. So, why not hope in him today and forevermore? The alternative is clearly a complete mess.

Hope in God. It's really a simple lesson, and yet it takes a whole lifetime to learn.

THREE QUESTIONS FOR YOU TO CHEW ON:

1. What in this short psalm speaks to you? At what point are you drawn in, or to what can you relate? Why?
2. There's something powerful about hearing someone's testimony (as David offers here). Have you ever shared your testimony, either formally or during the course of a conversation? How'd it go? Did working through your thoughts and experiences help *you* as well as others?
3. How is this similar to the lesson Job eventually learns (you can read Job 38–42 to hear where Job finally lands)?

A WORSHIPFUL PSALM
OF VOWS

Let's begin our reading today with Psalm 132.

This psalm is a psalm of vows. And while we don't know who the author is or what the setting was, we do have recorded here a vow from David (vv. 1–5), a vow from the people (vv. 6–10), and then an oath from God (vv. 11–18). It was David who made a vow to build a house for the Lord (see 1 Chronicles 17:4–15), God who responded by stating that it wouldn't be David but his son Solomon who would build it (which Solomon did do; you can read about it in 1 Kings 6), but then God who promised that a descendant of David would sit on the throne for eternity. God held up his end by providing a descendant upon the throne—a throne that would last forever! His name is Jesus (Matthew 1:1; Luke 1:32–33; Acts 15:15–16; Hebrews 1:5). So, vows made, vows given, vows upheld. Is this, though, simply a psalm of reminders of the importance of vows? Why do we have this psalm, and why did the people need the reminders?

While we don't know much about this psalm, we do know that it falls under the "psalms of ascents" category and thus that it was written as a song and remembrance that was used/sung by the people as they climbed up toward Jerusalem. It was sung by the people as they went to visit the temple, the dwelling place of God here on earth and the very place promised by David and delivered by Solomon. Maybe this was a song meant to encourage the people about what had gone before. Maybe it was a song to challenge them to relive the vows made by their ancestors and kings. Maybe it was a song they sang to God as they asked him to remember what he had promised in his vow, above: the eternal king to come. Maybe it was all three or a combination. Maybe. Did *God* need to be reminded? Certainly not, . . . but the people felt as though they needed to sing. I'm surmising, then, that this was probably more for *them* than for God.

It's funny how we feel the need to ask God for something we know he'll deliver on without a nudge from us. We affirm that God is the God of covenants (promises). And we know that, if God says he's going to do something, he'll do it. While we may not know *when* any given promise will come to fruition, we hold to the truth that it will. That's what our hope is built on: what God says will be. And yet, how interesting it is that there is still a felt need within us to speak of those needs to God and to ask him to remember them. To ask God to hold to his Word, as though he may have forgotten or been internally balancing whether he should move on and do something else instead. The reality is, even though this may seem counterintuitive to us, that we need to verbalize our hope even though all our hope and assurance are already placed in the God of vows (in fact, Jesus *instructs* us to do just that in the Lord's Prayer). If God's Word were not true or reliable, then Scripture, from the very beginning, would need to be tossed out. Everything we believe and hold as true is based on what God has done and declared. So, why did the people still ask God to *remember*? I don't know, as I wasn't there. But it couldn't be any different from what you and I do when we ask God to *forgive*. We know he does, but still we seek it.

As I reflect on this psalm and what the people were asking, I find myself coming back not only to *what* they were asking but *why* they were asking. They were asking God to remember his vow that a descendant of David would be on the throne for eternity. Why was that important? Because it meant they would be ruled over by one of their own (a Hebrew); because it meant that they would forever be in God's presence; and, ultimately, it meant that they would be able always to worship him. When I scramble that all together, at least in my own head, I come to the understanding that all the people wanted to do was worship God and that they knew, and declared, that God had to act in order for that to happen.

The work of Solomon in building the temple happened only because God said it would happen, allowed them to, . . . and made a vow about it. Without God's vow, and conceivably without God holding to his word, there would have been no future worship of him *in his presence*. That's what the people wanted. They wanted to worship God not only on that day, not only on their way up to Jerusalem, but in his presence for eternity to come. And so, their worship song became a song of hope for tomorrow. It became a song that brought peace to their hearts in the present and yet prepared them for what was to come.

Sometimes we simply need reminders that need to be verbalized. Sometimes we need to hear and even repeat the promises in order to comprehend them, to remind *ourselves* of them, and to put our souls at rest, even when we know they are true and will happen regardless. Our worship of God can get confusing and complicated, but this all stems from our desire to worship God. While we may confuse what we do with what God does, that doesn't remove the fact that we long to worship God. We can rest easily in the knowledge that God has done everything in order for our worship to continue on well past our lives on this earth today (into eternity and through infinity). Because that promise, that vow that one of David's descendants will sit on the throne forever comes to fruition in Christ. It is by way of Christ and what he has done that we will continue to worship God for eternity in his presence. So, go ahead and ask God to remember that promise—without forgetting that he already has, that his vow has long since been a "done deal."

THREE QUESTIONS FOR YOU TO CHEW ON:

1. What in this psalm touches you? Where are you drawn in? Why?
2. What are come requests you regular ask of God? Are they for the continuance, the replenishment, of blessings you already enjoy? For non-material realities? Or for something else?
3. Is it wrong to ask God for things we don't need but want?

A BLESSED PSALM
OF UNITY

Let's begin today's reading with Psalm 133.

In this short song of ascents, as the people of God walk together toward the house of God, David reflects on the joy that takes place when brothers and sisters live, work, play, and come together in unity. I imagine that David, as he walks with his brothers and sisters along this pilgrim route to Jerusalem, is able to hear their laughter and tears as they share. As he contemplates the journey ahead, maybe he overhears the hardships the people have experienced during the last year but then hears how a neighbor came and assisted them after the death of their loved one. Maybe there have been times when someone felt alone on the trek, but then the sisterhood and brotherhood of fellow believers, the doing of life together, provided peace, security, and happiness.

The imagery we get from David here—that of the oil flowing from Aaron's head onto his beard and robe—gets lost for us in translation. How does oil flowing down a nasty beard show unity (I say "nasty" because I once had a beautiful long beard and know how gross it can get—not that mine ever did or has . . .)? And the dew of Hermon falling upon the mountains of Zion? How do those images speak of the joy of unity?

Aaron represented the priesthood, and we know that the priests would not only anoint and consecrate the tent and burn offerings, lamps, and all other decorations for God's house; the priests *themselves* would be anointed with the oil and various spices (Exodus 30:22–30). Why? Because they had been made holy; they were set apart, consecrated, cleansed, and purified *for service* to God. They were his people and were marked as such. So, when

David brings up Aaron and the oil, it's because he, the other priests, and the house of God were special. They were marked and set apart for God.

But what do we do with all this oil flowing? David is giving an image of having not just a little oil but a whole lot of it! He wants not only Aaron's head but his beard and robe—all of him—to be drenched in God's holiness. David wants the oil to be poured lavishly on Aaron's head so it will drip down over his face and onto his beard before falling upon the collar of his robe. And what's under his robe? The breastplate with the names of the 12 tribes of Jerusalem inscribed on it. This is David's way of saying that, when God's people gather together, from every tribe, from every tongue that declares the living God, the assembly is so great, rich, good, pure, and precious that nothing can compare to it. Just as Aaron and his priests were consecrated for God, so too are all those who gather together in joyous worship.

The other part of David's analogy is that of the dew of Hermon falling upon Mount Zion. This imagery works quite similarly. Just as oil poured on the top of one's head eventually flows down the face and body (it's a gravity thing), so, too, does the dew that comes down from Hermon as it falls upon Mount Zion. Is it significant that Herman is mentioned? From what I can see, it isn't (although Herman was considered the highest mountain in the region). The imagery we are to take from this is that of the *dew* itself; if you have ever walked across the grass on an early spring morning, you know how wet it can be from the dew. The grass has been refreshed, fertilized, and invigorated.

So, here's what this all means: we are to worship as a teeming multitude, en masse. When we gather under God's name, when we sing and praise him and do life together, when we join in one voice and praise the Creator, Maker, Sustainer, Savior, Redeemer, and Lord *in everything we do*, then something unique and awe-inspiring happens. Some of the ramifications:

- We give and receive brotherly and sisterly love. (Hebrews 13:1)
- We are united as one. (John 17:11)
- Jesus joins and is present with us. (Matthew 18:20)
- We break bread together in Jesus's name. (1 Corinthians 11:17–34)
- We join in fellowship with each other and thus with the Father, Son, and Holy Spirit. (1 John 1:3)
- We are purified from our sin as fellowship with God and each other enables us to walk in the light of Christ. (1 John 1:7)

Ultimately? My relationship with God is not just about *me*—it's about *us*. Ultimately? Christ didn't die just for *me*—he died for the *Church* he calls his Bride (Ephesians 5:22–33). So, when we gather as one and lift his praises with a unified voice, . . . God finds joy. Just as the Father, Son, and Holy Spirit are separate and yet one; just as God created us as social, communal beings; just as we are created to love and worship God; and just as we declare that there is no place in our lives in which God doesn't work and the Holy Spirit isn't present—when we gather together we become one. We unite.

And guess what eternity is going to look like? A unified multitude of God's gathered followers—consecrated, set apart, made holy, replenished, fed, and having their thirst quenched by his eternal, life-giving water—shouting their praises with a unified voice. And what a joyous eternity that will be!

THREE QUESTIONS FOR YOU TO CHEW ON:

1. What in this psalm calls out to you? To what concepts or imagery are you drawn? Why?
2. If you think about being united in worship in the time to come, what is the most joyful aspect to which you're looking forward? Songs in other languages? Dancing with lots of different styles?
3. Can you think of other, comparable imagery to the word pictures David uses in this psalm? Perhaps imagery current to our context that would convey the same meaning?

A PSALM FOR
THE PRIESTHOOD

I invite you to turn with me to Psalm 134.

We are on the last of our "psalms of ascents" (Psalms 120–134), and we end with a psalm that is focused on the Levites and priests of God. The Israelite men and women traveling on their pilgrimage to Jerusalem and the holy sanctuary of God have sung of God's love and dedication and asked for his blessings on their own lives. They now turn their focus on those who will unite them, cleanse them, reconcile them, and pronounce the Lord's blessings on their lives. Their desire? Verses 1–2 are an encouragement for the priestly leaders to turn to God and lift up their hands on behalf of the people—who in turn (v. 3) ask God to bless these religious leaders.

As a pastor myself, I am always thankful to hear that people pray for me, think about me, and encourage me in my calling. It's hard work doing what we do each week, and so any encouragement, any prayers, any word of blessings from the people I serve always make me feel good. It's good to know they support me, care about me, and pray for my work, the people I meet with, and all the spit and grit that goes into what I do each week. In truth, all ministers hear the joking remark that we work only on Sundays and that during the rest of the week we golf/nap/rest/play. While we know it's a joke—it's an old and tired one. It's nice to receive acknowledgement of and encouragement for all the things we really do, but even just to hear that others are praying and asking God to bless us goes a long way.

There is also a beautiful challenge here; notice that the pilgrims first pray that the priests will lift up their hands and praise God. It's really easy to get into a rut each week of working and crafting a sermon for Sunday, while failing to spend time worshiping and praising God ourselves. It's easy to spend time in the Word for Sunday but fail to do so for my own benefit. The pilgrims, who need these "men of the cloth" to be in a right relationship with God, hope that the priests and Levites actually are in a healthy relationship with God. These men are their connection, their bridge, in terms of their hopeful relationship with God. They need the priests to be "on their game"—especially when they are making this massive pilgrimage.

What about today? We still need our pastors, ministers, and priests, all our men and women in this role, to be "on their game"—and, Lord knows, these members of the clergy need our prayers! They need them for their relationships with the people they serve, for all the varied work they do, but for their personal health and well-being as well. But we need to understand a distinction here. No longer do we as laypersons believe that the priests and Levites come between God and us. No longer do we believe that our pastors, like those ancient priests of God, help us atone for our sins by accepting our offerings. Because of Christ, because of *his role* as intermediary (1 Timothy 2:5), because he now is the High Priest in the Levitical order (Hebrews 4), because he makes *us*—*all* of us as Christians—a kingdom of priests (Revelation 1:6), a part of the royal priesthood (1 Peter 2:9), we—clergy and laity alike—have all taken on this role. So yes, we love our pastors and ministers and the work they do; we love that they have the education and training to minister the Word, open it up and reveal its truth to us, and lead our services and play their myriad other roles in our church, . . . but we must also recognize that *we too* have a role.

We come to church to hear the Word of God proclaimed by trained men and women of God. We gather together to be in his presence and bless him and be blessed *by* him. But we each have a priestly role, too. The barriers between us and God, just as the barrier between Jew and Gentile, have been demolished. The role of the priests long ago was primarily the work of reconciliation. As Paul writes in 2 Corinthians 5:18–19, all believers carry on this role now. So, in our work and play, in our church and community, in our homes and all other areas of our lives, we are called to praise, worship, give thanks, share, declare Christ, and praise him for *our own* role as prophets, priests, and kings.

So, *you*, child of the risen Savior, . . . praise the Lord!

You, child of the Lord Most High, . . . lift up your hands in the sanctuary (and in all other places).

You, daughter of Christ, . . . sing praises to the Lord.

You, son of Christ, . . . give thanks for the blessings of God.

May the Lord bless you from his dwelling place, he who is the Maker of heaven and earth.

THREE QUESTIONS FOR YOU TO CHEW ON:

1. What in this psalm grabs your attention? To what are you drawn? Why?
2. How can you pray for, and encourage, your minister or youth pastor?
3. *You* are a priest of God—so how are *you* doing in your prayer life? In your engagement with the Word of God?

A PSALM OF PRAISE

Please open your Bible and turn with me to Psalm 135.

Our psalm today begins and ends with praise. And all the stuff in-between? You guessed it: praise. Praise the Lord because we are his servants. Praise him because he is good. Praise him because he has chosen and redeemed you. Praise him because he is above all other gods. Praise him because he controls all things, both seen and unseen. Praise him because, when his people have been in need, he has provided. Praise him because he endures forever. When it's all said and done? Praise God.

The other day I was part of a conversation about God, predestination, election, and the general work of God, and I brought up the fact that the struggle *we* experience is that our answers to people's questions seem to have to do with what *we* know, perceive, or think. The questions we ask and the answers we seek are so often based on our own feelings and understandings. Still today, when it comes to those big existential questions, like why God allows suffering in this world or permits babies to die, unless the Bible itself has a clear answer, our answers tend to come only through our personal perception and thought. So, it's safe to say that, to a large extent, we learn and grow by what we observe and feel. When we start talking about why God would do _____ , our answers, more often than not, are going to be based on what we *feel*. The problem is that God doesn't work that way. God works in *his* way and not ours.

So, where am I going with this? *Because* God works in his way, I owe him praise. God is so far outside our realm of understanding that we *should*, and *can only*, praise him. I don't understand a lot of things in this world, but because I don't have explanations for why God does what he does doesn't mean I don't worship and praise him. I'm glad the Lord does whatever pleases him (v. 6) because I know that all he does is for the good of himself and his people. We may not feel comfortable with the fact that God in Old Testament times struck down many nations and killed many kings (v. 10), but we do know that he did these things to save his people; hold to his covenant; and remove sin, chaos, and destruction (the very things those kings and nations lived by). God is God, . . . and because he is—because of his love, knowledge, work, and sacrifice—we praise him.

Another challenge we have is that we sometimes don't *want* to praise him. Sometimes we go through experiences in life that bring to the fore all sorts of questions about God and his love. Sometimes the hardships we experience cause us to ask questions the answers to which are outside our comprehension of God. The untimely death of a loved one. The loss of a beloved job. Hardships of all sorts. All of these setbacks, in one way or another, make us wonder just how good God really is or how much he loves, cares, and watches over us. *Why* would God allow me to lose that job? *Why* would God take my loved one from me? While these are understandable questions—and legitimate questions we should ask God (he can handle them)—in the end we must still come back to praise.

We need to accept the reality that we simply cannot fathom the ways of God (read the ending chapters of Job, beginning with Job 38, for that one). For me personally, there is so much pain and suffering in this world that, if I were to allow it to, it would consume me. In the end the peace I have is in knowing that, regardless of what I know or don't know, God knows all and has it under his control. Nothing is outside God's purview, spectrum of knowledge, or plan—or beyond his ability to redeem or rectify. So, I praise him. Regardless of what I think is bad or tragic, I do know that God is still—is absolutely—good. So, again, I praise him.

Ultimately, if I declare that God is whole, perfect, holy, and completely good, then all that he does must fit into that understanding—even when I don't "get" it from my limited human perspective. A loving and holy God holds to his Word, his covenant, his love. And so, . . . I praise him. A loving and holy God pursues his people, his children, even though they constantly run from him. And so, . . . I praise him. And in the end, a loving and holy God, One who sacrifices himself for me (insert Christ here), deserves every ounce of my praise and worship.

So, praise him, all you people. Praise him!

THREE QUESTIONS FOR YOU TO CHEW ON:

1. What in this psalm speaks to you? What draws you in? Why?
2. How can you praise God even when you don't have the answers you seek?
3. How do we respond to others, especially seekers, when they are looking for specific answers in the Bible that the Bible doesn't give (or that the Bible doesn't give in the way that we want to read/hear)? How are we to come to peace with having no definitive answer?

A PSALM OF
ENDURING LOVE

L et's begin today by reading Psalm 136.
As usual, we want to know a couple of basic contextual details: who
the author is and what he is writing about. We don't know who the psalmist
is, but it would appear that this is a psalm intended for use in a liturgical
(worship) setting. Perhaps the choir is chanting back and forth with the
congregation, or maybe the temple priests are singing this in conjunction
with those streaming in to worship. What is the author writing about? That
one's easy: the worship of God for his enduring love. It's a song proclaiming
God's enduring love over all leaders (he acknowledges a few specifically),
over all creation (vv. 5–9), through the exodus (vv. 10–16), and in all those
conquest related situations the people of Israel went through (vv. 17–22).

What's beautiful about this psalm is that, while it's not explicitly
stated, and while we typically think of "good" things that came about
from these events (the exodus, for example, brought God's people out of
slavery and oppression, and God's people praised him for those conquest
victories), it is a fact that many times we overlook the harsh realities
surrounding those events.

In the exodus the people complained. A *lot*. This was neither an easy
departure nor a trouble-free journey for them. For hundreds of years the
Israelites had had a home in Egypt, and now they did not. For hundreds
of years, even though they had been slaves and treated horribly by the
Egyptians, they *had known* what each new day would look like. And now
they didn't. So, they grumbled . . . and grumbled . . . and were put through
a lot. And so, yes, we praise God for his enduring love and for extricating

his people from a terrible situation. Yes, we praise God for his covenantal love and for his binding word that he would *always* be their God, no matter what they might do to hinder that relationship. But that time was really hard for the people of God. Not so hard that the difficult overcame the positive—but a struggle nonetheless.

On the other side of the Jordan they were met with continual fighting, and the reality of war and battles is that nobody ever truly wins. People die on each side. Injuries happen on the battlefield that leave scars that last for weeks, months, years, and perhaps even whole lives. And I'm not just speaking of physical scars. What about emotional ones? We're learning more and more about PTSD and other mental and emotional battles; while these diagnoses may be relatively new to us, that doesn't mean they didn't exist back then. The reality is that wars hurt everyone. Yes, we are thankful that the "good side" ultimately came out ahead. Yes, we are thankful that when the "good side" won, the killing stopped. Yes, we are thankful that God went before the people and gave them the win, but people *still died*. Families were still ripped apart. Fathers and young boys were taken from their families, which in that day meant huge strains were put on those left behind. And what about the atrocious things done to women and girls? Again: nobody wins in war.

And *yet*, . . . we are still to praise God for his enduring love. Because, while we need to acknowledge the negative side to both the exodus event and the ensuing conquest, none of that compares to the goodness that came about. Especially in the case of the people of God who needed God to fight their battles, remove the whip from their backs, give them peace and a home of their own, and simply be their God and love them unconditionally. The truth is that the people of Israel needed God. They couldn't leave their slave masters under their own power, they couldn't win the battles that were before them in their own strength, and they couldn't exist without the God of creation providing all of their needs, both along the journey and in the promised land. As with so much of Scripture, we have to understand context and put ourselves in the people's sandals. They were extremely thankful that God's enduring love saved them time and time again. Did other people suffer—like those indigenous occupants of the land displaced by the new arrivals? Yes—but that's something we personally struggle with, while they did not. It's *my* issue to wrestle with—not God's.

So, how can you and I speak of God's enduring love through this psalm? Well, think about your own past. We can definitely agree on praising God for creation—so that's a great start. What about times of trial? What about times of darkness? Did you get through such periods? Then praise him. Are you still in one of them? Then you can still praise him because we don't believe God abandons us. Time may feel as though it's dragging as we are in this dark space, but dark spaces don't mean that we've been left alone. Think of yourself as being in that dark place with God at your side. What about your battles and those obstacles in your life that need conquering? Do we believe that God leaves us to handle those on our own? Do we believe God sits up in heaven waiting to see who wins so he can side with them? No. When God says "Never will I abandon or forsake you" (Deuteronomy 31:6; Hebrews 13:5), that's exactly what he means. From creation to the cross, from the grave to the sky, from the pits of despair to the heavenly realms of glory: God is there.

So, praise the Lord, for his love endures forever. It's a love that's based solely on him, his covenant, and his love. And for that alone we should praise him. For it encompasses our whole lives.

THREE QUESTIONS FOR YOU TO CHEW ON:

1. What in this psalm speaks to you? What draws you in? Why?
2. Have you ever been in a position where you had to look on the positive side of things in order to make it through a difficult spot? How did it help—or didn't it?
3. How do you praise God in the dark passages of human life (the lost loved one, the struggles with relationships, your own health, and others)?

A PSALM OF ANGER

I invite you to turn with me to Psalm 137.

Now that you've read this psalm, let's look at Lamentations 1:1–6 to help us with context and understanding:

> How deserted lies the city, once so full of people! How like a widow is she, who once was great among the nations! She who was queen among the provinces has now become a slave. Bitterly she weeps at night, tears are on her cheeks. Among all her lovers there is no one to comfort her. All her friends have betrayed her; they have become her enemies. After affliction and harsh labor, Judah has gone into exile. She dwells among the nations; she finds no resting place. All who pursue her have overtaken her in the midst of her distress. The roads to Zion mourn, for no one comes to her appointed festivals. All her gateways are desolate, her priests groan, her young women grieve, and she is in bitter anguish. Her foes have become her masters; her enemies are at ease. The LORD has brought her grief because of her many sins. Her children have gone into exile, captive before the foe. All the splendor has departed from Daughter Zion. Her princes are like deer that find no pasture; in weakness they have fled before the pursuer.

The city of God is in ruins, the people have been taken captive and are feeling abandoned by God, and now they are sitting by the rivers of Babylon, weeping, their captors taunting them with a mock request to "entertain" them. In response, there is not only this feeling of "What!? Are you kidding?" but a desire to dash their captors' infants against the rocks! And this is in the Bible.

The truth is that there is a ton of violent imagery throughout Scripture, and it doesn't end there. We witness people who get angry, become murderous, are deceptive, and have scheming hearts. What are we to do with them and those situations? Well, as one author writes, "Do we ignore those texts and move on? Do we turn our blinders on and pretend it never happened, those were anomalies, or that the Holy Spirit made a mistake and it never happened? Not at all. Those are real people, real events, and real violence—and that violence continues into this day." If Scripture is to give us not only Jesus but a rationale for our need for him, then we have to be honest with not only our feelings and emotions but the truth that even followers of God are broken.

Now, let's take that "remembrance" and put it in context for this psalm. The people of God were in exile. Their temple was destroyed, Jerusalem was in ruins, and the people were thus completely broken. All their hope had been dashed. All their emotions were raw. And they simply could not sing about their home that had once been. They couldn't get their fingers to play their once melodious harps. Their tongues were stuck in place; they couldn't seem to move them to bring forth words to sing. Nor were their memories coming like a flood in a way they would have liked. There was just too much that *had* happened and *was* happening in that moment.

This psalm speaks clearly of the psalmist's memories. Each stanza— vv. 1–4, 5–6, and 7–9—gives us a form of the word "to remember" in Hebrew, with nearly every word in this psalm being in the *past* tense except for the very end, where God's people wish that what has happened to them at the hands of the Babylonians might be repaid. Their pain and memories are raw and real, and we must acknowledge them. We need to understand not only where the people were but the feelings they were enduring. Sadly, for them, and for many people today, violence can be answered only with more violence.

What does that mean for you and me? First off, I would be deceiving myself if I were to claim that I would never voice the kinds of wishes these people had for their captors. I cannot imagine anyone harming, beating, or killing a member of my family. And I think my heart and feelings would, if I were honest, follow that same path toward repayment. We are all sinners, and brokenness affects all of us.

Second, we need to remember that the psalms are not a list of commands we must follow—they are the recorded emotions and thoughts of real people experiencing real life events (reading them is almost like reading someone's journal). The psalms are about who we really are deep down inside. Sometimes psalms are joyful, while other times they reflect anger. Sometimes they are calls to praise for what God has done, while at other times they are filled with confusion and angst. I'll say it again: *all people are broken.* I appreciate what one author writes in this regard: "The psalms are not our personal Hallmark cards to God. They are the cry to God of humanity as a whole."

Finally, I'm glad God doesn't follow through on all the wishes of his broken children. God doesn't play by our desires of violence for violence. We can be ever thankful that, while we may proclaim that "happy is the one who repays you according to what you have done to us," that response simply isn't in the DNA of heaven. God responds to violence with love. God responds to anger with peace. God responds to death with his own death, . . . which then brings life. What's important is that we recognize our own feelings and brokenness, . . . all the while holding firmly to God's work of love, peace, harmony, and redemption.

THREE QUESTIONS FOR YOU TO CHEW ON:

1. What in this psalm speaks to you? To what are you drawn? Why?
2. Should we avoid hard texts that don't sit well with us? Are we called to relate to their authors and attempt to understand their perspectives? Do we let them be as they are? Or do we look for honesty and truth in the writers' feelings and conclusions?
3. Have you ever asked something of God, only to have it *not* come to fruition, and then found yourself thankful for its not having happened? What was it?

A PSALM OF
OPEN WORSHIP

Our psalm for this reflection is Psalm 138.

We are now in the home stretch of the psalms—and these next eight psalms (138–145) are considered "Davidical psalms," as the belief is that David wrote them. When we look at the whole of them, we don't find any cohesive thought to unify the group, but we don't really need that. They simply are psalms from a believer that reflect his thoughts, praises, and needs. Doesn't that about cover all of our life (that's a rhetorical question)?

This psalm specifically has David singing praise to God, not only for what he has done but for the fact that God's works have *exceeded* anything David could have imagined. As we see in verse 3, not only has God responded to David's call to him—but he has done so with such power, strength, and swiftness that the strength of David's soul has been enhanced. Because of all of this, the psalmist praises God. But not only does he praise God, he also calls out in supplication, requesting that all the kings of the earth will praise God. He ends with coming back to his personal praise as the *reason* all the kings of the earth should follow suit. David goes from the personal to the corporate.

But that's not where I am struck or challenged. Verses 1–2a have really sunk a hook in me: "I will praise you, Lord, with all my heart; before the 'gods' I will sing your praise. I will bow down toward your holy temple and will praise your name."

Maybe it's me, but so much of my own praise is offered in the quietness of my self (at home, in the car, in my heart and head), in the gathering of my brothers and sisters on Sunday mornings (in a church service), or while I meet with people in my work (as a pastor). But this praise from David is none of those. When he speaks of the "gods" in verse 1, there are a couple of possibilities in terms of what he may mean: David may be referring to the pagan gods of the time or to human leaders who were being worshiped. Either way, David is declaring that nothing and no one will be worshiped except the one, true, living God. Now, *that* shouldn't hook any of us because we already declare it. We do not worship pagan gods, nor do we worship people and leaders. But the hook for me is what David does in *response* to the worship of gods around him; he bows toward God's holy temple. David is making a public statement against all gods who aren't God. Not only is he making a statement, but he's using a physical action, declaring his posture in this regard through an object lesson. Whether or not David is stating that he spontaneously bows toward God whenever John Smith engages in worship motions of a pagan nature—the challenge of his words is still before us. When any gesture or statement that is anti-God happens around him, David turns around and worships God. This is not only a response to the sins of others; it's a direct smack in the face of the pagan worshiper *and his god*, clearly demonstrating that David wants nothing to do with whatever is being done or said.

And that has challenged me. Not surprisingly, I do not participate in the worship of pagan gods. I do not bow down to them, talk to them, or give them any piece of my heart, my love, or my worship. But what do I do when *someone else* does? Do I ignore them? Do I speak softly under my breath against them? Do I chalk it up to the religious freedom to which we Americans hold so tightly (in truth, I'm thankful for this freedom, and yet heart-broken over some of its ramifications)? What do I do, what do *you* do, when the practice of religious freedom confronts us in ways that are uncomfortable to us?

David challenges us to respond by outright bowing down and worshiping God. Not as an insult, not as a "take this!" action, but because we want to and need to. In a way (as we see in vv. 5–8), this is a form of sharing who God is. David declares that he desires all the kings of the earth to praise God—and bowing to the true God in the presence of others can be an effective way of making a statement without being "in your face" about it. I'm not talking here about blatantly mimicry of what the other person is doing in response to *her god* but by following through without apology or any appearance of one-upmanship with our Christian worship and way of life. Because we *know* that our example is going to spark questions, which lead to conversations, which then lead to sharing about God, which then leads to more questions and the opportunity to share our faith. This is basic Sharing 101.

Sharing the Good News of God's love, poured out through Jesus Christ and indwelling us by the Holy Spirit, can be difficult or uncomfortable. I can find an opportunity to speak with you about Jesus via some natural turn in a conversation, but it's really hard to just walk up to you and ask point blank, "Do you know Jesus?" What I can do, though, rather easily, is live my life in your presence in response to God's love. I can understand and realize that all areas of my life have been impacted by Christ. I can declare that, no matter what comes at me in this world, no matter what I see or hear, do or say, I will praise and worship God. When someone *else* says or does something that is anti-God, I will respond by continuing to worship God.

Does our response to pagan worship even the odds, as though some invisible scale is balanced every time we respond by worshiping God when pagan worship is taking place around us? No. God doesn't need us to even the odds or balance the scales of worship. But I think that, in a way, *we* become stronger in our faith when we do respond to outside "anti-God" demonstrations or practices. The more we work that response "muscle," the stronger we become in our Christian walk. I also feel that, the more people see Christians unashamedly and without constraint practicing our beliefs, the more the devil gets kicked to the curb. I also wholeheartedly believe that the more I practice the "outward expression" of my faith, the more conversations will come up with non-believers about what I'm doing, why I'm doing it, what it means, and who God is.

So, bow away! Sing away! Do whatever you do in your worship of and service to God, not only in the confines of your home, your church, your car, and your *self* . . . but out there in the world and in the open for all to see! Because, Lord knows, this broken world needs more *true* and *open* worship of the only true God.

THREE QUESTIONS FOR YOU TO CHEW ON:

1. What in this psalm catches your attention? To what are you drawn? Why?
2. Do you find yourself standing up in religious freedom or withdrawing, afraid to inadvertently step on someone else's toes? Is it the possibility of confrontation from which you withdraw, or do you want to avoid curtailing the freedom of others?
3. How can you respond in a way that challenges, encourages, and yet loves to someone's hatred in response to your belief?

A BANNER PSALM OF GOD

I invite you to turn with me to Psalm 139.

This text has been dubbed the "crown of psalms," not only in that it is one of the best-known psalms but in that it comes across as a jewel that sits atop the crown that is the psalter. Why? Possibly, at least in part, because it's highly personal, broad in its focus, and yet narrow in its scope. This psalm touches upon who we are and goes on to declare that God is so much more. That he is all-knowing, all-powerful, and ever-present. That this all-powerful King of kings is at the same time intimately involved in your and my life. We use this psalm for so many different reasons. It's a banner psalm for those who fight for things they are passionate about. It's a banner psalm for those who struggle with sin in their lives. It's a banner psalm for those who are working through difficult emotions, the reality of creation, or an understanding of themselves. While many people may use this psalm as a battle *cry*, however, I would encourage us to use it as more of a battle *reminder*.

At first glance, this psalm could easily be read with me in mind (or you, for that matter). Is it about who I am; the brokenness within me; or the reality that, since it is God who created me, I am *perfect* in his eyes? (Unfortunately, the perfection part is *only* in his eyes—and that only because he sees his blameless Son when he looks at me. If you don't know this yet, then I guess I'll have to be the bearer of bad news: you are not *good*. You are not *complete*, and you're definitely not *perfect*. The only completeness in you is your complete brokenness. And guess what—it's the same for me. We see this clearly in our text.)

- To be hemmed in (v. 5) means being securely confined. Not necessarily in a bad way. We hem in little children when we swaddle them. When someone is physically struggling with someone else, we hem them in by holding their arms and legs together so they cannot hurt themselves or the person they are fighting. In our relationship with God, when he hems us in, he is wrapping us up to calm and ease us. We need him to hem us in because we're struggling with him, hurting ourselves, or hurting others.
- We read in verse 7 David's declaration that he cannot get away from God's Spirit. Which implies that there have been times when he's tried—ditto, I'll have to say, for me. Not because I've wanted to get away from goodness and love; it's only when I've done things I shouldn't have that I, like a child who knows he has been naughty, want to run and hide so that I don't have to face God.
- In verse 11 David declares that, should he say "surely the darkness will hide me and the light become night around me," he'll be saying it because, even though he also declares himself to be a child of God, there is sin and darkness in him that seek out more sin and darkness.

And yet, through all of this, David acknowledges that it's impossible to get away from God. So, getting back to my question, is this psalm *really* about you or me and our understandings of ourselves? Nope.

This psalm is an expression of praise to God, the One who knows me and searches me and yet still calls me his son. God is the One who knows me so well, and so deeply, that when I rise or fall the whole situation is already fully known and understood. In verse 3 we read that God "discerns" my coming and going and even my lying down, . . . which means that God not only knows my ways but the whole backstory of everything I do. And in the end *that*, and that alone, brings David peace. That God is so knowing, so present, and yet so beyond and above that even David's sin and brokenness can't push him away. We may not always appreciate this truth or find it convenient, but that's out problem and not God's.

But it doesn't end there; your sin and brokenness can't push God away, but God, through Christ, takes the proactive stance and runs toward you, right there where you're hiding. He runs not toward the sin but toward the person who has committed that sin. Maybe *that* should be our battle reminder and cry! That the God of the universe knows our hearts and thoughts intimately and completely.

I'll end here with words from Martin Buber's book *Tales of the Hasidim* (Buber was an early twentieth-century Jewish philosopher).

Where I wander — You!

Where I ponder — You!
Only You, You again, always You!
You! You! You!
When I am gladdened — You!
When I am saddened — You!
Only You, You again, always You!
You! You! You!
Sky is You, Earth is You!
You above! You below!
In every trend, at every end,
Only You, You again, always You!
You! You! You!

THREE QUESTIONS FOR YOU TO CHEW ON:

1. What in this beautiful psalm convicts you or draws you out? Why?
2. Some may feel as though not being able to "get away" from God is constricting and so have no desire to believe in him. How is being hemmed in a blessing to you?
3. I don't know about you, but sometimes it can feel overwhelming for me to recognize that God *knows* my thoughts. How about you? How can this, ultimately, be a comfort for us?

A PSALM OF SUPPLICATION

Please join me in reading Psalm 140.

Our psalm today reflects a person—in this case David—who is in the midst of pain and chaos. Evil doers surround him, violence keeps being directed against him, the tongues of his detractors keep lashing out and speaking ill of him, and he sees nowhere to turn but God. And so, he turns to God for mercy, for deliverance, and for God to fight this battle for him and restore him to safety. But why? What's going on in David's life?

As with many of the psalms, we just don't know. What makes this even more difficult, at least for me, is that I've never been in a situation where I was surrounded by evil. I've never had violence perpetrated against me or felt that the wicked were trying to trip me up. I do feel as though I have on occasion had "tongues as sharp as a serpent's" speak ill of me, but David's case seems to be a step up from whatever it was I've experienced.

Evil abounds in this life. There are people so focused on themselves that they consider all other people their enemies—their tactic to preserve themselves is to proactively attack anyone and everyone whom they don't presume to be on their side. This could be what was happening to David. One way or another, the situation had to have been hard on the king. It had to be hard ruling in a manner pleasing to both God and the people—the reality is that, while God's ways are holy, right, and just, they don't always sit well with those who want to do their own thing or who are bent on evil. At this point we can pull from the previous psalm (Psalm 139), since many feel that Psalms 139 and 140 work together.

In Psalm 139 we saw David petitioning God to slay the wicked because all those bloodthirsty people were surrounding him. In the end, while we don't specifically see that David was being attacked, he calls on them to step aside: any enemy of God is an enemy of David. This makes sense because any attack on God is also going to be an attack on his people. So, as we make our way *back* to our psalm for today, we can piece together a setting. David openly worshiped Yahweh, and all those opposed to God were doing their best to cut him down. Once again, an attack on God is also an attack on God's people. And, coming full circle, an attack on God's people is a direct attack on God. *That's* where we are to find our focus.

Not once does David demonstrate any intention to fight this battle. Never once does he ask for strength to attack his foes, slay his enemies, tear down the walls of his nay-sayers, or even tongue-lash those who are against him. What does he do? He seeks God's protection, safety, mercy, and deliverance. He seeks for God to do it all. David recognizes his place in this relationship. He realizes that his getting through this tumultuous time is not on him, that he cannot fight this battle, defend himself, remove the jackals that surround him, fill in the pit they have dug, or anything else. Any and all success is going to have to come from God. So, how are you and I to relate?

Times haven't changed as much as we may think they have. Evil is still rampant, people still try to trip up others, and if you proclaim the Lord as your Savior that triggers something negative in some people. People still tend to speak harshly or derogatively about believers. And just as in David's time, we must understand that taking things into our own hands is not the answer—though for some of us (myself included) that's hard *not* to do. I'm a proactive type of person. Yes, I pray. Yes, I seek God's will and answers. And yes, I ask God to intercede, but my real preference is to just "deal with it" when it comes to problem people. Why? Because I see the prospect of an immediate, satisfying outcome. While I do believe that there is a time and place for confrontation of sin and evil, it doesn't always feel convenient to wait for it. In the end? Scripture is pretty consistent in the sharing of the failures of God's people when they attempt to do things on their own. And Scripture is also consistent with the call of God for us to lean upon him in our times of need. This is a running thread from Genesis through Revelation. But Scripture also provides the resolution for this tension: Jesus is the answer to evil, life's problems, and the issues involved with our trying to do things on our own and never succeeding.

David's words are a reminder that evil exists and that it's hell-bent on doing anything and everything against God. Satan attacks David, attacks Jesus, is working hard against the Holy Spirit, and has cast his greedy eyes upon you and me. And the moment we think we can handle him, we've already lost. This is why Jesus came, . . . and this is why the Holy Spirit entered each one of us once Jesus returned to his throne. We need the sacrifice of Christ to win the ultimate battle of life over death, and we need the Holy Spirit to intercede today and give us the strength to stay focused on goodness, hope, love, mercy, justice, and peace. We simply cannot make it through the gauntlet of evil without our Lord and Savior. And that is where we ultimately find peace, as well.

THREE QUESTIONS FOR YOU TO CHEW ON:

1. What in this psalm catches your eye? At what point are you drawn in? Why?
2. Have you been in a space like David's where you felt yourself to be surrounded by evil? How did you work through it?
3. How do you discern when God is asking you to stand up and fight . . . or to sit back and allow him to fight for you? What does "fighting" even look like? Does it depend on the situation?

A PSALM OF PRAYERFUL REFLECTION AND PETITION

L et's begin our reading today with Psalm 141.

What do we know about this psalm that can help us find context, as well as application? The superscription (as is the case with Psalms 142–145) ascribes the authorship to David. And most commentators agree that this psalm is not only a prayer but an *evening* prayer. As we read this text, we find the wording not only reflective of what David is currently experiencing but a petition in preparation for what is yet to come. David asks God to protect him (vv. 1, 3, 4, 8, 9, 10) and to sanctify him (vv. 2, 5, 6, 10).

Every night, as I lie down to sleep, my final conscious thoughts/actions are prayer. Even after I pray with my wife, I still find time for my own prayer as I reflect on the day that has just gone by. I pray about the interactions between myself and others; I pray over the parenting fails of the day, as well as over the relationship fails and miscommunications; and I pray for others who have been in my thoughts. But never have I thought of my words to God as being an "incense" set before the Lord (v. 2) (an image not unlike that of Revelation 5:8; 8:3–4). But this is what we see in our text. David requests that his prayer be a sweet aroma that blesses the Lord. I don't know about you, but to me that's a beautiful image, one that challenges me to not only make good use of my prayers but also to recognize that even my own prayers can be pretty powerful. Not that they have power in themselves, not that they are beautifully constructed or worded, but that my prayers *mean something*. And the same applies to yours!

What I really appreciate, not only about prayer in general but about David's prayer here, is that David, while reflecting on the day he has had, not only prays about his interactions, not only prays that he has chosen the right words and actions toward people, but points toward the future. He not only prays that the words he *has used* but that tomorrow's words may be appropriate and on point. He wants to make sure that his lips not only were guarded today but will be guarded again tomorrow (v. 3). He wants his heart protected (v. 4), he wants *the rebukes of the righteous to correct and anoint him* (vv. 5–7), and he wants protection (vv. 8–10).

When we reflect back upon our day *and* look to the day ahead, we recognize that life has been hard. In a world that is broken and riddled with sin, we recognize that relationships are difficult . . . because people are difficult . . . because sin is present. When we go to work, we do so with people who are broken—and when *they* go to work, they too deal with broken people (this is my way of saying that you and I are broken, as well). We use the wrong words, harm people with and without intention, and take part in "wicked deeds along with those." And, just as David prays at the end of verse 4, we fall into the trap of those evil doers and "eat their delicacies." Which simply means that we *want* to hear that gossip, believe those lies, and play the office politics, even though we know it's wrong. Which is why David's prayer to be struck by a righteous person is powerful. He prays for someone better, holier, and stronger than himself to pull him aside and call him on the carpet for his actions. This is a powerful request that reminds us that we cannot handle a single day on our own. And since we cannot win all the battles, fight all the good causes, and stay strong—we need to surround ourselves with fellow believers who can hold us accountable and correct us when we take the wrong steps, say the wrong words, and fall victim to the evils of this world.

In my freshman year of college, I was in a fraternity that was supposedly Christian, and yet within a few weeks I found myself to be the lone active Christian who was trying to live out his faith. The other brothers may have believed in Jesus, but I appeared to be the only one living out my conviction each day. While I did not participate in events and activities I did not agree with, I quickly realized that I needed to get out of the fraternity because I had no brotherly support and encouragement there. And I did. I told the president of our fraternity that I couldn't keep doing this anymore and needed to leave. He begged me to stay because "We need more people like you so that we can change the culture" (his words), but my response was that "I can't be the only one—and the only one without support." So, I left. I recognized the harmful situation I was in and the fact that I was alone.

I firmly believe that, when we're alone in our faith and Christian stance, we become more susceptible to the temptations of this world. We need brotherly and sisterly support as we navigate, find strength, and display truth in our lives, and we need to be in prayer for strength and support. This is why Christ gave us the Church. It's why Christ sent the Holy Spirit to us. It's why I take comfort in the refuge we've been given and the fact that we haven't been given over to death (v. 8). For God sent his Son, Jesus Christ, to take on (and overcome) death for us. This is why we take comfort in knowing that God listens to our prayers and helps us in our times of need.

Psalm 141 is a beautiful reminder for believers to set our evening prayers and hearts upon God. To recognize that our interactions are completely broken and that we need the Holy Spirit to strengthen, guide, and fill us up. We need him to speak for us, through us, and in us as we navigate a broken world and try to speak the words of Christ—words of kindness, compassion, love, hope, gentleness, meekness, and mercy.

So, with that being said, would you join me in my Psalm 141ish prayer?

Come, Holy Spirit, fill me up with your presence. Guard my mouth and keep watch over the door of my lips. Focus my heart upon love and kindness so that I can take part in your ways and not the ways of this world. Surround me with holy, good, and righteous people who can help me each day—and strengthen me to speak into their lives as well. May all those who oppose you find that their ways and actions do not find traction, and may they come to know you and your love. Fix my eyes, each day, upon you, and may I live into your loving kindness and grace. Amen.

THREE QUESTIONS FOR YOU TO CHEW ON:

1. What in this psalm touches you most directly? Where are you drawn? Why?
2. What does it mean for God to sanctify you? Isn't this already happening via the Holy Spirit?
3. What can you learn from David's prayer and how it "blesses" God? How might blessing God be different from praising him? How can we instill that thinking into our own time with God?

A PSALM OF LONELINESS

I invite you to turn with me to Psalm 142.

The superscription (those words just beneath the psalm heading) attribute this text to David and add the detail that he penned this prayer while he was in the cave. Which cave? And why was he in the cave? Scripture does recount a time when David was in the cave of Adullam (1 Samuel 22:1–2), and Psalm 57 is a reflective psalm written during that time. Assuming this to relate to the same incident, we can surmise that David is in need of God to protect him. We read three different times that he cries out to God (vv. 1, 5, 6). And why? His spirit is devastated, his situation is dire, he needs rescuing, and numerous people are after him.

I don't know why, but verses 3 and 4 have rocked me. We know from the 1 Samuel text that there *were* people who were concerned for David. People who showed up, surrounded him, and were helpful in terms of his ability to move past that point. And yet, David *still* feels abandoned and alone. There is so much in David's cries that needs to be unpacked. There's so much to be understood from David's emotional outpouring, and yet the space I've given myself for this psalm doesn't allow for a deep dive. So, I'll speak to the one issue that draws me in: loneliness.

Loneliness, even when surrounded by family, friends, coworkers, and acquaintances, is still a real thing for many people. Simply because we are surrounded by people doesn't mean we cannot feel abandoned or alone. The reality of David's situation is that he *was* alone during much of his time in that cave; even when people did show up, and even though their presence was felt and appreciated, there was still this feeling of being isolated in that nobody else has been there with him *the whole time*. There is nobody at his right hand (v. 4), but his pain runs deeper than that; not only is it loneliness, but a genuine feeling of abandonment, of a lack of care and concern from other people. Scratch that—from *all* other people. Friends, family, staff, supporters—all of them. David needs someone to just be there with him . . . in the cave . . . during his suffering—and nobody consistently is.

To me this is just another reminder of the need we have for each other. The fact is that God created us as communal beings who *need* community. We need to be around people who love and care for us. We need to be there for each other, no matter what the circumstances. If you need me to come alongside you, for however long that is, I should be there, matching you stride for stride or sitting beside you in the darkness where you tremble. That's what friends are for. That's what a brother/ sister is supposed to do. That's what a community that is dependent upon one another should do, as well.

David isn't necessarily looking for someone to give him council, speak words of encouragement, or even entertain him during the long, tedious days. He just wants someone there because a simple presence can speak volumes. Now, don't get me wrong: a strong focus in this text is that God is the only One who will never abandon, the only One who can save, the only One who can deliver. We do not want to miss or dismiss these words from David. When we understand them, we begin to recognize that God, throughout Scripture, has revealed that very truth to his people—the truth you and I still live into today. From the garden to the promised second coming, the Bible is the story of God's love, as given and seen through Jesus Christ, the One who saves, redeems, delivers, and restores the soul and life of his people. Everything David needed, all the pain he was feeling, was not lost on God because God is in the business of handling all our needs and engaging with us and our emotions. Still, I'm drawn to the failure of David's community. *I'm struck by wondering how often I, too, have failed to provide support when people needed me.*

How often have I spent time with people and then left because I had "other" things to do? How often have I come alongside someone and tried to "fix" that person's situation, when the only action needed was for me to sit and listen?

Psalm 142 is a beautiful prayer for those who feel lost, abandoned, forsaken, and lonely. It's a challenging prayer that should encourage those of us in that kind of situation to feel comfortable lifting up our worries to God, calling on him to save us, . . . and finding peace and comfort in the fact that he does. And this psalm should challenge the rest of us to put the needs of our loved ones who are in that cave ahead of our own.

THREE QUESTIONS FOR YOU TO CHEW ON:

1. What in this psalm do you find convicting? What insights draw you in? Why?
2. Have you ever "been there" for someone, only to later find out that they didn't view your interaction in that way? Does that matter if your intentions were positive? How do we navigate those feelings (both theirs and yours)?
3. Have you ever felt let down by your community? How did you move past that? Did you find a new community—or did you reach out, share your feelings, and grow together as a body?

A PSALM OF DESPAIR

Our next psalm is Psalm 143.

Our psalm today continues on from the previous one. David, while hiding from his oppressors (most likely from Saul), is feeling faint in spirit. He's experiencing the pain of loneliness and sorrow, and his spirit is what we might call "shot" (vv. 1–2). He fully grasps the reality that he is not worthy of being saved (v. 2) and yet he knows that God can, and will, save him if he so desires. David isn't claiming that he's righteous enough *to be* saved, and yet he's hoping that God will still somehow find him worthy. This psalm is an expression of hope for deliverance and guidance from a soul that is in despair.

When we are distraught, in anguish, or full of sorrow—hope can seem like the furthest thing away. When misery runs deep, it can seem as though the place in which we find ourselves is the same space in which we will end up. Hope seems far off, joy is fleeting, and the only prospect we see for our future is more of the same situation we are already experiencing. That's the very definition of "despair," is it not? What's really interesting is that in verses 8–12 David calls out for God's love to come through, for God's directing hand to guide his path, for his arms to rescue him, for his words to teach and correct him, and for his own path to be flat. David is not only recognizing that his current situation is dire, not only declaring that God *can* extricate him from this situation, but acknowledging that the movement from here to *there* will come only from God.

This is all right and good—and completely correct. Our complete trust must only be in God. We need God to show us the right path because we constantly choose the wrong ones and need to recognize that our lives are in his hands (better his than our own!). We declare that God is the only One who can rescue us from the ills and dangers of this world, that what is right and true comes only from his Word and teaching. We acknowledge and proclaim that following God's will is the right course of action every time (we can usually find expression of that will in what God has already shared with us in his Word) and that we need the Holy Spirit to lead and guide our steps. So, why does David kick off these good declarations, hopes, and needs by stating that he *hopes* that by the morning God will bring him his unfailing love (v. 8)? Does God have to send a messenger? Maybe the Pony Express? Would a telegram take a long time to get from heaven to the cave? Would God need eight hours to get an email through to David declaring his love, his comfort, and his peace?

Despair is a really powerful place to be in—but not powerful in a good or wholesome way. It's a darkness that is all consuming. It's a feeling, a mindset, an emotion, a cave in which even the things we know are not true still find a way to sink their teeth into our flesh. So, David, despite all these truths he has rightly declared, still doubts that God's love, the one thing he needs most, will reach him. The truth David misses is that he already has that love—and has had it all along.

I'll be honest: I don't know where to go with despair because I've never felt it personally. I've witnessed it, spent time with people experiencing it, and tried to encourage people as they looked for hope—but that's where it has ended for me. What I do know is that despair is real and that simply because we are loved, held, and protected by God does not mean that its darkness won't sink into our hearts. One of the biggest fallacies when it comes to faith is that just because we profess our faith in God nothing bad will ever happen, . . . and that includes feelings of depression, desolation, or hopelessness. Anyone who has ever struggled with depression, lost a loved one, lost their job, or suffered through a medical condition that ravaged their body or mind can attest that faith and hope, while strong, do not in themselves push away darkness and anguish. For all the deep-rooted knowledge we have of God's faithfulness, love, and presence, sometimes darkness is just . . . well, dark. And no amount of God's declarations or demonstrations of love seems bright enough to dispel it.

The hope that you and I have goes beyond the reality and presence of God's consistent and ever-present love; our hope is also rooted in the fact that his love, his leading and guiding, his rescuing, his teaching, and his righteousness are not dependent on *how we feel*. His love doesn't come only when I can see it or feel it—it's always there, whether or not my eyes and heart recognize it. Paul writes in Galatians 2:16 that we are not justified by our works or by anything we can do, . . . and I would add that we are not justified by our 100% holding to what we believe or our unwavering steadfastness in our faith even when we are consumed by despair. If we confess Jesus Christ as our Lord and Savior, then our lives, our souls, are secure. That's it. Again, our present state of darkness does not mean that his continual light is not with and upon us. The pain of sin and brokenness means that sometimes we cannot see goodness even when it's right before and beside us, even when it's under us to support us or over us to protect. Again, my brokenness doesn't push his holiness aside—in truth, this is the very reason Christ came: to rescue us from the pit of despair. Not only that, but the Holy Spirit is our reminder that on that day of Pentecost (Acts 2), the love of God rained down upon his people. And it's been with and within us ever since—never leaving and always leading.

This psalm is a beautiful reminder that where we are and the feelings we experience do not make God any different from who he is—do not alter what he has done, the things he continues to do, the salvation he has granted by way of his Son, and the interceding work of his Spirit. My prayer for you, if you find yourself in a space like David's, is that you will cling to the Word and promises of God. That you will know and experience that, even in the darkness, his light is radiating. Even when you cannot see it, hold to the truth—it's still there.

THREE QUESTIONS FOR YOU TO CHEW ON:

1. To what in this psalm can you relate? What draws you in? Why?
2. Why is despair so strong and blinding at times?
3. How do we work through, and be honest with, our own feelings and still hold on to the truth of God when we find ourselves in one of life's dark caves?

A PSALM FOR A FUTURE

P lease open your Bible to the book of Psalms and read with me Psalm 144. Our superscription identifies this as a psalm of David, and there is no reason not to believe that it is—but what other information can we glean? Well, there is a lot going on here. We have David praising God for being his stability (v. 1); giving glory to God for his ability to fight and possess the skills for war (v. 1—if I may be honest here, I'm a little uncomfortable with that "praise"—but that's on me and not David); and declaring that God is his fortress, stronghold, and deliverer (v. 2). But the rest of this psalm has to do with God being the provider of peace.

- Verse 3 is about care.
- Verses 5–6 are about scattering enemies.
- Verses 7–8 are about deliverance from enemies.
- Verses 9–15 are about the joys that come with deliverance (you simply don't thrive, sing, or increase in numbers after your enemies have routed you).

I'm going to be honest with you—I can't stop going back to verse 1. It's simply not in my nature to think of war and battle, let alone personally having to go to it and through it. I *did* spend time in my younger years looking at the different branches of the military and trying to determine whether I was being called into any of them, but that didn't last long. When nearing the end of my seminary training, I also spent quite a bit of time focused on the Army and becoming a chaplain, but I ultimately recognized that God had something else in store for me. While I'm not against the military, . . . not against war when it is necessary (Is it *ever* necessary?

Good conversation starter there!), it's hard for me to swallow that God "trains" the hands of his servants for war or their "fingers for battle." Where is *that* conversation in the Gospels or in the New Testament epistles? Oh, it's there in the sense of preparing ourselves for the fight against sin and evil, but that's the extent of it. So, what do we do with David's words here?

Well, we first must recognize that times were different. Life and survival were all about killing or being killed. Second, we must recognize that God did in fact train David's hands. Think of all the time the young David spent as a vulnerable shepherd out in the fields. All that time he spent learning how to defend the sheep from large and ferocious animals that could easily take off with a sheep, . . . or conceivably even the shepherd! And yet it was during that time that God was training David to become the defender and protector of God's people. It was during those years that David acquired the skills necessary to eventually bring down Goliath (1 Samuel 17). But we must remember that the skills God gave to David were for protection, for preservation, for deliverance, . . . and for a future. They weren't to be used for vengeance or just because he could—this is reinforced for us when we remember that David had more than one opportunity to kill Saul but declined. Why? Because that was not the man God had called him to be or the reason he was to become king.

Despite many Old Testament appearances to the contrary, God is not in the business of war. God is not in the business of blood and guts and destroying people. God is in the deliverance and protection business. God seeks to give his people refuge, hope, and peace. A future where there is no war, no battles, no death and destruction—only life. The Bible is a story about hope, redemption, and salvation by way of Jesus Christ. Yes, all that war stuff is present, but it's there to show us how broken we are, . . . to demonstrate that, at our own hands, war doesn't stop, the endless and often senseless battles rage on, . . . and nobody wins. It is only through the Son of God that death and destruction are put to an end. And in the end? The Bible, by way of its central character and focal point, Jesus Christ, is a story about what we read in verses 7–15 of this psalm: deliverance, rescue, protection, joy, hope, worship, growth, life, and blessings.

This psalm is a great reminder that protection and a future come by way of God and God alone. This psalm is a great reminder that God is in the business of life and that he'll do whatever is necessary to destroy the evil forces of this world—so much so that he sacrificed himself to overcome the work of evil and Satan.

THREE QUESTIONS FOR YOU TO CHEW ON:

1. What in this psalm catches your attention? What draws you in? Why?
2. How do we see ourselves being "trained" for battle by way of the Gospel's proclamation of Jesus Christ? By what Christ teaches us, how do we combat evil and sin and its perpetrators? What does Paul have to say in Ephesians 6:10–20, and how can you and I live into that today?
3. How often, when faced with some type of "enemy," do you try to handle things on your own, instead of, or before, asking God to deliver, protect, and work this through?

THE PSALM OF PRAISE

I invite you to read with me Psalm 145.

Our psalm today seems like a needed break from the gloom of the previous few psalms; while they seemed dark and sad, this one if full of praise and hope. This doesn't mean that we shouldn't appreciate those dark psalms, because we clearly need them. But we should also find refreshment in the psalms of praise. What do we know about this psalm? We know that its authorship is again attributed to David, and we know that it's titled "A psalm of praise"—a generic sounding title that in reality belongs *only* to this psalm. From beginning to end, David is solely focused on declaring God's praise for all that he has done.

As I read this praise, I picture David trying his best to describe who God is, his love, his work, and his acts, . . . and yet fully understanding that his words are falling short. That his descriptions are not descriptive enough. That his praise is not exuberant enough or strongly enough expressed. That his joy, while he intends it to be complete, is missing that mark. In the last part of verse 3 David concedes, "his greatness no one can fathom." Nobody knows just how awesome God is. Nobody knows just how mighty God is. Nobody knows all that God does—so how can we even begin to fathom him and his work? I think of Job (though on the opposite end of the spectrum in his attempts to capture the essence of God and his works) when he is called out for his anger against God and God reminds him that not only is Job insignificant, not only does he have no clue who and what all God does, but he has no right to even claim to grasp the reality. But David doesn't care. What he does know of God and his works is enough for him to declare his majestic awesomeness.

I think that God, in a way, is like an iceberg, most of which is under the surface of the sea. There are wonderfully smart people who study scientific data and reveal much about the workings of the cosmos to us. And yet what we have discovered remains only a fraction of that which is knowable—or would be, if God didn't set limits on our ability to comprehend. There are things we see and know, and yet we acknowledge that these are just the tip of the iceberg, the peak that juts out from below the waterline.

But God is not an iceberg; he's infinitely more than this or any other analogy we can make in our attempts to quantify him. What about all the unknowns, and the not yet knowns? What about the realities we cannot see? What about all the things we've never thought of? What about the things we understand and yet cannot fully comprehend because they simply don't make sense to us—even though we know they're true? What about spiritual realities like grace, undying love, complete sacrifice, and eternity? These are things we know and declare and have the smallest fraction of a grasp on—as much as we need in order to relate to God and accept his salvation.

And yet David says that we are to not only praise God for all of these things but to *tell* others about them. We are to tell them from "one generation to the next"—to share not only who God is but all the things we know of him and yet cannot truly fathom. Things like, but certainly not limited to, his awesome works, his abundant grace, his goodness and righteousness, his majesty and glory. We are to tell of hope and joy and proclaim that his kingdom reigns forever and ever. We are to share the news that God is near when we call him, that he hears our cries and saves us, removes sin and wickedness from his world, and flat out loves his creation! So much so that he died to restore it—not only his people, but all of the natural wonders as well. To bring *creation* back into holiness and goodness, God sent his One and only Son, Jesus Christ our Lord, to redeem, provide, secure, and heal all those who call upon him.

So, where do we go from here with this psalm? *Wherever our praise goes!* Maybe we're challenged to recognize that there is so much more to God than we know. Maybe we're called to stop putting God in a box, to stop limiting his grace and love, to stop feeling as though we are "too far" away for his love to reach us. And why? Because we know that there's more to the iceberg than what we can see, . . . and there is *vastly* more to God than what we know and can comprehend. So, praise him. For what is known of him, what it not yet known, and what will one day be revealed.

THREE QUESTIONS FOR YOU TO CHEW ON:

1. What in this psalm of praise speaks to you? What is it David makes you feel called to praise? Why?
2. Where do you see God today, . . . right now? How can you praise him for those known and unknown things?
3. In what areas is it difficult for you to "see" God. How can you overcome those perceived obstacles?

A HALLELUJAH PSALM:

PART 1

I invite you to read with me Psalm 146.

We're nearing the end of our time in the psalms. The final five are considered "Hallelujah psalms" for a reason. They are songs about praise, glory, worship, and recognizing God as the Creator, sustainer, and upholder of all things. They recognize that he is above and beyond all. That he is our very breath, our hope, and our joy. But what about this first one—our psalm for today?

Maybe it's just me, or maybe it's just because of the times we live in, but I cannot help but read, reflect, and chew on this psalm in light of the world's political landscape. We put so much stock in our leaders to lead us that when they fail, we feel that we've been let down. Leaders are supposed to guide our country into good times by their sound decisions, hopeful words, dedicated and committed work, and self-denying sacrifices. They are supposed to help others outside our own country, too, and work well together with the leaders of other nations—for the betterment of the world. In essence: we expect our president and lesser leaders to *save* us. And then they don't. They never do—and there is no way they can. We put so much pressure on our government, all the while failing to remember that our leaders *will* let us down. Always. Though they are to rely on advisors, and often do, they will in the end do what *they* think is best. And why? Because they are broken. They are sinful. They are human.

The psalmist rightly asserts that all of our leaders (he uses the word "princes") will fail us. The psalmist doesn't declare *why* they cannot save us, but he goes on not only to declare that God is the only One who can rescue us but to specify *how* it is God saves. So, in essence, we can look at these words, consider the opposite of what God is declared to do here, and recognize that *that opposite* describes what our human leaders do for us. Here we go!

Can princes save? No.

When they die, are they really dead? Yup.

Have any of our earthly leaders ever created anything from nothing (like the heavens and the earth)? Nope.

What about the seas and everything in them? Did they make them, or can they do so? Not a chance.

Do our leaders uphold the cause of the oppressed? They try, but, ultimately, they fall short.

Do our leaders give food to the hungry? They do—but it's always temporarily and never enough.

Do any of our leaders set prisoners free? Not in the hopeful sense of which Scripture speaks.

What about giving sight to the blind or hope for those bowed low? Nada. Or at least not very often for that second category.

Do our leaders watch over foreigners? To some extent, sometimes (that's a whole different issue, isn't it?).

What about the fatherless and the widows? Again, social justice is on the agenda, but our leaders fail to see it through.

Do they see to it that the wicked are frustrated? To a certain extent, but never to the point of their destruction.

Our psalmist encourages us to really understand all the needs in this world and to orient our focus in the right direction, . . . and never should it be on broken human beings. The needs we have in life can only be fulfilled by the Lord. The worries we have in this world will never be taken care of by the next president, the next governor, the next leader—or any other person. Because they simply can't. This isn't a cop-out on their part, nor are my words here intended to be a downer. This psalm is simply one of recognition and praise that, while we are broken, God is not. While our leaders cannot give us complete hope, God can. This psalm is in praise of the God who loves, saves, feeds, protects, and restores people. This is a psalm that declares Jesus Christ.

Who saves? Jesus.

Who lives eternally? Jesus Christ.

Who gives us hope? Who made all things? Who is faithful forever, upholds the oppressed, gives food to the hungry, sets prisoners free, and restores sight to the blind? Who lifts all those up who have been brought down low? Jesus . . . Jesus . . . Jesus, Jesus, Jesus—need I say it again? Jesus.

So, as the psalmist calls out to us, praise the Lord. Praise him for all he does, for *he* reigns with justice and equity, forever.

As a closing side note, and something that's really cool and beautiful, . . . read this psalm followed by a reading of Mary's Magnificat in Luke 1:46–55. Notice any similarities?

THREE QUESTIONS FOR YOU TO CHEW ON:

1. What in this psalm speaks to you? What draws you in? Why?
2. Why do we put all of these expectations on our leaders when we know they will fail?
3. The end of verse 8 says that the Lord loves the righteous. What does it mean to be righteous? What are some "righteous" acts of God you see in this psalm? Does that mean that *we* are to do those? (in case you missed it, the answer: Yes!)

A HALLELUJAH PSALM:

PART 2

Turn with me to Psalm 147, and let's read it together.

From the opening "praise the LORD" to the closing ditto, this unknown psalmist recognizes, declares, and finds hope in the God of creation and restoration. Not simply because God creates and restores, but because he, the psalmist, and all those who hear his praises are benefactors of God's goodness, grace, and work.

Upon reading this psalm, we find some clues that help us understand its context in terms of voice and place. While we don't know by whom or when this was written, we do see that the psalmist praises God for gathering in the exiled people of Israel (v. 2). That alone narrows this down to sometime after the captivity of the Jews in Babylon. Some attribute it to the time period of Haggai (around 520 B.C.) or Zechariah (518 B.C.), while others push the timeline further toward Nehemiah's time (445 B.C.), as the writer praises God for returning, rebuilding, and watching over his people. While we may have discrepancies in opinion about the *when* and the *who*—the echoes of and the reason for praise still resound. God's people have returned after having felt that all was lost.

So much of Israel's life was dependent on where they were geographically, as God's presence was associated with his temple and its location. The reasoning was that, if you were not near the temple, and particularly if you were in captivity in a foreign land, then you felt as though God had abandoned you, forsaken you, forgotten you, and left you on your own. It may be hard for us to fathom this, but your *place* seemed to dictate God's care.

Can we relate? Most definitely.

When we've been in a rough patch for quite some time, it's really easy to wonder, "God—where are you? Have you forgotten me?" When we've been sick for a while or have lost a loved one, our minds easily begin to wonder whether God still cares and, if so, why he didn't prevent our loved one from dying. With all the death, starvation, destruction, and harm in the world, one can easily wonder where the God of salvation is and why he evidently isn't doing any saving. It's too easy for our minds to quickly go from knowing and remembering that God is always near to associating our current circumstances with God's apparent abandonment of us or others.

The psalmist acknowledges here, without blatantly stating so, that these conclusions are wrong. His very praise reflects his understanding that God has *not* abandoned, forsaken, or moved on. That the God of creation, the same God who provides food for the cattle (v, 9) and covers the sky with clouds and makes it rain (v. 8), is the God who blesses his people (v, 13), restores them from exile (v, 2), sends his word of hope to them (v, 18), and helps them along their journey to know, fear, love, and draw close to him (vv. 19–20).

This psalm should remind the Christian, too, that God does not abandon. That even when we feel we have been exiled by God, that's simply not true. If God is anything, he is the One who restores. If God is anything, he is the One who brings hope. If God is anything, he is the One who provides. If God is anything, he is the One who makes all of creation exist and function. And so, while all of this psalm is joyful and God-honoring—there is an incompleteness to it because you and I, as believers in Christ, are encouraged to see this psalm *in the light of* Christ.

For the people of Israel during this time, hope was not only about restoration but about the good news of the ability to go back home. The people longed to learn that their long captivity had run its course, that oppression had been removed and hope restored. But all of that was only temporary, as captivity, oppression, and fear would always be present in one form or another. What they needed—what *we* needed—was finality. A finality to the oppression by the permanent removal of the whips, chains, and hatred that existed. Humanity needs finality and removal of fear. Enter Jesus Christ, the One who alone does all those things for us.

So, our encouragement is to read this psalm through the lens of Jesus. Read this psalm with the understanding that God created all things *for*, and *through*, his Son. That God sustains the humble, casts down the wicked, and returns singing and dancing to his people *because* of what Christ has done upon the cross and through the grave and his departure from it.

So, "praise the Lord," all you people. For you have *not* been abandoned or forsaken. You have been restored into the arms of the God who loves, the God who creates, and the God who gives you peace.

THREE QUESTIONS FOR YOU TO CHEW ON:

1. What in this psalm speaks to you? Where are you drawn? Why?
2. If we *know* that God doesn't abandon or forsake us, then why does it feel as though he does when we are in those dark spaces for so long? Have you ever been in that space of feeling abandoned by God? How did you get through it? What, or who, helped you remember that his Spirit was with you?
3. How can you encourage someone who is in that dark space? How can you remind them of God's presence even there?

A HALLELUJAH PSALM:

PART 3

I invite you to turn with me to Psalm 148.

If Psalm 147 is a psalm of praise to God as the protector, defender, and comforter of his people—then Psalm 148 could/should be seen as a psalm of praise *from all* of creation. What's really beautiful in this psalm is not only that it is a sweeping, all-encompassing, full-on psalm of praise (from above and below); not only that we see in it beautiful images of stars, heavens, waters, sea creatures, hail, mountains, trees, and people—but that it is a call for *all* of creation, all creatures and inanimate objects, to glorify, praise, and honor the Creator, . . . from wherever they find themselves. If you happen to be above, . . . praise the Lord. If you find yourself below, . . . praise the Lord. If you were created a tree, a rock, a fish, a bird, a pig, a snail—it doesn't matter, because you were created by God and thus are called to praise him.

But the psalmist doesn't stop at praising God for (and by) all created things (though this is the majority of the psalm); the final two verses deal with the reasons for praising him: because he is exalted, because he has saved, and because he holds his people close to his heart. I find myself absolutely awe-struck right . . . there (at that image of God holding us close).

The sustainer of the universe, the Creator of the heavens, angels, and all the heavenly hosts . . . holds *his people*, you and me, close to his heart. The One who made the sun and moon and shining stars; the One who spoke them into being; the One who established them forever and ever, so that they cannot whither or die or be removed without his voice of authority; the One who created the smallest of things in the oceans to the biggest of things in the air and everything in between—*that almighty One* holds his people close to his heart!

It's easy to get lost in my own problems and concerns and wonder whether I really am important to God. I suspect that we all wonder whether our job glorifies God or brings him praise or whether our place in this world is really of any value, . . . because we want to be useful and worthy. As believers, we want to make sure that our work is beneficial to the kingdom, is bringing honor and glory to God. We can take this even deeper, questioning the value of our *life*, our *presence*, and our *being*. We can go so far ask to ask whether our life is worth the price Christ paid for it. Am I, *me*, worthy of what my Sustainer has done? Are my 8:00 a.m.–5:00 p.m. job, my family life, my community work, my service through my church— "good enough" for all that Christ has done for me?

The problem, of course, is that these questions are just rabbit holes after rabbit holes that do nothing but depress us. The problem with these rabbit holes is that they never stop, because our questions never stop. The problem with these rabbit holes is that I will consistently wonder but never find the answer I am looking for.

We're looking for answers within ourselves when we should be remembering the answer we've already been given. That the Creator of the universe, and of all other things, holds his people close to his heart. You and I, proclaimers of the One true God, believers in the Son of the almighty One, know that it's not only that God holds us close to his heart but that he redeems us and creates in us a new heart, one that is fully worthy in his sight, based not in any deserving on our part but in the worthiness of his Son, who paid the penalty for the sin of all who will believe. No rabbit hole will give you that answer, or the peace it brings. Only Jesus will.

So, praise the Lord, all you created children of God.

Praise the Lord, all you who are held closely to the heart of God.

Praise the Lord, for you were created, upheld, redeemed, and given life by the One who is above all, within all, and the splendor of all things.

Praise the Lord.

THREE QUESTIONS FOR YOU TO CHEW ON:

1. What in this psalm speaks to you? At what point are you drawn in? Why?
2. I like to imagine many things, but one of the things that has always fascinated me has to do with what praise and worship are going to look like in the New Earth. What will the praise from rocks look like? What about the cedars, or the hail or snow?
3. For further study, read Luke's account of Christ's birth (Luke 2:13). What parallel do you see between Luke's birth narrative and the psalmist's declaration?

A HALLELUJAH PSALM:

PART 4

We're nearing the end of our joint excursion through the book of Psalms. Please read with me Psalm 149 before considering this reflection.

It's always interesting to me what things get picked up when people, yours truly included, read Scripture. Sometimes it's a word that hits our heart, sometimes it's an idea or image that grabs us, and at other times there's just a peace that falls upon us. The Holy Spirit hits us with what we need, right where we are, . . . and right when we need it. He's pretty cool that way. I'm struck in this psalm by the second half of verse 5: "and sing for joy on their beds."

The bed has always been a comforting and important place—at least for me. I think it would be safe to say that, when we think of our bed, we think primarily of the place where we sleep at night—but our beds are so much more than that! As I think about my 41 years of existence and all my memories associated with me bed, so much comes flooding in. The bed was where I was sent when I was being disciplined (is it weird that this is the first thing I think of?). The bed was where I snuggled with my parents, cried, got angry, hung out when I was sick, memorized homework as I waited for sleep to overtake me (state capitals, Spanish words, sign language, etc.). The bed was where I thought about a lot of things, talked with whomever my girlfriend was at the time, had conversations with God, and now snuggle with my wife or my kids—or all of us (including the dog).

For the psalmist to mention singing for joy on his bed brings to mind the idea that he will go from mourning—the bed was, and possibly still is, a common place for that (see Psalm 6:6)—to hope and joy. But if the psalmist is anything like me, I don't visualize this image as straight-up singing for joy. It's more like jumping on the mattress, moving around, dancing, yelling, singing at the tops of your lungs—a you're-gonna-get-in-trouble-from-your-parents type of action!

Why? Because a *new* song is being sung (v. 1). Not one dwelling on sorrow and fear and dread—but a new one that is full of joy, praise, and happiness because of God, his Maker (v. 2), the King of kings (v. 8), and Lord of lords, who has crowned his humble servant with victory over his enemies (v. 4). *His* enemies. Because God takes delight in his people (v. 4). Because God crowns them with victory, and the people rejoice in this honor. Because God's sentence will be carried out against the enemies of his own. So, why not dance and sing and shout and bounce on the bed?

Another thing that struck me is the fact that the "praising" and singing "hallelujah" and dancing to God happen in the corporate space (the assembly of the people: church) (v. 1), but also in the privacy of one's own home (v. 5). This is clearly done by millions of Christians around the world to this day, but it reminds me of a few things:

1. There is *no* space in this world where the worship of God should *not* take place.
2. You cannot get away from God's presence, . . . so acknowledge this and worship him!
3. Wherever you happen to be, . . . worship God.
4. Our future with God is going to be *amazing!*

If your excitement about the future is based on an all-encompassing space of worship—then awesome. If your excitement about the future is all about some good ol' fashioned dancing and singing—then awesome. But if you're excited to sing and dance and jump on the bed and shout to the heavens and *not* get in trouble for it but, be encouraged, too! . . . I'll be there with ya!

I think we're gonna need a bigger bed . . .

THREE QUESTIONS FOR YOU TO CHEW ON:

1. What in this psalm energizes you for praise? Why?
2. What is going on in your life that causes you to mourn? Knowing the promise of Christ—how does that change?
3. The psalmist rejoices in verse 3 with a call to praise God's name with dancing. What would this look like for you?

A HALLELUJAH PSALM:

PART 5

We've about to reach the end of a pretty extensive journey together. Please turn with me to your Bible, and let's read Psalm 150.

Yes, this is the *last* psalm in the Bible. The one that wraps up all that we've read, all that we've processed together—and then some. As it should be, this psalm is not only a declaration of a hallelujah and a praise; it's a call to worship. And, while this last psalm is short in length, it's *huge* both in implications and in theological significance. We've considered psalms of joy, psalms of lament, psalms of confusion, and psalms filled with fear. We've read from psalmists who needed God to forgive them, as well as from writers who invoked God to judge their enemies. We've reflected on psalms that were simply a call to worship, . . . and on others that were a tear-jerking call to repentance. But all of them, from Psalm 1 through Psalm 149, have been about God, his loving grace, his relationship with his people, and their response *to* his grace.

So, why end with this hallelujah praise? Why bring it all back around to this? Because every emotion, need, and hope for the people of God was, and is, with and in God. We, the readers, are invited to enter into this praise—and to consider *why* it is we praise God. Ultimately, for each of us as Christians, we are invited to see Christ in this text and thus naturally come to the realization that we praise God *for Jesus*:

- For his atoning, sacrificial death, praise him.
- For his love and grace, praise him.
- For his redemptive, crown-bestowing, Satan-kicking, grave-leaping work, praise him.

- For his patience and love, praise him.
- For his adopting us as children of God, praise him.

I appreciate what Albert Barnes states about this psalm:

It was manifestly designed, whoever wrote it, to occupy the very place which it does occupy—to complete the volume devoted to praise. Praise is the suitable ending of the book; praise is what the Spirit of inspiration meant to secure in the heart and on the lips. In the review of the whole there is occasion for praise. In view of all that has been disclosed about God, about his religion, about the manifestations of his mercy and grace to this people, there is occasion for praise.[6]

Finally, I think this psalm truly answers the psalmist's original declaration from Psalm 1. Who is blessed, and why are they blessed? Why are we fed by streams of water? Who are the righteous, and who watches over them? (the answers, in order: the people of God are; because God loves us and blesses us; the people of God are; and God is). When you can answer those questions, you're ready for Psalm 150. Yes, every living and breathing thing is to praise the Lord with songs, harps, cymbals, tambourines, and anything else you can get your hands on. Praise him!

Praise him!

Praise him!

THREE QUESTIONS FOR YOU TO CHEW ON:

1. What in this psalm speaks to you? Where are you drawn in? Why?
2. Does this psalm reflect how *you* would have ended the book? If not—what would you have done differently?
3. How many times does the psalmist use the word "praise" in this short text?

6 Ellsworth, Roger. *Opening Up Psalms*. Leominster: Day One Publications, 2006. Print. Opening Up Commentary.

ACKNOWLEDGMENTS

I'm not sure where to begin with acknowledging and thanking people—but there are a few who specifically need to be called out.

Michelle, Lukkas, Taylor Jean—thank you. Your endless love, support, and encouragement are my daily rock. And I should probably thank you for allowing me to use you in some of these (even though I never asked permission—hope that's okay).

Mom, Dad—thank you for all your support. You raised Kay and me to love and fear the Lord and to worship and adore him, and I couldn't have asked for a better home because of it. You loved us without end, and who we are is because of who you are (at least the good stuff—right?).

Midwest BASIC Bible Camp family, and you know who you are, thank you. We started this journey together, and many of you stuck around week in and week out. This compilation of thoughts and meanderings was compiled because of you and our encouragement of one another *to remain* in the Word of God.

Donna Huisjen, your editing of my "writing" is beautiful, and you added a richness of wordsmithing that I could not have done. You clearly slogged through my manuscript and made me sound vastly better than I really am. Thank you.

Finally, Tim Beals and David Sanford, thank you for believing in my simple writings and reflections on these psalms. It was never my intention to land here, but you saw something different. Thank you.